P9-AFC-046

FOSTERING HEALING AND GROWTH

R

FOSTERING HEALING AND GROWTH

A Psychoanalytic Social Work Approach

EDITED BY
Joyce Edward, C.S.W., B.C.D.
Jean B. Sanville, Ph.D, B.C.D.

NATIONAL MEMBERSHIP COMMITTEE ON PSYCHOANALYSIS
IN CLINICAL SOCIAL WORK INC.
Affiliated with The National Federation of Societies for Clinical Social Work, Inc.

JASON ARONSON INC.
Northvale, New Jersey
London

This book was set in 11 pt. Bodoni by Alpha Graphics of Pittsfield, New Hampshire and printed and bound by Book-mart Press of North Bergen, New Jersey.

Production Editor: Judith D. Cohen

10 9 8 7 6 5 4 3 2 1

The editors gratefully acknowledge permission to reprint material from the following sources:

"In Defense of Long-Term Treatment: On the Vanishing Holding Environment," by William S. Meyer, in *Social Work* 38(5): 571–578. Copyright © 1993 by NASW Press. "Clinical Supervision: Its Role in 'Containing' Countertransference Responses to a Filicidal Patient," by Linda A. Chernus and Paula Grote Livingston, in *Clinical Social Work Journal* 21(4): 349–364. Copyright © 1993 by Human Sciences Press, Inc. Excerpt from "The Tree," by D. W. Winnicott, reproduced by permission of Mark Paterson and Associates on behalf of the Winnicott Trust, London. Excerpts from "Tired," by Gary Mackler, in *Newsline* #33, September 1988, reproduced by permission of *Newsline*.

Library of Congress Cataloging-in-Publication Data

Fostering healing and growth : a psychoanalytic social work approach / [edited] by Joyce Edward & Jean Sanville.

p. cm.

Includes bibliographical references and index.

ISBN 1-56821-723-4 (alk. paper)

1. Psychodynamic psychotherapy. 2. Psychiatric social work.
3. Psychoanalysis. I. Edward, Joyce. II. Sanville, Jean.

[DNLM: 1. Social Work, Psychiatric. 2. Psychoanalytic Therapy.
3. Psychoanalytic Theory. WM 30.5 P373 1996]

RC489.P72P78 1996

616.89'14–dc20

DNLM/DLC

for Library of Congress 95-30910

Manufactured in the United States of America. Jason Aronson Inc. offers books and cassettes. For information and catalog write to Jason Aronson Inc., 230 Livingston Street, Northvale, New Jersey 07647.

Contents

Preface ix
Joyce Edward
Jean B. Sanville

Acknowledgments xi

Contributors xiii

Introduction from the President of the National Membership Committee on Psychoanalysis xvii
Cecily G. Weintraub

Introduction from the Founding Chair of the National Study Group on Social Work and Psychoanalysis xix
Elaine Rose

Prelude xxi
Jean B. Sanville

1 Applying Psychoanalytic Principles to Social Work Practice: An Historical Review 1
Herbert S. Strean

2 Listening, Hearing, and Understanding in Psychoanalytically Oriented Treatment 23
Joyce Edward

3 Transference: A Key to Psychoanalytic Social Work 46
Daniel Coleman

4 A Clinical View of the Use of Psychoanalytic Theory in Front-Line Practice 59
Margaret G. Frank

5 The Good-Enough Social Worker: Winnicott Applied 77
Jeffrey S. Applegate

6 From Holding to Interpretation 97
Martha W. Chescheir

7 The Beginning Phases of Treatment of the Schizoid Disorder of the Self: A Developmental, Self, and Object Relations Perspective 125
Karla R. Clark

8 Maria's Second Chance: Resolving Oedipal Conflict in the Transference 152
Roberta Shechter

9 The Use of the Telephone as a Transitional Space in the Treatment of a Severely Masochistic Anorexic Patient 163
Joyce Kraus Aronson

10 Recovered Memories of Childhood Sexual Abuse: Problems and Concerns 179
Marilyn A. Austin

11 The Adult Survivor of Childhood Sexual Abuse: Linking Inner and Outer World 195
Roberta Graziano

12 Working with Dreams of Survivors of Violence: Facilitating Crisis Intervention with a Psychoanalytic Approach 212
Katherine A. Brunkow

13 A Psychoeducational-Psychodynamic Approach to the Treatment of Drug Addicts 226
Julie R. Miller

14 Psychoanalytically Oriented Psychotherapy with the HIV-Infected Person 244
Sheila Felberbaum

15 Leaking Walls–A Tale of the Unconscious: A Psychoanalytic Reading of a Case of Post-Partum Depression as Seen through the Perspective of Ignacio Matte-Blanco 261
Gail Sisson Steger

16 The Child Therapist and the Child's Parents: A Precarious Alliance Viewed from a Psychoanalytic Perspective 293
Diana Siskind

17 From Parental Failure to Foster Parent: Facilitating Development in the Life Cycle 312
Cecily G. Weintraub

18 Psychoanalysis and the World of Two: Object Relations Couple Therapy 327
Ellyn Freedman

19 Ending Where the Client Is: A Psychodynamic Approach to Forced Terminations 353
Margaret Coker

20 In Defense of Long-Term Treatment: On the Vanishing Holding Environment 372
William S. Meyer

21 Clinical Supervision: Its Role in "Containing" Countertransference Responses to a Filicidal Patient 386
Linda A. Chernus
Paula Grote Livingston

22 Collaboration between Psychoanalysis and Social Work Education 404
Carolyn Saari

Postlude 417
Jean B. Sanville

Glossary 443
Patsy Turrini

Bibliography: Related Clinical Social Work Writings 469

Index 475

Preface

This book has been developed by the National Study Group on Social Work and Psychoanalysis, an organization formed by the National Membership Committee on Psychoanalysis (NMCOP), to consider the ongoing relationship between psychoanalysis and social work. We include in the next pages a description of the NMCOP by its President, Dr. Cecily Weintraub, as well as an account of the Study Group by its founder and first co-chair, Elaine Rose.

Both the NMCOP and the Study Group attest to a long and valuable relationship between social work and psychoanalysis. Some members of the NMCOP are practicing psychoanalysts. Others work in public or private agencies or practice psychotherapy privately, and draw upon psychoanalytic theory in diverse ways.

In this compendium, a group of practitioners share their understanding of an ever-expanding body of psychoanalytic theory, and demonstrate the ways they have translated this theory in their everyday efforts to help the men, women, and children who seek their help. We hope that this endeavor will enrich the reader's knowledge of modern psychoanalytic theory and serve as a useful resource for enhancing clinical social work practice.

Joyce Edward, C.S.W., B.C.D.
Jean B. Sanville, M.S.W., Ph.D., B.C.D.
Editors

ACKNOWLEDGMENTS

We would like to express our gratitude to all those who helped with the realization of this book. First to the National Membership Committee on Psychoanalysis, Inc. (NMCOP), which is affiliated with the National Federation of Societies for Clinical Social Work, Inc. Its foresight in establishing the National Study Group on Social Work and Psychoanalysis and affording that group the opportunity to explore relevant issues and develop new projects has made this book possible. To the President of the NMCOP, Dr. Cecily Weintraub, we give special thanks. Always available and supportive, she acted with a light touch, encouraging us to find and pursue our own paths as we wended our way.

We are especially appreciative of Jason Aronson's belief in the value of this book and his willingness to publish it. At a time when many social work educators have dismissed analytic theory and discarded it from the curricula of our social work schools, it has been especially meaningful to have an enthusiastic publisher who recognized the merit of our endeavors and facilitated them.

We are also grateful to our production editor, Judy Cohen, who warmly responded to our concerns and helped us to proceed more effectively with our efforts. Her availability and wise counsel are much appreciated. To Norma Pomerantz, whose interest and assistance have meant so much, we also say thanks. We know that there are many others at Jason Aronson, unknown to us, who made the publication of this book possible, and we include them in our appreciation.

These acknowledgments, of course, would not be complete without a warm thanks to our authors who made this book possible. It is their effort, creativity, skill, and dedication that are at the heart of this undertaking. Finally, we know that if our writers could speak here, they would wish to express their deep appreciation to those clients and patients who have inspired and informed their contributions. We do so on their behalf.

Joyce Edward, CSW, BCD
Jean Sanville, Ph.D., BCD
Editors

Contributors

Jeffrey S. Applegate, D.S.W. Faculty, Graduate School of Social Work and Social Research, Bryn Mawr College, Pennsylvania; private practice.

Joyce Kraus Aronson, Ph.D. Editor of *Insights in the Dynamic Psychotherapy of Anorexia and Bulimia: An Introduction to the Literature*; Faculty, Center for the Study of Anorexia and Bulimia, New York City; private practice.

Marilyn A. Austin, M.S.W., B.C.D. Member of the Greater Washington Society for Clinical Social Work; private practice.

Katherine A. Brunkow, M.S.W., B.C.D. Clinical social worker and psychoanalyst in Washington, DC who serves on the faculties of the Washington Psychoanalytic Institute, the Advanced Psychotherapy Program of the Washington School of Psychiatry, and the Psychoanalytic Psychotherapy Program of the Washington Psychoanalytic Foundation.

Linda A. Chernus, M.S.W., B.C.D. Associate Professor of Clinical Psychiatry (Social Work) at the University of Cincinnati College of Medicine; private practice.

Martha Chescheir, Ph.D. Faculty member and supervisor, Washington School of Psychiatry; private practice.

Karla R. Clark, A.C.S.W., B.C.D., Ph.D. Faculty member of the San Francisco Masterson Institute, 1986–1994; private practice.

Margaret R. Coker, M.S.W., A.C.S.W. Department of Social Work, Albany Medical Center Hospital and Department of Psychiatry of Albany Medical College, Clinical Instructor. Adjunct Instructor, University of New York at Albany.

Daniel Coleman, M.S.W. Clinical social worker at the Child Guidance Clinic of Southeastern Connecticut.

Joyce Edward, M.S.S.A., B.C.D. Practices psychoanalytic psychotherapy and psychoanalysis. Chair of the National Study Group on Psychoanalysis and Social Work. Co-edited *Separation Individuation: Theory and Application* and is co-editor of this publication.

Sheila Felberbaum, A.C.S.W., R.N.C.S. Adjunct Faculty, Nassau Community College; private practice.

Margaret G. Frank, L.I.C.S.W., B.C.D. Coordinator and faculty, Boston University School of Social Work, Advanced Training Program in Child and Adolescent Therapy; private practice.

Ellyn Freedman, A.C.S.W., B.C.D. Clinical instructor at the Medical University of South Carolina, Department of Psychiatry and Behavioral Sciences; private practice.

Roberta Graziano, D.S.W. Associate Professor, Hunter College School of Social Work; private practice.

Paula Grote Livingston, M.S.W., L.I.S.W. Clinical social worker for the past eight years, focusing on work with children and their families.

William S. Meyer, M.S.W., B.C.D. Director of Training for the Department of Social Work and Assistant Clinical Professor in the Department of Psychiatry at the Duke University Medical Center.

Julie R. Miller, Ph.D. Adjunct Clinical Consultant, Greenwich House Counseling Center; private practice.

Carolyn Saari, Ph.D. Professor, School of Social Work, Loyola University Chicago; Editor, *Clinical Social Work Journal*; private practice.

Jean B. Sanville, M.S.W., Ph.D., B.C.D. Clinical social worker and psychoanalyst in private practice. Taught at the UCLA School of Social Welfare and in continuing education at Smith College School for Social Work.

Writings include *Illusion in Loving*, co-authored with Joel Shor, and *The Playground of Psychoanalytic Therapy*.

Roberta Shechter, D.S.W., B.C.D. Adjunct Assistant Professor, Hunter College School of Social Work; Faculty, Washington Square Institute, New York; private practice.

Diana Siskind, M.S.W., B.C.D. Author of various articles, a book, *The Child Patient and the Therapeutic Process: A Psychoanalytic Developmental Object Relations Approach*, and a forthcoming book, *Working With Parents*; private practice, New York City.

Gail Sisson Steger, M.S.W., Ph.D., B.C.D. Practicing, training, and supervising analyst at the Los Angeles Institute and Society for Psychoanalytic Studies, where she is currently faculty chair.

Herbert S. Strean, D.S.W. Distinguished Professor Emeritus, Rutgers University, Director Emeritus of the New York Center for Psychoanalytic Training; private practice.

Patsy Turrini, C.S.W., B.C.D. Practices psychotherapy and psychoanalysis. Member of the faculty of the Society for Psychoanalytic Study and Research and the New York School for Psychoanalytic Psychotherapy and Psychoanalysis.

Cecily G. Weintraub, Ph.D. Practices psychotherapy and psychoanalysis. Teacher, supervisor, and training analyst for the New York School for Psychotherapy and Psychoanalysis and the Society for Psychoanalytic Study and Research.

Introduction From the President of the National Membership Committee on Psychoanalysis

The National Membership Committee on Psychoanalysis in Clinical Social Work, Inc. (the Committee), was founded by Crayton E. Rowe, Jr., M.S.W., B.C.D., who recognized the pressing need for clinical social workers with a specialty practice in psychoanalysis and psychoanalytic psychotherapy to have a professional home within the social work profession. The Committee was formed in 1980 as a standing committee of the Federation of Societies for Clinical Social Work, Inc. (the Federation), the organization which represents over ten thousand clinical social workers across the United States.

By 1992, the Committee grew to approximately one thousand members with twelve area groups throughout the United States, and the Committee's scope of activity increased. The Federation voted the Committee its right to independent incorporation with an affiliative relationship to the Federation.

This 1993 restructuring affords the Committee collaboration with the national clinical social work profession as a whole and, simultaneously, the ability to promote psychoanalysis for our membership and to the public.

The Committee is the only national social work organization that promotes and furthers the understanding of psychoanalytic theory and knowledge within the profession and to the public at large. We represent, foster, and protect, by means of education, the identity, standing, and advancement of psychoanalytic practitioners and educators in social work. The Committee established the National Study Group on Social Work and Psychoanalysis to further strengthen this effort.

The Committee has taken an active role in promoting health care reform generally and advocated to guarantee equal mental health benefits for citizens. We have adopted standards to provide a basis upon which parity for social work psychoanalysts and psychoanalytic psychotherapists will be guaranteed. We publish an annual newsletter and conduct national conferences.

A further accomplishment of the Committee has been its founding role and collaboration in the Psychoanalytic Consortium, a group consisting of the American Academy of Psychoanalysis, the American Psychoanalytic Association, and the American Psychological Association, Division 39, Psychoanalysis. The Consortium attests to the common theoretical roots across professional lines, as well as the commitment to defend the integrity of psychoanalysis while advancing its common goals.

The Committee, clinical social workers who practice psychoanalysis and psychoanalytic psychotherapy, believe that the effectiveness of psychoanalytic theory as a conceptual base has too long been understood as confined to the private consulting room. Accordingly, in keeping with the aims of developing and applying psychoanalysis for the public good, the Committee has supported the development of this book through its national study group.

Fostering Healing and Growth fulfills a fundamental objective of the National Membership Committee on Psychoanalysis in Clinical Social Work, Inc., to foster the highest level of care to patients and clients through the application of psychoanalytic theory. We are pleased to offer this volume as a resource to the educational, professional, and lay communities.

Cecily G. Weintraub, Ph.D.

Introduction from the Founding Chair of the National Study Group on Social Work and Psychoanalysis

1990 was a time of turmoil and dichotomy in social work. On the educational front, schools of social work were phasing out courses based on psychoanalytic thought while students in the schools were asking for more psychoanalytic theory. Organizationally, social work psychoanalysts and practitioners of psychoanalytic psychotherapy were seeking more definition and recognition while the spectre of managed care was propelling clinical social workers, responsible for the majority of therapy in the nation, to find short and simple solutions to long and complex problems.

Against such a background, the National Membership Committee on Psychoanalysis created the National Study Group on Social Work and Psychoanalysis. We wanted to review the history of the influence of psychoanalytic theory on the development of social work. We wanted to discover what social work theory has contributed and can contribute in the future to psychoanalysis. We wanted to study the evolution of psychoanalytic practice within clinical social work with the focus of defining the identity of the social work psychoanalytic practitioner. We wanted to demonstrate how psychoanalytic theory is useful to social workers in diverse settings for treating the major maladies of our day. Finally, we hoped to make a contribution toward repairing and reweaving some of the split threads within our profession and to join in interdisciplinary alliances representing the social work psychoanalytic clinician to the broader community. To this end, we have conducted research and participated in the National Membership Committee on Psychoanalysis national conferences.

Now, culminating four years of thinking and planning, and through the work of our illustrious editors, we present this compendium. It reflects our interests and integrates them through the writings you will find herein.

This book is a milestone contribution from psychoanalytic social workers to the field of clinical social work and to all clinicians of whatever discipline laboring today to maintain standards and to hear and understand those seeking our help.

Elaine Rose, L.C.S.W., B.C.D.

Prelude

Psychoanalytic theory, growing from the conceptions of Freud, has matured into a many-splendored thing, often affirming the basic ideas of the originator, but sometimes extending or modifying them in accord with the times and the sorts of patients shaped by and, in some measure, shaping a changing social and cultural surround. The development of basic concepts about human life evolve in a dialectic, beginning always with the person or group that we professionals are trying to understand and help with the aid of extant theory. When previous concepts do not fit the person or situation we seek to alter them, returning to the patient or group to determine whether the modifications enable us to comprehend and respond more fully to them. No theory will ever capture all the possible relevant data; it will inevitably be made up of abstractions from which something is ever in danger of being omitted. Yet we cannot do without theory. We may be conscious or unconscious of the precepts from which we practice, but without them we would see nothing. The advantage of conscious theory is precisely in the ongoing testing and self-remedying that become possible.

The contributors to this book, mostly clinical social workers or social work psychoanalysts, all work from a psychoanalytic perspective, considering it the richest of ways to grasp the human condition, affording views both deep and broad. Perhaps we should not say that these authors apply psychodynamic theories; they apply themselves assiduously to the task of listening, understanding, and being helpful to their patients. They do believe and demonstrate to us readers that these theories have bearing on their professional tasks, but they also remain alert to the times when some modifications in prescribed approaches may be in order, either because of the idiosyncratic features of their clients or of those that characterize this particular therapeutic relationship. Many of them work in clinics and agencies of various kinds, inpatient and outpatient, but also maintain private practices. About half of the chapters draw on agency work and half on private practice. The latter describe work with patients who are strikingly similar to their agency counterparts, often with sordid histories and manifesting severe pathologies. Such patients, in their transferences, sometimes may provoke in the therapist reactions similar to those that were pathogenic on the part of figures in their early lives. We see these authors drawing upon analytic ideas also to understand themselves and to use their countertranferences in the service of understanding and responding in healing ways. Thus these practitioners disabuse us of the myth that psychoanalysis is relevant only for the privileged. Indeed, we are left with the suspicion that the notion that it is irrelevant for the underprivileged is itself a form of irrational prejudice.

Nearly all of these writers serve clients who, once upon a time, might have been deemed unreachable by a psychoanalytically informed perspective. One client is of another culture and comes with a suicidal depression and a history of physical and sexual abuse. One is a young man in a residential setting for sex offenders, forever getting into trouble with others. There is a black teenager who has witnessed the murder of her mother and her brother. We learn of a fragile 80-pound woman of 26, severely anorectic, functioning in social judgment rather like a girl on the verge of early adolescence. And we meet a tough, weather-beaten woman who had a violent father and a drug-addicted and alcoholic mother, and who herself has an air of violence and menace and an attitude of joyless self-sufficiency. A man with a history of difficulty sustaining intimate relationships is searching for the origins of his rage at his father and wondering whether he has been sexually abused. And a woman with similar complaints suffers flashback memories after being told by a previous therapist that she was an incest survivor. A health professional reveals, after some years of therapy, having been physically and sexually abused by nuns in an orphanage where she lived as a young child. We learn of three women who were raped and of a man once taken hostage while working in a distant country. We become acquainted with a single black woman, an HIV-positive heroin addict in recovery, with a life of street prostitution. Then there is a 22-year-old who has just discovered that he is HIV-positive, who is so flooded with panic, so ashamed of his homosexuality, that he flees treatment. Another homosexual was diagnosed with AIDS two years previously; we are with him over the fifteen months left of his life. One case is of a woman with post-partum depression and terrors that she would harm her infant; her abundant dreams revealed for a while "tidal wave emotions" and later the beginnings of structures to contain the leaks. Another young mother, quite unmotherly, is overwhelmed by having two children and comes into treatment because of the rebelliousness of her first-grader. A handicapped paraplegic woman, unable to care for her own son because she had infantilized him, becomes a successful foster parent. A homosexual man seeks therapy because of the threat that his partner of many years may abandon him through suicide, but the HIV-infected partner then also comes in, harboring a bottomless pit of grievances about his own life and about the relationship. We encounter a paranoid-schizophrenic patient who has a history of admissions to state hospitals and of "noncompliance with treatment," and who initially does not seem to want treatment at that time either. A woman referred by her daughter's psychiatrist seems agitated, terribly anxious; after some months she reveals that as a child she had been sexually abused by an alcoholic father. And, finally, we meet a woman who has murdered her own son.

We see also in several of these chapters how advances in analytic theory have enriched the psychotherapeutic treatment of those patients whom we ordinarily have considered neurotic. Recent developments, for instance, permit us to fathom more fully the co-existence of oedipal and preoedipal problems, and of their inevitable interconnectedness. There is the woman who seems to have trouble finding a man, and who "suffers from reminiscences" of an attraction to her father linked with fears of abandonment by her mother. Another woman suffers severe anxiety when her aged mother faces an operation, but along with her separation anxiety are memories of her mother's preferred place in her father's affections. In another patient, complaining of "crazy" nightgown-changing behaviors, and in the very constricted and depressed businessman, we see the intertwinings of conflict and deprivation.

The therapists who met with each of these troubled persons are seen drawing on various of the existing psychoanalytic schools of thought, some veering toward the classical, others toward ego psychology, or self psychology, or Kleinian concepts, or the British independent tradition, or the intersubjective approach, sometimes on his or her unique blend of these. All share an emphasis on the importance of early life experiences, especially on those within the family of origin. They draw on the burgeoning data from research into infancy and childhood as they make inferences about the effects of deprivations or conflicts. But all also attend to the here-and-now situation in which their clients find themselves. That includes prominently the therapeutic situation itself, with the transferences and countertransferences that constitute the drama of the treatment. All psychoanalytic theories have this in common, an alertness to the often subtle qualities of the relationship between therapist and patient, and to how the ways of each of the participants exert an influence on the other and on the process of therapy. The therapists seen here take responsibility for their own reactions and responses, analyzing themselves as they attempt to understand and treat these often difficult and provocative clients.

Each of the clinical chapters contains a rather detailed account of the interplay between a particular patient and therapist. So readers garner not only information about the theories that inform the action, but also about what actually transpires between the therapist and patient or, in several cases, a couple. Unlike many old accounts of treatment, where patients were pigeonholed into diagnostic categories and described in presumed "objectivity," here we witness therapists who confess their own humanness, and who regularly engage in introspection about why they may have missed something or made a move they later regret. They believe in the value of what they try to accomplish, that a greater degree of consciousness about what was originally unconscious affords one, whether therapist or patient, a greater sense of agency in constructing one's life.

The first chapter will give something of the history of the relationship between social work and psychoanalysis, and the concluding chapter will invite some rethinking about the implications of these ideas for social work education, and, we might infer, for the education of all those in the helping professions.

At the end, readers will find a glossary of psychoanalytic terms that have been used in the chapters, and the bibliography of related clinical social work writings may prove of value to psychotherapists of whatever discipline.

Jean B. Sanville

1 Applying Psychoanalytic Principles to Social Work Practice: An Historical Review

Herbert S. Strean

Although social work has its own knowledge base, its own set of values, and its own unique body of practice wisdom, since its inception the profession has been a constant borrower of knowledge. While there are those who contend that borrowing knowledge is a sign of social work's openness and flexibility (for example, Turner 1986), there are other social work scholars (for example, Kadushin 1959) who have averred that social workers are much too dependent on other disciplines and should concentrate more on developing their own distinctive knowledge base.

Whether we agree with those who admire our flexibility or with those who decry our dependency on other theoretical perspectives, it is a truism that social work practice and theory consist of strands of knowledge from many personality theories and social science perspectives. In the 1990s, the number of theories and perspectives borrowed by social work has reached an all-time high. The contemporary social work student, both in the classroom and in the field, is exposed to learning theory, system theory, role theory, communication theory, classical psychoanalytic theory, ego psychology, and self psychology, to name just a few perspectives.

One theory, psychoanalysis, has been utilized by social workers almost since the inception of their profession and remains an influence to this day. At times, that theory has been the perspective that most influenced social work theory and practice; during other periods, applying psychoanalytic principles has been limited.

It would appear timely to review and assess the seventy-year relationship between psychoanalysis and social work. First, I will attempt to define the terms *psychoanalysis* and *social work*. Second, I will examine the history of their relationship. Third, I will evaluate what social work can profitably utilize from psychoanalysis in the 1990s.

WHAT IS PSYCHOANALYSIS?

Psychoanalysis is a theory of personality, a form of psychotherapy, and a method of research. Although influenced by many theoreticians and practitioners, the findings of Sigmund Freud guide heavily its modes of diagnostic assessment, therapeutic treatment, and research methodology. As a theory of personality, the major tenet of psychoanalysis is psychic determinism. This principle holds that in mental functioning nothing happens by chance. Everything a person feels, fantasies, dreams, thinks, and does has a specific (if not specifiable) psychological motive. Freudian theory alleges that motives and behavior take form primarily within the unconscious, which consists of drives, defenses, superego mandates, and memories of repressed events. How individuals earn a living, whom they choose to marry or not marry, what kind of love they give and receive, how they interact with their children, and how much pleasure they extract from their work and love are all motivated by inner, largely unconscious, forces (Freud 1905).

Freud viewed the human personality from several distinct but intermeshing points of view: structural, topographic, genetic, dynamic, and economic.

The structural point of view focuses on the interaction of the id (which embodies the drives), the superego (which is composed of the conscience and the individual's ideals and ethical imperatives), and the ego (which mediates between the inner and outer world and has many functions, such as the operation and control of thinking, impulses, judgment, frustration tolerance, defenses, and interpersonal relationships). The topographic approach refers to the conscious, preconscious, and unconscious states of mind; the genetic point of view emphasizes that all human beings recapitulate their pasts in the present, while a developmental view allows for the epigenetic–the capacity of the person to alter the outcomes via his/her own efforts and decisions; the dynamic approach refers to the interaction between the instincts and other parts of the psychic apparatus. The economic perspective deals with how psychic energy is discharged and/or restrained. These points of view, when combined, form the psychoanalytic metapsychology, and all of them are considered necessary for comprehending fully the functions of the human personality.

According to psychoanalytic theory, how an individual relates to others is essentially based on how he or she experienced himself or herself during early life with family members. The vicissitudes of interpersonal relationships, in other words, depend on how the individual experienced himself or herself vis-à-vis parents and siblings. Freud further averred that the same psychological mechanisms could be found in all cultures. Although the same libidinal and aggressive drives exist in all human beings and in all cultures, they are molded in different ways by different societies (Freud 1904, 1905, 1926).

The psychoanalytic theory of therapeutic intervention parallels its orientation to personality functioning. Just as its theory of human behavior contends that the individual's adaptation to life cannot be fully understood unless the meaning of wishes, defenses, superego admonitions, and history are exposed, a similar perspective is needed in treatment. Individuals cannot be substantially helped unless they become aware of wishes, defenses, superego admonitions, and memories. In the treatment situation, the patient is asked to observe "the fundamental rule" and say everything that comes to mind. As patients study how they distort the analyst, that is, develop *transference* reactions to the analyst–and face how they resist in the therapeutic situation–conflicts become resolved and more energy becomes available for more productive work and love. As the aforementioned enactments are taking place, the analyst studies his or her own countertransference reactions so that he or she can more objectively intervene on the patient's behalf (Freud 1904, 1912).

Early in the history of psychoanalysis, it became apparent to Freud and his followers that the difference between the "patient" and the "nonpatient," or the difference between the "neurotic" and the "normal" is one primarily of degree. As psychoanalyst Harry Stack Sullivan (1953) stated it, "We are all more human than otherwise."

Psychoanalysis has pointed out that the difficulty with much research on human beings is that it must take full account of introspective data, yet it is exactly these kinds of data which are so difficult to test. If one human being asks another a question, the answer is a variable one—depending on the question and the relationship between the questioner and the questioned. If it is agreed that this idea is accepted even in non-psychoanalytic circles, it must be pointed out that this phenomenon depends on many psychoanalytic notions—transference and counter-transference factors, resistances, counterresistances, and a host of other unconscious variables. There is, therefore, every reason to continue to test psychoanalytic notions (Strean 1991).

A frequent criticism of psychoanalysis has been that it is untestable scientifically. In their book *The Scientific Credibility of Freud's Theories and Therapy*, Fisher and Greenberg (1977) tried to describe every reported experiment relevant to psychoanalysis. They concluded that it is clearly verified that Freud's ideas can be translated into testable hypotheses, many of which have indeed been tested. They show that the quantity of experimental research data on Freudian ideas greatly exceeds that available for most personality theories.

Despite the fact that most people come to a therapist only when they become desperate, there is evidence that individuals who undergo psychoanalytic therapy move toward what Reuben Fine has called the "analytic ideal" (1981); they can love more genuinely, seek pleasure, achieve sexual gratification, have a feeling for life maturely guided by reason, have a role in the family, work, be creative, have a sense of identity, communicate, and be free of symptoms.

WHAT IS SOCIAL WORK?*

In contrast to psychoanalysis (and some other professions such as medicine, law, the ministry), social work is difficult to define, even for its practitioners. Whereas most lawyers, doctors, and ministers probably share similar notions regarding their professional work, social workers demonstrate much variation in their responses when asked about the major tasks of their profession. Indeed, when the question was posed to a leading social

*Parts of this section were originally published in the *Journal of Social Work and Policy in Israel*, vol. 4, pp. 77–100, 1991. The article was entitled "Social Work and Psychoanalysis."

work educator, Professor Helen Perlman, she remarked that to attempt to define social work "takes courage or foolhardiness or perhaps a bit of both" (Perlman 1957, p. 3). The problem still remains. According to Frank Turner (1986), social work is still difficult to define and "social work practice does not have an accurate theoretical base" (p. xxvii). Similar sentiments have been expressed by social work scholars Hollis (1972) and Siporin (1975).

Social work has come to mean different things to many different social work practitioners and theoreticians. It initially meant alms to the poor and other forms of charity (Richmond 1922). It has meant marital counseling and child therapy (Hamilton 1947) as well as family therapy (Ackerman 1957). It has connoted income maintenance (Ginsberg 1983), health care (Germain 1984), work with the mentally retarded (Dickerson 1981), helping individuals and families in rural areas (Farley 1982), child welfare (Zuckerman 1982), clinical treatment of substance abusers (Brill 1981), work in the schools (Winters and Easton 1983) and more.

Different methods of working with people have been associated with social work. Casework (working with individuals and families in counseling and psychotherapy) has been one of the most popular specializations in social work, and for many years it was the sole method. Group work (working with individuals and families in social, recreational, and therapeutic groups), and community organization (planning and executing change in sectors of the community) have been traditional methods in social work for over fifty years. The methods keep proliferating; to these long-established specializations have been added social administration, social policy, and social work research.

Perhaps it is not possible to offer a definitive answer to the question, "What is social work?" because many different individuals, groups, and institutions define it depending upon the perspective from which they view it. Social work, with its multiple tasks, personnel, methods, and fields of practice, may have no simple definition and therefore can have no single, unique operational definition. Like psychoanalysts, many social workers focus on the internal lives of individuals in an attempt to improve their psychological well-being (Hollis 1972). However, like sociologists, many social workers concentrate on the situational forces in individuals' lives which cause stress, such as poor housing or deteriorated neighborhoods. In 1959, Alfred Kahn suggested that the unifying conceptual key to social work seems not to have yet been identified. Thirty years later, other social work scholars shared similar sentiments (Rosenblatt and Waldfogel 1983, Turner 1986).

Although social work, in many ways, seems to defy a firm definition and has a somewhat vague knowledge base with inadequate theoretical underpinning, it is a profession that has had a long and intense relationship with psychoanalysis. Let us now turn to a review and examination of this relationship.

SOCIAL WORK AND PSYCHOANALYSIS: AN HISTORICAL TOUR

Mary Richmond and "The Friendly Visitor"

When social work emerged as a profession in the United States, Canada, and England at about the turn of the twentieth century, its major goal was to "elevate the poor" (Richmond 1917). Although allowing in theory that a compassionate attitude was necessary, social workers who dealt with the poor often took a harsh stance toward them (Hellenbrand 1972). Mary Richmond, who wrote the first textbook on social work (*Social Diagnosis*, 1917), tried to infuse warmth and sensitivity, as well as an orderly and scientific perspective, into agency practice. She emphasized the individualization of each case and advocated a sympathetic relationship between the "friendly visitor" and the client. Her book was essentially a sociological attempt to locate the causes of the client's plight in an understanding of the transactions between the client and his or her reference groups. Therefore, much of the social worker's activity at that time involved intervention in the client's environment. Work with clients themselves consisted primarily of advice and moral suasion.

In her book *What is Social Case Work?* Richmond (1922) listed the kinds of case situations that were part of a typical case load of the friendly visitor.

> A small boy in need of a father.
> A husband and wife who cannot agree.
> A fatherless family with children who are not receiving proper care.
> A widow with children who is not an efficient homemaker.
> An older woman with difficulties which her relatives fail to understand.
> [p. 27]

Home visits were made quite frequently by the friendly visitor. Part of a case record by a friendly visitor is as follows:

> Ms. Young and her little daughter at home. Front room had been fixed up with some old prints, one or two runner rugs, and a few other things that made it appear homelike. The kitchen also had a strong home atmosphere. The wash tubs had been painted by Mr. Young. The dish cupboard . . . was full of shining dishes. . . . Mr. Young came in, it being lunch hour, carrying a load of wood on his shoulder. He showed a good deal of pride in what his wife had accomplished in the way of making the house look like home, and also in his own handiwork as a painter. [Richmond 1922, p. 56]

The friendly visitor of the 1920s eventually recognized that manipulating the environment of a client or giving him or her advice rarely altered a shaky self-image, a punitive conscience, or self-destructive behavior. The social worker needed a perspective that would not only provide some understanding of the social forces contributing to the client's maladjustment, but would also consider such crucial intervening variables as the client's motives, affects, anxieties, coping capacities, defenses, conscience, and personal history. Attempts were made to utilize dimensions of learning theory, Gestalt theory, and some concepts from the Individual Psychology of Alfred Adler, but these attempts appeared to be short-lived (Richmond 1922, 1930).

While social work in the 1920s was looking for assistance in understanding and helping its clients enhance their functioning (realizing that manipulating clients' social systems and giving them advice was insufficient), psychoanalysis was being noticed by social workers and others—professionals and nonprofessionals. Sigmund Freud, together with several of his colleagues, had appeared at Clark University in Worcester, Massachusetts, in 1909 and had talked about the unconscious, self-destructive behavior, anxieties, defenses, transference, and countertransference (Jones 1953). Some social workers were entering psychoanalysis themselves and a significant number of intellectuals found many of psychoanalysis's precepts valuable and interesting (Gay 1988).

Social workers liked what Freud had to say about the poor man and woman. The founder of psychoanalysis averred that one may reasonably expect that at some time or other the conscience of the community will realize that the poor man or woman had as much right to help for his or her mind as that person had for the surgeon's means for saving his or her life. Freud contended that by combining psychotherapy with material support, poor people might be able to enhance their functioning (Freud 1904).

Freud's theory, by the beginning of the 1930s, had a very dramatic impact on social work practice. Furthermore, Freud's role at any specific time in social work's history has tended to serve as an important barometer regarding social work's overall priorities, concerns, values, and focus.

During its long affiliation with social work, psychoanalysis has been esteemed and demeaned. Esteemed because it seemed to provide much help to the practitioner in understanding the meaning of the client's behavior and resolving treatment impasses; demeaned because its findings regarding the unconscious, sexuality, and aggression have been very anxiety-provoking and threatening to those who were unfamiliar with its aims and goals to liberate the human being from pain and conflict.

In the 1930s, Freud's perspective refocused the social worker's lens from poverty to the person who was poor, and from social problems like desertion and alcoholism to the individual personalities who were beset by them. Psychoanalytic theory helped transform a one-dimensional moralistic approach to human beings in trouble into a non-judgmental psychosocial process. Incorporating the notion of the unconscious into diagnostic and therapeutic plans encouraged social workers to be less self-righteous with their clients. Recognizing that unconscious forces stimulated maladaptive behavior, the worker could take a more realistic view of the human being and be more compassionate as he or she aided the client to struggle with inner and outer forces.

Perhaps one of the tenets of psychoanalysis that has influenced social work practice the most is the notion of compassion, that is, the therapist's willingness to identify and empathize with the client and be ready to acknowledge, "I could be this client. His (her) struggles are similar to mine and just as I would like to be understood in a non-judgmental manner, this is the attitude I will try to present to my client."

The social worker of the late 1920s and early 1930s also looked to Freudian psychology for other purposes. In contrast to some of the other concepts that came into vogue at the time, for example, behaviorism, psychoanalysis could demonstrate how the client's past experiences contributed in a major way to current malfunctioning. Many social workers since the 1920s and 1930s have been able to recognize that the same kind of attachments to parents and to significant others that were experienced in the past are constantly sought in the present, even if these attachments bring disappointing results.

By the late 1930s, psychoanalytic theory enabled social workers to realize that not only were external pressures major contributing factors in their clients' psychosocial problems, but so also were internal pressures, such as prohibitive superegos, weak ego functioning, and unresolved, infantile wishes. Psychoanalytic theory also helped social workers to recognize that apparently unredemptive individual suffering—such as the need for punishment or masochistic fantasies—can gratify unconscious wishes. Freudian psychoanalysis was by now being utilized by most social workers and, though its insights were often startling and frightening, it had the effect of helping social workers become more sensitized to the inner life of the client and to relate to that inner life with more discipline, understanding, and compassion.

The Growing Relationship between Social Work and Psychoanalysis

During the fourth decade of this century, psychoanalysis could be considered a sub-culture in America, Europe, and elsewhere (Gay 1988). Analytic teaching institutes were growing in number; psychiatrists, educators, social scientists, and even the clergy were incorporating psychoanalytic concepts into their work. Literature and politics were finding "the unconscious" quite palatable as an explanatory concept. Psychoanalysis was achieving a high status, particularly in North America and in Europe (Jones 1953).

In social work, one of the effects of the Depression was to bring clients from many walks of life to the profession's attention. Working with a varied clientele, social workers could better appreciate the psychoanalytic proposition that injured narcissism, anxiety, defensiveness over sex and aggression, unconscious guilt, and interpersonal conflict are universal phenomena.

During the 1930s and 1940s, social workers began to turn to Freudian psychoanalysis for therapeutic procedures to help their clients resolve problems. By appreciating the universality of transference, social workers began to comprehend why their clients' extreme love, hatred, or ambivalence toward them could be a distorted expression of immature cravings and maladaptive defenses and could then go on to help their clients learn how they might be distorting their perceptions of others. The psychoanalytic concept of resistance helped the social worker understand why advice was frequently not heeded, interpretations not heard, and environmental assistance not accepted. Psychoanalysis also provided procedures for helping clients resolve their resistances to change. They were encouraged to abreact important memories and feelings, particularly forbidden sexual and aggressive wishes.

Writing in 1940, Annette Garrett pointed out that Freudian theory had actually changed Richmond's *social* diagnosis and *social* treatment into a *psychosocial* diagnosis and a *psychosocial* treatment. By adapting Freudian theory to practice, the social workers could now individualize each person–situation constellation, recognizing that each individual reacts to crises in an idiosyncratic manner, and that each individual client, with a unique past and unique strengths and weaknesses, determines in many ways what happens to him or her in day-to-day functioning. By the 1940s, many of the psychoanalytic therapeutic procedures such as clarification, confrontation, and interpretation were being used to assist clients to understand themselves and achieve better mastery of their lives.

A More Discriminating Use of Psychoanalysis

At first, psychoanalysis was exclusively an id psychology. However, as psychoanalytic practitioners worked with patients, they began to learn that the awareness of drives created anxiety, and defenses were needed by the patient to protect himself or herself. Anna Freud was one of the first psychoanalysts to discuss this important human dynamic comprehensively in her classic work, *The Ego and the Mechanisms of Defense* (1946).

Social workers followed the same pattern as psychoanalysts. Many errors in practice occurred because practitioners did not always appreciate the protective function of defenses. The social workers in the late 1940s had to be taught and/or learn from experience with clients that defenses such as denial, projection, and repression were needed by the client to ward off the inevitable discomfort when a forbidden impulse reached consciousness. Toward the end of the 1940s, the social work literature contained many caveats from writers pointing out that the client's defenses had to be respected.

Within psychoanalysis the ego was becoming the more popular interventive target and the id tended to recede into the background. Ego psychology, as formulated by psychoanalysts such as Heinz Hartmann (1964), Erik Erikson (1950), and Anna Freud (1945), became quite popular among mental health workers in the late 1940s and 1950s. In contrast to an emphasis on the drives, ego psychology stressed the importance of the client's interpersonal relationships (object relations), his or her internalized interpersonal world, the importance of the client's reality functioning, and other ego functions such as strengthening the client's adaptive defenses, judgment, impulse control, and frustration tolerance.

Hartmann's, Erikson's, and Anna Freud's work was most compatible with dominant social work thinking in the 1950s. Not only was the preoccupation with the strengths and limitations of the client's ego compatible with the social work approach, but, perhaps of more import, social workers were pleased to have eminent analysts place emphasis on the client's social context and on the importance of significant others in making diagnostic assessments and in formulating individualized treatment plans. In the 1950s, buttressed by psychoanalytic concepts, ego supportive therapy, that is, strengthening the client's ego functions, became the modal intervention for social work practitioners (Bandler 1963). "Ego functioning" and "ego defects" became comman parlance. The social worker began to understand that many marital problems were established to escape anxiety, that children's ego problems could be an expression of unconscious identification with parents, and that one could support certain functions of the psychotic patient's ego by understanding the dynamic meaning of hallucinations and delusions (Federn 1952).

One of the major contributions of ego psychology to social work practice is that by emphasizing functioning and interpersonal relationships, it could help in the diagnosis and treatment of very disturbed clients, those frequently referred to as borderline or ambulatory schizophrenic. Ego psychologists emphasized direct observation of infants and children, refined considerations of early developmental phases, studied superego development more carefully, and researched narcissism, psychic trauma, and other kindred phenomena. All of this helped social workers better understand and treat the more disturbed client (Blanck and Blanck 1974).

Social Work and Psychoanalysis Diverge

While mainstream psychoanalysis continued to adhere to its major precepts with some further increments from object relations theory and other dimensions of ego psychology, social work practice and social work theory began to diverge from psychoanalysis. While Anna Freud (1965) was prescribing that the empathetic but neutral therapist should maintain an equidistance from ego, id, and superego, social workers concentrated much more on the ego, often depreciated the id, and tended to ignore the superego. This divergence of emphasis, in addition to many other factors, coalesced during the late 1960s and 1970s, causing much of social work to move away from psychoanalysis.

As social workers concentrated more on the client's ego, particularly its relationship with external reality, they became less interested in the individual and much less focused on his or her unconscious. Instead, they became much more interested in the kind of interactive processes where the ego can be directly observed, that is, in parent–child and marital dyads, family units, small groups, and communities. Long-term treatment was quickly being supplanted by short-term conjoint marital counseling, family therapy, and group therapy. The theoretical insights of psychoanalysis no longer seemed to be an appropriate underpinning for work with dyads, families, and groups; consequently, social work practitioners turned more and more to social systems theory, role theory, learning theory, and communication theory to study interactions and transactions rather than wishes, defenses, and superego commands.

The wider culture of the 1920s had emphasized introspection and self-sufficiency. Consequently, psychoanalysis was compatible with the major ethos of the time. However, the 1960s and to some extent the 1970s were times when looking outward became the dominant theme, and social workers refocused their lens on issues such as the War on Poverty, the community mental health movement, the domestic Peace Corps, and Vietnam. Psychoanalysis did not appear to provide much help for the social worker whose goal was to curb the effects of poverty in a community, reduce apathy in a suburb which sorely needed a community mental health center, or meet the needs of a whole tenement of welfare clients. Slowly, social problems became crucial to the profession, social planning became comparatively more prestigious than clinical work, and as the social sciences seemed to be a more appropriate knowledge-base for social work, it became fashionable by the 1970s for social workers to remove themselves from psychoanalysis.

During the 1970s, it was frequently alleged that social work's tie to psychoanalysis over four decades had stifled social reform, leading the profession away from addressing social problems with concern and competence (Borenzweig 1971). Some authors noted social work's disengagement from the poor and considered the field's alleged preference for middle-class clients the result of the profession's illegitimate preoccupation with the human being's internal life and the verbal technique of psychoanalysis (for example, Riessman 1964). Research that pointed to the ineffectiveness of social work intervention often ascribed the failure to social work's tie to psychoanalysis (Fischer 1976). It was asserted that the family was not being helped (Ackerman 1958), children were being insensitively placed in institutions and foster homes (Mahoney and Mahoney 1974), and environmental factors were overlooked in the assessment of clients' problems (Pincus and Minahan 1973)—all because social work utilized psychoanalysis as a theoretical underpinning.

Of course, the popularity of psychoanalysis in the wider culture also started to ebb in the late sixties and seventies. The long period of time that psychoanalytic treatment required was being deplored in favor of short-term therapy, family therapy, and group therapy (Turner 1986). Other theoretical perspectives such as learning theory and system theory were gaining more ascendancy. Feminists were attacking Freud and psychoanalysis for being a phallocentric ideology (Freeman and Strean 1981), and many university professors were questioning the validity of psychoanalysis as a personality theory, a treatment, or as a research instrument (Fine 1979).

During the 1960s, when the profession turned its lens outward and became engaged in the War on Poverty, racism, sexism, civil injustice, and other broad social problems, the status of the direct-service practitioner declined, and the positions of the social activist and social planner were elevated. Many social work educators, researchers, and administrators contended that the impact of social problems like poverty and mental illness could not be lessened appreciably by helping people through casework and group work, but that social action, social planning, and social legislation were required. Thus in the early 1970s, one of the oldest and most prestigious casework agencies in North America, the Community Service Society of New York, drastically altered its policies to give priority to social action and social legislation, abolishing many of its traditional direct-service functions. Many social agencies emulated the C.S.S. and began to confine their direct therapeutic services to crisis intervention and to short-term therapy.

The late 1960s and 1970s also witnessed another phenomenon which lowered the status of the direct-service practitioner. Many agencies that traditionally employed social work graduates of master's degree programs as counselors and therapists replaced these practitioners with personnel without graduate training in social work, that is, with B.S.W.'s. Schools of social work contributed to the trend by beginning to train and encourage graduate students to go into supervision and administration rather than direct service.

Helping professionals outside of social work also moved away from their therapeutic roles toward an interest in modifying the social framework. Furthermore, not only were therapy and social change perceived by many professionals as two different realms of endeavor, each with its own separate technical requirements, but practitioners of each began to appear as feuding political enemies. As one writer concluded:

> Two major orientations are observable on the contemporary scene. One stresses dynamic inner psychological forces, psychotherapy, and individual change. The other emphasizes external forces and social manipulation and is antitherapeutic. The behaviorist, organic psychiatrist, and social worker–social manipulator are in one camp; the psychoanalyst, dynamic psychiatrist, and therapeutic caseworker are in the other. [Fine 1975, p. 447]

In response to the above trends, the National Federation of Societies for Clinical Social Work was founded in 1971 to establish standards for direct-service practitioners and a peer-review system to serve the needs of providers and consumers of direct service. In this way, its founders were also expressing publicly their conviction that the leaders of the social work profession were paying limited attention to the interests of the clinical social worker. The founding of the journal *Clinical Social Work* in 1972 can also be attributed to the feeling among many social workers in direct services that their professional interests were insufficiently addressed in the established social work periodicals.

Social Work in the 1980s

Although the National Federation and the N.A.S.W. both legitimized the existence of clinical social work, this development did not bode too well for some of those social workers strongly identified with the overall social work profession. Many social workers in the 1980s renounced their identification with social work and tended to view themselves exclusively as psychotherapists and/or psychoanalysts. These disaffiliated social workers often appeared to move away from traditional social work concerns such as poverty, racism, and sexism. Furthermore, they tended to reaffirm a stereotype of the clinician as one working exclusively with middle-class patients who introspect and verbalize, but who do not suffer from basic economic and other primary hardships. In the 1980s, social work practice became quite enamored of a variety of symptom-oriented therapies such as sex therapy, primal therapy, sensitivity, and encounter groups. Behavior modification became one of the most popular forms of therapeutic intervention and short-term treatment increasingly became the treatment of choice.

Schools of social work tended to move away from emphasizing the assessment and treatment of the individual client. Instead, dyads, families, groups, and communities became the more dominant units of diagnostic and therapeutic attention. Casework was increasingly dropped as a method and was merged with group work as more and more students were trained to become generalists—experts on everything from the treatment of the individual to the organization of the community. As the unit of diagnostic and treatment attention became enlarged, psychoanalysis and ego psychology became more *passé*, and perspectives such as role theory, system theory, learning theory and organization theory became much more in vogue. *Ecology*, *eco-systems* together with *reinforcement* and *social learning* were the frequently used terms in schools of social work in the 1980s.

In the 1980s, the concerns of many schools of social work tended to be reminiscent of casework in the 1920s—short-term work with an emphasis on the client's situation, but with limited attention given to the client's unconscious wishes, defenses, superego reactions, transferences, and resistances. Few social work texts had anything to say about the client's sexual fantasies, sexual transference reactions, psychosexual history, or the worker's countertransference reactions. The social work student in the 1980s, like the aspiring caseworker in the 1920s, was frequently viewed as a general change agent who focused on the external social situation and manipulated the environment.

By the 1980s, social work encompassed a rich diversity of treatment modalities and theoretical perspectives. Many social workers began to practice psychotherapy, family therapy, and group therapy privately as well as in agencies. By the 1980s, the private practice of social work was growing by leaps and bounds and was being legitimized and legalized throughout North America. There was, however, a group of social workers, smaller in number than heretofore, who tended to decry psychotherapy and paid special attention to the pluralistic needs of clients resulting from ethnic and racial differences (Rosenblatt and Waldfogel 1983).

WHAT CAN SOCIAL WORK UTILIZE FROM PSYCHOANALYSIS IN THE 1990S?

At the beginning of this chapter, I stated that one of my aims was to try to respond to the question, "What can social work utilize from psychoanalysis in the 1990s?" Although social work practice has moved away from psychoanalysis, it is my thesis that there is a large body of psychoanalytic knowledge that is very pertinent to social work practice. Before discussing these pertinent contributions, it is important to differentiate between psychoanalysis as an intensive form of therapy on the one hand, and social work practice on the other.

While psychoanalysis seeks to alter basic character structure, social work practice as formulated for the 1990s aims to help the individual improve his or her functioning in social roles, such as spouse, employee, parent, and colleague, that is, enhance psychosocial functioning. The psychoanalyst, in order to help modify a patient's character, uses such procedures as free association, dream analysis, and an intensive exploration of the patient's transference neurosis. The prevailing style of the social worker, on the other hand, is to utilize face-to-face interviewing, to eschew dream analysis and intensive exploration of the transference, and to focus discussions on the client's day-to-day problems.

It should be noted, however, that psychoanalytic treatment, as Freud and the early analysts conceived it, has been modified by contributions from self psychology, object relations theory, developmental theory, and increments from ego psychology, to name just a few sources of modifications. The writings of Kohut (1971, 1977) have been very helpful in introducing students and practitioners to the injuries and deficits of the self in early development and to the consequences of such injuries. Kohut, who had a long association with social work and social workers, has emphasized popular social work concepts such as *empathy* and *attuning* onself to the client's concerns. Object relations theory (Blanck and Blanck 1974) has stressed the importance of the client's interpersonal relations, which has helped social workers better understand and treat the client's difficulties coping with his or her social roles.

Psychoanalysts have traditionally focused exclusively on the internal life of the client while social workers have focused on both the client's inner world and external reality. For example, in working with an unemployed or physically ill client, the social worker will focus diagnostically and therapeutically, not only on how the client experiences the self and his or her plight, but may intervene in the client's situation and work collaboratively with a prospective employer or a physician. Hence, social work is what Hollis (1972) terms *a psychosocial therapy*.

With increments of knowledge coming from self psychology, object relations theory, and ego psychology, social workers can relate to the person in his or her situation with more certainty, and help in such seemingly overwhelming situations as the treatment of incest, work with people with AIDS, or with violence-prone clients. These disenfranchised clients now have a chance (Shapiro 1983).

Recognizing some of the differences between current social work theory and practice and current psychoanalytic theory and practice, how can psychoanalysis contribute to all social work practitioners who work with clients in the 1990s?

What often occurs in many social work settings is that the prospective client leaves the worker prematurely. It is quite clear that fewer clients would leave treatment prematurely if more social workers could integrate the psychoanalytic notion that the client's presenting problems give him or her some form of unconscious gratification. The man who goes from job to job, the husband and wife who are constantly bickering, the parent and child who cannot communicate well, the family that is scapegoating one of its members, the group that cannot achieve much solidarity—all these individuals and groups, from a psychoanalytic perspective, are unconsciously participating in the creation of their presenting problems and receiving some gratification and/or protection from them. This perspective is of value in addition to whatever other perspectives the worker wishes to utilize.

It would also be helpful to keep in mind that when prospective clients make requests or demands, these requests and demands have unique unconscious meaning. Parents who wish to place a child in an institution may be unconsciously asking for help with their underlying hatred toward the child. A spouse who requests a divorce may be unconsciously asking for help with forbidden sexual wishes. Almost all applicants for social work help have resistances to facing personal anxieties and are usually interested primarily in defending themselves from seeing their own responsibilities for their problems. For example, the man or woman who has job difficulties often finds it easier to project these difficulties onto the boss; the troubled spouse frequently denies his or her own role and projects interpersonal difficulties onto the partner; parents may repress forbidden wishes and feelings that become activated in the parent–child relationship; and group members, through reaction formation, may condemn their colleagues without noting how they are protecting themselves. If the defenses of applicants are understood as necessary for their sense of self-cohesion at the time, and not attacked as though they were defenses against the social workers, they will find it easier to become clients, because their sense of vulnerability is being protected rather than being prematurely exposed.

Regardless of the social worker's unit of attention and field of practice, it is extremely helpful, perhaps necessary, to understand the unconscious meaning of a client's request and the unconscious contribution he or she is making to the problem. When the social worker does not accept the client's statements literally, but recognizes that they evolve partially from id wishes, superego mandates, defenses, and unique personal history, the client can frequently be helped to stay in treatment.

In making a diagnostic assessment of the person–situation constellation and evaluating how the two components interact, psychoanalytic theory can also be quite helpful. In fact, the complete metapsychological system referred to earlier can be utilized. For example, using the structural and topographic models, we can determine how chronic complaints of spouses about each other are very often expressions of unconscious wishes. The man who complains that his wife is a "cold, frigid bitch" may unconsciously desire such a wife. The parent who chronically complains that his or her son or daughter is too aggressive may be aiding and abetting the over-aggressive behavior. In fact, psychoanalytic theory constantly offers a guide in helping the social worker ask, "What is the client doing to aid, abet, and sustain the very problem about which he complains?" (Strean 1991).

In reviewing the client's history (the genetic approach), the social worker will want to assess how much the client is recapitulating the past in the present. Is he or she attempting to make a spouse, employer, or colleague into a parental figure? Or still seeking gratifications that were more appropriate in childhood? Or has some external stimulus that caused anxiety triggered a regression?

Two major contributions from psychoanalytic practice which are insufficiently utilized in current social work practice are *transference* and *resistance*. Social work students and some practitioners need help in facing the fact that all clients respond to their interventions on the basis of their current transference position. If the client wants to defeat the worker, the most brilliant interventions in the world will be defeated. Or if the client needs to idealize and love the worker, anything the latter does or says will be responded to positively. Social workers, when psychoanalytically informed, can help clients to see how and why they respond to assistance the way they do. Moreover, they may rediscover the idea that all clients fear change, at least to some degree. If this were not so, treatment would be a very simple procedure. Unfortunately, all clients have some fear to face themselves and their environment realistically, and social workers who are psychodynamically sophisticated can show them what they are afraid of–to love, to assert, to defend, to have sex–and why they are afraid.

Although social workers may draw on many perspectives to assess their clients comprehensively and to help them therapeutically, psychoanalysis has an enormous amount to contribute. Many social work practitioners continue to find the psychoanalytic perspective indispensable in assessing and treating clients in a variety of social work settings. Psychoanalysis aids the social worker in understanding the meaning of the client's presenting problems; it helps the practitioner understand the client's fear of involvement in the helping process; it intensifies and broadens the clinician's psychosocial assessment, sensitizing the worker to the client's conflicts and strengths; suggests possible modalities which will be of help; and provides technical procedures and technical understanding of the therapeutic process.

REFERENCES

Ackerman, N. (1958). *The Psychodynamics of Family Life*. New York: Basic Books.

Bandler, B. (1963). The concept of ego-supportive psychotherapy. In *Ego-oriented Casework*, ed. H. J. Parad and R. R. Miller, pp. 27–44. New York: Family Service Association of America.

Blanck, G., and Blanck, R. (1979). *Ego Psychology II*. New York: Columbia University Press.

Borenzweig, H. (1971). Analytic theory: a historical analysis. *Social Work* 16:7–16.

Brill, L. (1981). *The Clinical Treatment of Substance Abusers*. New York: Free Press.

Dickerson, M. (1981). *Social Work Practice with the Mentally Retarded*. New York: Free Press.

Erikson, E. (1950). *Childhood and Society*. New York: Norton.

Farley, O. (1982). *Rural Social Work Practice*. New York: Free Press.

Fausel, D. (1990). Profiles in independent social work: Herbert Strean. *Journal of Independent Social Work* 4:81–90.

Federn, P. (1952). *Ego Psychology and the Psychoses*. New York: Basic Books.

Fine, R. (1971). *The Healing of the Mind*. New York: David McKay.

—— (1975a). *Psychoanalytic Psychology*. Northvale, NJ: Jason Aronson.

—— (1975b). The bankruptcy of behaviorism. *Psychoanalytic Review* 62: 447–467.

—— (1979). *The History of Psychoanalysis*. New York: Columbia University Press.

—— (1981). *The Psychoanalytic Vision*. New York: Free Press.

Fischer, J. (1976). *The Effectiveness of Social Casework*. Springfield, IL: Charles C Thomas.

Fisher S., and Greenberg, R. (1977). *The Scientific Credibility of Freud's Theories and Therapy*. New York: Basic Books.

Freeman, L., and Strean, H. (1981). *Freud and Women*. New York: Ungar.

Freud, A. (1946). *The Ego and the Mechanisms of Defense*. New York: International Universities Press.

—— (1965). *Normality and Pathology in Childhood*. New York: International Universities Press.

Freud, S. (1904). Freud's psychoanalytic procedure. *Standard Edition* 7:249–256.

—— (1905). Three essays on the theory of sexuality. *Standard Edition* 7: 125–248.

—— (1912). The dynamics of transference. *Standard Edition* 12:97–108.

—— (1913). On beginning the treatment. *Standard Edition* 12:121–144.

—— (1923). The ego and the id. *Standard Edition* 19:1–66.

—— (1926). Inhibitions, symptoms, and anxiety. *Standard Edition* 18:77–174.

Gay, P. (1988). *Freud: A Life for Our Time*. New York: Norton.

Garrett, A. (1940). Modern casework: the contributions of ego psychology. In *Ego Psychology and Dynamic Casework*, ed. H. Parad, pp. 38–52. New York: Family Service Association of America.

Germain, C. (1984). *Social Work Practice in Health Care*. New York: Free Press.

Ginsberg, L. (1983). *The Practice of Social Work in Public Welfare.* New York: Free Press.

Hamilton, G. (1947). *Psychotherapy in Child Guidance.* New York: Columbia University Press.

Hartmann, H. (1964). *Essays on Ego Psychology.* New York: International Universities Press.

Heiman, M. (1913). *Psychoanalysis and Social Work.* New York: International Universities Press.

Hellenbrand, S. (1972). Freud's influence on social casework. *Bulletin of the Menninger Clinic* 36:342–359.

Hollis, F. (1972). *Casework: A Psychosocial Therapy*, 2nd ed. New York: Random House.

Kadushin, A. (1959). The knowledge base of social work practice. In *Issues in American Social Work*, ed. A. Kahn. New York: Columbia University Press.

Kahn, A. (1959). The function of social work in the modern world. In *Issues in American Social Work.* New York: Columbia University Press.

Kohut, H. (1971). *The analysis of the self.* New York: International Universities Press.

—— (1977). *The Restoration of the Self.* New York: International Universities Press.

Levin, A. (1976). Private practice is alive and well. *Social Work* 21:5–13.

Mahoney, K., and Mahoney, M. (1974). Psychoanalytic guidelines for child placement. *Social Work* 19:6–14.

Meyer, C. (1977). Social work practice vs. clinical practice. *Alumni NewsLetter*, Spring Issue, Columbia University School of Social Work.

Perlman, H. (1957). *Social Casework: A Problem Solving Process.* Chicago: University of Chicago Press.

Pincus, A., and Minahan, A. (1973). *Social Work Practice: Model and Method.* Itasca, IL: F. E. Peacock.

Reid, W., and Epstein, L. (1977). *Task-Centered Practice.* New York: Columbia University Press.

Richmond, M. (1977). *Social Diagnosis.* New York: Russell Sage Foundation.

—— (1922). *What is Social Casework?* New York: Russell Sage Foundation.

—— (1930). *The Long View.* New York: Russell Sage Foundation.

Riessman, F., Cohen, J., and Pearl, A. (1964). *Mental Health of the Poor.* New York: Free Press.

Rosenblatt, A., and Waldfogel, D. (1983). *Handbook of Clinical Social Work.* San Francisco: Jossey–Bass.

Shapiro, J. (1983). Commitment to disenfranchised clients. In *Handbook of Clinical Social Work*, ed. A. Rosenblatt and D. Waldfogel, pp. 888–903. San Francisco: Jossey–Bass.

Siporin, M. (1975). *Introduction to Social Work Practice.* New York: Macmillan.

Strean, H. (1978). *Clinical Social Work.* New York: Free Press.

—— (1979). *Psychoanalytic Theory and Social Work Practice.* New York: Free Press.

—— (1985). Clinical social work: What's in a name? *NASW News* 30:17 and 36.

—— (1991). Social work and psychoanalysis. *Journal of Social Work and Policy in Israel* 4:77–100.

—— (1993). Clinical social work: an evaluative review. *Journal of Analytic Social Work* 1(1):5–24.

Sullivan, H. (1953). *The Interpersonal Theory of Psychiatry.* New York: Norton.

Turner, F. (1986). *Social Work Treatment,* 3rd ed. New York: Free Press.

Winter, F., and Easton, F. (1963). *The Practice of Social Work in Schools.* New York: Free Press.

Wolberg, L. (1968). Short-term psychotherapy. In *Modern Psychoanalysis,* ed. J. Marmor, pp. 343–354. New York: Basic Books.

Zuckerman, E. (1983). *Child Welfare.* New York: Free Press.

2 Listening, Hearing, and Understanding in Psychoanalytically Oriented Treatment

Joyce Edward

Among Freud's most enduring contributions to the technique of psychotherapy has been the way in which he listened, heard, and understood his patients. The "science and art of therapeutic communication" (Perlman 1971, p. 9) that Freud formulated and the respectful attitude toward his patients expressed through his communicative approach continue to influence analytically and many non-analytically oriented therapists today, irrespective of their particular discipline or their theoretical outlooks.

Freud (1893) began to develop what was to become the psychoanalytic communicative process in his work with his very first patient, Frau Emmy Von N. A sharp and often angry critic, Frau Emmy complained that Freud's interventions in their sessions, his questions and suggestions, served only to interrupt her thoughts. Finally she admonished him to cease asking her where this or that came from and let her talk. Taking her advice seriously, Freud began to diminish his activity and started to carefully follow her ideas, taking particular note of the effect of each of his interventions on what she subsequently had to say. Through this process, patient and analyst reached an understanding of Frau Emmy's personality and difficulties that Freud's previous efforts had failed to provide (Kanzer and Glenn 1980). Out of this experience and others like it, Freud became convinced that within all patients there exists a capacity to contribute to their own treatment through saying whatever is on their minds.

It is the purpose of this paper to examine what it means when we speak of an analytic communicative process, to consider how clinical conditions for its development may best be promoted, and how an analytic perspective influences clinical listening, understanding, and intervening. To demonstrate the points to be made, I will include a fairly detailed process account of one session with a young woman in once-a-week psychotherapy, who was seen over a period of six months.

THE COMMUNICATING PATIENT AND THE LISTENING THERAPIST

The patient in an analytically oriented treatment is called upon to communicate in an unusual way. He or she is asked to relate everything that comes to mind without censoring any thoughts, to follow what Freud referred to as the "fundamental rule" (Freud 1912). At best, this is a difficult task to achieve. The very experiences, thoughts, wishes, fantasies, and fears that a person is asked to share are often those that he or she has sought to protect himself or herself from knowing. Thus, an important aspect of the therapist's task is to help each patient understand what it is that tends to limit the ability to communicate freely (A. Kris 1990).

The therapist, as he or she listens and observes, must in turn remain open to hearing and observing whatever the patient expresses, no matter how painful, objectionable, or discomforting that may be. In other words, the therapist seeks to follow the patient's thoughts without censorship (Freud 1912). This involves listening with an open mind and with what Freud (1912, p. 112) referred to as "evenly suspended attention." By this I understand him to mean that the therapist should avoid directing attention to anything in particular and instead remain open to all that the patient has to say. This allows both patient and therapist to discover that which is as yet unknown, and helps them avoid falsifying what is expressed in order to fit preconceived ideas.

An open mind, however, is not an empty mind. What a therapist hears and attends to in a session is inevitably affected by all he or she already knows about the patient, as well as by the therapist's theoretical outlook, personality, experiences, philosophy, and affective responses to what the patient is communicating. The recommendation that the therapist maintain "evenly hovering attention" nonetheless serves as a reminder not to abandon what we know, for we cannot, but to remain open to what we and the patient do not as yet know. It means a "wait-and-see attitude," a questioning on the part of the therapist as to "what else that we have never thought of might be significant at this moment?"

Just as it is difficult for the patient to speak freely, so is it difficult for the therapist to listen openly. As a fellow human being, the therapist shares with the patient a need to protect against knowing, experiencing, and feeling certain phenomena. That which we cannot as therapists attend to in ourselves frequently becomes difficult to comprehend in our patients. A therapist too must come to understand those unconscious issues that limit what he or she can hear and attend to. One's own analysis, continuing self-analysis, and at times consultation with peers or a more experienced colleague are means by which therapists ordinarily seek to ensure and expand their capacity for open-minded listening.

MODELS OF THE MIND AND THEIR INFLUENCE ON LISTENING

The way in which a therapist listens, and what he or she finally hears, is affected not only by intrinsic factors but also by extrinsic ones. This communicative process is, for example, significantly influenced by the models of the mind and the theories of pathogenesis that guide a particular clinician. These tend to sensitize a clinician to certain themes and issues. While today, psychoanalytic theory includes a variety of perspectives, there is significant common ground among analytic clinicians, which helps to determine what they hear and how they understand what is expressed in a session. Among these commonly held ideas is that a significant portion of human mental activity, character, and behavior is determined by unconscious phenomena, derivatives of which may be expressed in dreams and parapraxes, as well as certain linguistic devices such as metaphors, symbols, displacements, and condensations. Psychoanalytically oriented clinicians also share the view that what we as humans are and do as adults, what we wish for, fantasize about, fear, or castigate ourselves for are, more often than not, rooted in our childhood pasts; that most forms of psychopathology are likely to be the result of developmental vicissitudes resulting from innate or environmental deficiencies, traumas, conflicts, or any combination of these; and finally there is agreement that the analysis of the phenomena of transference, countertransference, and resistance are central to the treatment process.

In addition to these and other basic concepts, psychoanalytic theory now encompasses a variety of theoretical models that affect each clinician's unique way of listening and understanding. Self psychology, interpersonal psychology, ego psychology, object relations theory, relational theory, intersubjective theory, Jungian theory, Kleinian theory, and other outlooks have greatly extended the theoretical map. Each model has somewhat different implications for understanding pathology and treatment. For those who are strict adherents to one or another point of view, their particular theory tends to serve as the primary prism through which they observe the clinical data. Others, like Fred Pine (1985), propose that each of the major psychologies (self psychology, ego psychology, object relations theory, and conflict/drive theory) has relevance for the human condition and can be drawn upon at different therapeutic moments in understanding a given patient.

Clinicians must have theories to orient their listening. They serve as a structure that helps to "hold" us (Casement 1990). We cannot, in fact, according to Sanville (1987), function without theory. She agrees with Bruner (1977) that there exists a tendency within the human mind to form and test hypotheses about what is occurring in the world. The danger is that we will narrow our view, selecting only that information from exchanges with our patients that fits our theory. We are then faced with the possibility of losing the opportunity to "find out with the patient" as Freud (1895) did with Frau Emmy what is unique and new. Ideally, theories should help guide rather than restrict exploration (Reed 1987).

DIAGNOSIS AND THE COMMUNICATIVE PROCESS

The way in which we diagnose our patients is also likely to affect how we listen and what we hear. Psychoanalysis was developed initially as a technique for working with neurotic patients, persons who are ordinarily understood as having achieved adequate psychic development, but who have remained under the pathogenic influence of an inadequately resolved Oedipus complex. The treatment of the neurotic has therefore involved an effort to help the patient gain a more favorable re-resolution of that nuclear conflict and achieve more adaptive compromise formations. With this view in mind, therapists working with such individuals have tended to be particularly sensitive to communications that appear to contain derivatives of unconscious fantasies and wishes, to manifestations of conflict and prohibitions, and to expressions of defense against anxiety and depressive affect as they relate to the nuclear conflict of the neuroses, that is, the oedipal conflict.

In contrast to the neurotic, the histories of patients suffering from borderline and narcissistic pathology have led many clinicians to view those disorders as more likely to be the outcome of serious early developmental deviations. The findings of developmental researchers also support this view of such pathology as the result of failures on the part of those ministering to the child, severe early traumas, innate deficiencies in the developing child's capacities to utilize available developmental offerings, or any combination of these. This theory of pathogenesis has tended to sensitize clinicians to preoedipal developmental issues, to render them especially alert to indications of early transferences which are the outcome of the patient's need to relate to the therapist as a caretaker (anaclitic transference) or as a part of or complement to the self (narcissistic transferences). This outlook tends to lead to a focus on the relational needs of such individuals. Thus, for example, there are some therapeutic moments when the content of the patient's communications is thought to be less important than the relational aspect of the communicative exchange with the therapist.

A clear-cut demarcation between the neuroses and more severe pathology, with the former being distinguished by oedipal issues and conflict and the latter by preoedipal issues and deficit, has however been giving way. We are recognizing that individuals (Rangell 1979) all along the diagnostic spectrum can suffer from conflicts at each level of development, oedipal in borderlines and preoedipal in neurotics. We must be ready, therefore, to hear issues from all developmental stages and along all developmental lines in the material of all patients.

CASE EXAMPLE

I am reminded here of a young woman, with what I regarded as borderline pathology, with whom I had the opportunity to work for two different periods of treatment. The patient, Mrs. Miles, (Edward, Ruskin, and Turrini 1992) manifested complex developmental problems and had experienced severe deprivation and trauma from early on. Among the many concerns she expressed in our initial work was an obsessive need to change into a freshly ironed nightgown whenever she awakened during the night despite her awareness that her gown was not soiled. Drawing on Robert Knight's (1954) idea that certain neurotic-like defenses in borderline patients may serve important adaptive functions rather than constituting defenses against the drives, as well as Pao's notion (1979, p. 225) that symptoms frequently represent "the best possible solution the person can come up with at a given moment," I am especially sensitive to material that might explain a more troubled patient's behavior from an adaptive standpoint. Thus, when in one session Mrs. Miles complained about the "craziness" of her nightly gown changes, and next recalled a bed-wetting incident, I began to wonder about the connection between these two thoughts. As Arlow (1979) has reminded us, contiguous ideas are very likely to be related, and careful attention to the sequence of the patient's thoughts in the session can serve as a helpful guide to understanding. Mrs. Miles, in this instance, then began elaborating upon her bed-wetting. She spoke of how her mother had teased and beaten her until she finally stopped. She next spoke of how she had slept during the summers in a very hot attic and to cool off she sometimes threw a glass of water on herself. As I listened to this sequence, noting the contiguous ideas, and bearing in mind Spitz's (1965) proposition that young children seriously deprived of care may use their body products as a substitute object, I began to consider the possibility that her bed-wetting represented in part an early effort to comfort herself. I therefore told her that I had the sense that when she was little and all alone, being wet somehow made her feel good, and thus had something to do with her wetting the bed. However, what was once an effort to aid and comfort herself had ultimately become a source of shame and punishment. While she had finally controlled her urinating, perhaps the impulse to urinate had lingered on. Thus when she got up at night she felt she had or would wet herself, and this led, without her understanding it, to the feeling that she needed to change her gown. In time and with similar explanations regarding other efforts to compensate, Mrs. Miles was able to relinquish this behavior. Most importantly, her image of herself as a "dirty, bad" child became modified. Instead, she began to recognize herself as having once been a child who had tried to cope as best she could with the painful adversities of her early life.

Five years later, Mrs. Miles returned to treatment, following a serious automobile accident. While no longer changing her gown, she revealed in the course of this work another concern about her night attire. She found herself worrying that some emergency would require her to run out of her house during the night and her gown would be insufficiently attractive. We then began to understand a central unconscious fantasy, in which her father, who had abandoned the family when the patient was three years old, would return during the night to take her away with him. She must be ready to leave and attractive enough so that he would want her. Analysis of this fantasy put us in touch with some of the oedipal determinants of her difficulties, as well as enriching our comprehension of additional pre-oedipal determinants. From our work on this fantasy we could also see more clearly how pre-oedipal developmental vicissitudes had burdened Mrs. Miles's subsequent oedipal negotiation (Edward 1994). One sees in this case how important it is to deal with the conflicts of each developmental phase as they emerge. Perhaps Mrs. Miles's return to treatment was, in part, motivated by her own dim awareness that we had discovered only one part of the story in our first piece of work.

ATMOSPHERE OF SAFETY

The fact that there are inevitably both intrinsic and extrinsic obstacles to a free psychoanalytic communicative exchange makes it incumbent upon a therapist to do everything possible to create a therapeutic environment that maximizes the patient's sense of trust and safety. A person must feel safe if she is to relate her innermost thoughts no matter how reprehensible, exciting, shameful, or frightening they may be and to express through the transference often unacceptable needs, strivings, wishes, and fantasies. Roy Schafer (1983, p. 14) has argued that there is no better means of establishing a safe therapeutic atmosphere than for a clinician to adopt those attitudes of neutrality, anonymity, and abstinence that Freud recommended in his "Papers on Technique" (1911–1915). When not defensively maintained or rigidly adhered to, each of these attitudes helps to protect the therapeutic exchange.[1] Abstinence on the therapist's part ordinarily helps assure that neither partner's wishes or fantasies will be acted upon in the treatment. Neutrality means that a therapist keeps his or her own feelings in check, avoids imposing his or her own values, judgments, or desires on the patient, and maintains respect for the patient's wishes and capacities. It also means that a therapist remains impartial regarding the patient's mental processes, showing equal interest in activities of the ego, the id, and the superego. A therapist's relative anonymity makes it possible for the patient to use the therapist as a figure for unconscious fantasies and transference responses, and also affords additional protection against the therapist's unconscious efforts to use the patient for his or her own psychic purposes.

These "analytic attitudes" (Schafer 1983) also serve to protect the freedom of the therapist to listen, hear, and respond in an attuned way. While needing to feel with and for the patient, a therapist must also, as will be elaborated upon later, be able to step back from the patient and to think about him or her. To the extent that these analytic attitudes help maintain a sense of the therapist's own boundaries, they facilitate this capacity for shifting from "being with" the patient to observing, understanding and interpreting what "being with" the patient has yielded. Contrary to the impression of some critics, these attitudes do not preclude courtesy, responsiveness, cordiality, gentleness, and empathy (Schafer 1983). When Freud (1909) compared a therapist to a surgeon who needs to put his or her feelings aside, a comparison often interpreted as a sign of coldness and detachment, Schafer (1983) argues that he was suggesting that, like a surgeon, the therapist must concentrate his attention on a single aim: the carrying out of the treatment as skillfully as possible. While the surgeon recognizes the pain his or her procedures may temporarily cause a patient, he or she must not be put off from taking the requisite medical measures. So it is with the therapist who must inquire into matters that he or she appreciates may temporarily upset the patient, and maintain

1. It is beyond the scope of this chapter to consider the therapeutic value that often accrues from both carefully planned departures from these stances, such as when a patient needs the therapist to serve some real function, or from unintentional departures, which may come to be understood and effectively utilized as "diagnostic responses" (Casement 1990).

attitudes that are often difficult for the patient to tolerate, in the interest of advancing the treatment.

UNDERSTANDING

The patient's freedom to speak his or her thoughts and the therapist's open-minded listening pave the way for understanding but do not ensure it. How do we derive meaning from the patient's associations and behavior? How in particular do we understand the unconscious communications?

According to Freud (1912), the therapist's primary tool for such understanding is his or her own unconscious. Freud envisioned the therapeutic process as one in which the therapist turns his or her unconscious like a receptive organ toward the transmitting unconscious of the patient, adjusting himself to the patient as a telephone receiver is adjusted to a transmitting microphone. Just as the receiver converts back into sound waves the electric oscillations in the telephone lines that are set up by sound waves, so the clinician's unconscious is able, from the derivatives of the unconscious that are communicated by the patient, to reconstruct unconscious phenomena that have determined the patient's free associations. By paying attention to his or her own thoughts, associations, and daydreams while observing and listening to the patient, the therapist may then begin to formulate ideas about the significance and meaning of the patient's thoughts. It is assumed that what occurs to the therapist under the stimulus of the patient's associations, gestures, and behaviors tends to resonate with what is occurring unconsciously within the patient (Arlow 1979). In describing this unique communicative process, Theodore Reik (1948) has suggested that the analytic therapist listens with a "third ear," which alerts him or her to what people do not say, but only feel and think. This "third ear" can also be turned inward, allowing the therapist to hear those voices from within the self that are ordinarily obscured by conscious thought processes.

That the unconscious of one person can tune into that of another is not difficult to comprehend. As humans, we all share certain unconscious and conscious experiences, fantasies, wishes, and fears. Irrespective of culture, class, ethnic background, or economic condition, in one form or another we each have been through the same biological experiences. We have developed in the body of a woman, ordinarily as a result of a sexual joining between a man and a woman, and have emerged into the world the same way. We eat, we sleep, we eliminate, we have sexual urges. We have experienced hunger and pain as well as satisfaction and pleasure. Irrespective of our differences, all of us must face the limitations of our human power and our mortality. We cannot have been children without knowing what it is to fear abandonment, or the loss of a needed person, or the loss of the love of someone we value, or the fear of bodily damage, or the pain of narcissistic humiliation or feelings of exclusion. We each have had to contend with the recognition of our separateness and the longing for what we have lost. We have known the impossibility as children of fulfilling our desires and wishes to be in our parents' places, to displace and surpass them, as well as the fears and guilt such ideas arouse. We are all familiar with feelings of desire, envy, jealousy, hate, and wishes for revenge. Thus, a patient's thoughts and behaviors inevitably strike a familiar chord in us, though we too, like our patients, at times may need to resist knowing.

Closely linked with Freud's proposition that one's unconscious can tune into another's is the concept of empathy, a term that we hear much about today, though, like so many terms in psychoanalysis, it does not mean the same thing to everyone. According to the most recent glossary (Moore and Fine 1990), empathy is a mode of "perceiving by vicariously experiencing (in a limited way) the psychological state of another person" (p. 67). Literally the term means "feeling into" another person. The patient's verbal expressions, including such poetic devices as symbolism, allusion, and metaphor, as well as their nonverbal actions and their affective expression, impinge on the therapist at work, producing resonating internal parallel states. The therapist's self-perceptions or introspections can therefore serve as a source of information about the patient (Arlow 1979).

Empathy represents a temporary partial ego regression in the service of the treatment, permitting an easily reversible trial identification with the patient. Beres and Arlow (1974) propose that there are two distinguishing features of empathy, the transient identification just noted, and the fact that the empathizer preserves his or her separateness from the other. This sense of separateness is needed so that a therapist may appreciate that what he or she has felt has not only been *with* the patient but *about* the patient. As therapists, we must move beyond identification in order to reflect on what the patient is experiencing so that we may ultimately act to help him or her. This is similar to a mother who initially merges with her child in identification with his or her suffering, but who must at some point step away and suffer *about* the child in order to take steps to relieve her offspring's distress. Sanville (1991) has described this movement as an oscillation between empathy and alterity.

The capacity for empathy is thought to be developmentally related to the early mother–infant symbiosis (Loewald 1970). Therapeutic empathy, however, involves more than a temporary regression to a sense of oneness with another. For the cues of perception to lead to empathy, such functions as memory, thought, comprehension, and conceptualization must be in place (Beres and Arlow 1974). Empathy consists of more than an immediate affective response and it requires considerable development. According to Beres and Arlow (1974), the capacity for empathy ordinarily increases with age and experience, particularly with experiences of suffering.

In this emphasis on the use of the therapist's own unconscious processes and on the empathic mode of listening, the focus is on the inner experience of the therapist as a guide to understanding (Arlow 1979). While what transpires within the therapist's mind is of considerable usefulness, it cannot, however, be relied on alone. As in the case of the actual telephone, messages may be garbled, muddled, and indistinct when transmitted (Arlow 1979). As Arlow has noted (1979), one person's empathy may in fact be another's personal countertransference. In other words, not every association which comes to our minds during a session constitutes an accurate interpretation of the data presented by our patient.

Empathy as a tool for understanding, therefore, must be used in conjunction with other, more objective ways of gathering information about the patient's feelings and behaviors. The data derived from it must be reviewed and integrated with information based on cognition and the exercise of reason. Arlow (1979) has suggested certain criteria which he believes help to transform what would seem to be random associations or disconnected thoughts into supportable hypotheses. He advises that we consider the context in which ideas emerge and that we heed such phenomena as contiguity, repetition, and metaphor, which can alert us to the dynamic relevance of what is being said and may help validate or invalidate insights that are obtained through the empathic exchange.

CASE ILLUSTRATION

In order to demonstrate the foregoing, I would like now to offer a case vignette, drawing on process notes from one session of the five months of once-a-week sessions that I saw the patient. It is offered to demonstrate how I, as one clinician, have drawn on the communicative process, explicated here.

Background

Mrs. Foster was a 50-year-old businesswoman, married and the mother of one daughter. She sought treatment because of intense anxiety, which was impeding her overall functioning. We had worked together successfully some seven years previously for a two-year period. At that time, Mrs. Foster was concerned that after receiving a promotion she had found herself placing her job in jeopardy. At the time she returned for help, her elderly mother was facing a serious operation and she was experiencing the onset of menopause. As I listened to her relate these experiences and her responses to them, I thought of how early separation (Mahler et al. 1975) and/or oedipal issues might be being stirred up under their impact. However, I kept these and other speculations to myself as ideas to be tested over time and discarded in favor of understandings that I as yet could not foresee.

At the time of the session to be considered, which occurred about four months into the treatment, Mrs. Foster's mother's operation had been scheduled. The patient was making plans to be with her. Her older brother lived out of the country so that she had been largely the one responsible for her mother since her father's death ten years ago. An unusually caring and attentive daughter, who was greatly appreciated by her mother, Mrs. Foster wanted to be particularly supportive during this difficult time. Yet, despite her real concern and positive regard for her mother, she found herself frequently resentful of her. At times she experienced her mother as self-centered and intrusive. Yet, even as she spoke of this, she felt guilty, for she recognized that for a woman of her age and poor health, her mother was unusually undemanding and independent. "Was it really intrusive," she asked herself, "for a mother to want to know about her daughter's work or how her granddaughter was doing in school?" She thought not. While there were times when her mother would probably annoy anyone, she felt that somehow she was harboring an irrational anger toward her. She recalled beginning to feel this way sometimes during her adolescence. As a young child, she and her mother had been unusually close. She had warm memories of her early years with Mother who spent much time playing with her and taking her on many pleasant outings, despite a serious physical handicap that impaired her ease of movement.

She knew that she had sometimes been ashamed of her mother's handicap and felt angry at her difference from her friends' mothers. However, their real difficulties began when she was a teenager. They fought constantly. Mrs. Foster understood this as the outcome of her struggle to achieve independence from her mother, as a way of gaining distance from her in order to grow up. However, she now wondered why she had to go to such lengths to be independent. Her mother had not actually tried to keep her too close. She wanted help, she realized, not only to get through her immediate situation, but she felt she needed to understand more about her relationship with her mother in general so that she could feel at peace with her.

Treatment Session

Mrs. Foster arrived a minute or two late for the hour. It was foggy outside and she told me that she had not been prepared for the difficult drive. She advised me to be careful if I went out. She then spoke of a "strange" experience she had when she turned off one highway. She didn't know whether she should go east or west and began to feel disoriented. She feared being lost and was worried about being late for her appointment. I inquired about her thoughts while driving. She was thinking, she said, how miserable her job was. She had also been listening to a program on the radio in which a comedian was being interviewed. It was very funny. Both the woman interviewer and the man she interviewed were having so much fun. She thought to herself, "I am not having fun." She then went on to tell me of an acrimonious telephone exchange she had with a business associate. She had been very angry and told him so. When she hung up she was upset, and finally called him back. He too was disturbed and they agreed to begin their talk over again. She then started to say that she is a "receiver," changed her mind about the word, and groped for the proper term. The words "responder," "reciprocator" of other peoples rage and miseries came to mind. She still couldn't find the right word and looked to me. I pointed out that it was so uncharacteristic for her to have so much difficulty finding the right word and suggested that we might wonder why. She said she could not find the term but she meant that somehow she has to take in other people's miseries. I asked her if she was thinking of a "container." "Not quite," she responded. Mrs. Foster then told me that the surgeon who was operating on her mother phoned her this week. He was very nice. Everything was all right until he advised her that he was sending her mother for a consultation about her incontinence. She repeated, with obvious discomfort, what she had told me the previous week about her mother leaving a puddle of urine on the car seat during her last visit. Neither she nor her mother mentioned it at the time. That made her feel awful. She believed that this thought of her mother's incontinence had something to do with her feelings of disorientation. I wondered what that might be, and she replied that it suggested that her mother was losing some of her capacities. She realized that her mother was growing old and had only a limited number of years ahead. I recognized how painful it was for her to watch her mother's physical decline and yet I suggested that her incontinence must have some special meaning, in view of the powerful reaction it aroused in her. What came to Mrs. Foster's mind following my comment was her mother's telling her that when she was about 9 or 10 months old, her mother had toilet trained her. Mrs. Foster had a hard time believing that. "How could that be done?" She thought perhaps her mother really didn't remember correctly. She was clearly annoyed and suggested that she must have had "accidents" at that young age.

I asked what occurred to her regarding accidents. She began to speak at that point of friends who were getting a divorce. The wife had left her husband and she knew how abandoned and angry he must feel. They alternate weekends using their country house. Recently the husband called his wife to tell her that a mirror broke when he was in the apartment but he insisted that he had nothing to do with it. Mrs. Foster doubted that. "He probably did break it," she commented, "as an act of revenge."

My own thoughts at this point shifted back to all the trouble she had locating the proper word to describe her feeling that people were leaving her with their misery. It was not clear to me why this was so.

Was I seeking to avoid what Mrs. Foster last said, or was I intuitively making a connection between the idea of revenge and whatever she associated with the word she could not locate? Whatever the case, I did follow my own promptings at the time and returned to the issue of her forgetting, saying that I was still wondering about the difficulty she had had in finding the proper word for what she had in mind at the start of the session. Mrs. Foster responded that in some way the word was connected with what she had spoken of in the previous session, her wish for mutuality with her mother. There was then a long pause. "I have it," she said, "the word I was searching for is 'receptacle'."

In retrospect, I think it would have been useful had I wondered with Mrs. Foster why she had connected mutuality and the idea of receptacle. However, as therapists, we all must unfortunately live with missed moments. Instead, I was at that moment struck by the fact that she had again referred to the previous session. She had earlier referred to that session when she told me of her mother's incontinence. I suddenly was reminded that I had made a mistake in the previous hour, and her references to accidents and mistakes took on new meaning. I began to wonder whether my mistake and Mrs. Foster's reactions to it might not have provided the context for this particular session. What had happened was that I had had to see Mrs. Foster in another office for that particular session and had incorrectly written out the directions. She nonetheless found it and maintained throughout that session that it was no problem. When she mentioned something that she said in that previous hour, I now hypothesized that something in that hour connected with the issues of this session. I therefore said to her that in thinking about the word she had brought us back to our last session again. It had been an unusual one and I wondered if perhaps she had some additional thoughts about it later. She proceeded to tell me that she had been worried about finding the temporary office even before she realized that I had made a mistake in the directions. She shared that she was always apprehensive about finding a new place. However, she insisted, as she did earlier, that she was not angry at me. I took this to be a negation and hypothesized that indeed she was angry at me, though I did not say this to her. Mrs. Foster then went on to say that she actually had felt good. She has been so hard on herself and it relieved her to see that I could make errors. "Everyone," she asserted, "limps a little bit." I said, "limps a little bit?" That is a saying, she told me, that one of the salespersons used at work. She added that of course her mother really does limp, but it was her intention to convey that everyone made errors.

I said, "You think of your mother when you think of mistakes" (the reader will note that she also thinks of her therapist as she thinks of her mother). "Actually," Mrs. Foster said, "I thought of my mother as perfect when I was a little girl. It hurt when I realized she wasn't." She then had another idea about herself as a child. According to her mother, when they went to a bathroom away from home she would always ask if it were clean and would carefully place toilet paper on the seat. Her mother thought that was so "cute." Mrs. Foster angrily said that her mother put too much emphasis on such matters.

She suddenly thought of the fact that she was going to be missing several sessions when she tended her mother. She was sorry to have to do that. At this point she referred back to her past treatment with me, to a time when she had called for an extra appointment. She found herself at that time unable to work on her income taxes, needing to do and redo them over and over. She reminded me that I finally, as a result of something she had said, connected what was happening with ideas of masturbation. She thought it was strange that we never went back to that subject again. There then was a brief silence and she said, "I did calm down after that session and completed my taxes." What we talked about then must have helped. I took this as an announcement to me that what we were talking about in this session also connected with something sexual and that we should try to understand what that connection was.

"Why," I inquired, "do you think that masturbation comes to your mind at this moment?" She replied, "Well, sex is the last hard thing we need to work on. It is unbelievable that I, a modern woman, should be so uncomfortable talking about sex. I admire my daughter for being able to talk freely and thoughtfully about it. Yet it is impossible for me to do so. Even mentioning the word masturbation now is upsetting. Maybe I can bring this up today because I will not be coming for a few weeks while I am caring for my mother." In my mind I deleted the "maybe" and considered this an assertion that she needed to qualify. I also noted that, after speaking about sex, Mrs. Foster referred again to her mother, suggesting a relationship between the two ideas by virtue of their contiguity. I said that she seemed to connect her reactions to her mother with something sexual. "Might you have some thoughts about that?" I asked. She said she could think of nothing.

It was getting close to the end of the session at this point, and I decided to share what I understood from what she was saying. I said something to the effect that I had the sense that my mistake last week and her mother's incontinence, which she also regarded as a mistake or accident, had brought to mind what was, in her eyes, a more serious mistake, that of her mother's being sexual. I thought that when she discovered this she had felt rejected and abandoned, as she thought the husband of her friend had felt due to their divorce. Like him, she was hurt and angry and wanted revenge. Mrs. Foster then became quiet. After a few minutes she said she had been thinking about how, when her mother visited her recently, she had called Mrs. Foster to the window to watch two doves mate. In her mother's "typical lyrical, romantic way" she had described what was happening. Mrs. Foster found herself enraged. She could not figure out why. She then added that today was the anniversary of her father's death. "Isn't it amazing," she said, "what the mind can do? I think now of both my mother and father when I think of the mating doves."

After another few moments of silence she said, "Perhaps I wasn't so pleased with your mistake. I kept thinking that I don't proofread and you didn't proofread well. What difference does it make?" she asked herself. "But," she said, "if I had not figured out the mistake and gotten lost I would have been angry. I don't know if I thought it at the time but it occurs to me now that if I have to be here on time, you have to be good, too. I think I was angry." I said, "I think so too, but it is difficult to acknowledge that anger. If you are expected to be good then I, like Mother, should be good and not make mistakes, since mistakes make you think of your mother and father mating."

"Did I tell you," Mrs. Foster asked, "about the talk with my daughter about sex? She is so open and has such a positive outlook. She would not mind me knowing if she made love, but I would mind knowing. I know her attitude is healthy, but I have this punitive, unforgiving attitude about sex–about my own sex life in particular." I said, "You did not want to know about your parents having sex and you have not forgiven them for having it. Like the man and woman on the radio, your mother and your father seemed to you to be having fun and you weren't. You have been angry about that." I then went on to connect this with her often inexplicable anger, her compelling need to distance from Mother, and the painful guilt she experienced in relation to all of this. I pointed out that, thanks to her thoughts in the session, we could better understand how burdened her task of caring for Mother in her present health crisis has been by these previously unknown concerns. She said, "My poor mother!" She then looked at a book shelf in the office and laughed. "Would you believe it?" she said. "Of all the books on your shelf, my eye is lighting on the one entitled *Envy and Gratitude*. Those are the feelings I have for my mother."

Discussion

In considering this foregoing clinical effort, it is, I think, clear that the understandings arrived at in this short-term treatment owe much to Mrs. Foster's own contributions. She brought to our work a keen intelligence, a fine sense of humor, a sense of trust which facilitated her engagement in the clinical partnership, a capacity to reflect before acting, and a certain "psychological mindedness." The latter may be related to the fact that she had a prior treatment experience which prepared her for the work and led to a certain optimism about the possibility of another favorable outcome. Mrs. Foster's strengths, in my mind, also bore testimony to what I regarded as the adequate nurturing she had received as she was growing up and the favorable development this had facilitated. Having said this, I don't want to leave the impression that only patients with such competent ego capacities can engage in the work described nor that such work can only be done in a second round of treatment. I would only suggest that, had the earlier work not taken place and had the patient not been so capable of engaging in the treatment, the current effort might have required more time and the therapist might have needed to provide more of a developmental opportunity in the treatment than was necessary in this case.

With these caveats in mind, let me now consider how I arrived at the particular understandings that I did in this session. What were some of the ideas coming to my mind? Let me say that when Mrs. Foster initially told me of her disorientation and the fog, my thoughts had turned to historical material she had told me earlier. I knew that there were times when, because of her difficulty in walking, her mother had leaned on Mrs. Foster for help when crossing the street. Mrs. Foster was only a little girl when this began and she recalled being frightened at times that she might not be able to support her mother. Had her mother's infirmed state and her current responsibilities for her mother revived memories of a weak mother and the fright this aroused in her as to her own well-being? Had the current situation perhaps reawakened feelings of disappointment and fear in finding her mother weak and powerless, as opposed to being the illusory omnipotent mother that young children wish for and actually need for a time (Kohut 1971)? There were times in the treatment when an appreciation of such phenomena had seemed significant.

Yet Mrs. Foster had became disoriented on this occasion, according to her report, while listening to a man and a woman on the radio having fun and realizing that she was not having fun. It was followed by her account of the anger she experienced with her colleague and later with the thought of her mother's incontinence, which she linked to her strange feelings. The likelihood of this being a displacement of ideas about the parents' relationship with each other seemed probable to me. The difficulty she had in using the word "receptacle," which can possess sexual significance, seemed to me to further support the notion that thoughts about the primal scene had been stirred up. Mother and Father were having "fun" together and she was alone. Her conscious thoughts about sex and masturbation further strengthened this idea. It therefore seemed to me that it was sexual mistakes that were on her mind. Her mother could make serious mistakes but she was expected to remain a good, clean little girl. In introducing the theme of revenge into these associations, by way of her divorcing friends, Mrs. Foster appeared to me to be letting me know that she too sought revenge for the unfair treatment she thought she had been meted out. The feelings of disorientation I came to regard as defensive rather than an indication that her ego had been overwhelmed. This accords with Arlow's (1966) view that states of disorientation, either depersonalization as experienced momentarily by Mrs. Foster or derealization, may be employed defensively to protect a person from an inner danger. Such ego states can serve a reassuring function. It would be as if Mrs. Foster thought to herself, "I need not be bothered by all of this for it is not happening to me."

I therefore discarded the earlier hypotheses in favor of the later ones. I viewed the patient's direct introduction of sex into the material as affirming that oedipal rather than preoedipal issues were central in this particular session. I believe that Mrs. Foster was herself at least dimly aware of what had been evoked by the events surrounding the session and sensed that in some way her consciously unwarranted anger with her mother was related to her mother and father's "mating." It was as if she were saying, "We must look at this matter of sex now. It has something to do with my seemingly irrational anger at my mother. I also love my mother deeply and I want to be able to understand and deal with whatever is inappropriate in my rage so that I can sincerely offer her the help I want to."

CONCLUSION

The reader is likely to have observed and heard things in this session that I did not, and to have chosen other interventions that would have been equally helpful. I myself was aware of more than I responded to, though there were issues I missed for one reason or another. There was material that I heard but did not address in this session as, for example, Mrs. Foster's death wishes toward her mother. As a matter of fact, if one goes back to the beginning of the session, one can recognize the possibility that these death wishes were also being displaced on to her therapist. She began the session, if the reader recalls, by advising me that I should be careful if I went out. This, incidentally, is a reminder of the importance of paying attention to what the patient begins the session with, for it more often than not suggests the theme of the hour. I chose not to pick up on this material then, feeling that it would be preferable to enable Mrs. Foster to understand better the reasons for her anger before considering more specifically the destructive wishes it led to. We did get to them in time. My failure, however, to pick up on exploring the connection between mutuality and "receptacle" and to explore the interaction between us around the lost word were not deliberate. Why had I felt it necessary to supply this very bright, articulate woman with an extensive vocabulary, the word "container," as I did? I am still left to ponder these responses of mine.

Despite these and other possible technical flaws in this session, we were nonetheless able to draw from it a better understanding of one particular issue of great significance in the patient's mind and life, one contributor to her inexplicable anger toward her mother. According to Mrs. Foster, this effort led in time to a reduction in her anger and enabled her to support her mother through her operation and early recuperative period in a way that brought her mother great comfort and herself a feeling of pride and satisfaction. What was important was that she could feel her love toward her mother and was not just acting the role of a good daughter. She could take in her mother's courage, grace, and humor and was left hoping she could be like her if she had to face such challenges in her older years. Our work together appeared to have have helped fulfill Mrs. Foster's earlier expressed wish to find greater peace in her relationship with her mother.

An array of analytic theory was drawn on in this clinical work. Time does not permit a thorough consideration of the many concepts that guided my efforts. I was mindful, for example, of the way in which progression through separation-individuation (Mahler et al. 1975) and the negotiation of the Oedipus complex contribute to development and its vicissitudes. My effort to understand was influenced in varying measures by object relations theory, self psychology, ego psychology, and conflict drive theory (Pine 1985). What I knew about the phenomena of transference and the way in which the actions and attitudes of the therapist can evoke particular transference responses facilitated my understanding of the interactions between Mrs. Foster and me, which in turn led to some revision of the way she viewed her experiences and responses to the significant figures of her past. A reconciliation with the mother "in her head" allowed for greater ease with her mother "in person." I kept in mind that, like all people, Mrs. Foster employed displacements, symbols, metaphors, and condensations in expressing herself, and I tried to pay careful attention to those figures of speech. I relied on intuition and the empathic exchange, though there were moments when it was difficult to ascertain whether a response was in tune with her or whether it was the outcome of my own personal countertransferences. To the best of my ability, I sought to confirm my inner responses by checking them against the criteria proposed by Arlow (1979) and noted earlier. If one goes back to the session one can see that the sexual theme was repeated in both direct and displaced form, suggesting a dynamic significance to that topic. The context of the session was at least in part my "mistake" and Mother's "mistakes." A connection between sex and mistakes was suggested by their being contiguously expressed, as was the idea of mistakes (the broken mirror) and revenge. One might say that in my intervention I added connecting words. "You think of your parents' sexual life as a mistake they made which hurt and angered you *and* has led you to want to avenge yourself." I believe that Mrs. Foster affirmed the validity of this understanding with her association to the mating doves.

Finally, let me say that there is no question in my mind but that a non-psychoanalytically oriented clinician could also have provided Mrs. Foster with significant assistance. She was facing a life crisis that trained helping professionals of all disciplines are familiar with and skilled in relating to. Caring for one's elderly parents and facing the loss of them is a universally painful experience that can be significantly eased by an empathic helping person who can provide appropriate knowledge, support, and frequently much-needed concrete services. I would suggest, however, that the psychoanalytic communicative process described here, by revealing at least one heretofore unconscious source of Mrs. Foster's previously experienced incomprehensible rage at her mother, not only enabled this patient to negotiate a particular crisis in her life more effectively, but also contributed to important psychic changes. The lessening of her anger toward her mother enabled her to develop a more appropriate, satisfying, mature relationship with her before her mother died, an accomplishment that meant much in both of their lives. Mrs. Foster also became freer to identify with her mother's more valued attributes, especially with the courageous way in which she was facing the difficult tasks of her old age. Finally let me say that the understanding acquired during this session eventually helped to clarify one of the determinants of her less-than-satisfying sexual life. We began to see how her rage at her parents' sexual life, particularly her mother's, had seriously compromised her own capacity for sexual enjoyment. She could not have that of which she wished to deprive her mother. Thus, in making peace with her mother, Mrs. Foster became freer to enjoy her own adult sexual life. In short, I would say that listening and hearing with a "psychoanalytic ear" enabled me not only to help Mrs. Foster deal with the life crisis that brought her to treatment but led in time to an expansion of her sense of self-value, to an increased capacity to allow herself pleasure, and ultimately to an enrichment of her personality.

REFERENCES

Arlow, J. (1966). Depersonalization and derealization. In *Psychoanalysis–A General Psychology*, ed. R. M. Loewenstein, L. M. Newman, M. Schur, and A. J. Solnit, pp. 456–478. New York: International Universities Press.

—— (1979). The genesis of interpretation. *Journal of the American Psychoanalytic Association* 27:193–206.

Beres, D., and Arlow, J. (1974). Fantasy and identification in empathy. *Psychoanalytic Quarterly* 43:26–49.

Bruner, J. (1977). Early social interaction and language acquisition. In *Studies in Mother–Infant Interaction,* ed. H. R. Schaffer, pp. 271–289. London: Academic Press.

Casement, P. C. (1990). *Learning from the Patient.* New York: Guilford Press.

Edward, J. (1994). The interplay between separation-individuation and the oedipus complex: clinical implications. *Psychoanalytic Inquiry* 14:42–57.

Edward, J., Ruskin, N., and Turrini, P. (1992). *Separation Individuation: Theory and Application.* New York: Brunner/Mazel.

Freud, S. (1893). Preliminary communication case 2, Frau Emmy Von N. *Standard Edition* 2:48–105.

—— (1911–1915). Papers on Technique. *Standard Edition* 12:85–171.

Kanzer, M., and Glenn, J. (1980). *Freud and His Patients.* Northvale, NJ: Jason Aronson.

Knight, R. P. (1954). Borderline states. In *Psychoanalytic Psychiatry and Psychology.* eds. R. P. Knight and C. Friedman, pp. 52–64. New York: International Universities Press.

Loewald, H. (1970). Psychoanalytic theory and the psychoanalytic process. In *Psychoanalytic Study of the Child* 25:45–68. New York: International Universities Press.

Mahler, M. S., Pine, F., and Bergman, A. (1975). *The Psychological Birth of the Human Infant.* New York: Basic Books.

Moore, B. E., and Fine, B. D. (1990). *Psychoanalytic Terms and Concepts.* New Haven and London: Yale University Press.

Pao, P.-N. (1981). *Schizophrenic Disorders.* New York: International Universities Press.

Perlman, H. H. (1971). *Perspectives on Social Casework.* Philadelphia: Temple University Press.

Pine, F. (1985). *Developmental Theory and Clinical Process.* New Haven and London: Yale University Press.

Rangell, L. (1979). Contemporary issues in the theory of therapy. *Journal of the American Psychoanalytic Association* 27:81–112.

Reed, G. S. (1987). Rules of clinical understanding in classical psychoanalysis and in self psychology: a comparison. *Journal of the American Psychoanalytic Association* 35:421–446.

Reik, T. (1948). *Listening with the Third Ear.* New York: Farrar, Straus, & Giroux.

Sanville, J. (1987). Theories, therapies, therapists: their transformations. *Smith College Studies in Social Work* March, 75–92.

—— (1991). *The Playground of Psychoanalytic Therapy.* Hillsdale, NJ: Analytic Press.

Schafer, R. (1983). *The Analytic Attitude.* New Haven: Basic Books.

Spitz, R. (1965). *The First Year of Life.* New York: International Universities Press.

3 TRANSFERENCE: A KEY TO PSYCHOANALYTIC SOCIAL WORK

Daniel Coleman

INTRODUCTION

There are many in the mental health field who toll the bell for the death of psychoanalysis. This is unfortunate, for psychoanalysis provides tools that form a basis for understanding what goes on in the psychotherapeutic interchange, whatever the theoretical orientation of the therapist. For example, an understanding of transference/countertransference could save the behavioral therapist from recapitulating some relational dynamic from a client's past, and thus condemning the therapy to failure. Similarly, an understanding of transference/countertransference makes it possible for a caseworker to render advocacy for a client profoundly therapeutic.

The central purpose of psychoanalysis is to understand what exists, not to change things directly. It is in this that psychoanalysis makes the perfect companion to all human-interaction-oriented fields. For example, a teacher who explores the psychoanalytic meanings that her students attribute to her role through their transferences will teach more sensitively, but her insights will not transform the basic form of teaching, nor will they make it psychoanalysis.

This article sets out to give words to the graceful handling of therapeutic relationships done on a daily basis by social workers and other mental health professionals, frequently in environments which do not promote or appreciate the psychoanalytic process. The modern psychoanalytic understanding of transference and countertransference is shown theoretically and practically to fit the interpersonal situations encountered by social worker-therapists. The articulation of a theoretical model of transference-centered therapy that encompasses the necessary and expedient roles of the contemporary mental health professional provides a guide for coherent, insight-oriented practice in a wide range of settings. This synthesis sheds light on the work done by professionals practicing both within and outside of the traditional dyadic psychotherapy model.

DEVELOPMENTS IN EPISTEMOLOGY

The changes in epistemology that have been integrated into psychotherapy theory over the past several decades lend themselves to psychoanalytic social work practice. Constructivism and constructionism in psychology and the social sciences, post-modernism in the arts, and quantum physics are all reflections, in different fields, of human beings recognizing the limitations of linear, positivistic "knowing." Family therapy led the way in attempting to integrate this new epistemology, establishing itself on the recognition of circularity in family systems.

Slipp (1989), in describing his model of object relations family therapy, argued that the psychoanalytic attention to transference and countertransference works with subjectivity and circular patterns even more than other family therapy approaches. He drew a picture of the clinician as one part of the resonating family system, drawing the family's attention to their relational patterns through interpretation–including an ongoing inquiry into what familial roles and functions the therapist is playing out in the interpretative stance in the family.

Cooper (1987/1990) described the evolution of transference interpretation in analytic practice: the changes in general intellectual climate, with a movement away from positivistic assertions and assumptions, accompanied by a shift in clinical theory from intrapsychically based to interpersonal or object relational and self psychological models. In this account of theory development, a change is seen from the positivistic assertions of the scientific basis of psychoanalysis of Freud and others to increasingly subjective and relativistic theoretical developments.

Saari (1994) approached these developments in clinical theory by distinguishing between the hermeneutic (interpretive) and the scientific (causative) views of clinical process. The interpretive and narrative emphasis cautions clinicians from assuming that their constructions developed with clients are "scientific truth." As we will see in the next section, the therapist's acknowledgment of thc ambiguities and unknowns is an opportunity for clients to both create and know their reality–transference constructions.

As will be clear in the following section on theory and technique, transference interpretation that draws on contemporary epistemology places emphasis on respect for clients and their experience of reality. This approach encourages sensitive and empowering therapeutic exchanges between therapists and clients of different genders, ethnicities, and economic backgrounds.

THEORY AND TECHNIQUE

The Holding Environment

The central theme of this chapter is the theoretical and practical aspects of the interpretation of the transference. A piece of important background, however, is a brief look at the treatment relationship as a "holding environment."

In understanding the holding environment, Winnicott's (1956/1990) concept of the true and false self is helpful. This theory grew out of the influence of "baby-watching" on analytic theory (p. 246). He described how "good enough adaption" in infancy "enabled the individual's ego to come into being" (p. 247). If "adaption is not good enough . . . there is no true ego establishment, but instead there develops a pseudo-self which is a collection of innumerable reactions to a succession of failures of adaption" (p. 247).

The goal of therapy in this case is creating a "good enough" holding environment, which allows the "true self" to emerge out of its protective hiding behind the false self. The true self is associated with spontaneous emotional being and an ability to "feel alive" (Winnicott 1956/1990, p. 248).

Bollas (1992) built on Winnicott's true self:

> I believe each of us at birth is equipped with a unique idiom of psychic organization that constitutes the core of our self, and then in the subsequent first years of our life we become our parents' child, instructed by the implicate logic of their unconscious relational intelligence in the family's way of being. [p . 51]

Each of us, and all of our clients, comes to the therapeutic exchange with all of the intelligence of our true self and the layered education which made us our parents' child, then perhaps a favorite teacher's child, and later, a lover's child. The holding environment aspect of therapy is creating sufficient trust and empathic warmth to allow these patterns of relationship–what Freud (1915/1958) called the "pre-conditions of loving" (p. 156)–to come to consciousness.

Freud (1914) called the transference "an intermediate region between illness and real life through which the transition from the one to the other is made" (p. 154). In a similar way, Sanville (1991), drawing on Winnicott and Stern, paralleled the transference with the "transitional space" (p. 85) between an infant and a caregiver. The therapist's intent to help, while respecting the intentions of the client, allows the client to experience the authenticity and vulnerability of his or her inner life. The therapist ideally prepares a safe place for the client to enter into a spontaneous exchange that will highlight both the influences of the past and of the present, and thus contribute to the ongoing sense of an emergent self.

Transference and Interpretation

Cooper (1987/1990) wrote that amongst the wide diversity of therapists worldwide who identify themselves as psychoanalytic, the one area of agreement is the importance of interpretation of the transference. This section will glance at the history of these two concepts, en route to developing a workable definition for contemporary social work practice.

In Freud's lifetime and for several decades beyond, the transference was discussed as a distortion of the real analyst–patient relationship. In this understanding, the patient was corrected through interpretation to resolving his or her transferences, and to seeing reality (Cooper 1987/1990, p. 514).

Freud (1940) offered a definition of transference:

> the patient sees in him (the analyst) the return, the reincarnation, of some important figure out of his childhood or past, and consequently transfers on

to him the feelings and reactions which undoubtedly applied to this prototype. [p. 174]

The concept of transference found in much social work literature was consistent with the psychoanalytic literature of the time (Hamilton 1951, Sterba et al. 1948). It distinguished reality-based reactions and transference reactions as two distinct categories.

Following from this theoretical division of transference and reality attitudes was a technical approach in the social work tradition that advocated reinforcing the reality relationship and minimizing transference. Hamilton's (1951) suggestions for technique included the worker's referring transference developments to outside relationships, and the transference was "sparingly commented upon" (p. 257). She also stated that the transference was limited by the face-to-face interaction of casework (p. 31). This concept of transference as unrealistic, displaced feelings persisted in Woods and Hollis's (1990) revision of their social work textbook.

Gill (1982, 1988) de-emphasized transference-as-distortion by seeking to establish that the client's transferences are "plausible responses" (Gill 1988, p. 269) to the real stimulus of the therapist, but are nonetheless shaped by the client's unique past. Gill (1982) stated, "I conceptualize this indistinguishable interweaving of transference and realistic attitudes as the transference elaboration of a real situation" (p. 83).

Sanville (1991) wrote, "We are increasingly aware that the sense of the real is always created and that, from the start, fantasy also entered into it" (p. 89). Turning to the treatment relationship, she elaborated, ". . . in play we have some sense of timelessness . . . in psychodynamic psychotherapy, reconstructions of the past and their enactments in the transferential present are mutually interdependent" (p. 90).

There is, then, no neat dividing line between transference and reality attitudes. It is a simple fact of human experience that we blend transference and reality to create our own idiosyncratic experience. It is a sign of health to be flexible about these constructions, to appreciate others' viewpoints and to consider ways in which one's transference-reality constructions are limiting.

In discussing Gill's definition of transference, Levenson (1988) suggested an evocative paraphrase of a Marianne Moore poem: that the therapist is "a real frog in an imaginary garden" (p. 139) of the client's unique transference-reality construction.

The technical implication of Gill's position is that the therapist should actively explore the client's reactions to the therapist's character and actions. It is in the interweaving of examining contemporary life situations, the feelings brought up in the transference, and the genetic precursors of these that the healing takes place.

Oremland (1991) stated this delicate balance well, suggesting that the therapist stick to transference interpretations, allowing the patient to make the genetic connections:

> Reconstructive statements come largely from the patient . . . paradoxically, partly resistance to transference-centered interpretations. The psychotherapist further interprets the new information from the past and . . . interweaves the themes of the past with the themes of the present, each enriching the understanding of the other. [p. 47]

Kahn (1991), following Gill's work, suggested a technique of "searching" the client's associations for references to the transference. Like Gill, Kahn stressed tact and respect for the client in making interpretation to "awareness of the transference" (p. 60), saying "I can understand feeling x in that situation, and I wonder if you might have felt x about me as well?"

This emphasis on tact and respect for the client's construction of reality is an important departure from the "blank slate" school of analytic practice, and challenges the concept of transference as a distortion. Gill (1988) wrote: "the patient's experience is not correctly construed as a distortion of current reality in any simple sense but is rather an idiosyncratic construction of that reality with its own kind of plausibility" (p. 269). Kahn (1991) went further in stating that the client's construction is not only plausible, but when seen in light of the insight generated in psychotherapy, an inevitable result of the client's individual history.

One central psychoanalytic concept has taken a quieter role in this understanding of the psychoanalytic process: the concept of resistance. Schafer (1993) commented that he was finding the concept of resistance less useful. As we begin to acknowledge the involvement of the therapist in the client's repetition of past relationships, the concept of resistance moves from being seated in the client to being a limit on the shared understanding possible between the therapist and the client. Schafer questioned, "Whose defenses are we talking about anyway?" pointing out that the therapist and client create a unique interpersonal relationship that is a synthesis of both participants' psychological strengths and limitations.

The therapist's work of reflecting and interpreting to the client shows the therapist's effort to understand, the "adult equivalent of being held" (Ornstein 1988, p. 109). As Pulver (1992) noted, the therapeutic action of insight cannot be separated from the value of the "understanding relationship," but "*an understanding relationship cannot be maintained without insight into the dynamics of the relationship itself*" (p. 204, emphasis in original).

The effort to create insight into the dynamics of the here-and-now relationship between the therapist and the client also creates a holding environment for therapists to develop insight into their own psychic contribution to the relationship. These ruminations are likely to extend beyond the hour for the therapist, to supervision, self-analysis, or to the therapist's own therapy or analysis.

Lipton (1977b) cited an example which I find characteristic of the approach to therapy that I am developing. Lipton described a patient who came to a session with a severe cold and complaining of how ill she felt. The psychoanalyst–a medical doctor by training–offered her a thermometer. This incident, and the patient's feelings and thoughts about it, were explored just like any other issue in the analysis. There is a portion of the relationship, that human and personal relatedness, that is non-technical, but which nonetheless can be analyzed in the technical relationship (Lipton 1977a, p. 259).

The contemporary mental health professional, perhaps in particular in public agencies, is often faced with the situation of offering something analogous to Lipton's thermometer to clients. The effort to use a psychoanalytically based approach is not violated by these kinds of real assistance to clients. The challenge is to make the meaning of the interaction for the client as much as possible a part of the therapeutic dialogue.

THE PSYCHOANALYTIC SOCIAL WORKER

The social worker's role with socially disenfranchised clients provides a rich source of transference stimulants that can be transformed into therapeutic material through transference exploration and interpretation. The social worker's functions directed by the need of the client, for example, as an advocate, will evoke some of the dynamics of the client's past important relationships. As a part of the holding environment, the therapist's insight into these issues can help him or her function in a way that the client experiences as supportive and helpful.

A further step is to open up the discussion with the client about the thoughts and feelings about the social worker and the social worker's actions. Transference exploration of this kind offers the client the rare experience of being able to reflect openly about a relationship while it is happening. The social worker models what Kahn (1991) calls "nondefensiveness" (p. 15) in this dialogue about the client's feelings. This turning of awareness to the feelings happening in the moment affords new possibilities of insight that there-and-then reflection, encrusted with defensive rumination, can never approach.

In practice, a social worker applying these principles is an active participant in the therapeutic dyad. Real interventions such as offering support, discussing realities of outside relationships, and so on, are followed by collaboratively exploring with the client feelings and meanings. This exploration should naturally flow from transference issues to outside and historical relationships and back to transference. Interpretation is not dictating, like an oracle, to the client the inner meaning of the words and action, but is engaging in a collaborative effort to understand with the client. Interpretations develop in the shared interpersonal space of the therapeutic holding environment.

CLINICAL EXAMPLE

In this example, the therapeutic potential of the holding environment and of transference interpretation functions with a social work intervention of advocacy. The client, "Linda," is presenting herself in therapy with a deep depression, and with a wish to overcome the effects of her childhood experiences of physical and sexual abuse.

> Linda is in her early twenties, and has gone back and forth over her lifetime between living in her native Latin American country and the United States. The mother of a young daughter, the client has struggled with alcohol dependence to get through an abusive marriage. Prior to coming to therapy, Linda had stopped drinking through an alcohol treatment program after losing custody of her daughter. With bringing to an end a decade-long pattern of substance abuse, Linda began to con-

front some of her scattered memories of childhood, and, in one instance, experienced a flashback to an incident of being sexually abused.

At the time that the client came to therapy, she was living with her grandfather, who was supporting them both on a small monthly retirement check. She had come to the clinic at her grandfather's request, as he had become concerned about her staying in bed all day, not caring about anything, and making overt comments about suicide.

In the initial interviews, Linda presented several layers of concerns that contributed to her current depression. She was deeply troubled by her limited contact with her young daughter, and with her chances of regaining custody; she struggled with a pervasive hopelessness, that things had gone wrong beyond repair; and she felt at times that this fate was "right" for her, that she was "no good" and "deserved" all that befell her. The initial phase of the therapy focused on providing a holding environment on a range of levels, from the real to the symbolic. In the first weeks, additional sessions were scheduled until Linda's suicidal thoughts had ceased.

Linda's dawning awareness of her childhood experience was discussed, and she made efforts to understand this experience through friendships with several other survivors of abuse. An initial transference placed me with these friends, as I was familiar with the popular literature on childhood sexual and physical abuse.

The therapy with Linda followed a course that reflects the breadth of focus needed in psychoanalytic social work. Her initial depression was responded to with times of listening, times of action, and some time spent preparing for the psychotherapeutic work. Acknowledging and "sitting with" her pain at this time in her life was important in establishing a therapeutic alliance. Also important, and relevant to Linda, was aiding her in her deadlock with the social service system. This was accomplished by providing her with information, advocating for her, and facilitating movement in her situation. In the initial sessions, some time was spent exploring with Linda her feelings and reactions to me, in preparation for being able to talk about more powerful transferences as they developed later.

In an early session, the client was depressed that she would never see her daughter again, and would never have the legal resources to represent her interests. After a time of exploring these feelings and issues, I offered to the client that we phone a legal aid office. She agreed, and we were able to set up an appointment for her. Her affect changed from flat and depressed to buoyant and happy.

The final minutes of the session switched back to an exploratory mode. I questioned her about her feelings about my offer of immediate assistance, and the change in her feeling state from the beginning to the end of the session. She stated that she had always felt unworthy of help; she described her parents leaving her with extended family members, leaving her feeling undeserving of assistance, and of being at fault for her predicament. I suggested that she was afraid that I too would fail her in that way, and she expressed relief that this belief was not confirmed.

In this example the client was expressing an intrapsychic reality–that she felt unworthy–and that this reality was both a response to current conditions and a transference from her lifetime of experience. It is a reasonable and natural social work intervention to offer the client the assistance of the worker's knowledge of the social service system and the worker's class privilege in getting a response from that system. The therapeutic value of this interaction is brought back to the intrapsychic level by returning to an exploratory mode, questioning the significance of this interaction for the client.

This example of the therapeutic dialogue early in the treatment gave way to more sophisticated and affectively charged transference developments. The pattern of the transference was initiated by building a maternal, supportive, positive relationship.

Around this time, the client discussed a memory of some neighbors of her family when she was a child, several unmarried older sisters who lived together. As her memories of peace and acceptance in her visits to these older women were explored, and the transference implications questioned, she somewhat apologetically stated that she was feeling that I was like these caretaking matron figures. We shared some affectionate, humorous moments as this transference was elaborated and the juxtaposition of inner and outer realities became clear.

My countertransference feelings included a satisfaction with providing a safe environment for Linda, but there was an otherworldly, all-good

> quality of the transference. In supervision I discussed allowing Linda to move out of this idealizing transference in her own time. There were several indications that this time was approaching. Linda would periodically talk about her experiences with men, and her tendency to be seductive. For a number of sessions she denied any feelings of this kind for me.

As Schafer pointed out in asking "Whose defenses are we talking about anyway?" my own defensiveness around discussing the sexual feelings in the therapeutic relationship collaborated with Linda's defensiveness and use of denial. For both of us, however, this was a partially self-aware use of defenses, for the therapy was drawing steadily towards Linda's experience of inappropriately sexualized relationships with several adult male relatives. The time of this building and testing of a positive, holding transference was necessary to provide the safety for the sexual dimension of the relationship to emerge and to be worked through.

> A pivotal session occurred when Linda called requesting a session earlier in the week than her scheduled session. She complained of feeling anxious and fearful, and that she was wondering a lot about what had happened to her as a child. Linda opened the session describing fights with several significant male figures in her life. She began to cry and turned her body away from me and hid her face for several minutes. As her sobbing subsided, I asked her what she had been experiencing.
>
> Linda slowly straightened her body and smiled, her face streaked with tears. She said that as she talked about her recent fights with men, she had become afraid that I would be angry with her. She was silent for a moment. I reflected to her that she had partially curled her body, and covered her face, as if she needed to hide or felt ashamed. She described how, as she cried, the flashback of being sexually abused had come back to her. She laughed a little and said, "Part of me was afraid that would always happen again. Now I see that it is in the past."
>
> In the remaining time of the session, Linda and I put together some of the pieces of this experience: the blend of aggressiveness and affection in her close relationships, and the danger of sexualization that had all appeared in the transference. I felt privileged to have shared this therapy experience with Linda.

CONCLUSION

There is a wondrous gestalt to this process that embraces transference, interpretation, and the real relationship including social work interventions. Kahn (1991) used the metaphor of classical music, where a central musical theme is introduced at the beginning and then repeated with rich variations throughout the piece. He suggested that we live out similar relational patterns throughout our lifetimes. The social worker–client dyad will at least symbolically fit this lifetime pattern as surely as any other relationship.

Transference exploration and interpretation offers an opportunity for the client to have a glimpse of this pattern, introducing a new possibility for creative, more fully alive existence. It is in this way that the psychoanalytic social worker responds to the basic needs of clients, while providing a psychotherapy of quality and substance.

REFERENCES

Bollas, C. (1992). *Being a Character: Psychoanalysis and Self Experience.* New York: Hill and Wang.

Cooper, A. (1987/1990). Changes in psychoanalytic ideas: transference interpretation. In *Essential Papers on Transference,* ed. A. Esman, pp. 511–528. New York: New York University Press.

Freud, S. (1905). Fragment of an analysis of a case of hysteria. *Standard Edition* 7:3–124.

—— (1914). Remembering, repeating, and working through. *Standard Edition* 22:145–156.

—— (1915). Observations on transference love. *Standard Edition* 12:157–171.

—— (1940). An outline of psychoanalysis. *Standard Edition* 23:139–207.

Gill, M. (1982). *Analysis of Transference.* (Vols. 1–2). New York: International Universities Press.

—— (1988). Converting psychotherapy into psychoanalysis. *Contemporary Psychoanalysis* 24:262–274.

Hamilton, G. (1951). *Theory and Practice of Social Case Work* 2nd ed., rev. New York: Columbia University Press.

Kahn, M. (1991). *Between Therapist and Client.* New York: Freeman and Co.

Levenson, E. (1988). Show and tell: the recursive order of the transference. In

How Does Treatment Help? ed. A. Rothstein. Madison, CT: International Universities Press.

Lipton, S. (1977a). The advantages of Freud's technique as shown in his analysis of the Rat Man. *International Journal of Psycho-Analysis* 58:255–274.

——(1977b). Clinical observations on resistance to the transference. *International Journal of Psycho-Analysis* 58:463–472.

Oremland, J. (1991). *Interpretation and Interaction: Psychoanalysis or Psychotherapy?* Hillsdale, NJ: Analytic Press.

Ornstein, P. (1988). Multiple curative factors and processes in the psychoanalytic psychotherapies. In *How Does Treatment Help?* ed. A. Rothstein. Madison, CT: International Universities Press.

Pulver, S. (1992). Psychic change: Insight or relationship? *International Journal of Psycho-Analysis* 73:199–208.

Saari, C. (1994). An exploration of meaning and causation in clinical social work. *Clinical Social Work Journal* 22:251–261.

Sanville, J. (1991). *The Playground of Psychoanalytic Therapy.* Hillsdale, NJ: Analytic Press.

Schafer, R. (1993). *Transference, Countertransference, and Defense in the Treatment Situation.* Lecture presented at Smith College School for Social Work, July 11, 1993.

Slipp, S. (1988). *The Technique and Practice of Object Relations Family Therapy.* Northvale, NJ: Jason Aronson.

Sterba, R., Lyndon, B., and Katz, A. (1948). *Transference in Casework.* New York: Family Service Association.

Winnicott, D. W. (1956/1990). On transference. In *Essential Papers on Transference,* ed. A. Esman, pp. 246–251. New York: New York University Press.

Woods, M., and Hollis, F. (1990). *Casework: A Psychosocial Therapy,* 4th ed. New York: McGraw-Hill.

4 A Clinical View of the Use Of Psychoanalytic Theory in Front-Line Practice

Margaret G. Frank

This chapter will focus on the relevance of psychoanalytic theory to clinical practice on the "front line." Front line settings include, to name but a few, family and child welfare agencies, protective services, outreach programs connected to public schools, housing projects, shelters for the homeless, and day-care centers. Clinicians in these agencies perform the most important and needed therapeutic services throughout the country with the most vulnerable of our population. They offer these services while carrying the largest caseloads, receiving the least supervision, and with rules and regulations which often pull therapists in multiple directions. These pressures understandably tend to limit their ability to maintain a therapeutic focus and inevitably impinge upon their patients.

It is the purpose of this chapter to show how consultation with an analytically oriented clinician can serve to enhance the quality of treatment and in so doing relieve some of the pressures on the clinicians and help to prevent burn-out.

The writer will focus on three psychoanalytic concepts: the phenomena of transference, those of countertransference, and the role of the repetition compulsion. These concepts will be clarified, and, through the use of two case presentations, the writer will show the value of them in the treatment process. Many other psychoanalytic concepts will be observable in the text but will not be explicated.

PSYCHOANALYTIC CONCEPTS

The concept of the repetition compulsion represents a convergence of psychic forces which lead to the re-enactment of past life scenarios in the present formed in the earliest years of development. The pressure to repeat derives from the fact that human beings form views (representations) of themselves and others from infancy out of the affective exchanges they experience with significant others (Kris 1975). Thus children who experience more pain than pleasure may define themselves as "recipients of pain" and actually seek pain-inducing experiences. They expect pain, are familiar with this affective state, and can hardly envisage a different state of being. For them, the other, or object, is not to be trusted and can only be expected to inflict pain. Early experiences always associated with affect have coalesced (Spitz 1965) into complicated scenarios forming the representational world (Jacobson 1964, Sandler and Rosenblatt 1962). It is these representations which guide current interpersonal relations.

In the treatment situation, we can often see that dimensions of the patient's scenarios are being repeated. For example, I am reminded of a child who showered her therapist with compliments about her office and the toys in it. Since this was not a social worker who had somehow signaled her own need for such compliments, it seemed likely that this child was telling us that she needed to flatter in order to please others and possibly to hide other feelings she might have. We might then wonder if this was not a repetition of an early pattern of exchange in which the child felt that flattery of the object was essential for her own psychic or perhaps even physical survival. We are also familiar with the patient who demonstrates an inordinate amount of distrust of the therapist. Again, if the therapist has not provided any reason for the child to distrust her, it is likely that the child is communicating that he or she had little or no experience in his or her earliest developmental experiences to provide a foundation for trust in the present.

Central to the concept of the repetition compulsion is our observation that human beings are unconsciously drawn to recreate feelings and patterns of interactions associated with their formative relationships of infancy and early childhood (Blanck and Blanck 1986).

One of the goals of therapy is to end the repetition. To this goal, we seek to provide new object experiences. The tenacity of the need to repeat can be understood when we inquire into the psyche's investment in it. The definition of self and object and all the internalized object relations are the foundations of identity. Human beings cannot shed or rearrange their identities easily. No matter how painful the view of self and object may be, it is familiar. Of equal importance is the fact that affect serves as the connective link to the original caretaker. If the original connecting affect is predominantly pain, then pain will be sought as part of connections throughout later-life relationships (Valenstein 1973). Another perspective on the need to repeat envisages it as a reparative urge, an unconscious sense that something must be relived in a new context if deep changes are to occur (Sanville 1991). This writer offers yet another perspective to the psychic motivation of the urge to repeat. The psyche is known to be quite parsimonious and can use psychic phenomena for numerous reasons. Thus, the recreation of the representational world can at one and the same time reflect the earliest object relations and can also be used in conflict management. The person who seeks out painful experiences for the sake of attachment may at the same time be punishing him- or herself in order to manage intrapsychic conflicts (Frank 1995).

Transference emerges in these scenarios as transparencies that are unconsciously placed upon the being of the therapist, which make him resemble important early objects. It is the major vehicle of the repetition compulsion. In the first rather simple anecdotes cited above, one patient transformed the therapist into someone who needs to be pleased; the second turned the clinician into someone who is not trustworthy. The reasons for these stances remain to be understood in the therapeutic work. It is in this realm of our understanding that we gain the opportunity to end the repetition and to provide essential reparative experiences.

Countertransference relates to feelings and views of the patient experienced by the therapist, which may at one and the same time stem from qualities of the patient and from those qualities in the therapist that are the result of personal experiences with the early objects in his or her own life.

There was a time in the history of psychoanalytic thought when the patient's responses to the therapist and the therapist's responses to the patient were seen almost exclusively as the outcome of the intrapsychic issues of each. Today we are beginning to recognize that there are two psyches in the room and are looking more closely at the effect that therapist and patient are having upon one another. Merton Gill (1994, p. 17) has in fact redefined transference and countertransference as being "contributed to by both participants and shaped by one another." This recognition of "intersubjectivity" in the treatment situation, that is, of an interaction between the psychic reality of helper and helped (Stolorow et al. 1987), is altering the treatment situation. It is opening the doors for the therapist to make selective use of some of his feelings within the therapeutic interaction, which in turn can assist in the promotion of the therapeutic alliance.

The use clinicians make of this awareness of intersubjectivity must be approached with caution lest therapists move toward disclosure of self that may be anti-therapeutic. For example, the writer was recently preoccupied with events in her own life. A young patient felt her slight remoteness and wove this into her scenario of an expectation of abandonment. It proved useful, in this case, to share that I had, indeed, some things on my mind but that the conclusions she drew belonged to old experiences in her life. While I regarded it as important to acknowledge her correct perception that I was somewhat distracted, I felt it essential that I not divulge the reasons for my distraction but rather provide the opportunity for her to share her own fantasies about what was occurring. In this instance, my personal state of mind served as a stimulus for the patient's response to me as an abandoning person from the past. It provided the opportunity to show her how at times she misperceived the present as she transformed it in her mind into the past.

Countertransference, once seen as a toxic agent, is coming into its own in current psychoanalytic theory. While therapists are always challenged to monitor their own personal, idiosyncratic responses to patients and thus continuously attend to their own emotional well-being, countertransference is increasingly viewed as an important tool for learning about patients' feelings and for getting in touch with experiences from phases of their lives when they had no words (preverbal).

CASE PRESENTATION

Anne was a therapist in a residential setting for sex offenders. I came to know her and her work through my role as a consultant to her setting. Anne had many "masters" in this agency. There were rules and regulations which had been established to maintain order in the residence. In addition, Anne was the Chief Social Worker and had an understandable investment in doing well with her patients in the eyes of her staff. Last, but not least, she felt a sincere interest in her patient.

Her patient, Terry, was a young man in his early twenties with a long history of sexual exhibitionism, and some incidents of sex play with younger siblings and cousins. Unlike other patients in this setting, there was no history of actual penetration. Terry managed to provoke other patients to the extent that he was regularly beaten up when the staff were not looking and sometimes when they were looking. He troubled the system, lost privileges, disrupted his therapy group (led by Anne), and was alternately sullen or sexual with Anne in individual sessions. Transferential and countertransferential issues abounded.

Consultation helped Anne to see that Terry recreated (repetition compulsion) his life scenario within the milieu setting, his group, and his individual sessions. The staff, other patients, and his therapist had unwittingly become characters in his object relations scenario. Terry was particularly unable to manage any "hot" (sexual and angry) feelings. His history revealed that he came from a chaotic home. His mother had a number of children with different fathers. The "fathers" who came and went often beat the children. No one was present in his home to enable him to differentiate and manage feelings and impulses. The adults were unable to provide functions that he could internalize to help him manage his affective life. When the adult world fails to provide ego management, some children will devise their own methods. Terry developed a primitive ego stance, alternating between action and creating the need for punishment to curb himself. He unconsciously prompted the environment to act as a disapproving parent. Anne was caught in a further elaboration of his drama.

Terry's attachment to Anne was strong. He came to sessions, both group and individual, promptly and eagerly. Yet he unconsciously created a situation where she was viewed as a poor caretaker by the staff of the residence, which echoed his view of all caretakers. In approaching her feelings about this case, Anne was able to see that she felt a deep sense of failure. We can conjecture that she resonated with Terry's feelings about himself as well as his wish to convey that his caretakers failed him. She was angry with the young man even while she felt devoted to him and wished to help him. Her frustration and helplessness were the key to feelings in Terry. His story, at that point in treatment, could only be told in action, motivated by feelings emanating from the preverbal phase.

It must be quite clear that the therapist was caught up in a controlling and punishing stance vis-à-vis Terry.

> If we look through the window into a session from this phase, we can hear Anne beginning a session, as Terry slinked into her office. She remarked that Terry had really been getting himself into trouble that week. She wondered if he understood why she had to give him several demerits, which resulted in his losing privileges. Terry's response was sullen and almost nonverbal. Anne asked him why he did so many things to get himself into trouble. He replied that he didn't know and ventured that he could not help himself. He added a comment that he believed he was bad.
>
> Here, Terry was more on track than Anne. She spoke as if his behavior were within his control and could be reflected upon and he responded that it wasn't.
>
> Anne wondered what made Terry think he was bad. He replied that he saw how angry people were with him. He acknowledged that he felt mad too. He just wanted to hit out at everyone and show them who the strong one was.
>
> Anne commented that when Terry made people mad at him he couldn't feel good inside himself. She expressed her wish to help him not get into trouble and revealed a bit of her own frustration by commenting, "I end up having to punish you." Terry mumbled that he thought she cared more about the Center than she did about him.
>
> When Anne contradicted his conclusion, "No, that's not true, Terry, but you have to be able to fit into the rules and regulations of the Center or we cannot keep you here," she missed an opportunity to address the transference.

Anne had been caught up in her double role as administrator and as therapist. In addition, she was intervening at too high a level. Her remarks revealed her belief that Terry's actions were within his control and were subject to his reflection. In suggesting that his behavior made him feel bad, she was reaching for an observing ego which would experience the behavior as alien to the self. Her desperation is most dramatic in her threat of actual abandonment. She does not recognize that her threat meets his expectation to be abandoned.

Despite all, as noted above, there appeared to be a good enough connection between this young man and his therapist. Consultation involved reframing his behavior in developmental terms. A distinction was made between acting out and action. Acting out is a concept that belongs to patients of higher structure. Action suggests that development has not included the ego's ability to manage feelings and impulses. Language has not yet become a tool of the ego. The concept of developmental omissions in Terry was underscored, which in turn began to clarify the therapist's role. It was pointed out that her role with Terry need not be in conflict with the institutional needs. She was helped to see that Terry not only expected rejection (it confirmed his definition of self and object), he also needed it (it was part of his primitive self-regulation). Anne, because of her own despair, was unwittingly playing a role with Terry that replicated his family life. Discussions in consultation focused upon the difference between the adult who intends to protect the ego through teaching ego skills and control that is established through punishment (the ways of his family).

Observing patient and therapist some months later, we noted that Terry had continued his disruptive behavior but Anne had acquired a different understanding of it.

> In a session Anne addressed Terry, "You know what I think? I think no one ever helped you manage how you feel inside so you just let it spill all over." (This was an intervention informed by the therapist's increased awareness of the patient's ego development). Terry replied that he sometimes felt as if he were drowning. Anne continued the water imagery, "Well, I'll have to help you learn to swim. Sometimes, when I see you in the hall starting to grab another kid, I am going to stop you and help you say what you feel, to him or to me." We note her attempt to promote language to decrease action. Terry's response was negative and mocking. He saw the use of words as "sissy stuff" and thought "poking and pushing" were manly and showed strength.
>
> Anne again attempted to promote power within the ego: "That's what you think now, because you don't know how powerful a person can feel when they *choose* what they are going to say or do. Right now you don't have any choice." Terry was quiet and appeared thoughtful. Anne suggested that they use the office as a safe container (Winnicott 1989). "Let's try it here in the office. Yesterday, when you were trying to grab Paul's penis, do you know what you were feeling and thinking?" Terry replied that he wasn't sure. He knew that he was mad. He didn't like the way the other boy had pushed him around. The therapist, through her understanding, demonstrated considerable creativity when she

asked Terry how he might define "mad" to a kid from another country who might not know what it meant. Terry paused and replied, "Well, it's like bubbling feelings, all hot and scary. Maybe there's some fear in it." Anne wrote a list that Terry could see. She had headed it in large letters: MAD. "What else is in it?" she asked quietly. Terry added the word "sad" and Anne inquired, "How come?" Terry responded quietly, "Well, sometimes you want to be friends with someone but wanting things makes you feel weak, so you hit out at them and you feel sad 'cause that's not what you wanted; you wanted to be friends."

We would be quite correct if we were to note that Anne has been helping Terry with affect differentiation. She has been urging him to see the parts of what felt to him like overwhelming affects. In this way she was enabling him to get them to a manageable size (for the ego). We would be equally correct if we observed her creativity. Once she had a theoretical understanding of his behavior, she gained her sense of direction. As her anxiety decreased there was room for her creativity to emerge. I might add from our discussions that her frustration had been creating a sense of exasperation approaching burnout. She regained her excitement about the treatment process with Terry and other patients in the setting. She was able to see that she could maintain the order that the setting demanded by framing her interventions in ego-protective stances. "I have to help you calm down until you can do it yourself," she said to another patient. Here she lent herself as an auxiliary ego but included a sense of positive future. The child patient will be able to do this himself some day.

It is to be noted that Anne has not approached the sexualized aspect of Terry's behavior. Correctly, she has determined that this is too "hot" for him and that he has to gain some sense of self-management before she can proceed. Within a few months, Anne overheard Terry saying to a kid who was being provocative, "I don't have to hit you if I don't want to." The other child called him a fag and Terry, to Anne's amazement, replied, "I bet you're not strong enough to control yourself. You need people to beat up on you." Terry seemed to be gaining a useful knowledge of his own defenses. However, even though Terry's ego management had greatly improved, he seemed quite depressed and continued to disclose to his therapist his vision of himself as bad. Through her training, Anne had a basic foundation in ego psychology and the object relations theory which emanates from it. She had a less firm grasp of the interplay between developmental moth-holes (as I like to put it) and the realm of internal conflict (Pine 1985). She was in danger of feeling frustrated and exasperated once again, despite the improvements in Terry, because she did not recognize that his early definitions of self had been absorbed by his psyche and put to use to manage his conflicts. He clung to the concept of himself as bad and continued to "need" the environment to be mad at him. This was not simply a reflection of the angry, chaotic environment of Terry's earliest years. These views had an added purpose. In keeping with the principle of multiple determination, his negative image of himself served to help him manage conflict. Nothing in Terry's environment helped him to control his sexual interests and impulses. Since there were few models for management of impulse life, Terry devised his own. He used his negative self views and his punitive attitude toward himself to regulate his behavior. How does an understanding of this look in a treatment session?

Terry continued to incur the wrath of staff and peers, despite reduction in these incidents. In one session, Anne pondered out loud, "You know, Terry, I've been wondering how it is that you still get people to be mad at you. I've been wondering if there's something about those situations that you like."

Terry was annoyed with her and spoke defensively about wanting to be liked and that it was painful to have people mad at him. Anne went on with her musings. "Maybe I didn't put it well, Terry. Maybe it is not something you like but something you *need*." Terry became curious. "Well, suppose some part of you doesn't approve of some of your feelings and wishes. This is sort of you against you–not you against the world. But maybe you get the world about you to do the disapproving." The therapist "nudged" the patient to move from an external view toward an internal vision.

Terry wondered what he would disapprove of. Anne continued, "Well, you know, there's something we've never talked about. You are a healthy young man, and you used to get in trouble by coming on to people sexually. So I was wondering if you disapproved of your own sexual curiosity and feelings."

Terry replied quickly that such feelings are sins–even in the form of thoughts. He called forth the teachings of his church despite relatively little formal exposure to his religion.

Anne listened and finally commented, "Well, I guess we have found one corner in which you're at war with yourself." (Here she defines conflict to him).

Obviously, the intricate interweave of developmental deficit and conflict cannot be tackled in one session, but Anne and Terry have entered a new realm of exchange. There were months of discussion, all geared toward shifting what could be called Terry's self–self dialogue. It was, at first, a cruel dialogue with much self-hatred and scorn. As Terry exposed the fantasies and wishes and curiosity to Anne, her reactions and her ability to listen, perhaps even more than her words, began to soften his internal dialogue (through identification). Since he had accumulated experience in self-management, despite his voiced fears that he might be overwhelmed and go "crazy" with sexual acts all over the place, Anne was able to point to his capacities to exert power over himself. Ultimately, he acquired a kinder view of his inner life. The other way to view this shift might be to say that he no longer needed such harsh primitive ego and superego management of conflicts.

There is no question that this case had been on its way to being derailed. In the debris would have been a young man already on a crash course in life, quagmired in an interchange between a chaotic inner life and a distraught environment. In addition, there was a thoughtful and talented clinician working under the pressure of multiple roles with decreasing satisfaction in her work and increasing doubts about her ability.

One cannot discount the importance of the sheer presence of the consultant-mentor, but also Anne was able to incorporate what she learned into her own approach. The course of treatment was improved by Anne's increased clarity about Terry's level of ego development and function which led to a therapeutic focus more appropriate to his needs. Utilizing an object relations perspective helped to frame a chaotic series of interactions between the patient and his therapist, as well as the larger environment. Understanding that the reenactment of Terry's life scenario (object relations) in which staff, other patients, and the therapist were unwittingly playing old object roles enabled the therapist to extricate herself from the expected object position and provide new object experiences. The understanding of both transference and countertransference was used to bring about this clarity. Finally, as the therapeutic work progressed, the therapist was able to move even further with Terry as she came to appreciate the interplay between developmental deficits and internal conflict.

The second case involves a 14-year-old African-American girl, Amanda, who had witnessed the murder of her mother and, some time later, her brother outside their home, in a neighborhood where senseless murder is a daily event. Amanda was a bright, articulate young woman. Despite environs of poverty and violence, there was clear evidence of both good endowment and strong early nurturance.

The case had been assigned to a public school outreach program because very bright Amanda was beginning to show problems in her schoolwork. With this signal and the knowledge of the traumas that had befallen her, the agency intended to attend to the traumatic losses she had experienced. While Amanda retained her usual decorum at school, her loathing of people of color was expressed in an unbridled way. She refused her first clinical assignment to an African-American social worker, but connected in an extremely positive way to her second worker, "Adele."

Strongly attached to this white, blond-haired social worker, she disclosed her own deep wish to be white.

The agency setting was composed of multiple services. While therapy was offered and endorsed, the agency intended to help children of different ethnic and racial backgrounds find value in their racial origins. The therapist in this case was torn by what she understood to be the metaphoric meaning to her client of being a young woman of color and the social goals of the agency. The agency could too easily become the enemy of both patient and clinician in a world where there are more than enough enemies. Consultation aimed to help steer between essential psychoanalytic understanding and equally relevant social goals. Developmental principles were used to clarify the primary importance of establishing a valuable self. The goal of the self accepting the dimension of color was not viewed as a conflicting goal, but rather a long-range goal to be approached when the clouds of rage, hurt, and trauma were cleared.

Amanda, the patient, tearfully told her therapist how much she hated being black. Her therapist replied, "I think right now you hate being you. You have some very good reasons to wish to be someone else because so many things have happened to you that should not happen to anyone." The strong empathy in this response hardly needs to be noted. The therapist positioned herself with her patient, giving voice to her own outrage. The focus was upon the real external events which had befallen this child. This did not preclude the possible approach at a later time to issues which are more internal.

Months before, the therapist had tried to promote the value of Amanda being a person of color. In consultation, she talked about her feelings that this had been a misdirected approach. She felt angry that the agency imposed a goal upon her which she agreed with in principle but felt was not timely for her patient. The social worker saw as a priority getting to feelings within herself and within her patient.

Adele, like the clinician in the first case, was torn by pressures in her work. She had to cope with veiled resentment and disapproval from her African-American colleagues that she had been assigned to work with Amanda after Amanda's refusal to work with the first therapist. When her work was discussed in an agency case conference, she was subtly admonished for not focusing on Amanda's hatred of her color. She was urged not to comply with her patient's wish to walk along Newbury Street (Boston's Madison Avenue), where she would admire the white mannequins and remark on the peaceful looks on their faces. Adele felt pressured by the agency and somewhat guilty about Amanda's attachment to her.

The role of the consultant has many values. As an outsider the consultant can observe and address conflicts within a system. Both Adele and her agency were in need of shaping the frame of psychoanalytic theory for their work. Adele's instincts were in the right place but she could not articulate her reasons for wanting to soft-pedal the agency's goals. No one could argue with the agency's social purpose—only that these goals needed to be timed in relation to the patient's needs. The principle that value as a human being had to be established before attributes like color or gender seemed to be lost.

Adele reported an early session in which she and Amanda were walking along Newbury Street. Amanda was admiring Adele's earrings when her attention turned toward a group of mostly white young people having coffee. Amanda slowed their walking pace and Adele asked her if the group scene appealed to her. Amanda replied that they looked like they were having fun. Upon noting that the group included several blacks, Amanda frowned and remarked that she did not know why they had been included. Adele recalled being distressed and inquired of her patient why she had said that. Amanda replied to the effect that the blacks could bring them bad luck. The group looked so peaceful but maybe they would have to start looking around carefully.

Adele commented that that was what Amanda had to do on her block. Amanda responded with a quiet "yes." Adele continued that she imagined that Amanda wished her mother had been watching carefully before she was shot. Maybe she even thought had she been looking she might have escaped the stray bullets. Amanda nodded with sad agreement. The therapist's remarks were clearly empathic with Amanda's fears and wishes. Adele derailed her own attuned work in the following comment, "You know, Amanda, white people shoot each other on purpose or by accident too." Amanda demonstrated her response to the break in empathy by turning away to look at a store window.

In the discussion of this intervention later, Adele confessed to wanting to shift Amanda's views; they seemed too distorted and extreme. When she saw that she had interrupted an unfolding, she remarked that she wished she had led Amanda to begin to expose her fantasies about the real violence in her life and her environment. The consultant reassured her that she would have many opportunities to pursue her exploration further. She recognized her strong wish to remove pain from Amanda's life. She confessed that she was not eager to lead Amanda to revisit her feelings around the murders of her mother and brother.

Her overly positive countertransference was getting in the way of the child's need to grieve. Adele, herself, acknowledged her own reluctance to grieve losses of a different nature in her own life.

In a later Newbury Street session, Amanda stood in front of a mannequin dressed in a colorful block-print dress. She stood silently and Adele gave her lots of space. "My mom would have liked that dress," she almost whispered, with a single tear rolling down her cheek. Adele remained quiet while Amanda continued. "She would have loved the colors, she liked to dress up, she liked to dance, she taught me to dance, she was pretty, and she wanted pretty things for me."

Adele remarked that it sounded as though Amanda's mother wanted good things for her. Adele recognized that with the process of grief and the expression of anger, Amanda would be freer to gain access to identifications that could soften the enormity of her loss.

In another session, Amanda pondered that if she had been white maybe her mother wouldn't have been shot. Adele replied, "You know, we human beings have to try to explain things we don't understand. Sometimes we pick explanations just to make some order whether they are right or not." Amanda responded by telling her therapist that she used to think that if she were a boy like her brother she would have been able to go to the store and movies. She would have had the freedom that he had. "But look what happened to him. You know, if we were rich and white and didn't live in Roxbury maybe none of this would have happened to my family."

Adele described to the consultant her guilt about her own relative affluence and her wish to deny the undeniable reality of Amanda's remark. She spoke of having to force herself to say "perhaps." Upon returning to the office that day Amanda was able to weep. "I just don't understand–why her, why him, why me?" She gnashed her teeth in fury over the senseless violence in her neighborhood.

In the sessions that followed, she seemed to be able to use Adele's explanation of how the ego tries to make order out of chaos. She confessed to Adele that she thinks she first explained her mother's death by deciding it was because she was bad and ugly. It is important to recall that this is a young teen-age woman who is undoubtedly sorting out shifting self-images and increased competitive feelings towards her mother. While this level of understanding could not be approached at that time in the therapeutic work, it helped the clinician to understand the other forces which propelled the child into seeing herself as "bad and ugly."

Amanda had continued that she even thought that if she'd been there and watchful maybe she could have prevented her mother's death. Here we see the use of magical thinking in the face of intolerable feelings of helplessness, a level of thinking that often becomes activated after a traumatic event. Many people who have been mugged report dreams of beating up their assailant. The fantasied power provides a compensation for the real helplessness.

Amanda became intrigued with exploring her own explanations for unpleasant events which she didn't understand. Many sessions later she uncovered her deep conviction (part of her explanation) that the bad in her life was due to being black. Adele, in one of these sessions, remarked how hard it is to live with painful events and accept that there is no way to explain them.

It is often true that one does not see the usefulness of interventions until months later; sometimes we never see it directly. But some months later Amanda was back on track earning A's in school, writing freely, an activity for which she had a great talent, and became an active member of the city's youth movement against violence. She remarked to Adele, "You know, it's hard to live without clear explanation but it's better than false explanations; I don't want to feel bad and ugly."

She became fascinated with the Stewart family murder, where the husband shot his pregnant wife in order to get her money and, with the help of his brother-in-law, tried to blame it on a black man who supposedly attempted to rob the couple. The Boston police bought that story for quite some time. Later Mr. Stewart committed suicide. Amanda was irate at the misuse, as she put it, of "my people." In addition, she demonstrated extraordinary empathy for the surviving families. "That's another story in which they'll never be able to explain it to themselves—they'll just have to learn to live with their loss." We note Amanda's ability to obtain distance.

In her English class, Amanda wrote a prize-winning autobiographical story. Without clinical language, it demonstrated her mastery as she wrote of a little girl who had lost her mother and brother, and how she shielded herself from the pain through hatred of herself, her neighborhood, and her race. She had a friend who had a large lap (the therapist) and eventually the little girl felt her pain and her friend could feel it too. The little girl learned to live with her loss and the fact that she would never really understand it. When she could live with these awarenesses she didn't have to keep her false explanations.

DISCUSSION

The purpose of this paper was to show *in vivo* the important contribution of certain psychoanalytic concepts in therapeutic work with emotionally and environmentally inundated patients and their therapists, who often are equally, albeit differently, inundated. Amanda was a well-equipped and well-endowed adolescent. As she entered a phase of development that naturally involves much identity upheaval and reworking, she was struck by trauma beyond what most of us can imagine, the senseless and inexplicable murders of both her mother and older brother. The aftermath of these traumas threw her into self-hatred and racial splitting, and a loss of ability to use her capacities in a focused way.

One cannot say that Amanda had no earlier developmental issues which gave rise to her responses to the trauma. We are aware that the shapes of post-traumatic syndromes are always related, in part, to the person's earlier history. However, Amanda's reactions to trauma demanded immediate attention. Her racial split (which was viewed by the consultant as a defense) was of great social concern to the agency providing services. Through consultation, the split was seen as being designed to allow Amanda to cope with feelings of hatred that she could not integrate, for the moment, with her capacity to love. She placed her hatred upon her own race and retained her ability to love and admire (placing these feelings on the white world and therapist). Initially, the treatment setting did not grasp her need to grieve and to experience her anger. The goals and reactions of the agency placed pressures upon the therapist, which, combined with her overly positive feelings towards the patient, threatened to derail the therapeutic work. The clinician temporarily joined her patient in wanting to avoid re-experiencing the pain of her loss.

Whatever the wellsprings were in the therapist's history which prompted her own wish to protect Amanda from sorting out her pain, these were not germane to the work of consultation. However, awareness that she could use her own reluctance to approach pain enabled her to lead the way into explorations of Amanda's defenses against these feelings, her splitting, her explaining her losses through self-blame and racial hatred. Ultimately her grief could be approached, opening the way to reinstating her sense of a more valuable self.

In both cases the therapists had to cope with the needs and goals of their settings, which were experienced as interfering with their therapeutic focuses. In both cases countertransference, until recognized and used, produced barriers to therapeutic work. Finally, each therapist was able to gain greater access to her own creativity and energy through the illumination of psychoanalytic concepts.

This chapter was written with a sense of urgency. We are in an era in which psychoanalytic concepts are no longer studied in depth. This leaves the clinician on the "front line" with less equipment while dealing with profoundly challenging clinical and social situations. Seminars and in-agency supervision, once essential supports to staff, are no longer available. The writer has had the opportunity to consult with clinical and administrative personnel in a number of agencies. This chapter shows the value a clinician who is external to the service setting can bring in sorting out conflicts between agency goals and workers' and patients' needs. The psychoanalytic concepts which are essential to enhancing therapeutic work can, as demonstrated in this text, ease the burdens of front-line practitioners and their agencies.

The content of this chapter derives from a perspective which has been held by the writer for many years. I began practice like most of us, on the "front line" in times which were certainly less harsh economically and politically. In the 50s and 60s, one could work in community settings with outreach services and at the same time be afforded seminars, case conferences, and a variety of learning experiences, which softened the pressures of our work and added to our knowledge. In addition, despite our concern for social and environmental factors, they did not approach the current nightmare of drugs, AIDS, violence, and family deterioration that face the front-line practitioners of today. My career has afforded me the opportunity to teach in many leading schools of social work and I have watched the shrinkage of quality clinical courses offered to young people entering the field.

It seems ironic that when the environmental and psychological needs of the public are most challenging, preparation for this work offers less support to the clinician. This may well explain why social workers are the largest consumers of post-graduate analytic training of all the mental health professions.

REFERENCES

Blanck, G., and Blanck, R. (1986). *Beyond Ego Psychology: Developmental Object Relations Theory*. New York: Columbia University Press.

Frank, M. G. (in press). *The Interplay between Developmental Deficits and the Management of Conflict.*

Jacobson, E. (1964). *The Self and the Object World.* New York: International Universities Press.

Kris, E. (1975). *Selected Papers of Ernst Kris.* New Haven and London: Yale University Press.

Pine, F. (1985). *Developmental Theory and Clinical Process.* New Haven: Yale University Press.

Sandler, J., and Rosenblatt, B. (1962). The concept of the representational world. *Psychoanalytic Study of the Child* 17:128–145. New York: International Universities Press.

Sanville, J. (1991). *The Playground of Psychoanalytic Therapy*. Hillsdale, NJ and London: Analytic Press.

Spitz, R. (1965). *The First Year of Life*. New York: International Universities Press.

Stolorow, R., Brandchaft, B., and Atwood, G. (1987). *Psychoanalytic Treatment: An Intersubjective Approach*. Hillsdale, NJ and London: Analytic Press.

Valenstein, A. (1973). On attachment to painful feelings and the negative therapeutic reaction. *Psychoanalytic Study of the Child* 28:365–392. New Haven, CT: Yale University Press.

Winnicott, D. W. (1989). *Psychoanalytic Explorations*. Cambridge, MA: Harvard University Press.

5 The Good-Enough Social Worker: Winnicott Applied

Jeffrey S. Applegate

> Social workers need just now to look at the philosophy of their work all the time; they need to know when they must fight to be allowed (and paid) to do the difficult and not the easy thing; they must find support where it can be found and not expect support from administration. In fact . . . social workers need to be themselves the parent figures, sure of their own attitude even when unsupported and often in the curious position of claiming the right to be worn out in the exercise of their duties, rather than to be seduced into the easy way of inducing conformity.

This quotation trumpets a call to professional self-definition, self-advocacy, and pride that seems especially pertinent to the challenges social workers face in today's rapidly changing fiscal and political climate for service delivery. The words might well have been written yesterday. In fact, they were written more than a quarter-century ago, and not by a social worker, but by the psychoanalyst Donald Woods Winnicott (1969, p. 559).

How is it that a medically trained British psychoanalyst could have so pointedly captured social work's enduring struggle to define and assert its unique contributions to human well-being? In order to answer this question, I offer in this chapter a composite portrait of Winnicott as person, theorist, and clinician. This portrait serves as a backdrop for demonstrating the relevance of Winnicott's ideas for late-twentieth-century social work and provides some clues to the striking congruence between these ideas and the profession's values, principles, and mission. The case will be made that Winnicott's concepts have special applicability to the "silent" supportive and sustaining dimensions of social work and that they provide a language for articulating these seemingly ineffable qualities of our practice. Five of these concepts–the holding environment, ego relatedness, the transitional process, object relating and object use, and the true and false self–comprise the theoretical framework for demonstrating the ways in which Winnicott's work builds a bridge between psychoanalysis and social work practice. The chapter concludes with suggestions for incorporating these concepts into social work education.

BIOGRAPHICAL SKETCH

The Person

Several factors in Winnicott's personal history suggest explanations for his commitment to a professional life that embodied social work values. Born in 1896 in Devon, Plymouth, England, he grew up in a typical middle-class family living in economically comfortable circumstances. His father was 41 years old when Winnicott was born. A convivial, successful merchant who twice served as mayor of the town, he spent much time away from home, a circumstance that did not go unnoticed by his young son. As Winnicott later recalled, "It is probably true that in the early years he left me too much with all my mothers" (cited in Phillips 1988, p. 28).

Indeed, the Winnicott household was populated by multiple "mothers," including Donald's biological mother, an aunt, a female cook, a nanny, a governess, and two older sisters. As a boy, Winnicott spent much time in the kitchen, causing his mother to remark that he spent more time with the cook than with the rest of the family. He seemed drawn to the maternal, nurturant core of the house, a proclivity that may have influenced his later theoretical preoccupation with the vicissitudes of the child's relationship to the mother. His writing about this "first relationship" expresses an unusually intimate familiarity with the dynamics of maternal care, a familiarity likely rooted in a family situation that promoted his close identification with the feminine.

There is some evidence that the origins of Winnicott's finely tuned caregiving capacities can be traced to his perception of his role with his mother. This perception finds expression in a poem he wrote late in his life, quoted in Phillips (1988, p. 29).

> Mother below is weeping
> weeping
> weeping
> Thus I knew her
>
> Once, stretched out on her lap
> and now on dead tree
> I learned to make her smile
> to stem her tears
> to undo her guilt
> to cure her inward death
> To enliven her was my living.

This poem appears to give words to Winnicott's memory of "an early experience of his mother's depression, and her consequent inability to hold him" (Phillips 1988, p. 29). Phillips and other Winnicott biographers (Goldman 1993, Rudnytsky 1991) hypothesize that, having felt insufficiently "held," he may have made a career of "holding" others, thus vicariously gratifying unmet dependency needs.

The issue of dependency and its mastery surfaces elsewhere in accounts of Winnicott's youth. A broken collarbone sustained while playing rugby at boarding school, for example, played a role in his later career choice: "I could see that for the rest of my life I should have to depend on doctors if I damaged myself or became ill, and the only way out of this position was to become a doctor myself" (cited in Phillips 1988, p. 31). This early conviction did not waver, and Winnicott began reading medicine at Cambridge at age 18, eventually specializing in pediatrics. Freud's (1900) *The Interpretation of Dreams* introduced him to psychoanalysis at age 23, and he subsequently sought training in both child and adult analysis.

While Winnicott's professional life may have enabled him to tend to the child in himself, there is evidence that he continued in his personal life to live out a need to care for a troubled woman. His first marriage, at age 28, was burdened for its duration by his wife's mental illness

(Grolnick 1990). Masud Khan claims that Winnicott's young- and mid-adult years were devoted to her care (Clancier & Kalmanovitch 1987), and only when he felt she was strong enough emotionally to bear the loss did they divorce, when he was 53 years old. The strain of his wife's condition undoubtedly contributed to the couple's childlessness, a circumstance Winnicott may have been referring to when he wrote that "people with no children can and do find all sorts of other ways of in fact having a family; they may be found sometimes to have the largest families of all" (1957, p. 43). Winnicott seemed to constitute his "family" from the more than 60,000 children he treated in his career as pediatrician and analyst.

Early in his career, Winnicott left the boundaries of his office-based medical and analytic practice to enter and intervene in the wider social milieu of his time. Through working in the World War II Evacuation Project and at a pediatric clinic in London's poverty-stricken East End, he met families traumatized by homelessness, neglect, deprivation, and other sequelae of environmental failure. He became a spokesman and advocate for the mentally ill, dependent and neglected children, delinquents, and other members of vulnerable populations. He worked closely with social workers, one of whom, Clare Britton, became his second wife. They were apparently well matched personally and professionally, practicing and writing about what today is referred to as mental health case management (Kanter 1990).

Clare Winnicott's (1989) reminiscences about her marriage to Winnicott emphasize his spirited commitment to a life fully lived. There is a sense that his evolving life was expressive of an embodied reparative tendency at work. He employed a keen mind, insatiable curiosity, and a playful spirit to meet and transform adversity into creative living, His capacity for play was legendary, persisting into his old age despite worsening heart and lung problems. He liked to ride his bicycle downhill with his feet on the handlebars, prompting one policeman who stopped him to scold, "Fancy an old man like you setting an example to everybody" (C. Winnicott, in Rudnytsky 1991, p. 193). Through play, Winnicott stayed in touch with his true self. After his death in 1971, at age 75, a prayer that poignantly captures his approach to living was discovered in notes for his unfinished autobiography, tellingly titled *Not Less Than Everything*. The prayer asks simply, "Oh God! May I be alive when I die."

The Theorist

Winnicott's playful vitality also influenced his work as a theoretician, where his insistence on being himself provoked delight in some colleagues, dismay in others. He cut a rakish figure at professional meetings, and is often remembered as a "pixie" and "a bit of a Peter Pan" (Grosskurth 1986). Although retaining a degree of theoretical allegiance to his most influential mentors, Freud and Melanie Klein, he charted his own course, discarding or reinventing existing theory as he accumulated clinical experience.

This experience derived from his extensive work with infants and young children and with adults who presented problems related to psychosis, borderline vulnerabilities, and environmental deprivation or trauma. From his work with these patients he forged creative, strikingly innovative extensions of psychoanalytic theory. In applying analytic theory and technique to people traditionally viewed as too troubled to profit from in-depth work, he was induced to formulate "theories-of-action" (Argyris and Schon 1974) that take shape in the unfolding phenomenology of unpredictable professional episodes. Rather than moving in a linear way from theory to practice, he was often challenged by the immediacy and uniqueness of each new clinical encounter to develop theory and take action simultaneously. To paraphrase Schon (1987), Winnicott descended from the high ground of classical analysis to the swampy lowlands of clinical situations characterized by ambiguity and uncertainty and complicated by multiple environmental variables—a territory familiar to social workers. In this process, he worked with theory and practice dialectically: "What happens is that I gather this and that, here and there, settle down to clinical experience, form my own theories and then, last of all, interest myself in looking to see where I stole what" (Winnicott 1945, p. 145).

This quotation suggests that Winnicott seemed comfortable playing with theory as he and his patients mutually constructed meaning from the phenomenology of their interactions. He appeared to thrive on the spontaneity inherent in this endeavor and was enlivened rather than disconcerted by not knowing. Epistemologically, this approach places him ahead of his time in embracing a social constructionist perspective on theory building, a perspective increasingly recognized as congruent with social work principles, values, and methods of practice and inquiry (Dean 1993, Saari 1991). Moreover, the assumption of egalitarian clinician–client collaboration embedded in this approach reflects a feminist epistemological stance toward theory and practice that is rooted in the history of the profession (Freedberg 1993).

Winnicott's constructionist leanings did not signify, however, an eclectic or atheoretical orientation to practice. He embraced psychoanalytic theory and asserted that, for people whose problems stemmed primarily from neurotic intrapsychic conflict, classical analysis based on interpretation is the treatment of choice. But for those individuals whose troubles arise from more primary disturbances of self or from environmental deprivation and trauma, he believed that the consistency, continuity, and reliability of the therapeutic relationship itself could be mutative. He also believed in a systemic person-in-environment conception of human development and vulnerability (Grolnick 1990). Indeed, he perfectly captures social work's focus with his crisp observation that "the unit is not the individual, the unit is the environment–individual set-up" (Winnicott 1952, p. 99).

So long has the person–environment idea pervaded social work's epistemology that we take its centrality for granted. But in the psychoanalytic zeitgeist of Winnicott's day, consideration of factors beyond the intrapsychic world was revolutionary and controversial. In fact, when Winnicott mentioned to his second analyst, Joan Riviere, that he wanted to write a book on the environment, she warned, "You write a book on the environment and I'll turn you into a frog!" (cited in Goldman 1993, p. 79). Characteristically, he forged ahead anyway, theorizing and writing extensively about the interactional ecology of person and environment. With his now classic 1953 paper on transitional objects and phenomena, Winnicott became the first psychoanalytic theorist to develop a rigorous conceptual framework for understanding people's interactions with the nonhuman world.

Finally, Winnicott intuitively brought a strengths perspective to his understanding and treatment of troubled people. His language and concepts are inherently depathologizing, as exemplified by his use of the phrase "capacity for concern" to describe the stage of development which Klein (1964) called the "depressive position." He viewed aspects of autistic, schizophrenic, dissociative, and other disturbances as having elements of strength, in that they often serve to protect the vulnerable self of earliest dependency. And he insisted that access to primary process and other mental phenomena often seen in psychosis is essential to human imagination and innovation, quipping that "we are poor indeed if we are only sane" (1965, p. 61). From this rich combination of a focus on the therapeutic relationship, attention to the larger environment, and a strengths perspective emerges an approach to practice that resonates with the social work approach.

The Clinician

The essence of Winnicott's practice orientation is captured in his declaration that "cure at its root means care" (1970, p. 112). From his extensive observations of infants and their caregivers, he learned the complex language of primary care and translated it to clinical practice, where he emphasized the importance of a quietly alive, nonintrustive, facilitating presence with clients. Apparently he was a natural with children, seeming to have an entrancing effect on them and fully entering their worlds of play and fantasy. Clare Winnicott (1989) recalled that he never saw a child without giving her or him something to take away–a folded paper airplane or fan, perhaps.

Accounts by adults further document his capacity to become thoroughly immersed in the clinical encounter while simultaneously asserting his own presence. "Winnicott listened with the whole of his body, and had keen unintrusive eyes that gazed at one with a mixture of unbelief and utter acceptance. A childlike spontaneity imbued his movements. Yet he could be so still, so very inheld and still. I have not met another analyst who was more inevitably himself" (Khan 1975, p. xi). Accounts by other patients analyzed by Winnicott portray the genius of a clinician who, while well grounded in psychoanalytic technique, was free to experiment, to play with ideas and intuitively derived interventions (see Guntrip 1975, Little 1990). In the same way that his developmental theory describes and privileges the "real" or "environment mother" with human feelings and failings, Winnicott relied in his clinical work on the reparative potential of the "good-enough" therapeutic relationship. Commenting on his suspicion of the overinterpretive methods of traditional analysis, he wrote, "I have always felt that an important function of the interpretation is the establishment of the *limits* of the analyst's understanding" (Winnicott 1963a, p. 189, italics in original). For Winnicott, treatment was more a dialogue of mutual discovery than the exercise of interpretive finesse by a clinician-expert.

This spirit of discovery characterizes Winnicott's now well-known squiggle technique. In consultations with children (see Winnicott 1971d,

1977), he would make an impulsive, nonrepresentational line drawing and invite the child to turn it into something. The child's addition of a few lines would prompt Winnicott to make it into something else, and so on. Resulting drawings constituted both a mode of communication and a visual record of the unfolding therapeutic process. Deri (1984) suggests that, in Winnicottian clinical work with adults, a dialogic squiggling evolves as a sharing of verbal imagery fosters the client's symbol-building capacity and establishes both conscious and unconscious communication. In this interchange, Winnicott often sought to preserve rather than eliminate ambiguity. He aimed to retain "some outside quality by not being quite on the mark" (Winnicott 1962, p. 167), thus inviting his patient to contribute a new "squiggle."

Winnicott's emphasis on the curative potential of the therapeutic relationship predicted recent research suggesting that the supportive and sustaining dimensions of such a relationship are themselves mutative and contribute to the kind of structural change once thought to be possible only with interpretation of unconscious conflict (see DeJonghe et al. 1992). This revaluing of the reparative potential of the relationship qua relationship is a trend of crucial importance for social work, whose search for measurable outcomes, both to meet demands for accountability and to achieve scientific respectability, has fostered a recent focus on technical pragmatism and a general neglect of relationship factors (Coady 1993).

Winnicott's practice extended beyond the micro-context of the consulting room and clinic. As noted, he also worked for social change. He spoke out against psychosurgery and other forms of invasive treatment which he believed to be dehumanizing (see C. Winnicott et al. 1989). He gave educational radio talks, taught social workers at the London School of Economics, and engaged in spirited public debate in letters to newspaper editors and other correspondents (see Rodman 1987). Winnicott's dual approach to "people-helping" and "society-changing" (Goldstein 1984) mirrors social work's approach, and is embedded in several of his key concepts.

KEY CONCEPTS

The Holding Environment

Social work clinician-scholar Martha Chescheir (1985) notes that "Creating holding environments is the essence of social work and the beginning link between Winnicott's concepts and good clinical practice" (p. 220). From a century of accumulated practice wisdom, social workers know in their bones that our profession's primary role is to create and sustain holding environments for people whose stability, safety, and continuity have been disrupted or have never been firmly established. Historically, "holding" individuals, families, small groups, organizations, and communities has been the mission of many of the profession's service organizations, including the Charity Organizations Societies and the Settlement Houses.

Winnicott coined the term *holding environment* to capture the ways in which he observed caregivers tending to their infants. He then transposed this term to clinical work, asserting that the experience of being supportively "held" in the treatment context was central to everything else. While there is evidence that Winnicott occasionally held clients literally during their regressive episodes (see Little 1990), he primarily used the holding concept figuratively, underscoring the importance of clinicians "holding" clients in their full attention. Adequate clinical holding relies on the clinician's reliability, consistency, and empathy in much the same way that a baby's well-being relies on these qualities in caregivers.

Winnicott (1956b) also included larger systems in his view of holding: "One can discern a series–the mother's body, the mother's arms, the parental relationship, the home, the family including cousins and near relations, the school, the locality with its police stations, the county with its laws" (p. 310). He believed that interventions could occur at any or all of these levels. Referring specifically to social work, he suggested that "Casework might be described as the professionalized aspect of this normal function of parents and local units, a 'holding' of persons and of situations, while growth tendencies are given a chance" (Winnicott 1961, p. 107).

Social workers routinely encounter clients whose earlier or current holding environments have "dropped" them, compromising their capacity for basic trust and rendering them vulnerable to "unbearable agonies" (Winnicott 1968)–feelings of falling forever, falling apart, depersonalization, and disorientation. To defend against such catastrophic anxiety, such clients may fear and avoid interpersonal situations–including the clinical relationship–which make them feel vulnerable to becoming dependent and possibly "dropped" again. Even clients whose earlier lives have been relatively stable and secure can, under conditions of trauma or extreme environmental disruption or deprivation, experience regression to feelings of this primary separation anxiety to which we are all subject.

These clients present formidable challenges to social workers attempting to help them. Too anxious to articulate the nuances of their feelings, they often try to set up conditions designed to test the durability and sincerity of the worker as well as to communicate their inner experience. They can appear disconnected, preoccupied, sullen, or openly hostile. They come late to or fail to keep appointments, or storm out of the office in a rage, unconsciously giving the worker an experience of what it has been like for them to be dropped. Clinicians assisting these clients are called on to engage in a different kind of holding–a containment of their affective reactions to such provocations so that they may reflect rather than act upon them. When treated as "objects of contemplation" rather than "things of action" (Werner and Kaplan 1963), these affects become valuable diagnostic tools that inform the worker about the nature of the client's vulnerabilities and defenses. Resulting empathic attunement assists the worker in responding with acceptance rather than with punitive, retaliatory reactions that may replicate earlier empathic failures and confirm the client's worst fears.

Beyond the individual or family level, social workers in many settings are reminded on a daily basis that whole segments of society are being "dropped" by social institutions, policies, and programs that fail to hold them adequately. It is likely that there is a high degree of correspondence between the unbearable agonies associated with this experience and currently escalating levels of homelessness, addiction, child abuse and neglect, domestic and social violence, and crime. The implications of this conceptualization of societal dysfunction are clear: social policies and programs that assure the provision of food, clothing, shelter, adequate medical and mental health care, and other basics of an adequate social holding environment for every individual are essential. The professional responsibilities of the Winnicottian social worker reach beyond the office and the agency to include political activism aimed at establishing and sustaining these basic provisions.

Ego Relatedness

The provision of a holding environment, the first task of social work intervention, makes it possible for the client to construct a personal idea of the clinician and vice versa. This intersubjective construction arises from a condition that Winnicott (1956a) called "ego relatedness" in order to distinguish it from id or drive-based relatedness. This term keeps the focus on the client's ego strengths, adaptive capacities, and inborn propensities for connectedness and speaks to the possibility of the establishment of a profound mutuality between clinician and client.

Describing the developmental origins of this mutuality, Winnicott (1960b) once declared that "There is no such thing as a baby!" Elaborating this puzzling statement, he noted that "whenever one finds an infant one finds maternal care, and without maternal care there would be no infant" (p. 39). By emphasizing the mutuality of this "nursing couple," Winnicott did not negate the existence of separate, self-regulating individuals: "By the end of two weeks any baby has had plenty of things happen that are entirely personal" (Winnicott 1988, p. 29). But his focus was on their intersubjectivity, forged in countless mirroring interactions: "What does the baby see when he or she looks at the mother's face? I am suggesting that, ordinarily, what the baby sees is himself or herself" (Winnicott 1971a, p. 112).

Transposing this idea to social work, we can say that "there is no such thing as a client" and, by extension, no such thing as a worker. It is the mutuality between collaborative partners in the helping relationship, in other words, that makes clinical work possible. The worker mirrors what she or he sees in the client, thus acting as a reflective observing ego. This process has the paradoxical effect of helping the client discover a sense of self as separate and self-regulating. Winnicott (1958) believed that only when psychologically alone in the intimate presence of a concerned, nonintrusive other can infants discover a personal life. Similarly, only when they learn to tolerate the experience of feeling separate in the presence of an empathic other do clients develop the capacity for intimacy. Many social work clients have yet to develop ego relatedness; the therapeutic relationship may provide one of their first opportunities to experience it. When we "survive" and respond reflectively to clients' defensive attempts to ward off the fears associated with profound closeness, we demonstrate that it is possible to experience integrative solitude in the presence of someone–a lesson many clients' disruptive circumstances have prevented them from learning.

The Transitional Process

These experiences of separateness-in-connection lay the groundwork for the client to begin to make the transition to being able to function comfortably both in separateness and in connection, thus establishing a pivotal, life-long developmental dialectic between autonomy and intimacy (Applegate 1993a, Shor and Sanville 1978). As Winnicott understood it, this transition first finds expression in the baby's acquisition or "creation" of a transitional object. In the 1953 paper in which he coined this term, Winnicott observed that, as the developing baby becomes aware that the caregiver is a self-regulating other who does not always respond in synchrony with her or his needs, a new form of separation anxiety arises. This anxiety, less catastrophic than the "unbearable agonies" of earliest infancy but still acutely uncomfortable, leads the adequately equipped baby to reach into the inanimate environment for an object—a blanket, fragment of a blanket, or stuffed animal—that tastes, smells, and feels like the caregiver and becomes a symbolic substitute for maternal soothing in her absence. Such behavior signals the commencement of a transitional process which enables the child creatively to find and use her or his own means of self-soothing while enduring the vicissitudes of self–object differentiation.

Because the child imbues with powerful symbolic meaning an otherwise ordinary object, Winnicott believed that the development of a transitional object constitutes the first true creative act. While the fierce attachment to an original object fades, the internalization of its nurturant properties makes possible a life-long transitional process wherein reverie, fantasy, and engagement in such phenomena as art, music, and religious experience facilitate self-soothing. Neither self nor other, me nor not-me, such phenomena exist in an intermediate area or "potential space" between inner and outer reality that is the realm of play and psychotherapy. Winnicott (1971b) also located culture in this potential space, offering social workers a useful theoretical framework for considering contextual variables in their client's lives.

As social workers, we see many clients whose capacity for engaging in the transitional process has been compromised by chronic environmental deprivation or cumulative trauma. Their capacities for self-soothing, therefore, may be undeveloped. In practice with such clients, the Winnicottian social worker remains alert to junctures in intervention when they begin to express transitional relatedness. Sometimes workers or agencies may become transitional "objects" for certain clients; these clients may need to telephone between appointments, if only to hear a familiar voice on an answering machine, to activate self-soothing. A toy from the playroom, a photograph of the worker, or an appointment card can act as a symbol of relational connection and reliability between appointments (Applegate 1984).

Object Relating and Object Use

Winnicott (1971c) believed that the transitional process equips the developing child to undertake the crucial intrapsychic and interpersonal journey from object relating to object use. This journey is a metaphor for describing the move from the child's early conception of the caregiver as a subjectively constructed object based on projected omnipotence to a more objective perception of her as a real (fallible, imperfect) other whose separateness makes her available as an external resource for use in further development. Understanding this complicated process requires a consideration of Winnicott's (1971c) idiosyncratic views of aggression and destructiveness. He saw aggression, not as an instinctually-based antisocial drive, but as synonymous with the part of the life force that seeks differentiation and is expressed behaviorally in activity, motility, and vitality. Employing his most elliptical language, Winnicott submits that, in order to render the caregiving object usable, "the subject destroys the object" (1971c, p. 89). "Destroy" here means that, in moving toward acceptance of autonomy as part of the developmental dialectic, the child must in fantasy do away with the old version of the subjectively conceived, projective object. Behaviorally, this process finds expression in aggressive actions designed to test the caregiver's capacity to survive the "destructiveness." From cycles of aggression, destructiveness, and survival the child concludes, "You have value for me because of your survival of my destruction of you" (p. 90). Repeated experiences of the resilience and durability of the other provide for the child a model for survival in separateness. The boundaries of self become articulated through these experiences of alterity, and, paradoxically, this alterity inaugurates a new, more complex level of mutuality based not on survival, but on concern.

Social workers meet many clients whose early life experience has not afforded them opportunities to move from object relating to object use. Combinations of psychological vulnerability and environmental deprivation may have made it difficult for their caregivers to respond adaptively to their normal, self-defining aggression. Some caregivers may have reacted to limit-testing with retaliatory abuse or withdrawal. With clients subjected to these early conditions, social workers need to be prepared for repeated tests of their ability to survive without retaliating. This preparation includes a tolerance for and containment of powerful countertransference reactions to being "destroyed," including feelings of hatred toward the client (Winnicott 1947) that may be especially difficult for social workers to accept in themselves. Treated as possible "news from within" (Bollas 1987) about the nature of their client's inner life, such feelings can enable clinicians to understand and be accepting and non-judgmental of clients' provocative behavior. In turn, this response is believed to foster in clients a capacity to experience concern, guilt, and wishes to make reparation to others. This achievement initiaties a capacity for empathy and social responsibility.

The True and False Self

The developmental culmination of being adequately held, of establishing ego relatedness with another, of finding means for self-soothing, and of integrating libidinal and aggressive feelings is a sense of feeling real. As Winnicott (1971a) noted, "Feeling real is more than existing; it is finding a way to exist as oneself, and to relate to objects as oneself, and to have a self into which to retreat for relaxation" (p. 117). The basis for feeling real is the "true self" (Winnicott 1960a). With this concept, Winnicott attempted to describe how the self, at birth only a nascent potential, finds realization in the world of shared meaning. At first, the true self "comes from the aliveness of the body tissues and the working of body-functions, including the heart's action and breathing" (Winnicott 1960a, p. 148). It can come to full social expression only "through recognition by the mother of the infant's spontaneous gestures, through being reliably seen by her"; and, ultimately, "it is consolidated through aggression, the mother's survival–meaning her non-retaliation–of the infant and child's destructiveness" (Phillips 1988, p. 128). The result is a sense of being thoroughly alive that is grounded in the body and elaborated in dynamic, affectively complex relationships with others.

In social work, we see many clients whose true selves have been subsumed beneath a defensive "false self" posture. These are people whose caregivers, either because of their own early deprivation or environmental impingements, have been unable to support true self development in their children and have instead demanded compliance. Children with a compliant false-self defense often become adept at tuning into their caregivers' needs and learn to mirror and take care of them. Their hypersensitivity to others' feelings and needs can have the effect of alienating them from their own inner lives, an outcome social workers frequently see in adult children of parents with addictions or other vulnerabilities. With such clients, it is essential to make sure they do not need to comply with the worker's needs or in other ways act as his or her caregivers. Sensitive work with these clients calls for an understanding of their spontaneous gestures, both loving and hating, as signals that they are becoming comfortable in experimenting with their true selves in a safe, reliable, and non-demanding relationship. The true and false self concept captures the value of self-determination in its most essential manifestation.

IMPLICATIONS FOR SOCIAL WORK EDUCATION

Theory

Winnicott's developmental theory, with its emphasis on the person-in-environment "set-up," can be introduced at several points in master's-level Human Behavior and the Social Environment (HBSE) courses. Few theorists have captured so compellingly, and in such accessible language, the qualities and dynamics of the facilitating infant–caregiver relationship. A paper entitled "The Theory of the Parent–Infant Relationship" (Winnicott 1960b) provides an excellent introduction to his key ideas about early development and fits well other theory recently emerging from observational research on infancy. Compendia of his work such as the book *Human Nature* (Winnicott 1988) and a comprehensive summary of his entire developmental theory edited by Davis and Wallbridge (1981) are also helpful.

Winnicott's views on human vulnerability and disturbance can be included in HBSE courses in psychosocial pathology. His papers on work with people with schizophrenia and personality disorders provide a developmental perspective on these problems that helps students appreciate their origins, meaning, and survival value. Papers such as "Delinquency as a Sign of Hope" (1967) and "The Value of Depression" (1963b) offer a strengths perspective on antisocial behavior and affective disorders, respectively. In the last 10 years, considerable theoretical elaboration of Winnicott's concepts has appeared in published scholarship that can supplement traditional texts in psychopathology (see, for example, Fromm and Smith 1989). Some of Winnicott's work also lends itself to HBSE courses in social theory. Several readings in *Home is Where We Start From* (1986), for example, provide his unique view of issues such as war, democracy, and the meaning of freedom.

In considering Winnicott's work for HBSE courses, it is important to note that his and other object relations theorists' work has been criticized by some feminist scholars as reinforcing the patriarchal agenda (see Okun 1992). These critics express concern that the matrifocal emphasis of this theory contributes to gender-unequal childcare and, thus, perpetuates mother-blaming and other manifestations of the cultural devaluation of women. While other feminists such as Luepnitz (1988) take the view that Winnicott's work in fact privileges women, it is important that social work educators inform themselves about this debate and remain alert to the political messages embedded in the theory they teach.

Practice

Winnicott's ideas are also suitable for inclusion in beginning and advanced social work practice courses. Students readily grasp and appreciate the objective of establishing a holding environment for clients, from the micro to the macro level, as basic to all other intervention. The holding environment idea can also illuminate the details of relationship building, as can the concept of ego relatedness, with its emphasis on facilitating clients' innate reparative potential and other ego strengths. Students can be sensitized to recognizing points in their work with clients when they or their agency may serve as transitional objects to clients. And the concept of object relating and object use can be employed to help students develop and sustain empathy for clients whose behavior may appear to invite rejection. Finally, recognition of a client's right to "true self" determination will assist students in celebrating rather than retaliating against their clients' assertive efforts to claim themselves.

All these concepts help students keep the therapeutic relationship in the spotlight, regardless of the nature and duration of the intervention. Some educators believe that psychodynamic concepts are inappropriate tools for practice with people whose circumstances are so depriving or oppressive as to keep them in a chronic state of need or crisis. Certainly many situations social workers confront call for the provision of concrete services, environmental modification, and advocacy. What Winnicott's concepts offer is a way to attend to the *meaning* clients ascribe to their stressful situations and to the services provided to alleviate these situations. An assumption that chronically deprived or crisis-ridden families cannot benefit from such an in-depth approach may lead to superficial solutions that constitute a subtle but pernicious expression of discrimination and result in further oppression.

One potential danger of transposing Winnicott's work to social work practice courses lies in the homey simplicity with which he expressed some of his key ideas. This simplicity might lead beginning workers to adopt these ideas in a literal manner, promoting an infantilizing clinical posture that fails to capture the nuanced complexities of effective supportive work. Holding, caring, and nurturing are useful metaphors for supportive intervention, but they are vulnerable to reification and, as practice techniques, are not enough. In inexperienced hands, ideas that social workers can reparent clients or in other ways make up for seeming failures by earlier caregivers can promote fantasies of omnipotence and expressions of countertransference acting-out. Case examples of sensitive Winnicottian practice can help minimize this danger. Such illustrations can be found in the growing body of social work scholarship related to Winnicott's work (see Applegate 1984, 1993a, 1993b, Applegate and Barol 1989, Chescheir 1985, Kanter 1990, Meyer 1993, Sanville 1991).

CONCLUSION

Social work has a long tradition of borrowing psychodynamic theory to inform its practice and education. By now this body of ideas has pervaded the practice of social work psychotherapy, especially that conducted in private practice. In this chapter, I have employed the theoretical and practical concepts of Donald Winnicott to demonstrate ways in which psychodynamic theory can be applied effectively in agency-based practice and in master's level social work education. Winnicott's ideas offer tools for conceptualizing the range of social work practice activities in ways that can help prepare future social workers to uphold the profession's commitment to humane social services in increasingly challenging practice environments.

REFERENCES

Applegate, J. S. (1984). Transitional phenomena in adolescence: tools for negotiating the second individuation. *Clinical Social Work Journal* 12:233–243.

—— (1993a). The developmental dialectic: its place in clinical listening. *Clinical Social Work Journal* 21:125–135.

—— (1993b). Winnicott and clinical social work: a facilitating partnership. *Child and Adolescent Social Work Journal* 10:3–19.

Applegate, J. S., and Barol, B. I. (1989). Repairing the nest: a psychodynamic developmental approach to clients with severe behavior disorders. *Clinical Social Work Journal* 17:197–207.

Argyris, C., and Schon, D. A. (1974). *Theory in Practice: Increasing Professional Effectiveness*. San Francisco: Jossey-Bass.

Bollas, C. (1987). *The Shadow of the Object: Psychoanalysis of the Unthought Known*. London: Free Association Books.

Chescheir, M. W. (1985). Some implications of Winnicott's concepts for clinical practice. *Clinical Social Work Journal* 13:218–233.

Clancier, A., and Kalmanovitch, J. (1987). *Winnicott and Paradox: From Birth to Creation*. New York: Tavistock.

Coady, N. F. (1993). The worker–client relationship revisited. *Families in Society* 74:291–298.

Davis, M., and Wallbridge, D. (1981). *Boundary and Space: An Introduction to the Work of D. W. Winnicott*. New York: Brunner/Mazel.

Dean, R. G. (1993). Constructivism: an approach to clinical practice. *Smith College Studies in Social Work* 63:127–146.

DeJonghe, F., Rijnierse, P., and Janssen, R. (1992). The role of support in psychoanalysis. *Journal of the American Psychoanalytic Association* 40:475–499.

Deri, S. (1984). *Symbolization and Creativity*. Madison, CT: International Universities Press.

Freedberg, S. (1993). The feminine ethic of care and the professionalization of social work. *Social Work* 38:535–540.

Freud, S. (1900). The interpretation of dreams. *Standard Edition* 4 & 5: xxiii–627.

Fromm, M. G., and Smith, B. L. (1989). *The Facilitating Environment: Clinical Applications of Winnicott's Theory*. Madison, CT: International Universities Press.

Goldman, D. (1993). *In Search of the Real: The Origins and Originality of D. W. Winnicott*. Northvale, NJ: Jason Aronson.

Goldstein, E. G. (1984). *Ego Psychology and Social Work Practice*. New York: Free Press.

Grolnick, S. A. (1990). *The Work and Play of Winnicott.* Northvale, NJ: Jason Aronson.

Grosskurth, P. (1986). *Melanie Klein: Her World and Her Work.* New York: Knopf.

Guntrip, H. (1975). My experience of analysis with Fairbairn & Winnicott (How complete a result does psycho-analytic therapy achieve?) *International Review of Psycho-Analysis* 2:145–156.

Khan, M. M. (1975). Introduction. In *Through Paediatrics to Psycho-Analysis* by D. W. Winnicott, pp. xi–l. New York: Basic Books.

Klein, M. (1964). *Contributions to Psychoanalysis, 1921–1945.* New York: McGraw-Hill.

Little, M. I. (1990). *Psychotic Anxieties and Containment: A Personal Record of an Analysis with Winnicott.* Northvale, NJ: Jason Aronson.

Luepnitz, D. A. (1988). *The Family Interpreted: Feminist Theory in Clinical Practice.* New York: Plenum Press.

Meyer, W. S. (1993). In defense of long-term treatment: on the vanishing holding environment. *Social Work* 38:571–578.

Okun, B. F. (1992). Object relations and self psychology: overview and feminist perspective. In *Personality and Psychopathology: Feminist Reappraisals*, ed. L. S. Brown and M. Ballou, pp. 20–45. New York: Guilford.

Phillips, A. (1988). *Winnicott.* Cambridge, MA: Harvard University Press.

Rodman, F. R. (1987). *The Spontaneous Gesture: Selected Letters of D. W. Winnicott.* Cambridge, MA: Harvard University Press.

Rudnytsky, P. L. (1991). *The Psychoanalytic Vocation: Rank, Winnicott, and the Legacy of Freud.* New Haven: Yale University Press.

Saari, C. (1991). *The Creation of Meaning in Clinical Social Work.* New York: Guilford.

Sanville, J. (1991). *The Playground of Psychoanalytic Therapy.* Hillsdale, NJ: Analytic Press.

Schon, D. A. (1987). *Educating the Reflective Practitioner.* San Francisco: Jossey-Bass.

Shor, J., and Sanville, J. (1978). *Illusion in Loving: A Psychoanalytic Approach to the Evolution of Intimacy and Autonomy.* Los Angeles: Double Helix Press.

Werner, H., and Kaplan, B. (1963). *Symbol Formation.* New York: John Wiley & Sons.

Winnicott, C. (1989). D. W. W.: A reflection. In *Psycho-Analytic Explorations: D. W. Winnicott,* ed. C. Winnicott, R. Shepherd, and M. Davis, pp. 1–18. Cambridge, MA: Harvard University Press.

Winnicott, C., Shepherd, R., and Davis, M., eds. (1989). *Psycho-Analytic Explorations: D. W. Winnicott.* Cambridge, MA: Harvard University Press.

Winnicott, D. W. (1945). Primitive emotional development. In *Through Paediatrics to Psycho-Analysis*, pp. 145–165. New York: Basic Books, 1975.

——(1947). Hate in the countertransference. In *Through Paediatrics to Psycho-Analysis*, pp. 194–203. New York: Basic Books, 1975.
——(1952). Anxiety associated with insecurity. In *Through Paediatrics to Psycho-Analysis*, pp. 97–100. New York: Basic Books, 1975.
——(1953). Transitional objects and transitional phenomena: a study of the first not-me possession. *International Journal of Psycho-Analysis* 34:89–97.
——(1956a). Primary maternal preoccupation. In *Through Paediatrics to Psycho-Analysis*, pp. 300–305. New York: Basic Books, 1975.
—— (1956b). The antisocial tendency. In *Through Paediatrics to Psycho-Analysis*, pp. 306–315. New York: Basic Books, 1975.
——(1957). Integrative and disruptive factors in family life. In *The Family and Individual Development*, pp. 40–49. London: Routledge, 1989.
—— (1958). The capacity to be alone. In *The Maturational Processes and the Facilitating Environment*, pp. 29–36. Madison, CT: International Universities Press, 1965.
——(1960a). Ego distortion in terms of true and false self. In *The Maturational Processes and the Facilitating Environment*, pp. 140–152. Madison, CT: International Universities Press, 1965.
——(1960b). The theory of the parent–infant relationship. In *The Maturational Processes and the Facilitating Environment*, pp. 37–55. Madison, CT: International Universities Press, 1965.
——(1961). Varieties of psychotherapy. In *Home is Where We Start From: Essays by a Psychoanalyst*, pp. 101–111. New York: Norton, 1986.
——(1962). The aims of psycho-analytical treatment. In *The Maturational Processes and the Facilitating Environment*, pp. 166–170. Madison, CT: International Universities Press, 1965.
——(1963a). Communicating and not communicating leading to a study of certain opposites. In *The Maturational Processes and the Facilitating Environment*, pp. 179–192. Madison, CT: International Universities Press, 1965.
——(1963b). The value of depression. In *Home is Where We Start From: Essays by a Psychoanalyst*, pp. 71–79. New York: Norton, 1986.
——(1965). *The Family and Individual Development*. London: Tavistock.
——(1967). Delinquency as a sign of hope. In *Home is Where We Start From: Essays by a Psychoanalyst*, pp. 90–100. New York: Norton, 1986.
——(1968). Communication between infant and mother, and mother and infant, compared and contrasted. In *Babies and Their Mothers*, pp. 89–103. Reading, MA: Addison-Wesley, 1988.

6 From Holding to Interpretation

Martha W. Chescheir

My reason for writing this chapter comes from the belief that social work training teaches clinicians more about how to provide support and sustainment than it does about what constitutes a helpful interpretation. Historically, interpretations, especially genetic interpretations, were considered the bailiwick of psychoanalysis, whereas support, environmental provisions, and confronting reality were designated as the domain of social work. Clinicians certainly were taught to recognize transference and countertransference phenomena but were generally instructed to encourage the positive transference and only deal with negative transferences when faced with strong resistance.

Psychoanalysts generally believed that what cured their patients depended on the clinicians' management of the transference–countertransference and the accuracy of their interpretations, whereas social workers always have placed more value in the therapeutic relationship and were accustomed to working with more derivative forms of the transference. This writer hopes to bring these two perspectives closer together by discussing the meaning of "support" or "holding" and how we might expand that definition to include forms of interpretation that help patients get the most use out of the therapeutic relationship. In order to do this, the author will be drawing from the work of several object relations thinkers from the British Independent School. Four concepts: holding, transitional space, interpretation, and containment will be defined and discussed, then illustrated with an ongoing case.

Holding and Interpretation, written by Winnicott on the basis of notes compiled while working with the patient around 1954, was not published until 1986, fifteen years after his death. Notable about the case is that Winnicott made a great many comments and interpretations in a typically classical manner, while later in his professional career, with more experience behind him, Winnicott changed his mind about the purpose and value of interpretations and became much more parsimonious about his comments to patients. I will try to show how and why Winnicott's views shifted from more classical interpretation to one that is definitely more process centered (1964) and more like what social workers typically do. The change in his thinking came from his years of experience with severe borderlines, near-psychotic patients, antisocial personalities, and also, probably, from the influence of his wife Claire, who was a social worker.

DEFINITION OF HOLDING

For Winnicott (1965) the holding environment was the essential element needed to lay a secure foundation for ego integration and ego relatedness in working with severely disturbed and borderline individuals. The idea of the holding or the facilitating environment meant the total treatment situation, reminiscent of the atmosphere created by a mother caring for her growing infant. In this sense holding was a metaphor for the affective elements of treatment, not only the transference–countertransference phenomena, but also the potential space between the patient and therapist, which meant the fit between the two people and the way they are able to work together. Winnicott believed that psychological holding was necessary for the patient to experience some sense of continuity, "a going-on-being." It is the feeling that one is being held and a safety net is present that protects the infant or patient from impingements from both internal and external forces.

Initially, many emotionally deprived patients experience a sense of oneness with their therapist, which is reminiscent of the way we imagine an infant might feel in relation to a mother. During this earliest developmental phase (Winnicott [1964] likened this mother to the environment) the mother is perceived as simply being there to serve the functions of holding, protecting, and responding according to the needs of the infant. But as the infant matures, he or she gradually outgrows the need for an enveloping relationship with the mother and begins to explore the world more independently.

In a similar manner, during the initial phase of treatment, some patients need their therapist to function like an environmental mother, but as the treatment progresses and the patient begins to differentiate self from other, the patient pulls away from the therapist in search of more emotional space in which to examine personal experiences and to reflect upon different emotional states. When this happens, the mother's or therapist's task shifts, allowing for more psychological breathing room in which to examine contradictory and even opposite kinds of emotional states, like love–hate, security–risk, closeness–distance, order–chaos, and hope–hopelessness. This is the time when transitional phenomena begin to emerge within what Winnicott (1971) called the intermediate area of experience.

The similarity between a mother and her infant and a therapist and a patient does not imply that treatment is simply a matter of re-parenting. Rather, therapy can be viewed as offering a new kind of relationship which may be reminiscent of the past but which provides an opportunity and a new context from which to understand and reflect upon one's past life experiences differently.

When Winnicott spoke of holding, he was referring to the infant and mother together—a two-person unit—and also to the therapeutic environment. To foster this is the function that social workers seem to know best. Most clinical social workers seem naturally endowed with a capacity for holding. They know how to listen, provide support, and hold their clients through emotional crisis after crisis. But what has not been well articulated in social work education is what happens in the transitional space created within the therapeutic relationship. Consequently, Winnicott's teachings are particularly helpful for anyone interested in studying the intricacies of clinical practice. The case presented here illustrates a segment of long-term treatment with a severely depressed schizoid man. In order to maintain patient confidentiality, identifying information has been omitted or altered, but an effort has been made to preserve the mood and content of several clinical sessions that occurred over a three-year period.

CASE ILLUSTRATION

When Mr. B. entered treatment, he was profoundly depressed and only able to keep himself glued together with the help of antidepressants prescribed by the medicating psychiatrist. He described himself as constantly on the edge of anxiety, churned up inside, often sick in the stomach, having trouble staying asleep through the night, and worried about his capacity for intimacy with his wife, to whom he actually was devoted. He was a tall, handsome man in his mid-thirties who carried himself in a stiff, formal, almost robot-like manner.

He sought treatment about three months after his arrival in this area. Before coming here, he had been in psychoanalytic treatment for several years with an elderly male analyst. While he relocated here because of a new work assignment, he was also aware that moving was a way to distance himself from his intrusive and demanding mother and also a way to avoid having to face the possibility that his analyst might die. This latter thought was too painful to bear because he had lost his father during his late adolescence, and he did not want to repeat that kind of anguish all over again.

Some significant bits of history were that Mr. B. was the youngest of several boys fairly close in age. He often wondered if his parents might have preferred a girl after having so many boys. His father, a factory worker, was severely injured in an industrial accident that left him crippled on one side of his body. At that time Mr. B. was about three years old. His early memories of this event were of seeing his father carried home from the hospital on a stretcher and being devastated and totally mystified about what had happened. No one was there to talk about it with him. His mother was completely overwhelmed with responsibility for the house, the children, and now an invalid husband. In addition, she started to go to work on a regular basis. In spite of these realities Mr. B.'s father made quite a remarkable recovery, and, although unable to walk without crutches, he managed a small business from their home. However, after the accident, his parents never shared the same bedroom again. Mr. B. remembers that his father regularly slept on the couch in the living room.

He spent his childhood trying to be a good and dutiful son for his parents, hanging around trying to be helpful. While initially he had enjoyed school, as he reached puberty he began to get into trouble at school, which made him anxious and fearful about attending. He started to panic on his way to school because he was afraid that he would be lost in the mob of students, feel dehumanized, fade into the air, and then vaporize. As a consequence, he began cutting school and wandering the streets by himself. His favorite place was a forested area near a river where he felt safe. There he would sit on the bank, daydreaming and feeling quite mesmerized by the sparkling waters.

During that time he began stealing. At first he took small bits of change from his parents, and then he stole from a kindly bread man who gave him rides in his truck. Later during his adolescence he started hanging around with an older teenager and together they got into much more serious delinquencies, such as drinking, rabble-rousing, and finally shoplifting and car theft. He thought of this guy as a hero as well as his best friend. However, as a young adult he was devastated to hear that his good friend had been imprisoned in a maximum security jail for committing major crimes, including drug dealing.

By the time Mr. B. was 16 years old, he dropped out of school. When the authorities finally gave up on him, his mother helped him find work as an errand boy in a small family-owned factory, where he discovered much to his delight that the tradesmen really liked him. In looking back, Mr. B. believed that this was one of the few times in his life when he felt buoyed up and supported. Gradually he stopped getting into trouble with the law and within a few years began to work his way through college. He married in his early thirties and became quite successful at his work.

When Mr. B. was just about to get his life together, in his late teens, his father died. His father's death remained a deep sorrow. Several years later, as Mr. B. was completing his college work, his mother became gravely ill and incapacitated so Mr. B. felt obligated to move back home to take care of her through this major illness. During these years he became more aware of his mother's critically demanding nature. Whereas Mr. B.'s relationship to his father was generally idealized, his relationship to his mother was fraught with problems. He felt taken over by her, and, no matter how hard he tried to please, he could never satisfy her. Here he struggled with a split—one parent whom he perceived as good but weak, and another parent who he represented as bad and intrusive but powerful. His images of women were further split because, while he expressed real devotion to his wife in a brotherly fashion, their sex life left much to be desired. He was obsessed by fantasies about sexual experiences with small, dark, olive-skinned women, who physically seemed to resemble his mother.

Beginning Phase of Treatment

When Mr. B. left his former therapist, they decided together that it would be helpful for him to work with a woman. He seemed to have had a very positive experience with Dr. X., who appeared from Mr. B's description to represent a combination of a caring admirable father and a warm nurturing mother. Mr. B. met with Dr. X. five times a week and was encouraged to use the couch, where Mr. B. comforted himself by imagining he was a small infant. Therefore, having a woman therapist who expected him to sit facing her forced him to confront a number of realistic issues that he previously had avoided, especially his relationship with women. As you might imagine, the initial phase of our work together made him very anxious. He started most of those early sessions by telling the therapist how difficult it was to force himself to come.

Mr. B.'s job created further complications, since he was required to be out of town for two or three weeks at a time every few months. Taking these reality concerns into consideration, the best arrangement that seemed to work out was to meet intensely two or three times per week when he was in town, and deal with the trips and breaks in treatment as they came up. The schedule was Mr. B.'s idea since in his prior treatment he was accustomed to meeting more frequently. This therapist felt that such an arrangement might prove interesting, since Mr. B. had suffered a number of major losses, and the arrangement we negotiated included many comings and goings and was a way of drawing attention to the closeness–distance paradigm. Early on we began to notice that often he would bring up some significant piece of material shortly before he was scheduled to leave town. Also, he was frequently late for the sessions, which in the beginning phase of treatment had to do with his anxiety and ambivalence about coming. These complications set a tentative tone to the work. But in spite of his initial reluctance, Mr. B. persisted in wanting to be less depressed and feel better about himself. In fact, he generally used his time thoughtfully and well, but at other times when he arrived late or called at the last minute to say he couldn't make it, he was actively showing a concern about trust. Thus, he demonstrated two aspects of himself, his tendency towards compliance and his struggle with acting out.

After we had been meeting together for a few months, his wife gave birth to their first child, a daughter. Mr. B. was very attentive to his wife during the delivery and for the first few weeks after the baby's birth. It was remarkable how quickly he bonded to the little newborn infant. In fact those first weeks after the baby's birth were described as almost too blissful. It was not until two months later that Mr. B. dared to tell me about how really traumatic the baby's birth actually had been for him. All the blood and gore made him sick and intensely anxious because he feared that his wife's genitals were permanently damaged and mutilated, and he disclosed that he was having flashbacks as if he were a trauma victim. After talking about these frightening events, he mentioned a nightmarish dream that he and his old therapist had worked on during his previous therapy, which may explain why at times he needed a holding environment and a sense of a safety net under him.

This dream was set in an operating room. Here a woman was lying on her back about to deliver a baby, when a machine with a suspended arm came down and cut a circle into the woman's stomach. Mr. B. described having a terrible sensation as the machine came towards the woman. Then he said, "The baby is me, and I'm lifted up by this machine, suspended in air. I lose my envelope and the mother is brutalized by the procedure. I'm only in contact with the machine, suspended in air by a magnet. The baby is surrounded by air only and going higher and higher in an exposed state, more scary than the possibility of falling because there is nothing to surround the infant–only air, no coziness or sense of security."

Shortly after disclosing this frightening dream, he dreamed he was following a woman about his own age with black hair into a store. The room was full of shelves filled with ten-gallon tin cans. He stood and watched while the woman started to drink out of a large can of white paint, and he frantically yelled, "Stop, don't drink it! It's poisonous!"

The therapist asked if possibly the woman was looking for milk, not paint. He accepted that idea and went on to comment, "I guess I'm the one looking for good milk, but it certainly can't be found in that store room. In fact, I can get into trouble for even asking or wanting good milk." He went on to say, "My mother is an obstacle to my getting on with my life. If I could let her go, I would be happier, but I keep taking in her poison. To say what I really want is risky. It's better to hold down on desires so they don't get tested. I did what I thought mother wanted, giving up what I wanted. It's like there is a bad piece inside me, in the wall of my stomach." This was a theme that repeated itself during the course of the therapy. Another interesting feature was that whenever small dark females turned up in his dreams and fantasy life, he associated them with an image of an exciting but essentially "bad" mother.

Mr. B. described his wife as an unusually caring and motherly kind of woman, who was tall and blond. It should be mentioned also that the therapist was tall and blond. In general Mr. B. tended to idealize both his wife, Sally, and his infant daughter, Betsy. The only negative that Mr. B. could come up with about his wife was that she had a tendency to erupt in anger—a characteristic that she shared with his mother. While Sally did not flare up often, when she did, Mr. B. clammed up and immediately retreated into his shell.

From the very beginning he beamed with pride whenever he spoke of their little daughter. Shortly after her birth he commented, "Betsy is so little, everything is absorbed. She is so vulnerable, constantly needing love and assurance from us. That's what I didn't get. Kept me from starting out on solid ground, so I lost track of what might be me, forgot what I wanted, lost my core, and felt empty."

His initial anxiety was heightened by the fact that he was on probationary status at work that first year, and his supervisor, a small dark Vietnamese man, was constantly on his back. After a while it became apparent that this supervisor reminded him of his mother—rigid, demanding, never satisfied, always wanting more, and critical of whatever he did accomplish.

That first year in therapy was difficult for Mr. B. because of his hesitancy to trust the relationship. He feared that if he was not completely compliant his therapist might become demanding and critical like his mother and his current supervisor, or that she might get angry and lash out at him like his wife. From a countertransference point of view, the therapist felt rather tentative, and uncertain about whether she would pass the test, sometimes even wondering if he would be able to allow himself to remain in treatment at all. Generally it was clear that he needed support and psychological holding, but as yet he was not able to talk about his wants and needs for himself. He just reacted to others in his life and was not in touch with his inner life. The dilemma he struggled with was whether to remain the dutiful and compliant son or to act on his emotions, which to him meant following impulses which in the past had gotten him in serious trouble. During this first phase of treatment the therapist felt that her primary task was to help Mr. B. trust the relationship. Therefore, she tried to hold the situation over from one session to the next, establish continuity and predictability, and develop a sense that they could begin to work together.

FINDING A TRANSITIONAL AREA

Winnicott (1971) originally called this area *potential space* or the *intermediate area of experience* because he meant that it was neither in reality nor fantasy but somewhere in between. In his paper "Playing: The Search for the Self" Winnicott wrote:

> We experience life in the area of transitional phenomena, in the exciting interweave of subjectivity and objective observation, and in an area that is intermediate between the inner reality of the individual and the shared reality of the world that is external to individuals." [1971, p. 64]

Potential or transitional space implies a mix of inner and outer and self and non-self. Sometimes Winnicott (1971) called the space a third world or a play area, for this was the place from which transitional objects and phenomena originated. Transitional objects and transitional phenomena serve a bridging function between mother and infant and between therapist and patient and aid in the separation of self from non-self. Whereas transitional objects are tangible movable objects, transitional phenomena are activities, images, or patterns of behavior, but both are used to create an illusion both of being with mother, and, simultaneously, of a separate self.

Winnicott (1971) further suggested that this third area represented a metaphorical space between infant and mother where the capacity for illusion, play, and the creative imagination develops. According to Deri

(1978), transitional spaces are used for creative symbol formation because the function of a symbol is to connect and unite opposites. Thus, all transitional processes tend to symbolize the illusion of both separateness and togetherness. Transitional space is an intermediate area that does not represent self or object (me or you) but is a blend of both out of which something new, creative, or symbolic can be formed.

In his early experiments with mothers and their babies, Winnicott noticed that, when he placed a shiny object (like a spatula) within sight of the baby and then engaged the mother in conversation, the baby would glance at the mother's face to see if it was all right to grasp the spatula and enjoy playing with it by putting it in the mouth and drooling and slobbering all over it. Winnicott (1975) called this "the moment of hesitation." It is that brief second (in which the baby senses mother's permissive or controlling mood) that gets expanded into a larger space in which both mother and child learn to play and enjoy themselves, and real interaction begins. For the infant to realize and act on his or her own desires requires some sense of separateness and represents a kind of risk, because to say no to mother and yes to one's own desires can be dangerous, especially when faced with a possessive, emotionally needy, or demanding mother.

Winnicott's ideas about this potential space are particularly useful when trying to understand the interpersonal aspects of therapy, as it can be thought of as a kind of interpersonal experiencing. Modell (1976), for example, suggested that the therapeutic process itself is invested with transitional qualities. The space that develops from the interaction is created by both participants, who are engaged in the process and together create a safe place where personal or subjective meaning can be explored. The therapist's job is to try to follow the patient's thoughts and feelings and to help the patient explore different aspects of the self or, in object relations language, explore self–object representations.

Developmentally this phase follows the holding phase, which can be thought of as something like a cocoon where the infant and mother are one and, even though there may be some illusion of self-sufficiency, the infant is still dependent on the caretaking functions of the mother. As the transitional processes emerge, some separation between self and other occurs and a patient begins to acknowledge differences and negative or disappointing thoughts about the therapist begin to surface. Winnicott (1975) suggested that it was a time when the patient felt secure enough to "hate" the therapist. When the therapist survives being hated, the patient generally feels more at ease about sharing ideas because the therapist is now seen as separate from self and having more human qualities. Winnicott (1971) felt that a kind of playing takes place between therapist and patient in this intermediate area as transitional processes develop. He wrote (1971, pg. 54), "Psychotherapy is done in the overlap of two play areas–that of the patient and that of the therapist." When this occurs, ideas emerge that make sense to both participants, and the experience itself can more easily become internalized. These ideas may be a fragment of behavior, a new way of looking at things, or merely a spontaneous thought or feeling.

Christopher Bollas (1989) believes that infants do not simply internalize the image of mother as a person; they internalize the maternal process or the total experience of being with mother in this mutually created state. Once clear about how all this happens in the mother–infant dyad, the same process can be transposed into the therapist–patient relationship. What is internalized is the experience of working together.

In order to accomplish this task, Michael Balint (1968) recommended that the therapist be unobtrusively available by (1) reducing the inequality between patient and therapist, (2) being ordinary and unobtrusive, (3) paying attention to the meaning of silences and other forms of nonverbal communication, and (4) avoiding making interpretations that destroy the possibility of the patient seeking and finding out for himself or herself.

In Mr. B.'s case the therapist encouraged him to think about and try to understand some of his nonverbal behavior, more specifically what was behind his chronic lateness to sessions and why it was that he needed to bring up vital material just before leaving town. As we felt more comfortable in discussing his behavior, it became more apparent just how anxious he was about the therapy and how disappointed and frustrated he was to be working with me instead of his previous therapist. In short, the negatives in the transference that were discussed and accepted helped to create a different climate–one in which we could begin to work together in a new way. As Mr. B. became freer in expressing himself, the mood in the sessions gradually became lighter and more lively.

At the same time Mr. B. began to talk in more and more detail about his growing relationship with his little daughter, who actually was developing a mind of her own as she became a toddler and was better able to communicate with her parents. Actually, it was Betsy, his daughter, who taught Mr. B. about himself and how to find transitional spaces in which to play. When he brought this material into the therapy sessions we talked about what was happening with Betsy and in this way shared those experiences together.

Learning to Play

Shortly after Betsy's birth, it become quite apparent that this relationship was going to take on a life of its own. Betsy was the living incarnation of the little daughter Mr. B. believed his mother would have chosen as her last child. They even looked alike, with the same kind of light hair and coloring. As we started our second year of therapy, a few brighter, more playful moments began to show up in our sessions. Mr. B. brought them in whenever he talked about what he and Betsy were doing together. For instance, when she was an infant he commented, "Betsy gives me a kind of centeredness and continuity, especially when I'm walking along with her in a cuddly. However, it makes me realize that I didn't get the kind of nurturing that we are giving her."

When Betsy was 6 months old, Mr. B. remarked, "Betsy puts my life in perspective, finds the world a great place to be. When she is enjoying the moment, so can I. Then I'm remembering that a big part of me was just like that—enjoying new things and laughing at my own success." Then he added, "Wonder where my pleasure went?"

A month later, for the first time he seemed more upbeat and playful about his job as he commented, "Well, I'm more on a roll at work, even getting a bit more assertive." Then he said, "I found an article in a magazine about the life of Edvard Munch—you know, that depressed Norwegian artist—and for some odd reason, I put it on the floor of my office where I could just see it out of the corner of my eyes, but in my work I was feeling good—it was almost like I took a flight from bad feelings, so I could get the work done. Yesterday, I picked up the magazine, took it home, put it in the closet, then I handed in the paper I had been working on and felt satisfied."

When Betsy was a year old, Mr. B. realized that she was becoming more of her own person. "She lives in the here and now, innocently expects to be loved, but almost at the same moment she's loving, she pulls away and takes a step towards independence. I'm not sure I like her quite as completely as I did when she was so totally dependent on us." But about himself he remarked, "By the time I was a year old, my mother had managed to crush my sense of aliveness, my creativity. I don't want to do that to Betsy."

Six months later, when Betsy was about 18 months old, he commented, "I'll survive without my mother because Betsy is my connection to the future and she gives me a sense of growing." Then he seemed to compare his own depressive disposition with Betsy's exuberance for living. "There's a real spark of life in her. She is interested in every aspect of the world and always seems to see the funny side of things. Why is it that I can't seem to take the controls off myself?"

One of his favorite pastimes was playing with Betsy in the bathtub, making up stories about the toys, and having them magically dive and splash into the water. "We just have fun, and there is a wonderfully natural give and take as we play. Playing with Betsy is immediately fulfilling. The other day, I watched her playing in the leaves and admired her capacity to just throw herself into the moment. I think it's good for me to let myself enjoy her enjoyment."

During our second year of therapy, just before his birthday, Mr. B. bought an aquarium for himself and stocked it with delicate tropical fish because he found it restful and relaxing to watch them swimming around. This reminded him of the peaceful times he managed to find for himself when he played hooky from school and would sit by the river bank watching the sunlight play on the sparkling water. As he let himself relax, he enjoyed singing little songs with Betsy and making up nonsense rhymes that they could giggle about together.

He noticed that Betsy's dolls really came alive for her, and then he remembered that he had felt the same way about his teddy bear with an injured left paw that seemed to connect with his father's handicap. He said, "You know, I really thought that caring enough for Teddy's paw would make it well." The therapist remarked "That's the magic of childhood–much joy, but sadness when the magic doesn't work out." Mr. B. agreed and said, "It was sad to find out that I really couldn't make my father well. At one time I really thought I could." Then he added, "I have a lot of playfulness in my character but haven't let it come out. Playfulness keeps the lively stuff going." Shortly after this,

Mr. B. started to walk to work, saying that it made him feel good and slightly mischievous getting to work late. He was almost daring someone to question him about it, but no one seemed to notice. However, the therapist noticed that his lateness to the therapy sessions took on a different meaning. In the beginning of therapy his tardiness was about his anxiety and reluctance to be there. Now it had more to do with knowing that someone cared enough to mention it. At this point in the work the therapist began to sense that Mr. B.'s transference towards her was more paternal than maternal, so she asked what his father had to say about the delinquencies he had gotten into as a teenager. Mr. B. replied, a little sadly, that his father simply remained passive and let his mother handle things. In spite of his handicap his father seemed to find happiness in everyday life. He especially enjoyed doing some of the chores and puttering around the house.

When the family moved from an apartment to a house, Mr. B. began to show a bit of enthusiasm about fixing up his new house and particularly about providing more play space for Betsy. The first thing he did was to buy a little round tent with a zipper and was pleased that Betsy did exactly what he would have done had the tent been his. She went inside taking her favorite books with her, making it her private place. Then he said, "Like me, Betsy is finding a place for herself. I'm finally letting myself feel good about having my own space. As I put the pictures up in the new house I feel like I'm instinctively marking out my territory." While building a sandbox for his daughter, he fixed up a workbench for himself.

During one session he described how Betsy was frightened by thunder and lightning and the pleasure he got from comforting her. Then he added this comment, "My mother would have said, 'Don't be silly, pull yourself together.' You know it amazes me for Betsy to trust me to wash her hair. It's like she really believes me when I tell her that I won't let any soap get into her eyes."

What I have been trying to illustrate here is how important play can be, especially between people who share a common activity and in the process are creating a history of shared experiences together. While Mr. B. learned about himself through his play with his daughter, he also must have known that his therapist clearly enjoyed hearing about their activities together. In many ways, Betsy acted as a facilitator or a kind of co-therapist in the process, because as Mr. B. talked about his antics with his daughter he was making some keen self–other observations and delighting in the process, both the playing and having a chance to tell about it to an appreciative audience.

What is being described here is a kind of parallel process among three sets of people: Mr. B. and Betsy, Mr. B. and the therapist, and Mr. B. and the ghostly figures of his past. Mr. B's usual downhearted, depressed, and shadowy demeanor changed markedly whenever he talked about his experiences with his daughter. Here the mood of the sessions lightened up, even though at this stage he was generally quick to assure the therapist that the therapy didn't seem to be making much of a difference for him.

THE MEANING OF INTERPRETING

Just as Winnicott (1971) thought of the activity, playing, as more important than the content of the play itself, he believed that the process of interpreting was more valuable than the actual content of the interpretation. For Winnicott, interpretations defined the nature of the ongoing relationship rather than simply providing information or imparting knowledge. In this vein Winnicott (1989, p. 207) suggested five kinds of interpretation:

- Therapist simply gives back what is communicated.
- Therapist gives patient an opportunity to correct any misunderstanding.
- Therapist takes responsibility for adapting to the patient's way of relating so the patient can use him or her.
- When material comes up in a session that is not ready for interpretation, the therapist's task is to hold it back until it is ready for symbolic comment.
- Therapist and patient can learn to play together using comments from patient's observations about self and others or any material that comes up in the session, as well as dreams and fantasies.

By playing, Winnicott also meant exploring the different meanings of the material that turns up in a session. In writing his paper on "The Use of the Object and Relating through Identifications" Winnicott (1971) stated that:

> it is only in recent years that I have become able to wait and wait for the natural evolution of the transference arising out of the patient's growing trust in the psychoanalytic technique and setting, and to avoid breaking up this natural process by making interpretations. If only we can wait, the patient arrives at understanding creatively and with immense joy, and I now enjoy this joy more than I used to enjoy the sense of having been clever. I think I interpret mainly to let the patient know the limits of my understanding. The principle is that it is the patient and only the patient who has the answers. [pp. 86–87]

Patrick Casement (1991), a modern-day Winnicottian who freely acknowledges his indebtedness to Winnicott, also advocates the creation of play space. He described this space as something like Winnicott's squiggle game, in which one person draws a line on a paper and the other person turns that line into a picture or shape which then can be given symbolic meaning. He suggests that interpreting is not a matter of telling the patient but of discovering something with the patient.

DIFFERENCE BETWEEN INTERSUBJECTIVE KNOWING AND GENETIC RECONSTRUCTIONS

Dennis Duncan (1989), who studied with Anna Freud and considers himself a British contemporary Freudian, pointed out that interpretations can be viewed on a continuum from simple comments to complex formulations. He distinguished between interpretation by *force* or by *flow*. *Force* means that the interpretation comes from the outside in. The session stops for the statement from the therapist to the patient, which is clearly formulated and correctly timed. Duncan's notion of interpretation by force implies that the therapist is sure that a piece of clinical material fits a particular theoretical framework and thus makes a comment to the patient with certainty and conviction. This definition is closer to the traditional psychoanalytic understanding of the mode of interpretation. It is more of a pronouncement from on high and if the timing is right is intended to open up access to repressed material. A problem with these kinds of formulations is that unless they are exactly on target and stated at precisely the right moment, the patient may hear them as an intrusion or impingement on his or her personal space.

Flow refers to elements of a session that happen to be expressed by the therapist, seamless experiential movement naturally formed in the process of speaking. Interpretations by flow have elements of surprise, like a spontaneous comment that the patient can take in easily and use. Here the focus is on what makes sense to the patient rather than on the one "correct" theoretical explanation. These kinds of interpretations can be an incomplete thought or idea that the patient can complete, like a halfway step, allowing for small interpretations to develop until a mutual story develops and understanding increases.

Duncan (1989) acknowledged that interpretations at both extremes of the continuum were valid and have their place. He tended, however, to be more curious about the more effortless kinds of interpretation because he felt that patients could accept them more easily, and also, of course, there was always room for an improvement or correction from the patient.

Casement (1991) described the process by saying that he thinks of the therapist's presence as being potentially available, like the shiny spatula in Winnicott's clinical experiments, ". . . to be found and to be used in whatever way belongs to the patient at that particular moment. . . . I believe there is an important place for these incomplete 'shapes' in our work with patients; and this is what has led me to think of offering a halfway step to interpretation–for the patient to do something with rather than the analyst monopolizing insight in sessions" (pp. 196–197).

Therapists need to consider how the patient may be experiencing them in the present as well as the past. It is as if both patient and therapist are holding a mirror up to each other or, as Winnicott (1971) once suggested, like two daffy painters trying to create an image of one another.

An image that Mr. B. painted of his therapist (in the present), his mother (in the past), and himself as an adult and as an infant came in the form of a dream. In this dream, he found himself in a foreign city and following a wall down some stairs. He came into a public toilet in a basement, where there were both urinals and stalls. Two Asian men passed him as he entered the room. He thought to himself that this was Vietnam. While standing at the urinal he looked over the wall of the partition into a series of small rooms. They were all empty except one. In that room a small, dark Asian woman was seated and on her lap was a small child about a year old sitting cross-legged. He thought the child was a boy. Seeing this unnerved him, and so he decided to leave immediately, but walking out in front of the partitions frightened him even more, putting him almost into a panic state.

This dream can be interpreted a number of ways as it contains many symbolic elements. The question would be how to make an interpretation helpful to Mr. B. Some therapists might be quite sure that they had the right answer and after listening to the patient's associations tell the patient what the dream was about, taking into consideration the expressed anxiety, the repressed instinct, the organization of the patient's defenses, the past relationship with his mother, and his present situation with his therapist. This kind of understanding would be considered a genetic interpretation and might be useful for the patient to hear, but a more cautious approach might be equally helpful, and keep the dreamer from feeling that his dream was taken over by the listener.

After all, that therapist might not have the only correct way to handle the clinical material revealed in this dream. In listening to the dream, this therapist noticed that Mr. B. had created a word-picture and that the dream seemed to be saying something about his past sense of himself in his world, but also he was working on the nature of the current therapeutic relationship, which up to that point had seemed rather tenuous. In the dream, he indicated that he felt panicky, that in fact this might even be a war zone like Vietnam. So rather than move into his space the therapist simply waited to see what he wanted to make out of it.

Mr. B.'s first comment was, "The woman looked self-contained, but she was just looking at me." Then he noted, "The child was unnaturally still, like he had just perched himself up there on the woman's lap, but the woman looked as though she was sitting in God-like judgment and that she could see me as I am. She had a calm look, seeing and knowing, but not caring." He added, "The child is probably me—calm and protected. He is growing and somehow associated with this woman, born in her image, but I am frightened of her knowing me too well. I'm still struggling with knowing my own true nature, wanting to let go of male pretenses, but then I might become female."

Mr. B.'s comments disclosed a great deal about himself, as he seemed to be expressing two opposing sets of emotions. On the one hand, the dream made him quite anxious because it was cast in a war zone. The public bathroom seemed to imply that issues of control would be important and certainly danger seemed to be lurking about. On the other hand, the woman looked self-contained and the child calm and protected. When he mentioned that the child was unnaturally still, the therapist was reminded of Mr. B.'s general demeanor, as he carried himself in a stiff formal manner. When he said that the baby was perched on the mother's lap, he seemed to be suggesting that this might be a rather tentative gesture, almost as if the infant were testing to see if lap-sitting was going to be acceptable.

Mr. B.'s picture of the baby on the woman's lap seemed to fit Winnicott's notion of holding, that is, finding a safe place to be. So the therapist commented about the opposite kinds of moods expressed–the sense of safety and security, but also the danger and risk of being a boy in that woman's lap. After my comment he remarked, "Mother used to ambush me, no matter how good I was; if I stepped forward with my own ideas, I would be ridiculed. Mother's message to me was, 'Don't be assertive, be a wimp'." The therapist then asked, "Wasn't that a men's room? What do you think the Asian woman was doing in there?" Mr. B. replied, "It is strange that I would put my mother in a men's room because my mother was absolutely disgusted with male sexuality, but for some reason I seem to need to prove my maleness to her. But first I've got to disentangle my own beliefs from what my mother wants. I've allowed her to control my life."

Several weeks later, Mr. B. remembered the bathroom dream again, only this time he saw the scene differently. First he acknowledged that the presence of the child in the dream was a sign of hope. On this occasion, the dream suggested to him that his life could be renewed because he was revising his way of remembering and feeling about his own childhood. He said the woman was a part of himself and that both the woman and child had subdued looks on their faces. "The woman was contemplating me with a steady gaze and the baby's penis was exposed. She could see all of me–see me absolutely–especially my maleness. The child symbolized part of me, but the woman was the one that was showing him to me. This child needed to be revealed to me. It's an important child." This revised and more completed version of the dream seems to indicate that he was less concerned about exposing his sexuality.

Patrick Casement (1991) warned that when psychoanalytic assumptions are held beyond question, interpretations can be too easily imposed on patients and thus almost become cliches. He believed that rigid adherence to dogma might restrict the therapist's capacity to think imaginatively, and therefore the therapist might have to resort to stereotypic responses that were theoretically correct but received by the patient as off-base or even absurd.

Winnicott (1989) and Casement (1989) and many other modern-day object relations thinkers would agree that for something to become clinically useful it should be discovered, and that interpretations need to be open to correction and revision; in other words, understanding or meaning ideally grows out of the shared experience and is not imposed or implanted on the patient.

> Throughout his lifetime, Mr. B. had tried to do the right thing in taking care of his mother, with the faint hope that she would eventually love him. His memory, when he was 3 years old, of his father being carried into the house on a stretcher was just too painful and too vivid. The father that he had known might just as well have been dead, so he could not get angry at his mother because he might lose her also. These are Mr. B.'s words as he recalled that traumatic incident: "He didn't ever come home again. He was never a man again. He was such a quiet unassuming person, but he never was substantial." Some time later Mr. B. said, "There was no way that my father could show me how to be sexually alive as a male, as he was effectively castrated by mother who simply marginalized all men."
>
> As one might suspect, Mr. B. spent a a great deal of time grieving over not having the memory of a live, whole father, and a mother who could not seem to find anything good about him. Gradually, it became more apparent that his parents' roles got reversed. His mother became the energizer and harsh rule-maker, whereas his father provided nurture and care. For quite a long time, the therapist felt that her primary task was to help Mr. B. contain these tragic and painful memories.

CONTAINMENT

It is important to draw a distinction between *holding* and *containment*, because sometimes they appear to have similar meanings. As these concepts are applied in object relations theory, however, they are used differently because they refer to different contexts. While both concepts are necessary in managing anxiety or intolerable physical or emotional pain, *holding* is an interpersonal or relational term and implies the presence of two people interacting together (mother and infant or therapist and patient). *Containment* is an intrapsychic concept that refers to an internal function that first occurs inside the therapist and then gradually is taken in by the patient when it is expressed in a way that it can be assimilated, or as Winnicott (1971) suggested, when the patient has reached the state when he is developmentally ready to "use the object."

When Wilfred Bion (1967) developed the notion of containment, he was not simply referring to the therapist's passive acceptance of whatever emotionally laden material a patient brought to a session. He described containment as an internal process experienced by the therapist that involved taking in, absorbing, feeling, thinking, organizing, and giving back. During the course of treatment this function is gradually taken over by the patient, who learns from the experience as it is reflected back from the therapist who processed it. Thus, some different ways of looking at traumatic memories are created and more novel ways to process distorted images appear.

> The example of containment starts with another short dream fragment Mr. B. reported. "I am sitting at a desk with nothing on it but a telephone. My finger is poised over the hold button. I'm hesitating about whether to press or not to press, but I'm anxious and confused about what to do. Suddenly the perspective changes, when a woman comes into the room where my desk is. I notice that she has dark hair. At first I think she has positive intentions and wants to help me, but then I noticed that her skirt was slit up the front. The impression this gave me was that she was divided down the middle—a split person. That made me wonder if she really intended to be helpful, so I paused with my finger still over the hold button, waiting for her."
>
> Mr. B's associations to this picture were: "The telephone was a source of information. The question is whether I wanted to hear or not hear what the person on the other end of the phone has to say. I seem to be hesitating about whether to take it in or not. The divided woman connects to our last session, when we were talking about the fact that my father was the more nurturing parent and my mother the energizer and stern rule-maker. That woman could be part of me, but I also wondered if she did not stand for parts of both my father and mother

and the conflict between those two parts." The therapist nodded affirmatively, so he went on to say, "The good side that might help would be my father, and the bad side that would be harmful would be my mother. That telephone call is for me. I have not been having a conversation, but someone is there on the other end of the line, and I'm deciding whether to listen to what that person has to say. My desk used to be in a state of chaos, but it seems clear now. That phone connects down into what's underneath the desk and probably whether I can be in touch with my unconscious. My mother said no to her emotions, but my father accepted his situation and some of his emotional life, and of my two parents, my father was much more likely to say 'yes'." I said, "Do you think the dream is suggesting that you might be thinking of shifting some allegiance from your mother to your father?" The therapist questioned in her own mind whether Mr. B. would need to continue to hear his mother's critical voice or whether he would finally listen to his father or his therapist and begin to internalize a few of the things that had been discussed in their recent sessions.

Mr. B. then reminded the therapist that his father's disability made him more vulnerable than his mother. While the therapist agreed, she also suggested that both his parents were survivors. Thoughtfully Mr. B. added, "My father was a survivor because he was strong. His strength came from his acceptance of his own vulnerability. His strength was the more enduring. Mother's toughness was brittle but unhappy." But then he sadly added, "My father died."

Then the therapist asked, "So does that mean that your mother won?" He answered, "She won in the physical sense but lost emotionally. She had a longer but much more unhappy life. My mother made a big issue about winners and losers, and she saw my father as a loser—but there is no question that I would be happier being more like my father."

A while later, just before he was to go on a short business trip, the transference oscillated back from Father to Mother. Mr. B. began his session by announcing that he had mixed feelings about coming. He said, "The rules about the regularity of these appointments begin to feel like Mother's rules. I need a brief escape. It's like I'm stealing some time for myself. Been holding myself back from progress lately. For the last couple of days, I even felt close to my wife, but I can't seem to let myself express it. Somehow I associate Mother with coming here. I feel like telling you that I come here for your benefit. I resent all of you, my wife, my father, and you. It's like I must fit in with your expectations."

The therapist asked rather dubiously, "You mean there doesn't seem to be space for you to be here with me without losing yourself." He added, "I must pass this test and only then will I be well." Then the therapist asked, "Who is doing the grading?" Mr. B. went on to say, "Even if I get the right grade, I couldn't actually believe any grade you might give me." Then in a very angry tone he said, " I'm disowning the whole kit and caboodle of you. Feel like I don't have a reason of my own to do things. Don't have an idea about what I want to do."

The therapist asked, "If you did have an idea, do you have any faith that I'd be on your side?" He went on to say, "I'm comparing all of you to my mother, and she wins because she is the toughest, and you and my wife are weak. You can't get in the center of my life like my mother because of her absolute rigidity. No woman who is more accepting than my mother is worthy of my respect unless you are tough and negative."

Then the therapist commented, "Guess that keeps you from identifying with your dad also. It's like Dad and your wife and I are all softies." There was a long pause and the therapist added, "Could it be that we were right and mother was wrong?"

He replied emphatically, "I believe I am bad, and anyone who can't see my badness must be pretty foolish. If you are really taking me as I am, then I can't look at myself for any rules to live by, and I can't believe in the validity of my own desires." At that point his mind wondered and after a pause he said, "I've hit a blank."

"What is it that you want, at this very moment?" Then he surprised himself by saying, "I want to hold Dad's hand. I didn't get much chance to do it when I was a kid." He sat back in his chair a minute and then added, "When that thought popped into my head, somehow my body relaxed, and I felt connected and secure, like I have an anchor. I want to find that in my father, and all I'm allowed to do is to have relationships with you women. When I'm trying to find a way to hold my father's hand, I see my mother as a barrier keeping me from my father."

The mood shifted a little, and Mr. B. remembered that his father was always listening to a portable radio. "Now I'm doing it myself. Part of what's missing is having my father with me or in me. If he were here, I could get some guidance from him about how to live.

This is all complicated by the fact that I've sided with my mother against him."

The first thing he said at our next meeting after he had been away for two sessions was that having the break from our meeting was a good thing, a bit like a holiday. Then he added, "I teared up several times while I was away because I was reminded of little children. There were three, and they all had to do with orphans. The first two I saw on the TV. The last was a little 3-year-old girl and her family I happened to meet at the airport. This little girl didn't speak English, and I learned that these nice parents were adopting her and taking her home. I tried to entertain her as we waited in line and somehow ended up holding her hand. It felt nice and safe. But my reaction was to wonder what had happened to her in her short life. My thoughts were so unacceptable that I tried not to know. It was so monumentally unfair that I couldn't even keep that thought in my mind. I just knew that it was incredibly traumatic when you are 3 years old to be uprooted. I wanted to wish that it hadn't happened, because I didn't want to have to face it.

"Then after I got home, I had a nice little time with Betsy. At bedtime we had this talk about how much she wanted to go to work with me. The next morning she turned up to watch me tying my tie and asked again if she might go with me to work. For some odd reason I agreed to take her, and so Betsy ended up putting on a tie and a belt and her backpack, and we drove to my work for about an hour. She loved it and it was incredibly nice for me."

The therapist asked, "What do you think Betsy was wanting you to know about?" He answered, "I guess she missed me while I was gone and that she wanted to know what happened to me when I disappear out the door each morning. After all, the last time I left I had not returned for five days. I guess what she was saying was, 'Daddy I want to be exactly like you,' and that was pretty flattering." Then he went on to say, "I was reminded of the bond between us and that those other children that I teared up about on my trip had no one."

The therapist wondered if that event had reminded him of himself at about this age? Mr. B. nodded. The therapist then mentioned that at their last session he had wanted to hold his father's hand and was sad because he had not had a father to tell him about life. He answered, "When I saw those little homeless kids running the streets, I wanted to scoop them up and cuddle them. Even though they were forced to face incredible adversity, they had such bright little faces and seemed so pleased to be alive."

The case presented here is not completed, rather it is a segment of the work. The example ends with Mr. B.'s finding a sense of aliveness rather than feeling half dead or that he was drowning in his own depression. However, our work together did continue and Mr. B.'s depression gradually lifted and he gained more confidence in himself. This happened as he allowed himself to identify more with his father and was able to let go of the negative internalized image of himself that was connected to his history of interactions with his depressed and critical mother. In Winnicottian terms, this case is an illustration of the struggles of a patient trying to come to peace with several contradictory emotional states like love/hate, separateness/togetherness, and hope/hopelessness.

DISCUSSION

In this chapter, four concepts taken from the British school of object relations were examined: holding, transitional space, interpretation, and containment. These therapeutic processes then were applied to a long-term treatment case of a severely depressed man who had suffered considerable early trauma and who never allowed himself to feel really alive. We might say that he had never found a way to exist and also feel true to himself.

The first process, holding, is considered an essential part of the facilitating environment that Winnicott described when writing about the quality of the therapeutic relationship offered by a therapist to a patient that is reminiscent of the way a mother treats her small infant. It is a metaphor for the affective elements of treatment and refers to the therapist's reliability and capacity to understand what it is that the patient needs and to the therapist's ability to protect the patient from unnecessary frustrations or impingements.

During the first phase of treatment, the patient needed a holding environment to help him deal with his tragic and frightening memories of the past and his anxiety about being in therapy with a woman. His past experiences with a disabled father and an overburdened and critical mother left him feeling psychologically and emotionally damaged to such an extent that, even though he coped with his job and daily living, he had serious problems with intimate relationships and in knowing what he wanted for himself. Several times during the period we worked together he complained that he had never been able to feel substantial about himself. Instead, he grudgingly tried to do what others wanted him to do or he reacted against them by either rebelling or passively resisting them. Psychological holding was a necessary first step in the work we did together.

Transitional space refers to the metaphorical area between two people. Winnicott (1971) called this potential space or the intermediate area of experience, describing it as somewhere between fantasy and reality. It can be likened to a place where children play, and emerges during the separation-individuation phase when the distinction between self and non-self is not entirely clear. This space is filled with illusions and is the place from which transitional objects or transitional phenomena originate. Transitional space offers experiences where creative impulses and sensory aliveness come into play. Playing in psychotherapy generally implies that the patient and therapist find ways to enjoy moments together through the sharing of humor, metaphor, references to literature, music, art, or other cultural activities. In this case example, the patient progressed into a new stage in the treatment as he gradually discovered how much he enjoyed playing with his young daughter. His conversations with his therapist took on a livelier, more transitional quality as he regaled her with stories about his activities with his child.

Interpretation, as it was defined in this chapter (Balint 1968, Casement 1991, Duncan 1989, and Winnicott 1971, 1989), is a process that evolves during the course of treatment in which the therapist and patient discover or find out together the meaning behind the patient's patterns of behavior, thoughts, and emotions. These psychoanalytic writers all seem to agree that interpretations that flow from the fabric of therapeutic work are particularly valuable when working with seriously impaired or emotionally impoverished patients. In the chapter, an illustration is given about a dream in which important insights into the patient's feelings about himself as a male are disclosed. By asking a few questions, the therapist helped the patient to discover what the dream might mean to him. Several weeks later, when the patient referred back to this same dream, its meaning became even clearer, which seemed to be an indication of progress toward self-reflection on inner life.

In addition to holding, containment is also essential in helping patients to manage anxiety or intolerable physical or emotional pain. Here a distinction is drawn between these two concepts, because holding is more of an interpersonal or relational concept, while containment can be considered an intrapsychic concept that involves internal processing. The therapist takes in subjective thoughts, ideas, and feelings from listening to the patient, internalizes them, and then reflects them back to the patient. What the therapist returns to the patient is a slightly revised version of a perception or patterned way of thinking. Depending on the patient's receptivity at any given moment, the patient may receive or reject the new idea or interpretation. Eventually the patient begins to internalize the experience of being together. The last illustrations given about this patient are attempts to demonstrate how containment evolves from a mere thought or fleeting idea into a change in perception about the self and how those thoughts can shift into action and eventually lead to real improvement.

This quotation, taken from Winnicott's (1971) paper, "The Mirror Role of Mother," captures his thinking about therapy and seems to summarize some of the ideas that have been presented here.

> Psychotherapy is not making clever and apt interpretations; by and large it is a long-term giving the patient back what the patient brings. It is a complex derivative of the face that reflects what is there to be seen. I like to think of my work this way and to think that if I do this well enough the patient will find his or her own self and will be able to exist and feel real. Feeling real is more than existing; it is finding a way to exist as oneself, and to relate to objects as oneself, and to have a self into which to retreat for relaxation. [p. 117]

REFERENCES

Balint, M. (1968). *The Basic Fault: Therapeutic Aspects of Regression.* London: Tavistock.

Bion, W. (1967). *Second Thoughts.* London: Heinemann.

Bollas, C. (1987). *The Shadow of the Object.* New York: Columbia University Press.

Casement, P. (1991). *Learning from the Patient.* New York: Guilford.

Deri, S. (1978). Transitional phenomena: vicissitudes of symbolization and creativity. In *Between Reality and Fantasy*, ed. S. Grolnick, F. Barkin, and W. Muensterberger. New York: Jason Aronson.

Duncan, D. (1989). The flow of interpretation: the collateral interpretation, force or flow. *International Journal of Psycho-Analysis* 70:4.

Modell, A. (1976). The holding environment and the therapeutic action of psychoanalysis. *Journal of the American Psychoanalytic Association* 24: 285–308

Winnicott, D. (1958). *Through Paediatrics to Psycho-Analysis.* New York: Basic Books.

—— (1965). *The Maturational Processes and the Facilitating Environment.* New York: International Universities Press.

—— (1971). *Playing and Reality.* London: Tavistock.

—— (1986). *Holding and Interpretation: Fragment of an Analysis.* London: Hogarth.

—— (1989). *Psycho-Analytic Explorations*, ed. C. Winnicott, R. Sheppard, and M. Davis. Cambridge, MA: Harvard University Press.

7 The Beginning Phases of Treatment of the Schizoid Disorder of the Self: A Developmental, Self, and Object Relations Perspective

Karla R. Clark

To want and not to have, sent all up her body a hardness, a hollowness, a strain. And then to want and not to have—to want and want—how that wrung the heart, and wrung it again and again!

—Virginia Woolf, *To the Lighthouse*

INTRODUCTION

The person with a schizoid disorder of the self is usually apparently both self-sufficient and remote. I say apparently because this aloofness hides, as Virginia Woolf so beautifully expresses it, great thwarted longings for meaningful emotional communication. This kind of communication is difficult because efforts at it stir up painful fears of being enslaved by and/or ignored by the recipient. In consequence, schizoid people experience terrible feelings of futility and emptiness concerning efforts to express the authentic self without being able to eliminate the longing to do so. In response to this dilemma, they attempt to compromise by simultaneously psychologically hiding and maintaining some kind of emotional proximity to others. Such an individual longs for the help a therapist can provide, but also attempts to protect herself from painful feelings generated by self-disclosure and the discussion of feelings and fantasies about the therapist by keeping such expressions within an excessively narrow range. Thus, the patient's pain drives her to therapy and her fears stop her from using it effectively. She cannot be helped unless she is able—with the therapist's help—to understand the basis of her dilemma and to be supported in daring to increase her level and range of self-expression and intimacy.

In this chapter, I will present some ideas about the reasons for this disorder and how they translate into a working model of a characteristic intrapsychic structure. Using work with a particular patient, Ruth, as an example, I will show how this model of structure translates into a specific therapeutic approach which helps the patient to dare to identify and express her feelings, thoughts and needs more fully, thus opening the way to the help she longs for and the self-expressiveness and relatedness she needs and craves.

CASE DISCUSSION

I would like to begin by introducing you to the patient. Ruth told me, when she re-contacted me last year, that she had had a satisfactory time of it since last I saw her eight years before. Suddenly, however, she was being buffeted by terrible, seemingly inexplicable, feelings of anxiety. The precipitant quickly became clear—Ruth's mother was ill and dying. The anxiety she was feeling was inexplicable to her because Ruth had been denying the seriousness of her mother's illness and felt no conscious cause for concern about her. This made her anxiety doubly frightening and mysterious.

Ruth was a weather-beaten, yet attractive, somewhat masculine woman in her late forties. She was a top-ranked golf pro. Despite the obvious attachment to her mother that was reflected in her anxiety as she faced her loss, she rarely saw her parents or other family members. She stayed close but not too close to them. The same pattern of distance regulation was apparent in her relationship with her lover. She had a long-standing sexual relationship with Lisa, but Lisa was also involved in another committed relationship. Ruth and Lisa played professional golf together and managed to see one another around that activity several times a week. Ruth was comfortable with the arrangement for the most part, although she sometimes longed for more involvement and the two women quarreled over this issue. She would not have felt the need to return to therapy, she explained, if anxiety had not disturbed her equilibrium.

Her equilibrium had been hard won. When I first worked with Ruth, her presenting complaint had been that she was involved in a really cruel, exploitative relationship. The woman was making her miserable but she found herself unable to leave the situation. She eventually faced the abusiveness of her relationship with her lover and ended it. When she did so, she was able to acknowledge for the first time in her life that she had been physically abused when she was a child. Her father, determined to make a golf pro of his oldest child, had begun to teach Ruth the sport when she was only 3 years old. From that time on, he had forced her to practice for many hours a day, often forbidding her to stop for water, food, or to go to the toilet for eight or ten hours at a time. He berated and shamed her when her performance faltered. He beat her and locked her in closets.

Through all of this, her mother was lost in a fog of drugs and alcohol. Characteristically, she either ignored her child's suffering or caused her suffering in her own right. For example, Ruth had a severe allergy to eggs. Despite the doctor's repeated warnings and her obvious physical distress when she was fed eggs, her mother was convinced that Ruth was just being difficult and continued to give them to her in one form or another. Repeatedly she made the child ill and denied that she had done so.

The logical response to such abuse would have been for Ruth to become autonomous as quickly as possible. However she was undermined when she tried to do so. Her parents took credit for her accomplishments—such as her athletic ability—when they could, and when they couldn't they attacked her for attempting to express herself and develop her interests. For example, when she was 11 Ruth developed an interest in photography. One day as she sat in her room looking through recently developed pictures, her mother burst in and without warning or explanation smashed her camera and ripped the pictures to shreds. Over and over again, her experience was that she fared no better behaving autonomously than she did when she needed to depend on somebody. There seemed to be no safe way for her to be.

To deal with her dilemma, Ruth compromised. She established what was to become a lifelong pattern. She related by either being servile or antagonistic, thus disavowing her need for acknowledgment or support from others by keeping them at a safe distance without emotionally emancipating in any real sense. She did, however, become superficially self-reliant and competent—often outstandingly so—in all the activities that she attempted. Since she needed to be self-sufficient but experienced the autonomy which these qualities could have brought her as also dangerous, she compromised by simultaneously disavowing ownership of these self-same activities.

From this position, she was able to live up to her father's expectations of her as an athlete and, by the time that she was a young teenager, she was winning tournaments. She did extremely well in school, demonstrating a particular talent for writing.

She was, by this time—although often painfully lonely—quite remote in her dealings with others, isolating herself in their proximity when she would. When forced to relate directly she was either servile or a frightening person herself. She was never self-disclosing or expressive. For example, through these same years, her mother had become less and less functional and Ruth found a way to relate to her that did not involve them expressively with one another. Besides hours of practice on the golf course and doing her homework, Ruth took on many household chores, helping her mother out without telling her much about what she herself was thinking and feeling. When possible, for solace and relief, she went to a nearby creek where—alone with her reading and writing—she felt free to breathe. In addition to being self-effacing and subservient, she also kept people at a safe distance in more active ways. She was explosive and abusive to her siblings, so they were afraid of her. Because of her explosiveness, she was known as the family problem by the time she was 9 years old. Longing and fearing human contact, unable to either come close or leave, she felt the total despair of the leper.

At 17 she made an effort to emancipate herself. In a rage following a particularly difficult fight with her father, she threw her golf clubs away and vowed never to play again. At the same time—with what appeared at first to be a real stroke of luck—she was accepted at a prestigious women's college. With relief she went away to school.

She began to explore the world and tried to establish an identity of her own. She had her first homosexual love affair (which was, in those days, an extremely risky thing to do at a girl's college). Her lover wrote to her during the Christmas holidays while Ruth was visiting home.

Continuing the pattern of undermining Ruth's efforts to establish a separate, autonomous self, while simultaneously sabotaging her needs for care, support, and love, her mother found the letters and, without telling Ruth about it, reported her to the college. The dean reacted to the news that she was homosexual by moving her into a room alone and putting her on probation. This was particularly painful since at her school everybody had a roommate. Once again, Ruth was terribly depressed, lonely, and ashamed. Feeling like a pariah, she finished out the year. At that point, she dropped out of college altogether and her parents, furious at her "failure," kicked her out of the house.

Subsequently, rather than seeking to truly emancipate herself, she settled for the appearance of self-sufficiency without a real investment in herself. She reported amnesia for much of the next part of her life. She does know that she worked, returned to a local university and—after dropping out one more time—went back and graduated, but she doesn't remember how she accomplished this. She knows that somehow she found herself playing golf again. In fact, she supported herself in college by playing—winning tournaments, and teaching others to play. She was accepted to graduate school both in English and philosophy, but rather than commit to either interest, she became a golf pro.

Continuing the now well-established pattern of joyless self-sufficiency and relating servilely or abusively if at all, she made a success of her career as a competitive athlete but she had great difficulty with her attempts at relationships. She had physically violent and emotionally abusive relationships with a series of women, sometimes being the victim and sometimes the victimizer.

When I first met Ruth, I myself was struck by the extraordinary air of violence and menace that emanated from her. She was small, but tough and weather-beaten, her skin and hair roughened by constant exposure to the sun and wind. She very definitely had what is known these days as an "attitude." She slouched and glared. She was often explosively angry at me and I was, frankly, afraid of her. Sometimes she came drunk to sessions, so that I was forced to send her away. Sometimes she got up and, yelling, paced around the room so that I had to insist that she sit down. She shouted and slammed out the door when she got angry at me. For months, I dreaded the day of her appointment and braced myself for our encounters, never knowing when she would explode.

We were caught in a reenactment of her childhood in which she was the abuser and I the abused. It also worked the other way around. When I tried to help her set limits on her self-destructive acting out, I was frightened by her rage. Because I tried to hide my fear, I would set the necessary limits but in a rigid, angry, and controlling way. She, in turn, would bitterly submit to me. Thus it was that we traded the roles of abuser and victim up and back. For quite a while it seemed as though I would never extricate myself from my own defensiveness enough to be able to help her understand why she needed to behave so provocatively, although I knew that this was the exact problem that she had everywhere.

With a lot of work I was able to get my own acting out under control and to set limits in appropriate ways. By the time Ruth left therapy the first time, we had developed a healthy, but cautious, mutual respect on the basis of which she had calmed down and established a more peaceful, if isolated, existence for herself. I was able to experience the poetic soul behind the menace, the intelligence and essential kindness of this battered and battering woman, who was also willing, albeit cautiously, to acknowledge these gentler traits in herself. I was aware, however, that the violent, angry, and dark side of her had gone underground rather than having been worked through and that, perhaps because of this, in some ineffable way, treatment, although it had lasted for two years, had not touched her deeply.

She knew it too, but chose to ignore this. She told me that her monsters were still in the closet, but that, at least for now, she wanted to let them be and enjoy the first peace that she had ever known. When we parted, Ruth had a lover, Martha, whom she saw frequently. They had vague plans to live together someday, but the truth of it was that Ruth was quite content with their arrangement. She enjoyed her private time and space since she could simultaneously fantasize about an end to her time alone. Although she was still quite constricted in the use of her creativity and was somewhat unhappy about her athletic career, she said she felt content with both her relationship and her life-style.

I was only vaguely aware of the fact that I was not supporting real growth and progress, but, rather, her old compromise defense of undemanding isolation, self-sufficiency, and second-class status in relationships. Consequently, I supported her decision (feeling that it would be sadistic and/or intrusive to do otherwise), all the while wondering uneasily if I could be doing more.

From time to time through the intervening years I had received either notes from Ruth or messages on my answering machine. She made it clear that she did not want to speak with me, but only to let me know what was happening to her. She was holding me at an optimal distance–in her life, but not in it.

Through those same years, especially as I learned more about both the schizoid disorders and the effects of physical and sexual abuse on young children, I often thought of Ruth and wished for another opportunity to work with her. Consequently, I was very glad to hear from her when anxiety disrupted her fragile equilibrium. It now seemed clear to me that despite the explosiveness, volatility, and histrionic qualities that masked her detachment and had led me to diagnose her originally as having a borderline disorder (Masterson 1976), Ruth had a schizoid disorder, complicated, but essentially unchanged, by the dissociative-like symptoms—such as her amnesia for periods of her history—that were the results of childhood physical abuse.

Altering my perspective enabled me to engage Ruth on levels that had not been possible during her first period of treatment. Now I understood that, on the one hand, to acknowledge wishes to be known opened her to feelings concerning being controlled and abused; on the other, to express yearnings to be autonomous and unique opened her to feelings concerning being cruelly and mockingly ignored and/or destroyed—condemned to live outside human groupings, a stranger and a foreigner, isolated and alone—at worst, annihilated. Compromising—like the character of C. S. Lewis in the movie *Shadowlands*—she cultivated a half-life to avoid the pain of living.

When she returned to treatment, I understood her presenting complaint of anxiety as a signal that something—probably her mother's imminent death—had disturbed the fragile equilibrium of her compromise position. I hypothesized that the anticipated loss of this important person had stirred up her needs to be close to people as she tried to fill the space that she felt her mother's death would leave, and stimulated her fears of the consequences should she seek to be more involved. At the same time, Ruth was clearly terrified of the feelings of being alone that anxiety over her mother's dying had triggered. She was being driven toward others by her fear of that loneliness and away from them by her fear of the consequences of closeness. I also knew from things she told me that Ruth had used her involvement with her mother as an excuse not to explore career opportunities and creative possibilities which might upset her mother. I surmised that Ruth was also being driven away from connection to others by impulses toward greater creativity and expanded career choices and toward them by the fears which those opportunities generated. Therefore, I reasoned that in a way her anxiety, rather than being "the problem," might be a reflection of the fact that new opportunities had opened for Ruth in both her autonomous life and in the kind and quality of her intimacies.

I thought that understanding what was making her anxious could help her to make whatever adjustments she truly wanted in her life. On the other hand, treating the anxiety as the problem and using its cessation as the criterion for therapeutic success would, by definition, force her to retreat to the safety of her narrow, numb half-life without making conscious choices about what she really wanted. Therefore, my goal as I began to treat her in once-a-week sessions was to help her to understand and explore her anxiety and other feelings rather than to make them go away and thus to open up a wider range of lifestyle choices for her. The question, of course, was how to go about this, because such expressiveness is the very thing the schizoid avoids.

Why did I believe that these particular issues and concerns, out of all of the possibilities, needed to be addressed in order to help this patient? The answer to that question begins with an understanding of the schizoid's dilemma, and the nature of the false, defensive self developed in an attempt to solve it.

THE SCHIZOID DILEMMA

The schizoid person feels that expression of feelings and needs will have disastrous consequences. If she wishes to use such expression as a way to get closer to people, she fears being appropriated and blames herself for it. She reasons that because of some flaw in herself, internal representations of others, or objects, would want to treat her sadistically and controllingly. If her feelings and needs move her toward the experience of having a unique, autonomous self, she fears being isolated, abandoned, and left to suffer alone.[1] Surely, she reasons, the icy indifference and lack of responsiveness by her objects to her efforts to be self-expressive and real is due to some basic flaw in herself. Thus she is caught in a paradox

1. The reader may question this, in view of the schizoid patient's self-sufficient presentation. There is a considerable difference, however, between true autonomy and isolated self-sufficiency. Autonomy refers to the individual's capacity to experience himself as the owner of his own interests and unique personality and to express this ownership in a variety of contexts, many of which involve relating to other people. In contrast, the schizoid, while able to function physically alone, experiences the assertion of selfhood as leading to dangerous fears of invisibility and appropriation and, in consequence, avoids acknowledging these aspects of himself.

in which feelings of anxiety, lack of safety, self-loathing, and self-blame are triggered no matter in which direction she moves.

If, however, she mobilizes her real self and challenges the assumption that she herself is flawed, she destroys the basis of her relationship to the representations of important other people which she carries in her head. Losing them, she feels terrifyingly alone and empty. Her experience at those moments is of utter, bleak, insatiable yearnings for connection with a self-affirming object. This terrible, empty pain is the bitter price of separating from the object and acknowledging the separate self (see Clark 1994, for a clinical illustration of this process in another context). Because it is so painful, the schizoid person, fearing destruction by either getting too close or too far away from the other, retreats from a position of authenticity to one designed to maintain the ties to the object from a safe distance.

THE SCHIZOID COMPROMISE AND THE FALSE, DEFENSIVE SELF

Since the schizoid person thinks that genuine self-expression is destructive to the self, she must not attempt it. She develops a false, defensive self as an alternative way of relating to other people, as Ruth did, by "orbiting" them—both being there and not being there (Guntrip 1969). The patient experiences this position as safe and comfortable.

This orbiting compromise is reflected in the development of an elusive false defensive self, or selves. In her first course of treatment, Ruth gradually replaced her quarrelsome, off-putting false face with a self-effacing one. Both were, in fact, compromise positions, in which she revealed aspects of her needs for both relatedness and autonomy and yet concealed them by keeping people both in her life and not in it. The second manifestation of compromise seemed much more adaptive than the first. She seemed to be basically content alone in her little house, with her lovers, first Martha and then Lisa, frequent visitors, but visitors still—with her family nearby but hardly involved in her daily life—with her books, her garden, and her cat. Her life within her walls seemed to be a zone of safety and rest. She was only vaguely aware of longings for a freer and fuller life. She kept the loneliness and emptiness that was always under the surface in this position at bay with physical activity, drinking, fantasizing about Lisa in her absence (although she quarreled a lot with her in person), and psychic numbing. These activities kept her from becoming fully conscious of her deeper hungers for both relatedness and expressiveness.

Her self-effacing false defensive self provided Ruth, as it does many schizoids, with a way of relating that, in her mind, was acceptable to others and which did not involve what she anticipated as the inevitability of having genuine expressions of the self traumatically disregarded or used abusively. This compromise solution is contingent upon either suppressing or repressing feelings and needs. Therefore, no matter how tranquil the surface of the life, the individual does not feel truly alive, and suffers, as Ruth did, from feelings of emptiness, loneliness, and inhibitions of creativity when alone and anxiety, sometimes bordering on panic, when she tried to allow other people near her.

How does one treat such paralysis—such detachment and numbing and fear? To answer this question, the first issue I will consider has to do with the origins of the disorder. Do the faulty assumptions about the pains and pleasures of relatedness and self-experience reflect a primary developmental deficit or do they consolidate later, so that this condition reflects more of a developmental arrest than deficit? The answer to this question has crucial implications for treatment. Are we fundamentally trying to create a self or free up one that—while perhaps enfeebled—already exists? I believe the latter to be the case and have based my treatment approach on that belief.

DEVELOPMENTAL HYPOTHESIS

In my view, this condition results from problems between caretakers and child resulting in distortions in the healthy development of the verbal self (Stern 1985). During that period in his life, the child's own, inborn thrust toward the establishment of a separate autonomous self (Mahler 1972) is powerfully supported by his development of the capacity to express feelings and needs to others with words. It is the parent's, or primary caretaker's, responsiveness to his efforts that supports him and helps him to consolidate this crucial aspect of the sense of self. This developmental need makes him particularly sensitive to inconsistent, jarring misattunement from parents around his efforts to communicate with words. Misattunements in this area, because they are so painfully out of sync with the child's own most important needs at that time, are extraordinarily painful, and thus are especially prone to internalization where they assume a particularly fixed quality. This makes them difficult to modify or alter subsequently.

INTRAPSYCHIC STRUCTURE

These painful experiences of failure to support the development of such essential aspects of the self become part of the child's inner world. She carefully keeps "good" experiences–in which she is rewarded for unobtrusive, self-effacing behavior–separate from "bad" images–in which she is punished for expressing both her needs for care and closeness and her developing individuality (see Masterson 1977 for a discussion of a similar organization of the personality in the borderline disorder). The child's wish to depend on another person triggers an image of an omnipotent "master," linked to a self-representation of a "slave." The feelings which go along with this include anxiety, rage at being controlled, shame and humiliation, and feelings of hopelessness. You will recall this configuration in my discussion of my first experience of working with Ruth. Both master and slave were reflected in how I felt about her and how she felt about me.

Wishes to become an autonomous, expressive individual evoke an accompanying image of a cold, cruel person, looking with icy indifference upon a self that is exiled from others and, in consequence, feels weak, incompetent, despicable, invisible, and desperately, dangerously alone. The feelings that go along with the experience of cosmic isolation and invisibility associated with this configuration include anxiety, shame, helplessness, rage, and utter futility (Klein 1983). This configuration was reflected in Ruth's description of her mother's attitude toward her allergy to eggs, in the college's attitude toward her after her homosexuality was exposed, and in her parents' subsequent, unfeeling expulsion of her from their home.

It is important to remember that the self-hatred associated with both of these configurations is a defense. It preserves a kind of relatedness to internal objects (Guntrip 1969). Hence the investment in maintaining the safety of a half-life, in which the dangers of the futility and emptiness associated with self-expression are minimized and in which the sense of being defective and undeserving, against all apparent logic, is preserved.

These ideas about development, the nature of the self representation, the nature of the false, defensive self, and of intrapsychic structure heavily influence how one conducts psychotherapy.

TREATMENT

To understand oneself–indeed, to feel that one has a self at all–one must be able to identify thoughts and feelings, tolerate them, express them, and, simultaneously, think about them. This process of introspection and expressiveness about feelings and ideas is the first requirement of psychoanalytic psychotherapy–and this process of using the verbal, expressive aspects of the self is the very thing that evokes such painful feelings in schizoid people that they avoid it. Understanding this will help the clinician to understand why this group of patients finds it so difficult to involve themselves in their treatment, impelling them instead, to "orbit," to circle around without confronting core issues. The success of the therapy depends upon the patient making the shift from orbiting to investment in the real self and relating from that position. Consequently, the first task of therapy is to help the patient to control distance-regulating defenses and become actively interested in expressing her needs and feelings in an emotional and engaged way. She must accept the necessity to do this despite the discomfort that this generates. Until this happens, there can be no effective therapy.

THERAPEUTIC MANAGEMENT OF THE FALSE DEFENSIVE SELF

The therapeutic stance that makes it possible to interpret orbiting defenses is therapeutic neutrality. By strict, kindly adherence to the therapeutic frame, the therapist provides the patient with the safety of a predictable and consistent environment that does not resonate with her projections. Against the screen of the therapist's even-handed interest and availability, the patient can experience and eventually discuss her distance-regulating devices. Thus acting out–which merely repeats self-destructive defensive behavior–is converted into transference and therapeutic alliance, where the patient is free to simultaneously feel his painful feelings and impulses toward self-eroding behavior and explore their origins in safety (Masterson 1976).

In this context, the interpretation of the false defensive self (i.e., transference acting out) proceeds in four overlapping stages: (1) the interpretation of the need for safe distance, (2) the identification of the master/slave and self-in-exile/sadistic object relations units, (3) the interpretation of the dilemma. This includes tracking the circular process of self-expression, depression, and defense and making explicit the shame the patient feels for being unable to choose–as she believes she must–between dependence and autonomy (Clark 1994). The final stage is (4) a deeper interpretation of distancing defenses as an attempt to resolve the dilemma through compromise (see Klein 1993 for a related perspective).

Although, as I have stated, these stages overlap and interweave, I will discuss them separately.

1. *Interpretation of the need for safe distance.* At the start of treatment, the patient's idea is to feel comfortable by being in the therapist's presence without expressing feelings and needs. The therapist, knowing that this comfort offers only the illusion of safety, wants to disrupt the orbiting. She does so by interpreting that the patient's need for safety overrides all other concerns, including the wish to be self-expressive.

First, I must emphasize that *the focus of the interpretations is always on the function of safety rather than on what the defense covers up.* This is a crucial point. Why is it so important? There is a saying, "Give a man a fish and you feed him for a day. Teach a man to fish and you feed him for life." The therapist's interventions, in the main, should teach the man to fish. Since the patient's problems revolve around the identification and expression of feelings, he needs to practice doing so. The therapist must not provide him with interventions that do the work of identifying and expressing feelings and needs for him. Rather, by providing him with information about what he does to stop the development of these available if enfeebled abilities, one hopes to provide him with the tools necessary to do things otherwise if he so chooses (see Masterson 1976).

This stance also helps one to avoid resonating with the patient's projection of the appropriating master who can read minds and thus control one. In this climate, the balance begins to shift. The desire to be hidden loses its dominance as the patient begins to try to express her feelings and needs.

What do these interpretations of the need for safety look like? What can we expect the patient to do with them? Let us return to a consideration of Ruth's treatment as a way of answering these questions through example.

When Ruth first returned to therapy, she felt overwhelmed by anxiety. She wanted to "understand" her anxiety, but not as a way to know herself more deeply or to make a deeper connection with her lover Lisa, her friends, or me. She wanted to "understand" her anxiety intellectually, so as to bind it, stop it, get away from it, and thus re-stabilize. Why? Because while she was facing the imminent death of her mother–which terrified her–and wanted the solace and comfort of being able to turn to another person, she also assumed that, should she continue to feel anxious, I would distance from her and fail to respond to her need. Alternatively she feared that I would use her dependency to control and humiliate her. Intellectual understanding was her compromise: it allowed her to express her anxiety to me and simultaneously, by not feeling it, to conceal it.

Ruth was unaware of the dilemma underlying her need to "orbit," but she was aware of the attraction and need she felt for the safety that intellectualization provides. I therefore began at that point. My interpretations had the following elements: I stressed (1) the idea that expressing feelings and needs in particular generates feelings of unsafety, (2) the feelings that she must therefore protect the self, and (3) she was using particular distancing defenses–like intellectualization–to provide her with this protection. For example, one day, right after she resumed treatment and shortly after her mother died, I said, "When you show me your anxiety and try to talk to me about it, something happens which, I believe, makes you feel unsafe, and to protect yourself, you talk about the feeling without feeling it. This keeps you at a safe distance from the feeling and from me."

Ruth replied, "When I can't use my mind to understand things, I am not in control and I hate it. I don't understand why I'm feeling the way that I do and I can't fix it."

The timing and accuracy of one's interpretations are confirmed if a schizoid patient responds to interpretations by elaborating on elements of the need for safety, with increased access to feelings about her experience. I knew that I was on the right track with Ruth because she picked up on the notion of her need for safety and began to expand her understanding of it in a feelingful way. She talked about how upset she was at the outpouring of cards and letters of sympathy from friends and students and her wish to push them away. She began to explore why expressions of people's caring and concern made her uncomfortable. Then she spontaneously supplied her own genetic explanation for her discomfort. "I am not absolutely sure my mother ever really loved me. She would always say that, but she never did anything to prove it. I can't remember anything good she ever did for me." She concluded that maybe when other people showed concern, it triggered painful feelings of being unloved by her mother and that she pushed people away to stop that feeling. This thought was too painful, and she cut off emotion and began again to speak without feeling.

Rather than interpreting her resistance to facing her mother's failures to respond to her, (i.e., taking over and directing her) I repeatedly interpreted the defense and it's purpose–intellectualization as a way of reestablishing optimal distance and safety. "I notice," I said, "that, as you started to explore this idea and you began to feel some emotion, you got real intellectual. I think that something about your exploration must have made you feel unsafe so you went into your head for safety." She returned to exploration, experienced a renewed feeling of unsafety, protected herself with new intellectualizations and I once again interpreted. Gradually, over the first several months, she began to track her own intellectualization and tried to control it.

2. *Identification of the Master/Slave and Self-in-Exile/Sadistic Object Relations Units.* Almost from the start, I was also able to use these opportunities for beginning to work on the second stage of managing the false, defensive self–delineating the projected representations of self and other. For example, shortly after her mother died, Ruth's father sent her a check for a small amount of money. Angrily, she said, "Lisa thinks that I could take the money. I don't know what I think. I feel trapped, so I tabled it until I got here. I don't think that I can take his money if I despise his guts. I can barely resist asking you what *you* think."

When she went right on, acting as though comments from me were unthinkable, I interrupted her. "I think the idea of asking me for help with your feelings around this issue made you feel unsafe." Beginning to delineate the nature of the projected object representation, I said, "Perhaps you were concerned about my response, which kept you from turning to me and gave you some protective distance." She replied that, actually, she knew what the right thing to do was–return the money, because she hated her father and would not feel good about accepting it from him, but that she felt that nobody, including me, would understand and approve of her action. Underlining this, I interpreted, "When you can identify a course of action for yourself that is based on your own wishes and needs, and try to talk about it, it seems to me that you immediately have a picture of me not understanding. Anticipating this, which would leave you feeling unsafe, you distance by not revealing your feelings and intentions."

She agreed that I was right, but immediately shifted to projecting the master/slave unit. She began talking about her father and his brutality toward her rather than her own difficulties in expressing herself to me. Angrily, she said that she hated her father and went on to talk about a fight she had with her siblings. In this fight, she had managed to antagonize everybody in her family. She was very self-righteous and saw herself as a martyr to their delusions and illusions about their father. To continue to highlight the nature of the projected units I replied, "When you identify a course of action for yourself, based upon your own feelings and needs, and try to tell your brothers and sisters about it, just like here, what immediately comes up is the feeling that you will not be understood, like you feared a moment ago with me, or, alternatively, that you will be attacked and controlled, as by your dad. In order to keep yourself safe from revealing the feelings which these thoughts bring up, you talk about how put upon you are. That is safer than revealing your own feelings about what happened. That way, you create some distance from me and you can protect yourself from your anxiety and feelings of unsafety by doing this."

Constantly linking her efforts to identify her feelings and needs with the specific nature of her projections onto others and her distancing defenses in this manner occupied us for a number of months. This was not always a calm or easy process. At first, as the incident above suggests, she was volatile and, as in her first period of treatment, sometimes provocative with me and with other people (i.e., acting out). Because of this provocative behavior, she sometimes ended up in really painfully humiliating situations. During this time, it was important that I stay on task, constantly interpreting her need for safety and her projections.

For example, about a month and a half into treatment, Ruth was home alone on a weekend when she also knew that I was out of town. There was a power failure and her telephone line went dead. The combination of these events precipitated anxiety, unconsciously associated with being cut off and unable to elicit a response from anybody to her very existence. Her fear of being overwhelmed by her anxiety caused her to panic when she began to feel it, rather than sit still to try to understand what was causing her to feel so frightened. She quickly had a great deal to drink to try to stop the anxious feelings, got in her car, and drove off to find a booth from which she could call the telephone company and get information concerning what the problem was and when service would resume. She must have sounded terrifically upset when she placed her call, because the person she spoke to notified the police. They traced the call, found her, and drove her home. As soon as they left, she got right back in her car and started off again—desperately searching for information about her interrupted service. This time, when they caught her, the police tried to subdue her. More and more panicked, and very drunk, Ruth fought them and ended up handcuffed and jailed overnight. She was in a rage at the way the police treated her. She completely denied the dangerousness and destructiveness of her behavior and was unable to recognize her extreme provocativeness. She was furious that her sentence was that she lost her license for six months and that she had to pay quite a sizable fine and attend a therapy group.

I took the stance that when she found that the telephone wouldn't work, painful feelings of unsafety had come up around being cut off from people. Unable to comfort herself, I said, she had immediately managed her feelings of unsafety by both drinking and causing people to fight with her.

She was not terribly pleased with me. She told me indignantly that she had expected some sympathy from me (transference acting out by projecting the indifferent object onto me). I maintained my stance, though, and Ruth rather quickly came around. She was able to see that, far from being a victim in this incident, she had put herself in a really dangerous position and then in a humiliating one and that I, far from indifferent, was quite concerned for her. She stopped drinking. She abandoned her original plan to act obnoxious and superior in her therapy group, but—still distancing—opted for the safety of silence. Desperately, she told me that she hated the group and the group therapist. She had a therapist—me—and didn't want to talk with them.

I thought that, in reality, this expression of what she saw as loyalty was indeed a projection of the master/slave unit onto me. Rather than accept what I saw as protestations of enslavement to me, I said that her silence and her justification of it were a way to protect herself from the feelings of unsafety generated by a situation in which she was expected to disclose things about herself. I said that I thought that she was using her relationship with me as a way to create safe distance from the group, since obviously speaking to me and with them were not mutually exclusive. In response, over the weeks, she tracked her aloofness in the group and allowed herself to feel and be touched by some of the other members' experiences, although she never became really forthcoming about her own. Grudgingly, she admitted that she had learned a lot in the group and that it hadn't been a waste of her time.

During the same period of time, Ruth was quarrelsome and argumentative with her brothers and sisters and with her father. She rebuffed their efforts to see her and then felt martyred because they didn't include her in holiday planning. She was similarly difficult to get along with in her relationship with Lisa. Repeatedly, I interpreted her angry assaultiveness, martyrdom and distancing as ways to manage her feelings of unsafety about identifying and expressing feelings and needs in her relationships. I traced each distancing event, when I could, to its specific precipitant. I continuously stressed that she placed what she saw as her safety first, even when she behaved in ways that were very unsafe and often self-destructive.

Although I felt distressed about her when she got herself into painful and humiliating situations, I trusted that repeated interpretation would help her to control her behavior without retreating to the safety of her half-life. I held onto my hat and I kept my fingers crossed and, most importantly, I kept tracking for her that the very act of self-expression is what caused her to feel unsafe and made her distance or get herself into trouble. My interpretations eventually helped her to understand the schizoid dilemma that underlay her defenses. The process through which this occurred had two components: the delineation of the dilemma itself and the uncovering of the shame generated by acknowledging it.

3. *Interpretation of the Schizoid Dilemma. (A) The Schizoid Triad: Self-activation (self-expression) leads to depression (shame, emptiness, sadness, insatiable longings for unavailable supplies, anxiety, and rage) which lead to defenses designed to stop the dysphoria by stopping the expression of the self (i.e., seeking safety).* The delineation of the dilemma begins with the process of tracking the processes that unfold after the patient attempts real self-expression. Masterson, addressing this phenomenon as it appears in the treatment of borderline patients, has called this "tracking the triad" (Masterson 1981, p. xi). This process involves the following components: (1) an aspect of self-activation or expression, which (2) triggers feelings concerning object loss or unavailability, which in turn

triggers (3) a renewal of defensive behavior in order to avoid the painful feelings.

This process is at the heart of therapy and is crucial to the success of the endeavor. The mobilization of this triad explains why Ruth repeatedly returned to self-destructive acting out, although she appeared, almost from the beginning, to feel distressed by her own behavior. Ruth was reacting to the feelings associated with being savagely attacked and controlled or ignored by internalized representations of other people when she tried to express her feelings and needs. The unpleasant feelings she experienced when she expressed herself were, in effect, self-generated. Thus, when she stopped efforts to express needs and feelings, she also stopped the feelings of rage, fear, and self-hatred associated with self-activation.

Over the months, as I repeatedly linked self-expression, dysphoria, and defense I established a relationship in Ruth's mind among these three aspects of her experience. When she saw the linkages, she began to feel motivated to try to search for and express her feelings rather than always to put safety first. This set the stage for her to become aware of her dilemma and for us to discuss the shame she felt for vacillating about what she wanted and needed from other people when she expressed herself (Clark 1984).

(B) *Identifying the dilemma and the shame associated with acknowledging it.* As Christmas approached, she grappled long and hard with whether to spend the holidays with her family. Initially, she took a martyred position as a defense against the feelings of unconscious shame she felt about not really knowing what she wanted from them. "I'm really angry," she said. "My sister called to invite me to Christmas dinner with the family. I was furious. Lisa said, 'Grow up. They're trying to accept you as you are and you won't let them.' I got so angry at her for saying that I threw her out of the house, but then I thought, maybe she's right." Having said this (i.e., begun to explore herself), she immediately distanced by cutting off all feeling and I, tracking the triad, asked her whether she noticed what she had been feeling that generated the need to protect herself in this way. She answered that actually she felt ashamed of herself because she didn't really know what she wanted.

In the passage that followed, she showed me that she had integrated previous interpretations of the triad and could use her understanding in her own behalf. In this instance, what followed was her first exposition of her shame at being "indecisive." Weeping, she continued, "When I say I have that feeling that I will be discounted and anticipate either mockery or being discounted so that I don't know what I want, I feel also embarrassed, like I should be decisive—do I want to spend Christmas with them or not? This makes it hard for me to express myself. If I focus on myself so that I can try to figure that out, I feel too important, and that doesn't feel right. Again, I come back to embarrassing. . . ."

She abruptly relinquished efforts to explore her feelings here. I interpreted the triad, "When you focus on what you want and need, it stirs up wishes to be with them and wishes to be on your own, and uncomfortable bad feelings about yourself both ways. It seems like your indecision in and of itself also feels unacceptable and makes you feel bad about yourself as well, and to protect yourself you want to make the whole thing moot by reinterpreting events so that you see yourself as the victim of their exclusion—only reacting, rather than having to exercise choice and feeling unable to do so." Eventually, after thinking long and hard about what would be in her best interests, Ruth wrote notes to her family thanking them for their invitations but explaining that she did not feel ready, at this time, to see them. She spent Christmas in the safety of her home: alone with her cat and her music, consciously lonely but aware that she was there by her own choice.

Thus Ruth ended the year, seven months after she had returned to treatment, much better at controlling her acting out, alternately retreating to a safe distance while investing increasingly in expressing herself. She was also newly conscious of her reluctance to focus on herself and make herself important. She was aware of continuous feelings of self-hatred and self-blame. Occasionally, she was even questioning the accuracy of her harsh self-assessment. She had strengthened her observing ego and had become interested in how she blocked self-expression and was attempting not to do so. She was poised to recognize that her distancing defenses were efforts to compromise between needs for dependency and autonomy. She was about to begin to undo her fantasy that she had to choose one over the other to the detriment of her real self (Klein 1993).

4. *Deeper interpretation of distancing defenses as an effort to resolve the dilemma through compromise.* To help her to be able to choose expressiveness over safety should she wish to do so, I used her strengthened observing ego to expand my interpretations of her distancing de-

fenses, when necessary, by labeling them as an attempt to resolve her dilemma through compromise. At this writing we are involved in this process as each new attempt at introspection and self-expression triggers conflicts about closeness versus autonomy and defensive flights to the safety of compromise. There are increasing evidences of therapeutic alliance and deepening self-expression with each go-around as Ruth, exploring what the experiences are which make her wish to retreat to compromise positions, feels less of a need to actually do so.

For example, not long ago, Ruth's beloved cat Bonnie became ill. She had terrible diarrhea. She was losing weight and was increasingly weak and lethargic. Ruth was frantic. She was on the phone to the vet constantly. He was very patient and reassuring. Despite his respectful treatment, she was afraid to trust or rely on his responses to her. She analyzed her conviction that he would be unable to help and that, furthermore, she was a pest and that he was laughing at her for being so concerned about a cat (projection of the self-in-exile/sadistic object relations part unit). Over several sessions, I repeated how, when she was convinced that she would be humiliated, she retreated and suffered in silence as a way to make herself feel safe. I went on that she then felt too isolated, with a problem she couldn't resolve on her own, leading her to once again want comfort and help. Then, I continued, feeling anxious about the need for comfort, she negated it by behaving antagonistically toward the vet, Lisa, or me, rather than expressing her distress to any of us.

This led to her explication of the other side of the dilemma, the experience of being ignored in distress. "I just can't bear that I can't fix her," she wept. "I suppose it makes me feel that even if I do my best that it doesn't matter. . . . It's this helplessness. And I feel so alone. I get myself convinced that they don't know what they're doing, and then I get myself convinced that there's nothing anybody can do. It's very scary. I also think it has something to do with how pitiful she looks. I really identify with that. . . . I can't do it, I can't make it better . . . and I really can't tell how much is Bonnie and how much is other stuff. I know there's a feeling of fear that's beyond the fear that she's gonna die." She began to spin wheels here, taking literally her own feelings of futility. Taking the feelings literally was really a compromise defense. She protested that she was just stuck with these feelings, even though she thought that they were irrational. In other words, there was no point in either exploring or feeling them.

"I think," I said, "that you have backed up into a sort of protectively futile position for safety, but I don't know why."

"Well," she replied, "I think it started when I said that she is totally dependent on me and I can't fix it."

I replied, "It seems like you are caught between a rock and a hard place—if you ask for help, you are convinced that you'll be made fun of and if you try to do it yourself, you feel incompetent and painfully futile and ineffectual. To keep yourself safe, you tell yourself that expressing your concern is, in reality, futile, and you freeze."

This interpretation led her to a powerful explication of the feelings of emptiness and futility that accompanied the emergence of her real self. She continued, "It makes me want to feel sorry for myself. There is a familiar feeling of feeling pitiful. It's worse than that. It's worse than feeling alone. It is like feeling that if I picked a flower, the wind would come up and blow it to shreds." She began to cry. "This is very painful. I can feel it. It's an image of an old woman sitting on a park bench with a little bow around her neck and the kids come by and make fun of her. I can't describe what it is, but it's how I feel. . . . Small, important things that get made fun of. Looking stupid. Looking foolish. And I feel that way because I can't fix Bonnie. It's embarrassing. The world is laughing at what I think is important, and I look stupid and foolish to care so much.

"I dragged out some stories that I wrote in school. One was about a little boy, 8 or 9 years old, who was playing on the edge of the ocean, and his sister told him that it was okay to walk out, that the sand was level. So, of course, he did—and he fell in and scrambled back and, of course, the story ends (that) he'll never trust anybody again.

"Okay. That is one of the most painful of *all* of my feelings. The one I always have to fight. Because I get into this cocoon where I feel sorry for myself. It makes me run away. Like, standing there with this feeling—my jacket is scruffy and old—or wanting to give somebody a flower, and feeling stupid. . . . I can't stand to feel it for long, but the funny thing is that when I can, I almost like it because it is my own." Then, suddenly feeling unsafe, she turned to me, consciously asking for a response but obviously feeling that, like the object in the self-in-exile position, I wouldn't have the slightest idea what she was saying. "What am I talking about?" she asked. "Do you know?"

"Your self," I answered, simply to show her that I was with her, for I was fairly certain that, if I did so, it would support her own momentum—

and indeed it did. She went on to delineate the difference between the false, defensive self and the real self.

"I've always felt that part of me was crazy. That this person is incompatible with who I have to be in the world. The dichotomy is very confusing, but they're equally there. I suppose," she sighed, "I'm describing myself as a kid but I don't feel that connection at the moment. This feels like a whole separate thing. . . . I like this person and I don't want to lose it. And I've always thought of it as my 'bad person!' That makes me feel very sorry for myself. That's one part of me that never grew up, and I like that part, but this is the part that wants to shut the gates" (i.e., protect herself).

Despite this insight, she went on to do just that. She said, self-deprecatingly, "I just thought, you just feel sorry for yourself. I don't know, there's something comforting about being that person, but it may be the comfort of being a victim."

I tracked the triad and interpreted the compromise as follows: "I think that expressing these ideas about who you really are made you feel unsafe and embarrassed again, and that to protect yourself you labeled your experience in a self-denigrating way, as 'being a victim.' This allows you to both express it and take it back, speaking to your need to express this part of you and to protect it simultaneously."

In response, over the next few sessions, Ruth started to explore the genetic basis of her self-hatred as a way to explain her parents' terrifying inconsistencies and, thus, to be able to feel connected to them. "It's very confusing to me, because I think that I'm a pretty candid, open, frank person. I've even been accused of being witty. And I keep thinking it's gonna be taken away.

"There were my opera records. My mother made me take them back. Did I ever tell you that? It was pretty embarrassing. I had bought all of these records, and she made me return them all. And the record store was in our neighborhood too. The thing was, I never knew when these things would happen. It was my own allowance too that I had saved up. Sometimes it was okay Sometimes it wasn't. I never knew. I tried to think about the quality of the thing, but I never could figure it out."

Notice here how her focus shifts to her own experience in a newly strong, confident, and introspective way. "Anyway, the key thing is not so much the discussing it. My actual terror is bringing my interest to somebody's attention, because if they don't know it exists, they can't take it away. . . . "

Ruth related her memory to an event that had just occurred. "I went to Tower Records looking for a recording of the Messiah and I found this wonderful old recording of Callas doing Tosca. I told no one I had it. Not Lisa, not Martha, nobody. I told myself I was embarrassed that I spent the money, but that's not true."

She defended (i.e., transference acting out by orbiting rather than identifying and exploring her feelings), looking at me provocatively and defiantly. "I am not gonna tell anyone. I just have to start small so I don't make another mess, okay? I don't trust myself at all."

I wanted to draw her attention again to her distance-regulation and need for compromise, so I said, "I think that maybe you pushed out onto me that image you have of someone trying to control you and then tried to pick a fight to give yourself some space without totally negating what you were saying."

"I agree," she answered. Reestablishing transference and therapeutic alliance so that she could explore her wish to fight with me in order to take a safer distance rather than simply act on it, she went on, "And it started as soon as I told you about the record. God! Some things take an incredible, conscious effort to change!"

This is an effort, however, which Ruth is clearly willing to make. At this writing, Ruth has come to understand that the anxiety which brought her to treatment was precipitated by her mother's death and her subsequent need to reorder her relationships. Based on this understanding, she has re-negotiated her relationship with her lover so that it is more satisfying. She has discovered new and, to her, unexpected richness in her relationships with other friends, colleagues, and students whom she had always kept at arm's length, so that she is much happier in general and is much less lonely and isolated. She is grappling with the approaching end of her athletic career as she ages and is exploring several creative alternatives which take into account the parts of her athletic life she truly values, amalgamated with her creative pursuits. Most of the time, she is willing and able to identify and express an ever-expanding range of positive and negative feelings about me and about other people in her life in a way which allows her to introspect about her attitudes as well as have them. She has become interested in herself as a living, feeling human with needs and feelings and curiosity. Almost all of this was news to her.

What lies ahead for her if she is to fully reclaim her real self is the working through of the fantasies which prevent her from developing and expressing herself. This working through involves the sad and painful work of exposing the painful yearning for an object who is responsive to her needs for both intimacy and autonomy as a precursor to the development of the self; the recognition that the time for the satisfaction of this need by other people as a prelude to the development of the self is past; the relinquishment of the hope of these self-defining supplies from the mother; the explication of the futility and emptiness that this realization carries in its wake (so beautifully described by Woolf); mourning, and the acceptance of the need to be mother to herself. Mourning and acceptance of the need to mother herself, in turn, will reduce her feelings of unsafety and open the door to the possibility of truly sharing emotional experiences with other adults.

Because of its painful nature, such work usually requires several sessions a week and an analytic frame. This level of therapy and the full extent of self-reclamation which comes out of it may not be possible, in the light of Ruth's limited financial resources. Nonetheless, her life is much enriched by the changes that she has made. Her relationships are far better, her creativity is stirring, her sense that she has real choices is much more highly developed. She is deeply moved by her growth, as she should be. Like the thaw at the end of winter, this process is not always pleasant. I can sense, however–with what pleasure and with what awe, as one does in spring–the immense vitality and energy stirring as she looks at her life and her loves and tries to create a life that feels authentic and meaningful for herself.

CONCLUDING REMARKS

This presentation is about work with a patient who could only afford therapy once a week and yet was able to make considerable progress in less than a year. While her work is far from complete, the quality of her life has changed markedly. This has been possible because of the systematic exploration of her compromise, distance-regulating defenses, her increasing, willing control over them, and her growing awareness of the nature of the internal world that has kept her distorted self-representations in place.

The rapidity of Ruth's response is somewhat unusual. It was based, I think, in equal parts on her own high intelligence, motivation, and talent for introspection and on her prior, basically positive, experience with me. The *nature* of the response, however, is not unique. I have seen similar positive responses from any number of schizoid patients over the last few years. Their successful treatment depends upon the therapist's ability to grasp the nature of the patient's desperate need for safety, to communicate to the patient the importance of being self-expressive despite the pain of being so, and to do this both systematically and tactfully from a therapeutically neutral position. This is accomplished through the steps that I have outlined in this chapter. Is the process, then, cut and dried–simply a matter of applied technique? I do not believe this to be the case at all.

I have presented some of the science of my work. I have spoken of part self and part object representations, defenses, intrapsychic structure. I have talked about interventions such as systematic, deepening interpretations of defenses against underlying experiences of unsafety. I believe that all of these elements can make the difference between a therapy that has a chance of going someplace and one that does not. Of course, that is not all that is going on.

Ultimately, all our theories and techniques are only the scaffolding underpinning the structure of a well-conducted therapy. Without them, therapy would be a hit-or-miss proposition. However, even if the theory and technique are good and valid, things we cannot control and actively factor in–like fate, or the chemistry between therapist and patient–will influence the outcome of our efforts. These elements are the basis of the great mystery of therapy.

In the mid-ground between the science of psychotherapy and the mystery of psychotherapy, is the domain of psychotherapy as art. Here, the therapist's ability to use her own real self exerts a powerful influence–specifically, her ability to take the scaffolding provided by theory and technique and use them as the basis of a creative, human, and humane encounter that transcends it. It is co-determined by the patient's ability to learn to do the same–to take the clay of the encounter and to use it creatively and personally.

If we use our theories to support us in the thick of it, without assuming that they represent the full extent of revealed knowledge, our theories will inform us and allow us to transcend them.

REFERENCES

Clark, K. R. (1994). The Nowhere (Wo)Man: the fear of vacillating feelings and needs in the schizoid personality disorder. Unpublished.

Fairbairn, R. (1952). *Psychoanalytic Studies of the Personality*. London: Tavistock.

Guntrip, H. (1969). *Schizoid Phenomena, Object Relations and the Self*. New York: International Universities Press.

Klein, R. (1993). Schizoid personality disorder. In *The Emerging Self*, ed. J. F. Masterson, pp. 39–50. New York: Brunner/Mazel.

Mahler, M., Pine, F., and Bergman, A. (1975). *Psychological Birth of the Human Infant*. New York: Basic Books.

Masterson, J. F. (1976). *The Psychotherapy of the Borderline Adult*. New York: Brunner/Mazel.

—— (1981). *The Narcissistic and Borderline Disorders*. New York: Brunner/Mazel.

—— (1985). *The Real Self: A Developmental, Self and Object Relations Approach*. New York: Brunner/Mazel.

Seinfeld, J. (1991). *The Empty Core: An Object Relations Approach to Psychotherapy of the Schizoid Personality*. Northvale, NJ: Jason Aronson.

Stern, D. (1985). *The Interpersonal World of the Infant: A View From Psychoanalysis and Developmental Psychology*. New York: Basic Books.

8 Maria's Second Chance: Resolving Oedipal Conflict in the Transference

Roberta Shechter

INTRODUCTION

We all agree that a well-functioning mother–infant dyad is important to later mental health. Some clinicians believe that failures in adult intimacy are solely attributable to preoedipal difficulties, problematic nurturing during the oral, anal, and phallic psychosexual stages of development—ages 0–3. While this may be true for some patients, others have been profoundly affected by slightly later childhood experiences: the triadic struggles of competition and identification that spring from longings for parental love and fear of its loss. If unresolved, these struggles—occurring between ages 3 and 5 during the oedipal phase of life—also have an impact on intimacy achievements. Oedipal contributions to a patient's inability to love are often neglected by clinicians. Case material in this chapter will show how understanding and interpreting a central transference fantasy as an oedipal dynamic helped resolve a patient's core conflict, enabling her to achieve the capacity for heterosexual intimacy. The treatment perspective is contemporary Freudian—weekly individual psychoanalytic psychotherapy.

THEORETICAL FRAMEWORK

Transference fantasies are feelings and thoughts about the loving and/or frustrating figures of childhood that are displaced onto the therapist in the course of treatment (Moore and Fine 1990). A transference fantasy is a regressive phenomenon. Its ideation is typical of the infantile time of life, giving voice to a patient's most repressed conflict, incompatible libidinal wishes, and abiding fears. Developmental in origin, the painful conflicts expressed in a transference fantasy are often based on early childhood trauma. To work clinically with this phenomenon, it is helpful to understand the hypotheses of psychoanalysis that describe how and why a particular transference fantasy comes about. There is an important link between the content of a transference fantasy and the early childhood trauma of a patient. For the purpose of a focused exposition of ideas in this paper, the term *trauma* has been given a limited definition. Trauma refers to the excessive frustrations of childhood, interferences to libidinal gratification that can occur at any point in the course of development, hampering an individual's fulfillment of nutritional, love, and security needs.

With this definition of trauma in mind, the ideation of transference is viewed as unique to each patient. Much depends on early life history and the quality of object relations. Every patient who enters treatment has incurred some amount of early childhood trauma. No childhood is perfection. Even in a family where early relationships have been favorable, a child must contend with interferences to libidinal gratification (Nager 1966) that are experienced as traumatic. While passing through the maturational phases of childhood–the oral, anal, phallic, and oedipal–blocks to libidinal gratification lead to trauma. This trauma results in an intrapsychic weakness known as fixation. Fixation, like trauma, is also inevitable, the fate of humankind. Consequently, every adult patient has buried within his or her psyche fixation points, pockets of repressed memory that are invested with energy, the vestigial remains of early trauma. It is to these fixation points in development that a patient regresses at the height of daily-life anxiety. It is to these fixation points that a patient retreats when an analyst fails to satisfy the infantile longings that surface in treatment. The repressed memory of early trauma moves from the unconscious, into the preconscious, and invades consciousness, shaping transference fantasies (Arlow and Brenner 1979).

The most empathic analyst, like the good enough mother, is bound to fail. Interferences to libidinal gratification in the analytic relationship are unconsciously experienced as a replay of childhood frustration (Menninger 1958). Relationship with the analyst is then invested with transference ideation that reflects core conflict, wishes, and fears that are the product of early trauma and influence the nature of psychic structure. The failures of early childhood, then, come alive in adult treatment. Fantasies based on early trauma are given genetic or experiential interpretation by the therapist. Core conflicts expressed in these fantasies are, in time, resolved, and structural change occurs. A more adaptive balance within agencies of the mind–the patient's id, ego, and superego–is achieved.

The slow working through of multiple transferences that are derived from childhood trauma describes a key contribution to change in psychoanalytic psychotherapy. Regression into transference is necessary for progression into health (Loewald 1980).

In the case study that follows, wishes and fears based on early trauma brought the patient into treatment. These conflicts, predominately oedipal in nature, underpinned the ideation of her presenting problem. She suffered from reminiscences (Freud 1893), repressed memories of age-appropriate sexual attractions to father, and fear of retaliatory abandonment by her competitor, mother. This oedipal drama was the source of current maladaptive behavior. Preoedipal fixations, based on oral and anal trauma, colored the oedipal and lent it strength. Eventually, oedipal conflict was enacted by the patient in transference. A screen memory emerged from repression. All was interpreted by the analyst. Change proceeded in the patient's psychic structure. Core conflict abated, her anxiety lowered, superego softened, and drive was channeled into more adaptive behavior. The patient's libidinal needs could then be satisfied in the present.

THE CASE OF MARIA

Initial Portrait of an Oedipal Patient

A petite, slender woman, no more than 5'3" in height, with short black hair that capped a porcelain face scrubbed free of makeup, Maria, in her navy suit and high-necked white blouse, appeared younger than her 32 years. She seemed the earnest child, straining to play the efficient investment banker, all business, using her well-cut clothes to lend stature.

I had introduced myself casually in the waiting room, Maria smiled warmly in response, and, with halting steps, followed as I proceeded to my office. Maria's face was impassive; she lowered herself stiffly into a chair, depositing a black briefcase carefully on the floor beside her. She looked around the room, then directly at me, and her eyes filled with tears. To put her at ease, I asked softly, "What brought you here today?" What followed came in a rush of words that flowed more out of need than trust.

"All I do is work. My hours are long. The boss is demanding. Other people from my office seem to have a social life. I know that it is possible, but I haven't dated since I broke up with Dave 16 months ago. We were together for two years. I had expected to marry Dave. It would have been his second marriage, and my first. He made promises, then waffled. He said that he loved me, but couldn't make the commitment. It took me some time, but I realized that he would never be ready. I broke up with him. It was a relief when he was transferred out of the bank's New York office. The scumbag!" Maria paused, her voice became barely audible as she continued. "We still talk, Dave and I, by e-mail. I still think about Dave. I long for him when I'm alone at night. I wish that I could find someone else." Now, at full volume, she said, "I hate the singles scene. I even tried a dating service. That was a waste of money. Singles dances are like a meat market. And I'm no gourmet morsel. As my mother used to say, I lack the right curves. When I was younger I thought of having breast implants. Now I'm afraid to do it. I know the idea of implants is silly. I wouldn't do it. It's just that I feel so anxious in new social situations with men. I don't think I can rely on my charm to attract them. Meeting Dave was easy. We worked together; he charmed me." She paused and sighed. "I'm so lonely. I want to get married and have children. I'm 32 years old. If I don't find the right man soon, that may never happen. I may grow old alone. That's my dread, growing old alone, and if that happens I don't want to live." Maria's voice had grown gradually louder and more strident. These final words were said as she looked at me full-face, her eyes blazing with challenge.

I met her gaze and said softly, "Endless loneliness is hard to contemplate. Tell me about your past, how you seem to have come to this dilemma in life." My empathic response to her anxiety calmed her. Maria reached for a tissue, unbuttoned her suit jacket, and proceeded to dip into the history of her present pain.

The younger of two daughters, Maria described her parents as "typically Sicilian-American. They love my sister and me, but they would have been happier with sons." Father, now retired, was a barber; Mother, a housewife. Father was a loving, quiet, and kind man, who came home early each night. His presence in the kitchen had a "calming effect" on the family, especially at homework time. In contrast, Mother was described as excitable, critical, and invasive. She had ambitions for her daughters. Doing well in school and having the right friends, people socially well-placed in the community and central to the youth group in the local Catholic church, was important to her. Mother closely monitored how Maria and her sister performed in school. "It was a pressure, but maybe it was a good thing too," Maria said. "I've done a number of important things with my life, I have an M.B.A. degree, and I make good money. Mother's vigilance has something to do with that."

Maria's earliest childhood memory, at intake, involved Father. She remembered sitting at the piano, in fading afternoon sunlight, playing duets with him and singing. The keyboard was high above her fingers, and her feet hung over the edge of their shared piano bench. The memory dated from age 3. She associated to later memory, Father taking her to Central Park for a horseback-riding lesson. Seven-year-old Maria sat on a dark pony, terrified. The teacher said she was a natural. Her fear slowly changed to exhilaration, as teacher and father admiringly watched her go around the paddock.

Maria's affect was wistful, as she floated in phallic–oedipal memory. Developmental time receded for a moment, then came to the present with a jolt. "My life has changed. I must take care of myself. If I don't, who will?" Her eyes focused now on the floor of my office and seemed to trace the patterns of my Persian carpet as a way to avoid the anguish that threatened to overwhelm.

The Vicissitudes of Oedipal Transference and Points of Change

In the first eight months of treatment, Maria seldom mentioned her family, nor spoke directly about the pressures of building a social life. This anxiety was expressed in displacement. Her weekly sessions were filled with the trials and tribulations of office life at the bank. She mentioned men and women, some with the close relatedness of intimate contact. One man, Joe, was repeatedly mentioned. But, again, her focus was on work, their shared tasks and competitions. Slowly, Maria began to describe Joe physically. She found him handsome. He had a good sense of humor. He had what she was "looking for in a man." I waited for some indication of a romantic involvement between these two, which was never mentioned.

Maria went out with girlfriends for brunch and on weekend trips. If she met men, the information was withheld from me. When my curiosity got the better of me, and I asked a direct question about available men at a weekend party, I was met with silence. That silence was telling. I underscored it as an oedipal transference resistance with the comment, "It seems difficult for you to talk to me about available men."

One morning Maria entered her session in a fury. "I have something to tell you," she said, in a challenging voice. "I plan to put an ad in the personal column of *New York* magazine." She told me this as if she were planning a heinous action, something that would meet with my total disapproval. When I wondered why she needed to tell me this news in such an angry voice, she said, in a startled surprise, "I thought you would be angry with me. You really are different from my mother. She flew into a fury when I told her about the ad. 'Proper Sicilian girls don't meet men in such a fashion,' she said. My mother is such a lady! It makes me sick. I explained to her that it is not easy to meet men in Manhattan. Does she expect me to become a nun? I felt mortified discussing this with my mother. This whole thing is ridiculous!"

Addressing oedipal–superego derivatives, behavioral manifestations of unconscious conflict in the experiential transference, I said, "It may seem ridiculous to discuss the ad with me as well. You are fearful that I, like your mother, will disapprove of your efforts at forging a love life." Challenging Maria's defense, the disowning of fear by projecting it onto others, I continued, "Perhaps the real issue is your own conflict about placing the ad. You want to do it, but are worried. What might that be about?"

Maria freely admitted that the prospect of coffee dates with strange men terrified her. Mother seemed worried that she could not take care of herself. She, too, wondered if this were true. In the weeks that followed, Maria discussed her anxiety about men. She became keenly aware that she relished intense friendships with married men in the office. These friendships were "safe," oedipal choices. She need not worry about intimacy. They could "only go so far"; she remained "daddy's girl." Slowly the full force of Maria's libidinal longings emerged. From repression came a screen memory. One morning, focused on the painful longing in her attraction to "an unavailable colleague," Maria's thoughts suddenly shifted. "Funny, I just remembered something that happened when I was a little kid. I don't know if it is a memory or a dream. I think it really happened:

> "It was a hot summer afternoon. My parents' bedroom had the only air conditioner. Their door was closed. I must have been 2½ or 3 years old. I reached up and turned the knob. The door opened. Father was lying on his back across the bed, nude. One leg bent, his eyes closed, his breathing shallow in sleep. In the dim light his skin seemed luminous and smooth. He was beautiful. Then I saw his penis. It was rounded, soft, slightly darker in color. I longed to touch it. I reached out and laughed. He stirred. I was afraid that he would wake up and be angry. I thought of my mother and realized that she would be angry if she found me there. I ran out of the room. No one knew that I had been there." [Long silence.]

Following the flow of Maria's sexual longing, excitement and anxiety, I said, "It is not unusual for a little girl to be drawn to her father. Would mother have been angry if she had caught you looking at your nude father?"

"Yes," Maria continued, "that scene would have been entirely too sexual for her. She would have killed me! Tamer stuff angered her. She wondered what I was doing if I spent too much time in the bathroom alone. As if I needed a bathroom to masturbate. Closed doors infuriated her. She yelled, 'What are you doing in there?'"

In the sessions that followed, Maria described a sexually preoccupied and oppressive mother. "My sister and I used to laugh about her. She was so proper. Father teased her about it." Maria's mother didn't talk about sex, she questioned and badgered, and was suspicious of her daughters, especially as adolescents. Maria's elder sister was pregnant out of wedlock and married at 18. Fifteen-year-old Maria felt abandoned by her sister and was determined not to "add to the family shame." "I was sexually active but careful with boys," Maria said. Maria's deep-felt guilt diminished, bringing her libidinal longings to the present. "I'm ready to experiment a bit on how to meet a man." And she did–an ad in *New York* magazine brought John.

From the onset, meeting John was true excitement. The details of John–who he was, his interests, his past life experiences and current demands in their relationship–seemed less important than his willingness to be in her life. Maria complained about John in the way that she complained about anyone in her life. Occasionally she compared him to past boyfriends, but never described the details of their intimate time together. I became aware that Maria could be talking about a friendship with a woman. The fact that John was an adult male seemed to be irrelevant to their relationship. She mentioned once that she found his beard attractive. She took him home to meet her parents, and they found him charming. But the description of Maria's time with John was much like watching a 1950s movie—sex was simply deleted.

This changed on the eve of Maria's 34th birthday, two years into therapy. The night before that auspicious day, Maria and John had an argument. Maria had wanted John to take a shower before retiring to bed. John refused. In the details of this argument, John for the first time took on physical dimensions. Maria said, "He always smells so peculiar; it's hard to be near him. I can't figure it out. I used to think it was deodorant or a soap that had a particularly pungent odor. I am just not sure why it's hard for me to tolerate his smell." When I commented that it seemed difficult for her to be physically close to John, she responded, "At times I am unsure about whether I'm really attracted to John. I like him, he's a good man, but I've never felt a certain excitement that I always thought would be there when I found someone to love. I know that my parents have that romance in their marriage. My father cuddles my mother still today." Maria acknowledged, for the first time in treatment, that her closeness to John lacked something essential. They were good friends but unsatisfactory lovers. He was not much interested in sex. Maria enjoyed sex when they had it, but she was not driven to pursue it as she had been with other boyfriends. John's lack of interest was troubling. When I asked, in some wonderment, if this pervasive sexual dissatisfaction with John was a new development, Maria said, "No, I always felt this way." I wondered, again, why she had never mentioned it in therapy. She said, "You were so encouraging of John, I felt ashamed to mention that I had questions about him. My parents like him. Even my sister, Louise, thinks he's a lovely person. I want to marry a lovely person, I just don't know if it should be John." Tears now flowed. Interpreting her transference defense, I said, "I guess it's difficult to go after the sexual excitement and romance that you want, particularly when you're so concerned about our disapproval, your family and myself."

In the weeks that followed, Maria explored her feelings about John. She became aware that she felt, in their relationship, trapped in a vacuum of loneliness. She feared abandonment if she made a change: abandonment by her family, and disregard from me. We all, in Maria's fantasy, wanted her to marry at any cost. We expected her to compromise in her choice, giving sexual satisfaction a low priority. When she first thought of leaving John, the loneliness of her days without him seemed to outweigh her dissatisfaction with him. Tolerating this loneliness, and the dread of nothingness in the future, mirrored the plaintive fear that Maria gave voice to in our intake session. Eventually I interpreted this oral-level fear as a regressive defense against true closeness and other anxieties that it might bring. It was difficult, but Maria broke up with John, and mourned the loss of their relationship.

In the months that followed, Maria met a new man—in fact, several. She joined the Sierra Club and went on hikes and ski trips. She joined a professional organization and had late-night dinners and evening cruises on the Hudson River. Ed is Maria's latest boyfriend, a man she discusses in therapy sessions. He is a year and a half younger than Maria. He graduated from her business school just last year. Ed comes from a working-class family of Yugoslavian background. He is the pride and joy of his parents. Maria enjoys "the smoothness of Ed's skin. He is a sensual man. And the fact that he has brains too is helpful."

In our last session, Maria said, "I bought a beautiful peignoir yesterday. It's green, Ed's favorite color. I know it's frivolous to spend $400 on a nightgown and robe, but I like the matching effect. The combination of silk and lace makes me feel elegant. It will be our first weekend away together." As she reveled in telling me about her shopping spree, Maria was enjoying the instinctual satisfactions that her story supplied. We could look together, analyst and patient, at the prospect of her coming pleasure. There is work to be done, but Maria feels more comfortable in the sexual arena now, more accepted as a woman, by herself, her analyst, and the introjects of childhood.

CONCLUSION

Maria began treatment mired in the interpersonal quandary that plagues 90 percent of our young adult patients—a longing for stable intimacy. She entered treatment in a regressed state. Oral and phallic longings were on top. These issues acted as a defense against deeper oedipal strivings, strivings that surfaced in the initial session as early memories of being Father's special girl. In her work world, Maria fluctuated between being either a phallic woman, one of the boys, competing on their turf in their way, or she was a harmless, oedipal flirt, pursuing the unattainable married man. These behaviors constituted a defense, a relational wall that kept adult genital strivings at bay.

When Maria began treatment she was ripe for therapeutic engagement, and transference quickly unfolded. It reflected, from the first year onward, her core conflict. I was Mother of the oedipal phase–critical, competitive, the projection of her own punitive superego. I was the oedipal introject of unconscious fantasy, at the apex of her triangulations, the mother from whom she must keep her sexual striving hidden, her interest in men shrouded in silence. When I interpreted this transference, trust deepened and a screen memory (Freud 1899) emerged from the unconscious.

At the heart of Maria's screen memory we see the trauma (Greenacre 1949) that is the source of her core conflict: satisfaction of incestuous longing through voyeurism. In this memory Maria was, for one moment in time, the oedipal victor. Father was hers to view. She had satisfaction of component instinct (Freud 1905). This libidinal gratification produced guilt. She mortally feared Mother's retaliation for her transgression. The intensity of drive–barely contained sexuality on the rim of expression between father and daughter–invested Maria's screen memory with vividness. Mother, in the associations that followed the report of the screen memory, was a sexually oppressive shrew who threatened abandonment and worse–annihilation if her rival, the little daughter, grew too strong.

Hearing this memory I wondered, "What does Maria need now and from whom? What are her wishes and fears? Who do I represent on the canvas of conflict?" The answers to these questions diagrammed the transference interpretation most likely to bring change. Maria now needed an abiding presence (Winnicottt 1965), one that was tolerant of her incestuous longing, addressed her superego fear, and stayed close to her anxiety. My empathic comments gratified the positive side of the oedipal transference. Maria's response was a decrease in guilt. She moved forward in development. She acted on oedipal strivings and entered the competitive singles world with an ad in the personal columns of *New York* magazine. The tenacity of Maria's attachment to John was based on oedipal conflict. Her silence about sexual dissatisfaction with John was a testament to the tenacity of oedipal transference as a defense. With John on the scene, Maria's inner world was populated by adults who wanted to deny her sexual fulfillment. Interpretation of the conflict beneath this defense softened Maria's superego and fostered the beginning of a less repressive sexual attitude. Maria's treatment continues. Transferences ebb and flow, as she continues to work through oedipal conflict and build her life.

REFERENCES

Arlow, J., and Brenner, C. (1979). The topographic theory. In *Psychoanalytic Concepts and the Structural Theory*. New York: International Universities Press.

Breuer, J., and Freud, S. (1893). On the physical mechanism of hysterical phenomena: preliminary communication. *Standard Edition* 2.

Freud, S. (1899). Screen memories. *Standard Edition* 3:301–322.

—— (1905). *Three Essays On Sexuality*, ed. J. Strachey, vol. 7, pp. 125–245. New York: Basic Books, 1962.

Greenacre, P. (1949). A contribution to the study of screen memories. In *Psychoanalytic Study of the Child* 3/4:73–84. New York: International Universities Press.

Greenson, R. (1967). *The Technique and Practice of Psychoanalysis*. New York: International Universities Press.

Khan, M. M. R. (1960). Regression and integration in the analytic setting. *International Journal of Psycho-Analysis* 41:130–146.

Loewald, H. W. (1980). On the therapeutic action of psychoanalysis. In *Papers On Psychoanalysis*, pp. 221–256. New Haven/London: Yale University Press.

Menninger, K. (1958). *Theory of Psychoanalytic Technique*. New York: Harper.

Moore, B., and Fine, B. (1990). *Psychoanalytic Terms and Concepts*. New Haven/London: The American Psychoanalytic Association and Yale University Press.

Nagera, H. (1966). *Early Childhood Disturbances: The Infantile Neurosis and the Adulthood Disturbances*. New York: International Universities Press.

Winnicott, D. (1965). *The Maturational Processes and the Facilitating Environment*. Madison, CT: International Universities Press.

9 The Use of the Telephone as a Transitional Space in the Treatment of a Severely Masochistic Anorexic Patient

Joyce Kraus Aronson

INTRODUCTION

How do you work with a patient who refuses to come in to see you? This chapter is about a dangerously ill anorexic who began therapy and became so afraid of her needs–of what might be aroused in the contact between us, the possible threat to her schizoid withdrawal into anorexic preoccupation, and her unconscious fear of the inevitable disappointments in the potential intimacy between us–that she refused to come in to see me. However, she discovered the use of telephone sessions and the answering machine as a transitional space. On the machine she could hear my voice in an absolutely predictable way and establish an illusion of my constant availability. She could be as needy as necessary. This regressive experience allowed her to enact early developmental needs and begin to give up masochistic and omnipotent anorexic defenses. The holding qualities of this safe transitional space allowed a developmental thrust that eventually made these parameters unnecessary.

WORKING WITH THE SEVERELY DISTURBED ANOREXIC

Patients with anorexia exhibit a broad range of ego functioning. Their capacity for object relations can vary considerably, as can their developmental deficits (Aronson 1986). Chassler (1994) has suggested that the starvation of the anorexic elicits caretaking behaviors from significant others and is an expression of an unconscious hope to repair unfulfilled needs with important early attachment figures. Consequently, the therapist must be flexible, responding to where the patients are and to what their needs may be.

Diagnoses range from psychoses through character disorders to neuroses. Some patients, like this one, are at the low-level borderline and psychotic end of this spectrum and are not treatable within the traditional psychotherapeutic framework. These are patients who are unable to engage in a therapeutic relationship, don't get into treatment, avoid hospitalization unless forced by the family, avoid contact with hospital staff, and, although they comply with refeeding, upon discharge resume defensive anorexic patterns and remain chronically and dangerously emaciated. These patients flirt with death and sometimes die.

This chapter reports on therapeutic work with a psychotic, extremely masochistic, anorexic patient, and the use of telephone sessions and the telephone answering machine to create a flexible therapeutic hold. Winnicott (1951) used the terms *transitional objects* and *transitional phenomena* to describe an intermediate area of experience created by the infant, a way station in the transition from inside to outside, "between the thumb and the teddy bear." This concept of transitional space between mother and child is useful in understanding this patient's use of my telephone. She created this transitional space out of her needs; it was not something I suggested. On the machine the therapist's voice was always present in a totally predictable way and the illusion of constant availability could be maintained. Speaking aloud to the machine was entirely under the patient's control. Used between sessions, in states of depression or excitement, it helped her discover what she was thinking and feeling. Since she could not tolerate face-to-face contact, the telephone sessions and the answering machine allowed an intermediate area of experience in the therapeutic relationship.

In recent years, the work of infant researchers has made us aware of the impact of mother–infant dyadic interaction in the first years of life.

Highly restricted patterns of self- and mutual regulation can occur in infancy and be minimally transformed through adult experience. Kiersky and Beebe (1994) describe how understimulation in infancy may result in the lack of a sense of mutuality and effectiveness in dyadic exchange and subsequent avoidance of mutually regulated affective contact. For some severely disturbed anorexic patients, there has been a paucity of the interactional sensory–motor experiences which are the precursors of psychic structure. These deficits in dyadic experience can lead to inability to tolerate face-to-face contact in ongoing psychotherapy. This patient had to be allowed to titrate the amount of contact she could tolerate.

Interpretations were meaningless to this patient. For example, I could tell her that she wanted to have me endlessly, but it had no effect. She needed to enact it for a mutual engagement to evolve. Since she found a face-to-face encounter overwhelming, the following parameters were used: permitting telephone sessions; allowing the therapist's telephone answering machine to be used as transitional space; letting her limit the time of sessions, and set limits on the therapist's affect; being available to help the patient deal with the immediate and overwhelming anxiety aroused as she tried new experiences; avoiding hospitalization insofar as there was no threat to life; and having telephone contact during vacations for the first four years of treatment. Each parameter became unnecessary as the patient grew emotionally.

PRESENTING PROBLEMS

Ms. K. was referred to me for outpatient psychotherapy and I first saw her in preparation for her discharge from a hospital, where she had been for two months. She had had many previous hospitalizations. Ms. K. is a 4'10", 80-pound, 26-year-old with a strikingly high pitched, childish voice. She was dressed in odd, shabby clothing. Physically she looked prepubertal. She has never menstruated and has no breast development. She has lovely features–big dark eyes and waist-length black hair, which is unkempt, with large, bloody scabs visible on her scalp. At 80 pounds, she looked painfully thin and delicate. Her weight had been as low as 54 pounds. Her speech was pressured and she jumped from one topic to another without completing any thought. She seemed very anxious and timid, averted her eyes, and spoke with false hopefulness about her discharge plans. I felt as if I were talking to a poorly functioning 11-year-old child as far as her social judgment was concerned. The one thing she talked about in an affective way was her love of skating. She had taken lessons as a child, but her parents had not let her train as an adolescent.

Ms. K. lived an isolated, schizoid life alone with her cat, who she felt shared her human feelings; she was preoccupied with hurting him emotionally if she wasn't affectionate. She had money available to her from the family, but she felt that she had no control over it, had to save it for her old age, and lived like a bag lady, dirty and in old clothes. Her apartment was hot, dirty, disorganized, and rat-infested. The television was always on. Most of her time was preoccupied with what she could or would not eat, and with her upset stomach or diarrhea. Ms. K. would spend her time exercising or stretching, sometimes sitting in a split for hours chewing on ice cubes, her legs aching. If she did a good split she believed that the cars outside were honking their approval. If lights went off in a neighboring apartment, she thought that neighbor was watching her disapprovingly. She would, at times, search for and listen to music with lyrics that expressed her mood. Her hyperactivity, exhaustion, starvation, and pain kept her empty of thoughts and feelings most of the time. She was terrified that neighbors could see her, hear her, or know her thoughts and they would be angry. She frequently heard voices saying disapprovingly, "She's an anorexic." Unwashed and unkempt, she lived in an autistic, sensory-dominated mode (Ogden 1989). She was agitated, incapable of reflective thinking and frightened of human contact.

PREVIOUS TREATMENT

Socially isolated throughout her childhood, Ms. K. developed anorexia at 11. She was treated by a psychiatrist who was also her parents' friend. As part of the treatment, he came to family meals and encouraged her to eat. She recalls following his advice, eating voraciously, gaining 30 pounds, feeling out of control, and resuming her anorexic behavior. At 17, her anorexia became worse. She saw a therapist five days a week for five years. She described him as often silent. She too was silent. She said that her parents insisted she go and she complied. She recalled how she hated him and her pleasure in defecating on his chair. She was in and out of the hospital during this five-year period, often hospitalized when he went on vacation, although she denied that his going on vacation had anything to do with her hospitalizations. During the last year of treatment, it was suggested to the parents that they hire someone to watch her eat—which they did for one year. At age 22, she adamantly refused to see him. For the next two years she was seen by the internist who had worked collaboratively with this psychiatrist. Ms. K. said that she went to his office several times a week, he ate with her, and told her that she had to get well because he cared for her. Eventually he became enraged when she didn't gain weight and refused to see her. For the next two years she was in and out of the hospital on medical units, at times close to death. Eventually she was so malnourished that she had to have a surgical hip replacement. She also had surgery to correct her severely crossed eyes, which she had had from birth. After this corrective surgery she was hospitalized on an eating disorders unit because her weight was dangerously low. While hospitalized, Ms. K. avoided contact with other patients and with staff. For the most part she would stay in her room, isolated and come late for activities. When she met her goal weight of 80 pounds, she was referred to me for outpatient therapy.

I thought that with such serious developmental deficits she should be seen three times weekly; she should also see an internist regularly to follow her physical condition, and a psychiatrist for medication. She agreed. Her parents were to be seen monthly, but after a year of this, the parents' therapist refused to work with them because of the father's rages.

EARLY LIFE

In the course of treatment it emerged that Ms. K. is the middle daughter of five children. The siblings are three years older, two years older, three-and-a-half years younger, and five years younger.

Born with severely crossed eyes, she started out at some disadvantage in face-to-face experience. The mother had told the patient that she was preoccupied with the care of her other children, especially one who was continuously ill, and that after the first few weeks Ms. K. refused the breast and had to be bottle-fed. She was left alone a great deal, and was a quiet baby who never cried—even when wet or hungry.

The family moved during her first year, a change that was anxiety-provoking for both parents—making them even less available. They said she was such a good, undemanding, quiet baby that they could take her to restaurants and she wouldn't make a peep. At 1½, Ms. K. was diagnosed with failure to thrive.

It is probable that with her crossed eyes and Mother's unavailability, the patient had experienced very little dyadic, face-to-face gazing and vocalization—the interactional sensory-motor experiences that are the precursors of psychic structure. In this mother–child dyad there was little mutual gazing, mutual smiling, and sharing of excitement. This was not only true in infancy but an ongoing deficit throughout her childhood. The paucity of affective dyadic interaction came across poignantly when the patient told me that she never had fun with her mother. She remembered going to the playground and watching a child holding a penny and playing a game on a swing where as she came close she excitedly gave her mother the penny, then swinging back and forth exchanging the penny, laughing together. She asked her mother to play the game but it was no fun.

In our sessions, Ms. K. was unable to engage in conversational dyadic interaction. In her high-pitched, pressured voice she didn't converse. She often spoke whenever I began to speak; and she would rarely complete a thought. There was no eye contact. She seemed extremely vulnerable to overstimulation in face-to-face contact.

Ms. K. described herself as "very quiet" during her childhood, spending most of the time in front of the TV while mother was in the kitchen. A recurring memory is of her younger brother being held by a nanny who was employed to take care of that sibling, while she sat alone with the TV. The parents were often out, leaving the children with babysitters.

At 11, she became anorexic and dressed in rags. She reported that for one year she didn't bathe, and her parents said nothing. When she became dangerously cachectic, they were very responsive. Mother went to school everyday to feed her. Father became enraged at her for not eating—saw her as a willful, rebellious, defiant child who refused to take on his intellectual pursuits.

A test report at age 12 noted she was an estranged, depressed, fragile girl with borderline features, whose love for ice skating contained elements of desperation. "It keeps this estranged girl alive and also serves as a medium for human contact, however tenuous and impersonal."

PSYCHOTHERAPY

Initially, she came to some sessions, although very late. She had a difficult time just organizing her daily life, shopping, eating, and getting to my office. Terrified of the unexpected, she was totally preoccupied with others' perceptions of her, and often heard voices saying, "She's an anorexic." She expected rageful responses if she asked for anything.

In this beginning phase, she talked about her love of skating and gradually, with enormous anxiety and fear of criticism for being too thin and not being perfect, she started taking skating lessons again. Terrified of any new experiences, she would come home flooded with feelings and leave lengthy messages on my answering machine. She was obsessed with being criticized, felt people could read her mind, were calling her sick and anorexic, and were silently denigrating her skating.

I went on vacation for a week. Although I did preparatory work, telling her months in advance, she handled the impending separation with denial, increased psychosomatic problems, and overt psychosis. She was hospitalized and, although I saw her regularly during her hospitalization, after discharge she refused to come to sessions but would call me during the time we were scheduled to meet, often at the very end of the hour. At other times she would leave messages or ask desperately that I return her call. I often spoke to her on an as-needed basis until she calmed down (sometimes it took a half hour or more), then I'd suggest we talk further at the next scheduled session.

Ms. K. felt that if she came to see me in person there was something very wrong with her; she did not want to be aware that she needed me. She would rarely call at the beginning of a scheduled phone session. She would do exercises and then decide when she wanted to initiate the contact. For the next three years most of our sessions were by telephone.

I did insist that we meet in person once a week, but most of the time she would come to the last fifteen minutes of the session. She would spend the first five minutes in the bathroom and, after leaving, would return to the bathroom for ten minutes. She sometimes missed even those weekly sessions and expected a rageful response from me. In session, if I was animated or used my hands, she asked me not to do so. In a similar way she became afraid to go to the movies and would only watch films on television. She was generally afraid of being affectively overwhelmed by positive as well as negative affects.

Although ostensibly seeking help, for the first few years this patient was totally absorbed in hopelessness and self-destructive activities: starvation, hair pulling, creating bloody scabs on her scalp, drinking large amounts of bitter coffee, excessive, exhausting exercise, obsessive rumination about her life, and cutting herself off from all relationships and from therapy. This behavior produced in me a sense of hopelessness, despair, and ineffectiveness which I had to contain during the several years I worked with her by phone. This countertransference gave me an awareness of her own hopelessness, despair, and ineffectiveness.

Betty Joseph (1982) states, "It seems to me the near destruction of the self takes place with considerable libidinal satisfaction" (p. 450). These patients are enthralled by the pain. No ordinary pleasure offers such delight as exciting self-annihilation. The analyst is the only person who is actually concerned about progress. The patient pulls back into deadly passivity. The wanting parts of the patients are split off and projected. The patient goes over and over her failures and attempts to induce the analyst to become critical, despairing, and hopeless. Joseph (1982) says that these patients lacked warm contact and often had a violent parent. This is true of Ms. K. Her early life was remarkably bland and void of positive affect. The major emotional intensity in the family was her father's rageful reactions. Her parents' primary experience of her was as their dangerously sick child. In a recent paper Elliott Markson (1993) described how shared suffering is the essential emotional connection in families of the masochistic patient.

The classical position is that failure of infantile omnipotence forces the child to turn to reality. My experience with this patient is in line with the Novicks' (1991) view that the failure to achieve competent interactions with others forces the child to turn to omnipotent solutions. They argue that masochism can be best understood as the result of a multidetermined, epigenetic sequence of pain-seeking behaviors, which start in infancy and result in fantasies, modeled on the beating fantasy. The Novicks (1991) note that transitory beating fantasies could be seen in some form in all children. Fixed beating fantasies are derived from disturbances in the first year of life. In a sample of ill children indexed at the Anna Freud Center, there was a mutual lack of pleasure on the part of mother and baby in the earliest months of life in those children with a fixed beating fantasy. This patient's beating fantasy took the form of a constant preoccupation with a man who would be unpredictable and enraged at her. This fantasy often kept her terrified and immobilized. For several years, it was the head of the skating school who once commented on how strange she looked. The beating fantasy also included her coach feeling sorry for her, comforting her, sticking up for her, and reprimanding the head of the school.

The infancy of the severely masochistic patients the Novicks (1991) saw was marked by significant disturbance from the first months of life. They point out that self-esteem, confidence, and effectance are rooted in the child's real capacity to elicit the appropriate response from the mother. All of their masochistic cases had parents who were intermittently caring, but in response to the parents' needs, and in a way that gave the children little confidence in their ability to evoke a response. These parents, too, were intermittently caring. Ms. K. recalls being scheduled to be with her father a few hours one Saturday every month, but this was often cancelled. The Novicks speculate that externalization of hated, devalued aspects of the self onto the child serve as the mother's main mode of relating to the child who later develops masochistic pathology. Ms. K.'s mother's main need in relation to this daughter was to see her as a poor, sick, helpless, anorexic child.

These patients used the experience of helpless rage and pain magically to predict and control their chaotic experiences. The early repetitive traumata forced the child into an imaginary world where safety and omnipotent control were magically associated with pain. When Ms. K. was a toddler and young child, her mother was available only when this child was sad, unhappy, sickly or in pain. Moves toward autonomy and self-assertion were not encouraged. Mother was also physically intrusive, demanding to see her bowel movements up until latency and preoccupied with cooking and feeding. This physical intrusiveness contributed to the child's inability to integrate body and self.

She had a poor capacity to tolerate anxiety, as well as little ability even to begin to organize her cognitive and emotional responses to situations to which she was exposed. If she put off talking about her immediate experience it was lost to her. She could not hold it in her mind and talk about it later during a session. The immediate contact with me through the answering machine was used to explore both what she was experiencing and the tentative and fragile possibilities for connectedness and separateness from me. She could not begin to let herself experience anything new unless she had a means by which, on an as-needed basis, she could organize her life. She used my answering machine to do this.

During the first year of treatment she was hospitalized during my two vacations. After that I realized that she needed ongoing contact. For the first three years it was impossible for her to handle lengthy separations without psychotic withdrawal into a self-contained state. A treatment relationship could only begin to be established once the patient was assured that ongoing phone sessions would be maintained during vacations.

Even with phone sessions, Ms. K. was scheduled to come to a session after one vacation. Instead, she called and said she had been sleeping. There was no way she could get there. It was only on the phone that she discovered she was angry at me for having been away on vacation. "I didn't know I was angry until now that I'm saying it." Even with that awareness she did not hold onto it. She also missed her next session. She came at the last few minutes of the hour, expecting me to be angry.

Several years later after much discussion, we agreed that she would not contact me in person on vacation but could leave phone messages on my machine and I would call in to receive them every few days. I found myself enraged at the repetitive, endless rambling, unlike her usual messages. I felt nothing was enough for her, that she was endlessly demanding and insatiable and had no notion of what was reasonable to expect. I found myself talking out loud–furious, impatient, feeling that she'd drained me dry. Phone messages lasted for almost an hour. She was angry at me for leaving and was putting her anger into me, a characteristic pattern for her. I could detect it first in my countertransference, and only then help her express it to me.

This patient attributed magical omnipotent power to her own feelings and fantasies, and consequently carried around a terror of her anger. A key element in treatment was for her to be able to express anger at me and experience my tolerating what the original objects couldn't.

ENACTMENT AND COUNTERTRANSFERENCE

Christopher Bollas (1987) has written,

> By permitting himself to be used as an object the therapist facilitates the patient's sense of self. . . . We are made use of through our affects, through

> the patient generating the required feeling within us. In many ways, this is precisely how a baby "speaks" to its mother that either inspires some action in her on the baby's behalf or leads her to put the baby's object usage into language, engaging the infant in the journey towards verbal representation of internal psychic states. [pp. 203–204]

As a therapist, what I said did not matter as much as what I did. It didn't help to tell Ms. K. that I felt she wanted me available unconditionally. Interpretation of this was not meaningful. I had to be available as much as possible to maintain the illusion of optimum availability. I did not charge for phone time since I was being paid my full fee for three sessions a week. Ms. K. needed to feel that I wanted to talk to her for nothing in order to maintain the sense that I cared for her–a prerequisite for the relationship. She later spoke of her skating instructors, who stayed with her a few minutes more at the end of her lesson, as possibly caring. Eventually I addressed this in the transference. Initially, and for several years, it was essential to the treatment that this illusion of caring availability, which she had never experienced with her mother, be enacted over a long period of time.

In much the same way as the mother of an infant is first all available on demand feeding, and then the sound of her voice can let the infant know that she will be available later to soothe and help the baby contain and delay the satisfaction of its needs, I initially spoke at length to Ms. K. when she called (mostly to clarify affects and help her organize her thoughts). When later it became possible, I would put off a lengthy phone contact to when we could talk during our next scheduled session. For the first two years this patient would call, leaving lengthy messages several times during the middle of the night and as much as ten to twenty times over weekends. I arranged to listen to these at my convenience, or else I would have found it an unbearable intrusion. At many points early in treatment, I would come to the office and find that a dozen messages had been left for me during the night, all from Ms. K. Often there was more than a half hour of messages. At times I found myself angry at this intrusion. Did she feel she was the only person in my life? Was she testing to see if I'd be sick of her? Intellectually, I knew that as she gave up the anorexia more of her infantile demandingness and rage would come out. It helped me to contain my annoyance to know that she needed the answering machine as a transitional space in which to organize her thoughts, fears, feelings, and fantasies. If she asked that I call her back, I did so at a time that was comfortable and leisurely for me.

I had to be able to live through her pain, despair, depression, self-destructiveness, and demandingness. There was a period of several months where I felt that she was trying to provoke the kind of rage response that was typical of her father. It became apparent with Ms. K. that the major affective response from her parents was related to her illness. They came running when she was hospitalized, although expressing rage that she was ill. After years of illness, when she gave a public performance, preparing months in advance and telling them about it, the parents not only didn't come, but didn't even ask her about it. This is consistent with Markson's (1993) findings. With severely masochistic patients, pleasurable states are ignored by the parents.

Understanding my anger as a countertransference guide to what's going on has helped me to contain it. After a successful and satisfying skating lesson, Ms. K. came to our session 43 minutes late, terrified that I would be enraged at her "like her father would be." She walked into my office cowering, saying she expected "the wrath of God." I had felt angry at her lateness, but, knowing that this was connected with her terror of success, the anger dissipated. I told her that when she is satisfied and has a sense of accomplishment it seems to be followed by a barrage of uncertainty. She defended against this frightening uncertainty by trying to provoke the only thing she could count on in her family, an angry response. Over time we came to see that every successful interaction was followed by some self-destructive incident. Ms. K. would eat only melon, causing diarrhea, take the wrong subway, or overflow her bathtub.

Many traditional theorists (Wilson et al. 1983), emphasize the self-destructive behavior in anorexics as aggression turned against the self out of fear of expressing it directly. In addition, this patient had a childhood of bleak emotional monotony, where anger was the only emotional response that she could be sure of evoking. When she had some slight success, she became anxious, feeling that she could not believe it was happening, or would continue to happen. It was unlike her familiar experience and she returned to home base by a masochistic provocation.

When Ms. K. started to come to full sessions about three years after treatment began, I found myself dreading our sessions. In anticipation of seeing her, I wanted to eat something to store up energy so I wouldn't feel depleted. I had the fear that I wouldn't be able to get rid of her—that she wouldn't leave. I felt burdened, tired, as if I'd be drained. This countertransference feeling put me in touch with the voracious neediness for human contact, which she had been keeping at bay.

Ms. K. attempted to maintain a sense of constant availability of the object (therapist) while denying dependency on or need of the object. By actually physically coming to sessions and then leaving, she experienced both her need and then her loss. She would start to talk and then have to tear herself away when contact was satisfying. After sessions she would exercise in the waiting room for fifteen minutes before she left. Only recently was she able to say that if she has a good feeling with me she wants to stay as much as she wants to and not have to leave. She would rather not feel that she wants than to feel that she wants and can't have. This is true for food as well. She would eat only cold food, because hot food smelled so delicious.

THE PATIENT'S GROWTH

In the sixth year of treatment, Ms. K. began to face her hopelessness, despair, depression, the bleakness of her childhood, and the emotional emptiness she experienced with her parents. She's been able to become aware of her hatred, envy, and aggression. She came to each of her three sessions a week, and rarely used the telephone. When she faced an experience which she anticipated she would have difficulty handling emotionally, she scheduled a telephone session after it, for which she paid. She said this helped her calm down and put things in perspective.

There was a shift in her capacity for more human relatedness, which could be seen in her move from the isolated, controlled world of skating to the dyadic world of ballroom dance. Initially she only worked as an instructor with the elderly, because she was sure they would be responsive to her and they didn't engender envy in her.

CONCLUDING COMMENTS

As the reader will recall, in the past this deeply troubled patient had attended for five years all of her five-times-a-week therapy sessions without apparent change. It was the regressive experience of the treatment described herein that allowed improvement to occur. Regression allowed an enactment of developmental needs and growth. The emotional availability and the holding qualities of the therapist facilitated a relationship in which the patient could feel understood and begin to give up her masochistic, omnipotent, anorexic defenses.

In this treatment situation we can see, in particular, the way in which a carefully planned parameter can be usefully employed to advance the treatment of certain patients. Ms. K.'s use of the telephone answering machine to speak to me whenever she wanted to allowed her to speak to me as if I were present and as if I were her omnipotent creation. It served as a transitional object that enabled Ms. K. to build up an internal object. As she became able to talk to me in her mind, her voices disappeared.

Winnicott (1968) embedded the idea of the transitional object in a developmental theory of object relations. Initially, the subjective object is created by the infant with no independent existence. Then there is an omnipotently controlled object, perceived as outside the self, existing as a pole for identifications and projections. Finally, there is a movement to an object that is an independent part of external reality. According to Winnicott, this transition is the result of the subject's fantasized destruction of the object and the object's survival.

In keeping with Winnicott's ideas, Ms. K. had a version of me that belonged to her like a teddy bear. She could be as destructive as she needed to be. She would call me via the answering machine at 2:00 A.M. and talk to me for as long as she wanted. Just as with a teddy bear, there was the illusion of the responsive object. She could be as needy and as greedy as was necessary, and got to use me without using me up. The answering machine provided a transitional space that was uniquely under Ms. K.'s control. It allowed her to play with being connected, and to explore what she was thinking and feeling as she was experiencing it.

This patient could not tolerate the usual comings and goings of the treatment situation, which impose an experience of separateness. She needed the possibility of having me endlessly, which she could do by talking to my answering machine as if she were talking to me, and she could do this in an abusive, provocative way without destroying the relationship.

The transitional object is a possession used by the child to negotiate the area between the experience of inner and outer reality. Transitional objects are used, as the telephone was in this case, in the development of reality acceptance. In this transitional space Ms. K could accept therapy while rejecting it, accept the therapeutic relationship while at the same time rejecting the terrifying closeness to another person. Just as a transitional object becomes unnecessary and is relinquished in the course of development, in time this patient no longer needed to use the telephone as a transitional space.

Treatment of anorexic, severely masochistic patients is long and difficult because the self-destructive nature of the psychopathology has its roots in every developmental phase. Ms. K. continued to retreat to the magic of pain, but it was possible in the context of an ongoing relationship for her to put her experiences into words.

The telephone as a transitional space was not suggested by me. It was found by the patient, arising out of her deep, unmet needs.

REFERENCES

Aronson, J. K. (1986). The level of object relations and severity of symptoms in the normal weight bulimic patient. *International Journal of Eating Disorders* 5:669–681.

Beebe, B., and Lachmann, F. (1988). The contribution of mother–infant mutual influence to the origins of self and object representations. *Psychoanalytic Psychology* 5:305–337.

Bollas, C. (1987). *The Shadow of the Object: Psychoanalysis of the Unthought Known.* London: Free Association Books.

Chassler, L. (1994). "In Hunger I am King." Understanding anorexia nervosa from a psychoanalytic perspective: theoretical and clinical implications. *Social Work Journal* 22(4):397–415.

Joseph, B. (1982). Addiction to near death. *International Journal of Psycho-Analysis* 63:449–451.

Kiersky, S., and Beebe, B. (1994). The reconstruction of early nonverbal relatedness in the treatment of difficult patients. A special form of empathy. *Psychoanalytic Dialogues* 4(3):389–408.

Markson, E. R. (1993). Depression and moral masochism. *International Journal of Psycho-Analysis* 74:931–940.

Novick, J., and Novick, K. (1991). Some comments on masochism and the delusion of omnipotence. *Journal of the American Psychoanalytic Association* 9:307–331.

Novick, K., and Novick, J. (1987). The essence of masochism. In *Psychoanalytic Study of the Child* 42:353–384. New Haven, CT: Yale University Press.

Ogden, T. H. (1989). The autistic-contiguous position. In *The Primitive Edge of Experience*, pp. 47–81. Northvale, NJ: Jason Aronson.

Wilson, C. P., Hogan, C., and Mintz, I. (1983). *Fear of Being Fat: The Treatment of Anorexia Nervosa and Bulimia.* New York: Jason Aronson.

Winnicott, D. W. (1951). Transitional object and transitional phenomena. In *Collected Papers: Through Paediatrics to Psychoanalysis*. New York: Basic Books.

——(1971). The use of an object and relating through identifications. In *Playing and Reality*. New York: Basic Books.

10 Recovered Memories of Childhood Sexual Abuse: Problems and Concerns

Marilyn A. Austin

One of the most emotional issues of the present time and one that is commonly reported on the newsstands is the incidence of child sexual abuse. Lectures, workshops, support groups; journal, magazine and newspaper articles; TV and radio talk shows–all have devoted time and attention to this widespread problem. It has become a current shock and horror topic, and unfortunately at times has been designed to sensationalize and merchandise this human tragedy. But if this widespread awareness serves to halt the beliefs commonly heard not too long ago that a child is the property of the parents, to do with as they please, then it is time and effort well spent. The private space within the walls of one's home can no longer be accepted as an unquestioned area barred from the norms of what we know to be healthy and growth-promoting. Home is to be a place of nourishment and support, not a den of physical or emotional gratification at the expense of the weaker members of a family.

This chapter in no way is meant to imply a lack of reality or seriousness about the outrage against the abuse of children, or of anyone who has been made a victim of another person who is in some way more powerful. However, the eagerness and fervor of some people involved in the current movement to ferret out all present or past perpetrators of any sort of behavior which could be termed abuse has even resulted in a parody of the situation in a recent comic strip (Outland, *Washington Post*, May 1, 1994). In this strip, the young hero rouses his father from his sleep by declaring that he must be recovering long-repressed childhood memories: "It's all coming back in a rush," he says, "long boozy nights when I was 14 months old . . . how you filled my bottle with harvey wallbangers," and goes on to say that his father tried to sell him in the white slave market as a midget eunuch, and that his father had put a goat's head on him during a satanic ritual when he was 4 years old. He then claims that those memories were triggered by a recent emotional trauma. Father finally rallies himself enough to say "Your allowance is still canceled," as our hero contemplates contacting Geraldo and the police.

Even though this comic strip deals with the subject of recovered memories of abuse with satire, at times the emotionally charged enthusiasm of some of those involved in the uncovering of past abuse bears a certain resemblance to the witch hunts of former years (Gardner 1993).

To avoid the dangers of a witch hunt, we must give careful consideration to some factors that are rarely talked about. These factors have to do both with the influence of the emotional nature of the issue and with the effect of the therapist or counselor who suggests in specific or even in more subtle ways to the troubled client or patient that sexual abuse must lie at the heart of their personal distress. It has been found in the research of Elizabeth Loftus (1991, 1992) and others, that for some people, suggestion can actually produce "memories" that the person believes are true, but that in reality are not.

To illustrate this situation in a therapy setting, I will give examples of two cases in which sexual abuse was considered; then we will look at how the so-called false memories can occur, and possible reasons for the spread of this phenomenon.

CASE ILLUSTRATIONS

The Case of Mr. B.

Mr. B. is a middle-aged professional, an intelligent man with a history of difficulty in sustaining intimate relationships. He was the older of two sons in a stable middle-class family and grew up in a quiet neighborhood of a large city. His symptoms included feelings of great anxiety and sexual dysfunction when in a close, committed relationship with a woman. He had tried various brief therapies, and was well acquainted with theories of human growth and personality development. Other attempts to alleviate his anxieties had had little lasting effect and he was considering resigning himself to a fate of limited personal contact and a life of loneliness. Early in his most recent therapy, he suggested that he thought that he had been sexually abused by his father and had a mental image of oral sexual experiences. He seemed to be searching for some event which could account for his anger at his father and for his overwhelming feelings of having been intruded upon and personally violated. On his own he decided to join an anonymous support group of men who had been sexually abused. Throughout this phase of his treatment, I, as his therapist, maintained a stance of interest, exploration, and openness to whatever might be uncovered, and demurred from taking a stand on the historical reality of his images of sexual abuse. In the course of his treatment I invited him to explore more fully his relationships with his parents and his own inner feelings. He talked more of his memories of a somewhat eroticized and erratic relationship with his mother, and of his resentments toward his father, who reclaimed his mother when father returned home from travels abroad. In addition, his father made a special effort to mold this older son to be the kind of man idealized, but never achieved, by father. His father even seemed to feel he had the right to enter the boy's bedroom at any time and to lecture him on the interests he should have. The result for this patient was an abiding feeling of having been emotionally violated and robbed of a chance to form his own interests and direction. After a few months he stopped going to the support group, saying it wasn't really satisfactory for him. The inadequacies of his father's parenting were enumerated in a multitude of small memories as he continued to free associate during his therapy sessions. He gradually abandoned the belief of a sexual trauma, and said one day that he no longer thought that his father had sexually abused him. As he was free to think his own thoughts and have his own memories, without suggestion from me as his therapist, it became more clear that there probably were substantial parental insufficiencies, an eroticized environment, and arrested personality development, especially on the part of his father, but that the sexual abuse images were not true memories. The focus on the possibility of sexual abuse lost meaning for Mr. B. as a much more full picture of the developmental environment unfolded. It is possible that what this patient experienced as the excessive intrusion by his father and the eroticized relationship with his mother resulted in a belief that there must have been sexual abuse. This thought could easily be suggested by the current pop-psych literature and media presentations which offer a quick answer for anxieties and other problems.

The Case of Mrs. C.

Mrs. C. is a married woman in her mid-twenties. She was the next to oldest in a family of five children. Her parents were highly educated and stressed the importance of the fine arts. She had a history of troubled relationships with schoolmates and often reacted with much defensiveness in situations of relatively ordinary give-and-take. Difficulties continued with many of her later personal relationships with both men and women, and she experienced increasing levels of anxiety, especially around men. A few years after her marriage her anxieties increased to a point where the symptoms interfered with her ability to work and with her relationship with her husband. She went to a therapist who, after listening for two or three sessions, made the pronouncement that she had "all the signs of someone who had been sexually abused," and sent her to a support group for incest survivors. After attending those sessions for nearly a year, she had a "flashback memory," which was in the form of a sudden rush of emotion and a visualized scene of some sort of sexual abuse by a male babysitter when she was 12 years old. A few weeks later she had another "flashback" following a brief visit by her father. This "memory" was of the same incident in a similar setting, but this time she believed herself to be 6 years old and the male figure to be her father. With the encouragement of her therapist and her group, she confronted her parents with the supposed abuse, then cut off all communication with both of them when they denied the validity of the charges. The tragedy is that there is no corroboration of the supposed events, and there was an absolute denial by the parents accused of either conducting or condoning the abuse.

A more full exploration of the dynamics of this person's life revealed that she had been a very active child, who was difficult for her depressed mother to deal with in the context of several other children and an emotionally withdrawn father. This patient reached an early puberty but was unable to talk to her mother about her developing sexual feelings and impulses. Her father related to the children in a casually physical manner by frequently touching and hugging them even after they had grown beyond the childhood years. He denied any sexual contact, but it is possible that this daughter misinterpreted his physical contacts or was sexually stimulated by them. Before Mrs. C. began to attend the support group, she had related to a family member that beginning in early puberty she had been faced with a small group of boys who made lewd comments and touched and stroked her body. This occurred frequently in a setting from which she had felt unable to extract herself, even though it was a public place. She attempted to tell one of her parents but was not able to say specifically enough what was happening, so that she essentially was not heard and not protected. While she was growing up, neither parent was able to discuss matters of sexuality and sexual feelings with their children, so the nature of the difficulties which this child was experiencing remained unknown to the parents.

In both of these cases we see a confusing and sexually charged atmosphere without adequate emotional support from the parents. It may be an easy step for any person searching for a simple answer to their inner distress to seize upon the possibility of sexual abuse, especially when such stories are currently prevalent and when the ideas are suggested by a therapist or a support group. A great variety of contributing factors can be lost to the therapeutic process if the patient is encouraged to focus mainly on the possibility of sexual abuse and to concentrate on the recovery of memories, whether real or fantasized.

The therapist who is sensitive to the possibility that there may be other factors which have led to the affect and the conflicts which the patient is experiencing will better be able to hold various hypotheses in mind while providing the needed "holding environment," as advocated by Winnicott (1971).

The case of Mrs. C., unfortunately, is not rare, as has been confirmed by the records of the False Memory Syndrome Foundation, which is headquartered in Philadelphia and has been gathering much similar data from all over the United States. They also have collected numerous articles from various newspapers and publications which have told of other situations much like the one of Mrs. C.

One article which appeared in the *Los Angeles Times* in 1991 (Wielawski 1991) reported that George Ganaway, a professor at Emory University and an expert in psychiatric aberrations of memory, said that the people who claim falsely that they have been victims of abuse are not necessarily lying. They may have been persuaded by someone, such as a therapist, or even something they have read or seen on television, that the explanation for whatever emotional distress they are experiencing is due to childhood abuse. He said that poorly trained therapists may lead patients to believe falsely that they were abused. The seeds for false memories can be planted by tone of voice, a question phrased in a suggestive way, or by an outright statement such as happened with Mrs. C.

Elizabeth Loftus, of the University of Washington in Seattle, is a psychologist who has done extensive research on memory (1979, 1992, Loftus & Ketchum 1991, Loftus & Loftus 1980). An article which appeared in *Champion* magazine (Daly and Pacifico 1991) reported that Dr. Loftus believes that recall of memories that have not been repressed is tenuous at best, and that recall of repressed memories can be even less reliable. The process of trying to uncover repressed memories is filled with inherent difficulties if the therapist, implicitly or explicitly, suggests anything about the nature of the memories to be recovered. The expectations and pressures felt by the patient within the therapeutic relationship, and perhaps to an even greater extent in certain types of support groups, can lead to memory embellishment, expansions, and even false memories.

The zeal of the current efforts to expose and confront all perpetrators of sexual abuse of children has obscured some of Freud's basic thoughts. In 1897 he wrote, "It seems once again arguable that only later experiences give the impetus to fantasies, which [then] hark back to childhood. . . ." Later, in referring to the effect of the mother's attentions to cleaning the young child's genital area, he wrote, "The fact that the mother . . . unavoidably initiates the child into the phallic phase is, I think, the reason why, in fantasies of later years, the father so regularly appears as the sexual seducer. When the girl turns away from her mother, she also makes over to her father her introduction into sexual life" (Young-Bruehl 1990, p. 335). In a footnote to this quotation Young-Bruehl said,

> When, in his early analyses, Freud's hysterical patients told him that they had been seduced by their father in childhood, he accepted these tales as the truth and regarded the traumas as the cause of their illness. It was not long before

> he recognized his mistake, and he admitted it in a letter to Fliess [of September 21, 1897]. . . . He soon grasped the important fact that these apparently false memories were wishful phantasies, which pointed the way to the existence of the Oedipus complex. [p. 335]

In the fifth of the seven *New Introductory Lectures* (1932), Freud wrote,

> . . . you will recall an interesting episode in the history of analytic research which caused me many distressing hours. In the period in which the main interest was directed to discovering infantile sexual traumas, almost all my women patients told me that they had been seduced by their father. I was driven to recognize in the end that these reports were untrue and so came to understand that hysterical symptoms are derived from phantasies and not from real occurrences. It was only later that I was able to recognize in this phantasy of being seduced by the father the expression of the typical Oedipus complex in women. . . . [p. 120]

Freud, of course, did not abandon the idea of the reality of seduction in some cases, and of the influence of the environment and trauma on the development of pathogenic states. In his 1931 paper, "Female Sexuality," Freud acknowledged that seduction does occur and that the effects can be quite damaging: ". . . when seduction intervenes it invariably disturbs the natural course of the developmental processes, and it often leaves behind extensive and lasting consequences" (p. 232).

This brief elaboration of some of Freud's thoughts is not meant to suggest a return to the era of disbelief of anyone's accusations of sexual harassment, abuse, and rape. The current awareness of sexual violations and the credibility afforded to a woman who makes such allegations must not be sacrificed. We need to be aware, however, that there are innocent families that are being accused and presumed guilty on the basis of the assumed validity of retrieved memories. These are not the cases where there is recent or current abuse, nor the cases of childhood sexual abuse which cannot be forgotten no matter how hard the person may want to forget. What we need to reconsider are the accusations that result from "retrieved memories" without any corroborating evidence or exploration of the facts of the situations or of the personalities of the people involved. In order to consider the accuracy of such accusations, a thorough exploration must be made of time and place, of records of doctors and schools, of relatives and neighbors, and so on. The therapist who becomes involved in such an inquiry, however, would be forgetting what the patient came to therapy for. Some therapists and groups have indeed been acting as investigators. Starting with the premise that a particular patient's symptoms are suggestive of sexual abuse, they have sought to "discover" its existence. When parents say they are not guilty of abusing a child, they may be told that they are "in denial." When a family member or friend does not believe the story of the "victim," that person may be cut off from all future contact. Even when the "victim" does not quite believe what she is being told she must remember, she may be directed to try harder to remember, and to visualize the possibilities.

These are methods used by some therapists and groups which use ideas supported in the popular book, *The Courage to Heal,* written by Ellen Bass and Laura Davis (1988). This and other related books were reviewed last year in an issue of the *New York Times Book Review* in an article by Carol Tavris, a social psychologist, which was titled "Beware the Incest-Survivor Machine" (1993). Tavris reviewed many of the current books about surviving childhood sexual abuse and incest, and concluded that many of them promulgate faulty ideas of the nature of memory and methods to retrieve repressed memories. They also create a whole self-reinforcing movement centered on one's own sense of unhappiness and the blaming of parents and family. When, according to some of these therapists, anyone who suffers from symptoms such as a feeling of being bad or ashamed, a feeling of being powerless or like a victim, a feeling that there is something deep down inside that is wrong with you, a feeling that you are unable to protect yourself in dangerous situations, that you don't have a good sense of your own interests, abilities or goals, that you have trouble getting motivated, that you feel you have to be perfect, and so on–then you most likely were sexually abused as a child, and probably were a victim of incest. Unfortunately, the truth of a possibly very complex substrata of competing conscious and unconscious factors can be too easily overlooked in the pursuit of the particular preconceived notion of a therapist. To paraphrase a statement in a book on research methods (Pedhazur 1991), if we have difficulty thinking of at least three sensible explanations for any observations we make, we should probably choose another profession.

Quite apart from the more unconscious aspects of one's mind, we can look at the writings of Jean Piaget. He wrote that suggestion is a potent disrupter of truth, and he told of a memory he had retained for many years that can illustrate this point. When he was 2 years old, he could recall, he had a brush with a kidnapping attempt. He could remember the place of the event, the strap that held him in his carriage, his nurse valiantly trying to fend off the would-be kidnapper, the scratches on her face sustained during the struggle, a crowd that gathered around, and a description of the policeman who came to their rescue. But many years later, after he had grown and his nurse had retired, his parents received a letter from the old woman confessing how she had made up the whole story to impress her employers and had herself scratched her face to help substantiate the story. Piaget said of this, "I therefore must have heard, as a child, the account of this story, which my parents believed, and projected it into the past in the form of a visual memory" (Piaget and Inhelder 1969). This is a convincing illustration of the power of the mind to create pictorial images of verbal suggestions.

Human suggestibility should not be underestimated as a powerful influence on memory. With no original memory of an event, misleading information can create a belief, according to Toland and colleagues in a chapter of Schumaker's book *Human Suggestibility* (1991). A strong influence on memory is the believed expertise of the source of the misleading suggestions. It is easy to see how a therapist, to whom a person has turned for relief from emotional pain, can be in this position of great influence. Anna Freud pointed out that the person's need to be loved and the fear of object loss take the form of suggestibility and compliance toward the therapist (1965). The therapist who starts a therapy with the presupposition that certain symptoms are most likely indicative of repressed memories of sexual abuse overtly or subtly shapes and reinforces the patient's memory retrieval. The patient, in the attempt not only to be rid of the symptoms but also to please the therapist, may eventually create memories of abuses that never occurred.

The phenomena of memory, how it works, how it is stored and retrieved, have been studied for years. The former belief was that memory stores exact information, and if one can just retrieve a memory (even through hypnosis), then it is a truth and a fact. More recent research, however, has led to a different view of memory. Alain Robbe-Grillet, in Robyn Dawes's book *Rational Choice in an Uncertain World* (1988), said that memory belongs in the realm of the imagination. Human memory should not be thought of as a computer that records things; it is part of the imaginative process and can be considered to be similar to invention. Memory can be seen as a reconstruction, not a reproduction. Memory integrates the past with the present, so that the desires, fantasies, fears, moods, and so on of the present and the past can become merged in the form of a seemingly accurate memory.

Ernst Kris (1975), in his paper on the recovery of childhood memories, said, "Not only does the present experience rest on the past, but the present supplies the incentive for the viewing of the past; the present selects, colors, and modifies. Memory, at least autobiographical or personal memory, . . . is dynamic and telescopic" (p. 303).

Anna Freud, in referring to analysts who tend to be misled by the telescopic character of memory, said,

> . . . the single dramatic shock, e.g., seduction at an early age, usually does not appear in sharp outline; the experience is overlaid with its aftermath, the guilt, terror, and thrill elaborated in fantasy, and the defense against these fantasies. We are misled if we believe that we are able, except in rare instances, to find the "events" of the afternoon on the staircase when the seduction happened. . . ." [Kris 1975, p. 324]

Shengold (1989) raised the question "What is truth? Can the observer be sure that what has been recounted has actually happened?" In Freud's theory, "a psychic life of fantasy, in large part unconscious, developed in the course of transforming instinctual drives and body feelings. . . . He never minimized the role of the environment or of traumatic intrusion and interference in pathogenesis. He was aware of the past and continuing actuality of 'seduction by the father' for some of his patients" (p. 15). Shengold also said that "Differentiating fantasy from memory to determine if an event really occurred is never easy and sometimes impossible. Memory and fantasy are always intertwined. . . ." (p. 16).

In *The Analytic Attitude*, Roy Schafer (1983) held the view that accounts of the past are a reconstruction and a recontextualization. There may be a thematic revision and a filling in of details from present experiences. There is no paucity of similar thought among analytic writings concerning the workings of the memory.

But how does it occur that so many people can begin to believe that they have accurate memories which have suddenly been retrieved after decades of absence? How is it that memories can go astray?

Paul Watzlawick (1984), in *The Invented Reality: How Do We Know What We Believe We Know?*, talked about self-fulfilling prophecies. Expectations play a role in bringing about what has been expected. Einstein observed that the theory with which we start can determine what we are able to observe. Or as one person so cogently observed, "Believing is seeing" (Pedhazur and Schmelkin 1991, p. 181).

Physiological research has recognized that the limbic structures are important for emotional experiences. Pierre Gloor and colleagues, in Montreal, wrote that "unless limbic structures are activated . . . experiential phenomena do not occur" (Rosenfield 1988, p. 164). Affective or motivational significance may be the limbic element involved in the process of recall.

An experience to be recorded permanently makes a biochemical impression in the hippocampus, which then sends the sounds, sights, and smells through a network of nerve cells to various areas of the brain. Our recall consists of fragments of past experiences or memory traces, and these are biased by our current beliefs or feelings concerning what must be true. The patterns and constructs of what is recalled in memory-image are even more influenced by present moods and beliefs, especially if the affect is relatively intense.

The emotional and motivational components of the incest survivors movement provides limbic activation. When this activation is combined with the fragments of memory, which are then interpreted, elaborated upon, and integrated or constructed into a whole, we can see how these false memories can come about, and can have little or no resemblance to past experience. This emotional context could be sufficient to reconstruct bits of memories into an inaccurate whole. We are likely to recall in ways organized to make sense to a present expectation, in ways that reinforce our belief in the conclusions we have already reached about how the past determined the present. Without consciously doing this, we actually make up stories about our lives, the world, and reality in general. But often it is the story that creates the memory, rather than the other way around, according to Robyn Dawes (1988).

On the permanence of stored information, Loftus and Loftus (1980) wrote, "Not only might the originally acquired memory have departed from reality in some systematic way, but the memory may have been continually subject to change after it was initially stored" (p. 419). Daniel Friedman, a professor of psychiatry at UCLA, said that we can never recall things purely. Memory is a creative process which is built up with layers of successive experiences and interpretations (Wielawski 1991).

In *The Psychology of the Child* by Piaget and Inhelder (1969) there is an account of some of the experiments of W. G. Penfield in the early 1900s. Penfield reactivated memories by use of electrical stimulation of the temporal lobes and was able to confirm the existence of false but vivid memories. The experiments confirmed the views of Pierre Janet that memory is a reconstruction. Image-memory is governed by schemes of a person's understanding rather than pure perception of an object or event.

Working in the field of psychology and information processing, Atkinson and Shiffrin (1968) have been studying long-term memory storage. It was their view that this type of stored information does not decay, but that it is stored in pieces. People remember fragments, and then they will construct the fill-in material.

Paris and Lindauer (1977) enhanced Piaget's view of memory by saying that what is to be remembered must be assimilated. Assimilation is a process that involves comprehending and encoding; it is a "constructive memory." That is, something must be perceived and interpreted to make sense and may even add features to make the event comprehensible. In this view, retrieval of memory is also a reconstruction. According to Flavell (1985), ". . . the memory machine is nothing at all like a tape recorder or camera. We most emphatically do not simply take mental photographs of inputs at storage and then simply develop them at retrieval" (p. 215). Retrieved memories will be in fragments, with present understanding and inferences molding the pieces together to make what seems to be a unified whole—one that makes sense to the person at this present time.

Cognitive psychologists, such as Brewer and Treyens (1981), would say that we use schema in memory; we put together the fragments retrieved and fill in the blanks according to schemas which make sense to our understanding. We select, abstract, interpret, and elaborate, then integrate it all into a whole, that is, into what we are prepared to understand.

Elizabeth Loftus (1992) said that there are conflicting views on repressed memories which one day rise up from some recess of the mind into consciousness. The clinical anecdotes are legion, especially in the literature of those dealing with survivors of childhood sexual abuse. However, there apparently is no controlled laboratory research which confirms the concept of repressed memories. Loftus has received numerous letters from parents who were suddenly accused of having sexually abused a child, maybe twenty, thirty or forty years ago. Those memories frequently had emerged during the course of a therapy.

Ganaway (1989, 1991) suggested that an abuse memory may be manufactured from an inner motivation to provide a screen for more prosaic but actually less tolerable factual traumatic material. The details of the supposed incidents themselves can be suggested from such literature as the plethora of books and articles about sexual abuse, as well as from the suggestions of therapists and group members.

Memory blocks shut out significant parts of one's history, according to Loftus, and leave a person without a good explanation for negative feelings about oneself. When suggestions are made, subtly or insistently, some patients oblige the therapist. When the list of symptoms that supposedly are indicative of sexual abuse is read, almost everyone fits because they include most of human woes.

Loftus and Ketcham (1991) reported that there are hundreds of studies that support a high degree of memory distortion, and that post-event information can become incorporated into memory, filling in blanks, reconstructing, and transposing.

Many of the memory distortion studies involve incidents without much personal trauma, but a study of a violent event in 1984 when a sniper shot at children on a school playground (Pynoos and Nader, as cited in Loftus 1992) showed interesting results. The researchers interviewed ten percent of the student body, six to sixteen weeks after the event. What they found was that even some who were away from the site, and one boy who actually was away on vacation, had "memories" of being there, of hearing shots, and seeing people lying on the ground.

In experiments, "memories" have been implanted of "getting lost when you were about 5 years old." Loftus's work involved five pilot subjects who were told by a trusted relative about an event, using familiar settings, when the subject supposedly got lost. The subjects, who were from 8 to 40 years old at the time of the experiment, at first had no memory of the event. Then within a span of several days, they began to "remember" the event, what was said, details of the setting and people, what they wore, where they went, and how they were rescued. But the entire suggestion was fantasy; there was in actuality no such time when they were lost.

As stated earlier, there may be a similarity between the pursuit of the possibility of sexual abuse in one's past, and the pursuit of witches in the middle ages. Trevor-Roper (1967), the eminent British historian who wrote extensively of those witch hunts, considered the witch craze to be a social movement. Can we today think of the search for sexual abuse to be a social movement?

Certain contemporary factors may be contributing to the simplistic way of thinking which is involved in some of the characteristics of the movement to search out sexual abuse. One is a rather human temptation to view all things on a balance of cause and effect. This classical linear causality creates a split between subject and object. The subject becomes inert or, in this case, the victim; the object is the active perpetrator. A bright flash or loud noise, for instance, brings an autonomic reaction to prepare for fight or flight. However, we should not forget that a person's interpretation of a situation as dangerous also brings about a similar autonomic reaction. It cannot be assumed that there is a particular cause to any particular effect. This would mean disregarding the interrelating aspects of the human system and denying the contribution of physiological preconditions, which interact with the many inner urges and conflicts and with a multitude of environmental influences.

In addition to the easy appeal of reductionist thinking, it can also be easy to think of oneself as "victim." Young (1992) wrote about the position of victimhood as being powerful. To see oneself as victim can provide the illusion of a shield against the difficulties of assuming appropriate personal responsibility for one's own feelings, actions, or even inactions. To many, it may seem not at all appealing to take a painful look at one's own decisions and to consider how these may have contributed to one's own unhappiness. Seeing oneself as "victim" can enable one to retain an illusion of innocence and a belief that a perfect world can exist if only others were perfect in providing the sort of life we would like to have.

Tragically, physical and sexual abuse does occur far too often, and the aftermath of this distortion of human relationships must be dealt with in appropriate and sensitive therapeutic ways. But, in our thinking as a society and a culture, and in our work as therapists and researchers into the human condition, we do not want to become caught up in simplistic thinking and blaming. We have learned to appreciate the complexities of human life and development and of the multitude of factors involved. Enthusiasm does not replace careful exploration.

As therapists, we need to keep in mind the essential factors in mental and emotional health, which include responsibility for one's own emotional well-being. The patients or clients who come for therapy have placed their vulnerabilities in our hands as trusted professionals. Knowing what we know of some of the mechanics and fallibilities of memory, we are obligated to use caution in treating these memories as fact. The concentration of our efforts should be on working with the emotional state of what the memories represent. Human problems are most often complex issues, replete with ambiguities and murky memories, and usually not based on simple cause and effect.

REFERENCES

Atkinson, R., and Shiffrin R. (1968). Human memory: a proposed system and its control processes. In *The Psychology of Learning and Motivation,* ed. R. W. Spence & J. T. Spence. New York: Academic Press.

Bass, E., and Davis, L. (1988). *The Courage to Heal.* New York: Harper & Row.

Brewer, W., and Treyens, J. (1981). Role of schemata in memory for places. *Cognitive Psychology* 13:207–230.

Daly, L., and Pacifico, J. F. (1991). Opening the doors to the past: decade delayed disclosure of memories of years gone by. *Champion,* December, pp. 43–47.

Dawes, R. (1988). *Rational Choice in an Uncertain World.* New York: Harcourt Brace Jovanovich.

—— (1991). Biases of retrospection. *Issues in Child Abuse Accusations* 1(3): 25–28.

Flavell, J. H. (1985). Memory. In *Cognitive Development.* Englewood Cliffs, NJ: Prentice Hall, pp. 206–241.

Freud, A. (1965). *Normality and Pathology in Childhood: Assessments of Development.* Madison, CT: International Universities Press.

Freud, S. (1932). New introductory lectures on psychoanalysis. *Standard Edition,* 22:3–182.

Ganaway, G. (1989). Historical versus narrative truth: clarifying the role of exogenous trauma in the etiology of MPD and its variants. *Dissociation,* 2:205–220.

—— (1991). *Alternative hypotheses regarding satanic ritual abuse memories.* Paper presented at the American Psychological Association Annual Meeting, San Francisco.

Gardner, R. (1992). *True and False Accusations of Child Sex Abuse.* Cresskill, NJ: Creative Therapeutics.

—— (1993). Modern witch hunt–child abuse charges. *Wall Street Journal* Monday, February 22, p. 10.

Kris, E. (1975). *Selected Papers of Ernst Kris.* New Haven: Yale University Press.

Loftus, E. (1979). *Eyewitness Testimony*. Cambridge, MA: Harvard University Press.

—— (1992). *The reality of repressed memories*. Paper presented at the American Psychological Association Annual Meeting, Washington, D.C.

Loftus, E., and Ketchum, K. (1991). *Witness for the Defense*. New York: St. Martin's Press.

Loftus, E., and Loftus, G. (1980). On the permanence of stored information in the human brain. *American Psychologist* 35(5):419.

Paris, S., and Lindauer, B. (1977). Constructive aspects of children's comprehension and memory. In *Perspectives on the Development of Memory and Cognition*, ed. R. V. Kail, Jr., and J. W. Hagen. Hillsdale, NJ: Lawrence Erlbaum.

Pedhazur, E., and Schmelkin, L. (1991). *Measurement, Design, and Analysis: An Integrated Approach*. Hillsdale, NJ: Lawrence Erlbaum.

Piaget, J., and Inhelder, B. (1969). *The Psychology of the Child*. New York: Basic Books.

Rosenfield, I. (1988). *The Invention of Memory: A New View of the Brain*. New York: Basic Books.

Schafer, R. (1983). *The Analytic Attitude*. New York: Basic Books.

Schumaker, J. F. (1991). *Human Suggestibility*. New York: Routledge.

Shengold, L. (1989). *Soul Murder: The Effects of Childhood Abuse and Deprivation*. New Haven: Yale University Press.

Tavris, C. (1993). Beware the incest-survivor machine. *New York Times*, January 3, pp. 1, 16–17.

Toland, K., Hoffman, H., and Loftus, E. (1991). How suggestion plays tricks with memory. In *Human Suggestibility*, ed. J. Schumaker, pp. 235–252. New York: Routledge.

Trevor-Roper, H. R. (1967). *Religion, the Reformation, and Social Change*. London: Macmillan.

Watzlawick, P. (1984). *The Invented Reality*. New York: Norton.

Wielawski, I. (1991). Unlocking the secrets of memory. *Los Angeles Times*, October 3.

Winnicott, D. W. (1971). *Playing and Reality*. New York: Basic Books.

Young, C. (1992). Victimhood is powerful. *Reason*, October, pp. 18–23.

Young-Bruehl, E. (1990). *Freud on Women: A Reader*. New York: Norton.

11 The Adult Survivor of Childhood Sexual Abuse: Linking Inner and Outer World

Roberta Graziano

> There is, in each survivor, an imperative need to *tell* and thus to come to *know* one's story, unimpeded by ghosts from the past against which one has to protect oneself. One has to know one's buried truth in order to be able to live one's life.
>
> –Dori Laub

Trauma, and the violence it often wreaks on the human psyche, has become open of late to renewed attention by such disciplines as sociology, psychology, and psychoanalysis, as well as becoming a focus of inquiry and exploration in history, literature, and film. Such interest, however, has not yet led to explanations, cures, or solutions, perhaps because traumatic experience does not lend itself to linear or logical explication. In this chapter, I am concerned with the inner space and the outer world of the survivor of childhood sexual and physical abuse. Like Caruth (1991), "I am interested not so much in defining trauma . . . than in attempting to understand its surprising impact: to examine how trauma unsettles and forces us to rethink our notions of experience, and of communication, in therapy . . . as well as in psychoanalytic theory" (p. 2).

This chapter describes the interaction between two key issues, trust and fragmentation, which I believe are of central importance in working with abuse survivors. After examining pertinent psychoanalytic concepts,

I will then relate them to specific issues in the treatment of adult survivors of childhood sexual and physical abuse. An extended case study and discussion will follow.

TRUST

One of the most striking phenomena encountered in dealing with adult survivors of child sexual and physical abuse is that of mistrust. The child who develops in an "average expectable environment" (Hartmann 1958) has reason to believe that significant adults will protect him from danger and pain, rather than inflict the same. The child who grows up in an atmosphere that includes disregard of her needs for security and nurturance, where body and even mind can be regarded as the property of those older and more powerful, may not only not trust others, but also mistrust her own perceptions, needs, and wishes.

The difficulty in trusting others, as well as in the validity of one's own rightful needs, may begin, for some adult survivors of child abuse, in very early developmental experiences, such as "cumulative trauma," as described by Khan (1963). Here, breaches in the "protective shield" of the early and ongoing environment, caused by the intrusion of the mother's personal requirements and conflicts into the sphere of the infant/child's needs, lead to an ongoing failure to adapt to those needs. This leads to a precocious development, in which the child becomes especially responsive to the mother's needs.

Similarly, Winnicott (1960b) describes the development of the true self as taking place in an adequately caring and empathic early environment, and the evolution of a false self to protect the true self when such an environment does not exist. Kohut's (1971, 1977, 1984) formulations about parental mirroring and its role in recognizing and communicating to the child his or her own uniqueness are also pertinent to the early development of trust in others and self.

For other survivors of childhood abuse, lack of trust may be the outcome of traumatic events which occur somewhat later, but which may be violent and/or confusing enough to affect, most adversely, the individual's subsequent beliefs about the safety of events, situations, and people. Ferenczi (1933), who reintroduced the seduction hypothesis and hoped to reintegrate the reality of childhood sexual abuse into the mainstream of psychoanalysis, noted that children want tenderness, not sexual passion, from their parents, and that the pathological adult responds with aggression and the intrusion of adult sexual needs. However, afterward "Almost always the perpetrator behaves as though nothing had happened . . ." (p. 162). Sexual misuse is often accompanied by or followed with physical punishment of the child. "The consequence must needs be that of confusion of tongues. . . " (p. 164). Further, "When subjected to a sexual attack, under the pressure of such traumatic urgency. . . . One is justified–in contradistinction to the familiar regression–to speak of a *traumatic progression,* of a *precocious maturity*" (p. 165, italics original), similar to Khan's formulation.

Rather than trust, then, we can expect the adult survivor of childhood sexual and physical abuse to approach therapy and therapist with extreme caution. There may be an exquisite attunement to the therapist's needs as well as disbelief in the therapist's care and concern, a concomitant disregard of or lack of conviction about the patient's own needs, and the use of defenses and ways of relating which are designed to protect against further traumatization. These may include compliance, denial, and dissociation.

FRAGMENTATION

The phenomena that may be observed in therapy when the abovementioned defenses and modes of relating are activated, in reaction to the threat of retraumatization, have been described and conceptualized by psychoanalytic theorists in a variety of ways.

Winnicott (1949) describes a splitting of mind from emotions in response to trauma: "It seems to me that *it is in relation to the border-line of intolerable reaction phases that the intellect begins to work as something distinct from the psyche*" (p. 191, italics original). Further, the mind can be said to split from the body.

> There is a state of affairs in which the fear is of a madness, that is to say, a fear of a *lack of anxiety at regression* to an unintegrated state, to absence of a sense of living in the body, etc. The fear is . . . that there will be a regression, from which there may be no return. [Winnicott 1952, p. 100, italics original]

Winnicott uses the terms *unintegration, disintegration,* and *depersonalization* in connection with these processes.

Kohut (1977) discusses "a deeper unnameable dread experienced when a person feels that his self is becoming seriously enfeebled or is disintegrating. . . . the dread of the loss of his self—the fragmentation of and the estrangement from his body and mind in space, the breakup of the sense of his continuity in time" (p. 105). It will be noted that the larger context of the above statements refers, in general, not to overwhelming traumata from events in the larger environment, such as those experienced by survivors of war, the Holocaust, natural disasters or accidents, but to failures in parental empathy and the early caretaker–child interaction, ranging from moderate to severe. For concepts specifically dealing with the intrapsychic impact of severely traumatic experiences, it is necessary to turn to the work of psychoanalysts who addressed these events and their relationship to fragmentation.

Ferenczi (1933), specifically in relation to child sexual abuse, identifies what might now be called the genesis of Multiple Personality Disorder, the extreme outcome of dissociation:

> If the shocks increase in number during the development of the child, the number and the various kinds of splits in the personality increase too, and soon it becomes extremely difficult to maintain contact without confusion with all the fragments, each of which behaves as a separate personality yet does not know of even the existence of the others. Eventually it may arrive at a state which—continuing the picture of *fragmentation*—one would be justified in calling *atomization*. [p. 165, italics original].

Krystal (1978) traces the development of Freud's thinking about trauma from his work with Breuer in *Studies on Hysteria* (1893–1895) and describes "one paradigm of psychic trauma: an individual is confronted with *overwhelming* affects: in other words, his affective responses produce an unbearable psychic state which threatens to disorganize, perhaps even destroy, all psychic functions" (Krystal 1978, pp. 82–83, italics original). If the traumatic situation, as the individual appraises it, is overwhelming, according to Freud (1926), the admission of helplessness implies a change from anxiety to surrender, submission, emotional blocking, and inhibition. This process is discussed by Krystal as "becoming a threat to the functioning, integrity, and even survival of the individual" (1978, p. 93), who may display a "psychic closing off . . . a virtually complete suppression of all affect expression and perception" (p. 95). Those who have experienced severe childhood trauma may exhibit chronic anhedonia, perhaps attributable to their lifelong dread, as well as continuing expectation, of the trauma's return. Fragments of memory may rouse intense affects, but "the capacity to tolerate emotions becomes diminished. In addition, there is a regression in the affects themselves, both their cognitive and expressive aspects. This regression accounts for the high incidence of psychosomatic disorders, and the disturbance in affectivity and capacity for verbalization which Sifneos (1967) called *alexithymia*" (Krystal 1978, p. 109). In alexithymia, which literally means "without words for feelings," emotional arousal is responded to by a denial not of "the reality of the triggering event but a denial of the emotions aroused by it" (Jones 1991, p. 239). This disavowal severs the connection between incident and affect.

TRUST VS. FRAGMENTATION: DILEMMA, PARADOX, AND THERAPY

The lack of trust, fragmentation, and associated alexithymia exhibited by many survivors of childhood sexual and physical abuse pose a central dilemma, namely: in therapy, undeniably a verbal medium, how do we deal with a lack of words for feelings, if the merest movement toward expressing them produces overwhelming fear of, as well as demonstrable episodes of, fragmentation? Put another way, with an individual who has ample reason to be mistrustful, how can we establish enough trust to engage in a working relationship, which will then entail verbalizing affects which are perceived internally as lethal?

There exists, however, beneath the mistrust and inability to put words to feelings, an unremitting need to tell, to have another bear witness. If this life task remains undone, for many survivors life will become an ongoing battle between the push to reveal, the terror of fragmentation and the inability to explain:

> There are never enough words or the right words, there is never enough time or the right time, and never enough listening or the right listening to articulate the story that cannot be captured in *thought, memory*, and *speech*. The pressure thus continues unremittingly, and if words are not trustworthy or adequate, the life that is chosen can become the vehicle by which the struggle to tell continues. [Laub 1991, p. 77, italics original]

The task for the therapist, then, is to provide *enough* time, *enough* listening, so that at the *right* time, with the *right* kind of listening, the memories and their associated affects can be put into words and experienced in the presence of the therapist-as-witness. This may entail making provisions for listening that differ from the traditional parameters of time and space in analytic psychotherapy.

Clearly, it may take a long time for a survivor to develop trust, in spite of the therapist's efforts to create a safe, nonthreatening atmosphere. The paradox may be that, the more the survivor begins to trust, and to believe that indeed therapy may be a safe place, the more intense will be the thrust to disclose, and the more profound the threat of fragmentation, which will produce more mistrust. (How can this therapist, who is saying, at least implicitly, that "it will help to talk about it" and "trust me that talking will help you to feel better," be really trustworthy if I feel like I will fall apart, or be destroyed, die, or go crazy, if I tell?) The trust–fragmentation–mistrust cycle may continue for some time, and needs to be tolerated, until very gradually the survivor may establish enough trust to risk trying to link words and feelings. Until then, alternating episodes of telling details or pieces of memories in a strictly narrative, affectless manner, and displaying evidence of overwhelming affects without any memories of what brought them on or words to describe them, may take place repeatedly.

Time, especially under circumstances where a survivor is not in analysis and/or cannot have several therapy sessions each week, may need to be thought of in terms of the length of a given session. I have found that, especially with survivors who have moved toward "telling" but are clearly involved in the cycle I described above, a longer session has proved helpful. Survivors with whom I have used a weekly two-hour session have been able to become comfortable enough to risk disclosing details and talking about memories, experiencing powerful emotions and recovering from their effects, during this longer time-span, when they were unable to do so in two one-hour weekly sessions. (One survivor commented, after we began to use two-hour sessions, that a one-hour session gave only time to talk about the everyday, unimportant details of her life, and that just about the time she began to feel safe enough to hazard talking about overpowering feelings associated with years of sexual abuse by two older brothers and both sexual and physical abuse by her mother, it was time to end the session.)

The trust–fragmentation–mistrust cycle reflects issues of closeness and distance, especially apt for adult survivors of child sexual abuse, the majority of whom were abused by a family member. Most of the survivors I have worked with have serious problems with intimate relationships, and are intensely fearful of closeness, emotional as well as physical and/or sexual. I have discovered that, as a survivor begins to feel more trusting, there is often a physical movement toward the therapist which may be a more reliable indicator of increasing comfort than surface verbalizations. With that in mind, I put a small sofa into my office a while ago. Before then there were only two chairs to choose from, one somewhat further away from my chair than the other. Since the change of furniture, the survivors I am currently working with have chosen various degrees of distance from me. Those with whom I have been working longest and who have moved considerably along in the cycle have sat on the sofa near my chair, and on occasion have asked me to sit next to them. Those who are still furthest away in terms of trust and fear of fragmentation tend to sit farthest away and never ask me to sit near them. I believe that it is important to let the survivor choose and change the physical closeness, and that this can affect the development of trust.

The dissociation, depersonalization, and fragmentation experienced by survivors can extend into the verbal realm in more than spoken language. I have learned from many of my clients that they have kept journals and/or written stories or poetry at many times during their lives, but that they did not connect the meaning of what they wrote to the abuse experiences, and often did not remember writing it. I have encouraged them to write, especially when fragments of abuse events begin to resurface in nightmares and flashbacks, as a way of bearing witness to the reality of what happened to them. On many occasions, they have brought their current writings into the sessions and we have worked together to link the written words with spoken ones This may cause more memories to emerge, temporarily leading to reactivation of the cycle, but also providing more writings and opportunities for linkage.

Another procedure that, though much debated, has proven useful in providing connections between affects and words, is physical touch. Winnicott (1960a) has discussed the need for providing "the environmental condition of *holding*," which may take a physical form when verbal soothing is insufficient. Little (1990), an analyst herself, has described the effect on her of physical holding in her analysis with Winnicott, as well as the effect of holding in her work with patients. Ferenczi, in his article entitled "Child-Analysis in the Analysis of Adults" (1931), discussed the use both of a longer session and of physical touch when a patient is demonstrating "the reproduction of the mental and physical agony which follows upon incomprehensible and intolerable woe. . . . Tactful and calming words, reinforced perhaps by an encouraging pressure of the hand, or, if that is not enough, a friendly stroking of the patient's head, helped to mitigate the reaction to a point at which he again became accessible" (p. 138). Horner has described the lasting adverse effects of the refusal of two of her therapists to meet her need for physical holding (Kupfermann and Smaldino 1987). I have found that holding a survivor's hand, if asked to, or putting an arm around a shoulder, when requested, helps both to decrease the intense terror manifested during flashbacks and, perhaps more importantly, to enable the survivor to put the feelings being experienced into words.

In order to illustrate the clinical application of the foregoing material, I would like to provide a case example. The following is the story of a survivor currently in treatment.

EVA: A SURVIVOR OF SEVERE CHILDHOOD ABUSE

Eva, now 50 , is a widowed Cuban health professional who was referred to my private practice over nine years ago. In our first session, she told me that her reason for seeking therapy was that her husband was terminally ill. He had been comatose for six months, and Eva was finding it increasingly difficult to deal with this situation. Eva did not tell me much about her early life, except to say that she was "raised by nuns who were punitive and abusive," and that she had attempted suicide a number of years before, while at work. This action had led to the suspension of her professional license, and she was now surviving on her husband's disability and supplementing that income with occasional part-time work at minimum wage. It became increasingly clear in the session that she was extremely suicidal and, after immediate consultation with my psychiatrist colleague, she was hospitalized. When she was discharged, on antidepressants, four weeks later, I asked whether she would like to resume seeing me privately, or would prefer to see me in the hospital's outpatient clinic, where I worked part-time. She chose the clinic, where her medications could be monitored and there was a sliding fee scale.

The first two years of our work together consisted of sessions where Eva was often unable to speak for long periods, despite considerable encouragement on my part and my conscious efforts to be soothing and nonthreatening. When she did talk, it was about her marriage, in which she had been verbally, sexually and occasionally physically abused by her husband (who, himself Caucasian, made disparaging remarks about minorities, forced intercourse against her will, and once held a gun to her head, among other things). On rare occasions, she would speak of her life at the orphanage where she had spent the years from about 5 to 14. Then, she would look unbearably distressed, and at least twice she fainted in my office. Nevertheless, she went off medication after a few months, under psychiatric supervision, and continued coming more or less regularly to her sessions.

After about two years, Eva became involved in an affair with someone she had met through her employer. It soon became evident that this was yet another abusive relationship, and I experienced considerable frustration at not being able to help her to connect her past experiences (with the nuns and her husband) to her current distress. After a year of increasing unhappiness, however, and what I discerned as a concomitant increase in her suicidal potential, she finally, with tremendous shame, told me that she thought she had a drinking problem, and didn't know what I would think of her. After I assured her that I was glad that she had told me, that I would help her to get help, and that I would continue to work with her, I made a collateral referral to a colleague at the clinic who was an experienced substance abuse counselor. With her encouragement, despite great trepidation, Eva was able to go to AA, and has been sober for many years.

Sobriety did not bring Eva immediate relief from her problems. It did, however, enable her to terminate the abusive relationship within a few months, and to deal with her husband's death a year into her sobriety, despite flashbacks before the funeral. (By that time, he had been in a coma for more than four years.) Further, as she emerged from her pattern of drinking and/or drugging to numb the flashbacks and memories, she was able to give a somewhat more coherent account of her life, though, given her "avoidance of the recognition of the nature of inner reality" (Krystal 1991, p. 115), there were still many gaps and inconsistencies. Eva's earliest memory was of her mother trying to kill herself by jumping out of a window, and of herself, aged 2½, trying to stop her. (Her mother, a recent immigrant who was barely 20, deserted by her husband, already had three children. She was taken to a state hospital, where she remained for more than twenty years.) Eva and her siblings were taken in by an aunt who had several children of her own, but after a period of time this arrangement became unworkable. At that point, Eva and her siblings were brought to "the Home," a large Catholic orphanage far away from the city, where the children were separated by age and sex.

What Eva was able to tell me, in very small doses, about life at "the Home" was that the regimentation was total, punishment was constant, and there was no escape. In addition to beatings and sadistic punishments, such as kneeling for hours on gravel, the nuns had also sexually abused Eva. She wasn't sure why she was the target of this treatment, and felt "different" because she didn't know of anyone else who had had that experience. Was it because she was one of the few minority children in a Catholic institution of the 1940s and 1950s? Was it because, at least early on, she spoke out against the harsh treatment she saw being inflicted on other children? In any case, the same nuns who slept and ate with the children also taught them in the classroom, where physical abuse and verbal humiliation were commonplace.

Over time, Eva told me of at least one childhood suicide attempt (drinking a large bottle of cough medicine), as well as self-destructive behavior, such as lacerating the inside of her mouth with a sharp metal object. She also witnessed the accidental death of other children on two occasions, as well as having to be present at the funerals of nuns. My reaction to these pieces of information was as much related to her manner of telling me, which was in a monotone, in fragments, interspersed with information about her everyday activities, as it was related to the information itself, which was almost too much to comprehend. As Eva herself said, "They told us we were children of God, and they were there to be like our parents. Where was God, if they could be doing things like that to us? They were the representatives of God, so they couldn't do anything wrong, which meant I was bad for hating them and what they did."

Some years ago, I left the clinic. Eva continued to see me as a private patient. Shortly after this arrangement began, the malpractice suit that she had instituted in connection with her husband's "wrongful death" was settled for a large sum. For the first time in many years, Eva was able to live comfortably. She decided to go back to school to obtain a college degree, a longstanding dream. She also decided to petition the state licensing department to restore her health care license, as her career and professional identity had been a great source of pride to her.

Eva has succeeded in getting her license restored, despite the terror of the appeal process (which was extremely adversarial in nature, and at which I testified on her behalf). She has attended college part-time and is now majoring in history, a strong interest which she has pursued with great energy. She has made many enduring friendships in both AA and college, and lately was involved in a brief sexual relationship in which, for the first time in her life, she was able to enjoy sex with no flashbacks or fears. However, as she has expanded her activities in her outside life, and moved closer to others in relationships, the memories, flashbacks, and nightmares have intensified, becoming more intrusive and vivid. Until recently, she had been unable to give a coherent account of any of them, though with the use of longer sessions and flexibility of closeness and distance in the office it was clear that she was moving toward integration of memory and affect. She began writing letters and poems about two weeks before the session I am about to describe.

At the beginning of the session, Eva sat in a chair across the room from me, which was different from her usual position. (For several months, she had sat on the couch, and had asked me to sit on the couch as well.) I sat down in my chair. Eva appeared tense and drawn. She began talking about not feeling comfortable inside her own skin, having trouble with flashbacks. She had brought me a poem that she had written a few days before, when in distress, along with a letter to me. She asked me to read the poem aloud:

One, two, three, four, five, six
Start the count over
Stay still, don't move
When will it be over?

Sad, sad, you are bad
You're not to speak
You have been had.
I'll leave for awhile
I have to, you see
No one here
To hold me.

Stop, stop, don't hit me anymore
I don't care what's in store.
Dead, dead, yes that's what I am.
She wonders no more.
Her soul is in a distant land.

I have a question: "Why?"
No one is in.
Oh well, just more lies.

As with other items she had written in the past two weeks, Eva stated that she had no memory of writing and did not recognize the material afterward as having been written by her, though it was clear to her that each time she had written about incidents which aroused powerful, immediate memories and feelings.

Eva moved to the couch and asked me to sit there. She went on to say that she had felt distant from me at the beginning of the session because she was afraid. She had been thinking about stopping therapy soon but realized that this was in large part because she was terrified of her feelings. I asked her what kind of feelings caused such terror. She was unable to speak for a few moments. Her face expressed deep sadness and foreboding as she stated that she had been on the edge of telling me some memories for weeks now, but that she was convinced that if she did, she would die or explode like a volcano: "I feel like a little kid–helpless and terrified. They're still going to get me." I replied that though I knew she felt like a small, helpless child when her memories overwhelmed her, she was really an adult. I asked whether she thought grownup Eva and grownup Roberta together could help the little kid. Eva was silent. I went on, "I know the little kid was terrified into silence and believed that terrible things would happen to her if she ever told–like maybe she would die. But all the people that did those things are not here any more. Do you think that we are strong enough to help the little girl? Perhaps we can start by helping her talk to one of them who maybe wasn't as scary as the others."

Eva was silent again. When she began to talk, her face wore a faraway look, as it had many times before when she was immersed in a flashback. This time, her pain and fear were even more evident. She said, "Sister Rose Kathleen." She stopped abruptly, looking terrified. I said, "You named a name and you are afraid that something will happen to you."

She said, "I thought I would go straight to hell. But it's a worse hell not being able to talk." I replied, "You're still here. I know it's scary."

Eva went on, after a pause: "I thought I would die when I saw her in the hospital. She was dying of cancer. It was my first year as a health professional and she ended up on my unit. She was all skinny then. I remembered her as being very large and heavy. When I saw her in that bed, I wanted to kill her. I couldn't tell anybody. Nobody knew about my past. I fell apart–I didn't really drink much then, but I went out after work and drank to forget. I was so frightened and so angry, and I had nowhere to go with my feelings."

Eva paused again, and went on in a whisper: "She was the head of the whole Home. If you got in trouble, you had to come up against her. I remember being dragged to her office many times, thinking I would be dead, wanting to die, telling them to go ahead and kill me and get it over with. This one time. . . ." Her voice trailed off; she looked utterly terror-stricken, and shifted her gaze from the floor to me. I said, very quietly, "You have named a name. You're still very frightened, but we are both still here. If it's too scary, we can try to get the little girl out of there right now."

Eva looked down again. I asked, "How can I help?" She asked me to hold her hand, and went on, after some moments: "It's the middle of the day. I don't know why, but I'm in the dormitory, with another girl. This person, who was the dormitory mother . . . Sister Adele something . . . I remember, she was younger than the others, and at first I trusted her, and followed her around, wanting her to like me . . . anyway, this time she tells us that we were laughing about her behind her back, and that she knows we were making fun of her, and she would make sure we wouldn't do anything like that any more. Then she starts hitting us . . . and then I'm being touched [sexually abused] . . . (long pause) . . . the other girl chickened out, but I broke away and started running. Some other kids chased me and held me down. Then I was being dragged to Sister Rose's office. I remember seeing this enormous desk . . . I'm sitting on this chair, and I can see myself like that little kid that Lily Tomlin portrays, you know, a little girl on this huge chair. I keep hearing this voice, 'Get over here,' and I can't move. . . ."

Eva paused again, trembling violently. I asked again, "How can I help?" and she said, "Please hold me." I put my arm around her shoulder. After a few moments, Eva continued, with great hesitation, "Finally she dragged me out of the chair and started beating me. Then several other sisters were there, all hitting me. I gave up. Something shut down. And after they were finished, I was sent back to the same dormitory with the same Sister Adele. I had no way out. I stopped learning around that time because the same people were teaching me in the classroom. I just kept trying to find a way to die and end it all. . . . I used to think of how I could hang myself from the light fixture in the dormitory, and I had visions of myself hanging there naked, left to rot."

Eva put her head on my shoulder, and I held her for some moments. When she raised her head, though she was still agitated and fearful, she looked around the room as if bringing herself back to the present. I said, "We're still here. You were able to tell me things that you know really happened, and to name names, and you didn't die. Nobody came back here to get you, the earth didn't swallow you up, and lightning didn't strike you." She said, "I know I'm in your office, with you. I never thought that could happen. I swore I would never tell anybody because I was sure I was bad and would go straight to hell if I said anything about them. I thought I would die if I told. But the memories have been so close to the surface for a while now, and I've held back for weeks because I was so afraid. I didn't know if I could trust you, even though I know I can trust you. Does that sound crazy?"

We spent the remainder of the session processing what had happened, and Eva made many connections between the poem and the incident that she had just described. We both felt that this had been a momentous session, and Eva said that, though drained, she felt relieved.

When Eva left, she assured me that she would be all right during the ensuing week. As I have often done before, I let her know where she could reach me if necessary. She did phone me later that evening to say that she was feeling very shaken. She added, "It's like being two people–before the trauma happened, what could my life have been like? I'm trying to recapture the child who was happy, full of life, laughing. I have this desire to live, not to be hanging from someplace. I've opened the door–taken a risk."

DISCUSSION

The session recounted above illustrates the flexible use of time, physical space, written words, and touch in work with a survivor of severe, sustained sexual and physical abuse in order to reverse the internal experience of fragmentation and repair linkages between affects and words. The poem was an obvious account of the sexual and physical abuse experience, though Eva did not "remember" writing it when I read it to her in the session. The session itself lasted two hours, and even then it hardly seemed long enough to allow for the development of enough trust to decide to go through with "naming names" and the intense feelings (fear, disgust, pain, anger, hatred, terror) generated in the process. Further, the time necessary for Eva to "wind down" from the experience was an important factor as well.

Eva's move from the distant chair to the sofa, and then the request for me to sit nearby, indicated not only the existence of trust, but also the need for my physical presence as concrete support as she risked psychic annihilation. At moments of extreme terror (or fear of actual destruction, as she expressed it), my sitting next to her was not enough, and physical touch, and then holding, served as a bridge both between the intensity of the flashback and the present, and between affects and words. (It was clear that at two points of her narrative, Eva was *in* the flashback, not *observing* the events. She shifted to the present tense, her facial expression and breathing changed, her body was motionless, and she appeared far away.)

SUMMARY

In this chapter, I have attempted to describe some of the internal phenomena experienced by adult survivors of traumatic childhood abuse. I have related these phenomena to psychoanalytic theory regarding both trauma in general and what Krystal (1978) terms "catastrophic trauma" in particular. I have discussed the sometimes paradoxical nature of attempting to approach the survivor's inner space from my position in the outer world. I have ventured to link the intrapsychic experience of one survivor, which resulted from severe environmental trauma, to the external environment of analytic psychotherapy, as I endeavored to link affects with words, so that, through my bearing witness to the reality of "unspeakable" occurrences, she could move from isolation inside the events toward a fuller life in the external world. "The survivors did not only need to survive so that they could tell their story; they also needed to tell their story in order to survive" (Laub 1991, p. 77).

REFERENCES

Breuer, J., and Freud, S. (1893–1895). Studies on hysteria. *Standard Edition* 2.

Caruth, C. (1991). Introduction. *American Imago: Studies in Psychoanalysis and Culture*, 48:1–12.

Ferenczi, S. (1931). Child analysis in the analysis of adults. In *The Selected Papers of Sandor Ferenczi, vol. III: Final Contributions to the Problems and Methods of Psycho-Analysis*. New York: Basic Books, 1955.

—— (1933). Confusion of tongues between adults and the child. In *The Selected Papers of Sandor Ferenczi, vol. III: Final Contributions to the Problems and Methods of Psycho-Analysis*. New York: Basic Books, 1955.

Freud, S. (1926). Inhibitions, symptoms and anxiety. *Standard Edition*, 20:77–175.

Hartmann, H. (1958). *Ego Psychology and the Problem of Adaptation*. New York: International Universities Press.

Jones, D. M. (1991). Alexithymia: inner speech and linkage impairment. *Clinical Social Work Journal* 19:237–249.

Khan, M. M. (1963). The concept of cumulative trauma. *The Privacy of the Self*. New York: International Universities Press, 1974.

Kohut, H. (1971). *The Analysis of the Self*. New York: International Universities Press.

—— (1977). *The Restoration of the Self*. New York: International Universities Press.

—— (1984). *How Does Analysis Cure?* ed. A. Goldberg and P. Stepansky. Chicago: University of Chicago Press.

Krystal, H. (1978). Trauma and affects. In *Psychoanalytic Study of the Child* 33:81–116. New Haven, CT: Yale University Press.

—— (1991). Integration and healing in post traumatic states: a ten year retrospective. *American Imago: Studies in Psychoanalysis and Culture* 48:93–118.

Kupfermann, K., and Smaldino, C. (1987). The vitalizing and the revitalizing experience of reliability: the place of touch in psychotherapy. *Clinical Social Work Journal* 15:223–235.

Laub, D. (1991). Truth and testimony: the process and the struggle. *American Imago: Studies in Psychoanalysis and Culture*, 48:75–91.

Little, M. I. (1990). *Psychotic Anxieties and Containment: A Personal Record of an Analysis with Winnicott*. Northvale, NJ: Jason Aronson.

Sifneos, P. (1967). Clinical observations on some patients suffering from a variety of psychosomatic diseases. Proceedings of the 7th European Conference on Psychosomatic Research, Rome. *Acta Medica Psychosomatica*, pp. 452–458.

Winnicott, D. W. (1949). Birth memories, birth trauma, and anxiety. In *Through Paediatrics to Psycho-Analysis.* London: Tavistock, 1958.

—— (1952). Anxiety associated with insecurity. In *Through Paediatrics to Psycho-Analysis.* London: Tavistock, 1958.

—— (1960a). The theory of the parent-infant relationship. In *The Maturational Processes and the Facilitating Environment.* New York: International Universities Press, 1965.

—— (1960b). Ego distortion in terms of true and false self. In *The Maturational Processes and the Facilitating Environment.* New York: International Universities Press, 1965.

12 Working with Dreams of Survivors of Violence: Facilitating Crisis Intervention with a Psychoanalytic Approach

Katherine A. Brunkow

INTRODUCTION

An experience of violence disrupts both physical and psychic equilibrium. The immediate sense of helplessness and the ongoing task of sorting out the meanings of the experience challenge the psychological defenses.

Working with survivors of trauma for the past fourteen years in the context of brief, intensive crisis intervention, I have found the patterns of disorganization and reorganization of the defenses to be impressive signs of the mind's capacity to find its own means of integration. As clinicians we are all familiar with the process of working through a disruptive crisis. But we cannot predict the form of the working through since the specific outcome is unique to each individual.

One striking aspect of this working-through aspect of the integration of trauma is the emergence of dream material in the clinical work. In this chapter, I will describe four examples of working with dreams within the limits of short-term treatment of survivors of violence. I will explore the ways dream material can shed light on the management of anxiety through reassurance and mastery, the role of previous crises and developmental conflicts, and the reorganization of the defenses around the process of integrating the experience of violence. This exploration proposes a model of crisis intervention which goes beyond the usual expectable goal of restoring the prior level of functioning. It views crisis as an opportunity for growth while the defenses are loosened and old wounds reopened. A psychoanalytic perspective with an ear to unconscious conflict as well as to conscious fears and transference/countertransference themes facilitates the work.

I will offer a selective review of literature on types and functions of dreams related to trauma. The case material will describe the nature of the violence, timing of the dream material, and some of the developmental dynamics but will not discuss symptoms, character structure, or outcome in detail. Identifying data are disguised.

SELECTIVE REVIEW OF LITERATURE

Freud offered us basic guidelines for work with dreams in the principle that dreams are directed toward wish fulfillment (1900) and in his attention to the presentation of the dream material in the clinical process (1923). For example, the timing of the discussion of the dream may represent a gift to the therapist or a defensive use of disguised material or a resistance to free association in the moment in the room.

In 1920, Freud emphasized the reassurance function of anxiety dreams, such as examination dreams—a typical one being the situation of discovering that you have been signed up for a class which you have not been attending and now it is time to take the exam. Freud's point here is that when we wake up from such a dream, we are reassured with a feeling of relief that the feared situation has already been mastered—Oh, I did pass my exams, I did graduate from college; probably I can master what I am currently anxious about also. Ernest Kafka described examination dreams as an intermediate form between traumatic dreams and anxiety dreams (1979).

Freud distinguished repetitive traumatic dreams from other dreams in several ways. The manifest content is often undisguised. For example, the dreamer experiences over and over the frightening events of the trauma. The functions of these dreams are to master the external danger, to achieve some belated discharge of tension, and to regain a sense of control by repetition of the trauma (Freud 1920).

Owen Renik (1981) explored the related mechanisms of examination dreams, "superego dreams," and traumatic dreams showing how all contain disguised wish fulfillments. One of his conclusions was that people who have undergone truly damaging experiences tend to have the kind of post-traumatic dreams in which the trauma is wishfully distorted.

Dreams which appear to repeat trauma but actually distort certain aspects of the experience were also described earlier by Loewenstein (1949) and Levitan (1965). The distortions made it possible to work clinically with the dreamer's anxiety and underlying conflicts.

A detailed example of such clinical work was given in a case study of a Vietnam veteran by Adams-Silvan and Silvan (1990). They found that the veteran's repetitive traumatic dreams and some of his symptoms represented wish fulfillment as well as the attempt to master overwhelming stimuli. This patient's associations during therapy led to unconsciously pleasurable experience of childhood and adolescence that were revived by his traumatic war experiences.

CLINICAL VIGNETTES

In my own work with victims of violence, I have found the emergence of dream material a useful clue to how the patient's mind is working to manage anxiety, what developmental issues have been reawakened, and some aspects of transference/countertransference themes. The following clinical vignettes describe four people who survived violence: three women who were raped and a man who was taken hostage while working for an American firm abroad. Due to circumstances unique to each case, these patients were seen for brief psychotherapy. The treatments ranged from four to twelve sessions. In this type of short-term work, I use an active technical stance with frequent questions and a conversational tone to engage the patient, establish an alliance, gather information, elicit affects and encourage free association. When inquiring about experiences and symptoms (such as sleep disruption, loss of appetite, dissociation, hypervigilance) since the traumatic event, I often ask if the patient has remembered any dreams or nightmares. This has implications for the transference, since it establishes my interest in certain phenomena. This differs from my approach in longer-term work where the remembering or reporting of a dream would emerge spontaneously as part of the developing process between patient and therapist. In the brief treatments being described here, my asking about dreams gives them added importance depending on the individual patient's view of the nature of the authority and interest of the therapist. The timing of subsequent dreams or the remembering of previous dreams is important to note as an aspect of the developing alliance.

Miss A.

Miss A. and a male companion were assaulted and robbed by five men with a gun. They tied up Miss A.'s friend and forced him to watch while each of the five men raped Miss A. It was not clear for several hours whether Miss A. and her friend would be killed. Eventually they were released. The circumstances of the assault required Miss A. to move to the city where I practice. The medical referral described Miss A.'s unusual calm and her inability to feel much anger about the violence.

In the first two sessions of our twelve-session treatment, Miss A. expressed deep sadness at the loss of her work setting, the projects for which she felt responsible, and the friends and colleagues who had been so important to her, in particular a male supervisor. She expressed the wish that the violence could be isolated and not connected to time and history.

She felt she had learned a lot about coping with tragedy and loss. Her mother died when she was quite young and a brother was killed in Vietnam. But she realized that in this current experience she was removed from many of her feelings about the violence. She described the sadistic brutality of the gang rape in a distant way and gave rational explanations for criminal behavior. Here was a clear example of the way the mind can use isolation of affect, denial, and intellectualization to protect itself from overwhelming affect.

In the third session, Miss A. reported a dream.

It was very simple. It was Matthew (the close supervisor friend). He came to me and was telling me how things were going. Basically, he was saying, "It's okay here." For some reason, I felt some sort of resolution. When I woke up, I felt calmer and more rested than I have in a long time.

In the sessions following the presentation of this dream, Miss A. began to experience a wide range of feelings. This began with tears at remembering her companion's rage and helplessness at being forced to watch the rapes. She lamented, "He was so young and naive about evil and the terror of inhuman people. At least I was prepared by some of the bad things in my life."

Such projection of her own vulnerability and helplessness is common in rape victims (Rose 1986). For Miss A., it was a useful defense now and also during the rapes when focusing on her friend helped protect her psychologically from some of the more demeaning and life-threatening behaviors of their attackers. Gradually Miss A. was able to shift from her friend's helplessness to her own, to shift from the familiar altruism of her usual role taking care of others to exploring the meanings of this terrifying experience. In listening to Miss A., I struggled with my own shock at the sadistic activities of the assailants and felt this paralleled much greater shock in the patient. I assumed when enough of an alliance was established, Miss A. could allow herself to feel more.

The seemingly simple dream of Matthew signalled the shift in Miss A.'s defenses. The manifest content restored a lost loved one who reassured her and represented a "good" man of the same race as the assailants. I heard the dream also as a transference statement of trust and relative safety in the treatment, an undoing of the crimes of "bad" men, and a condensation of the wish to restore lost objects.

Miss A. could now explore the themes of loss and disruption at various stages of her development. As she experienced her anger and helplessness about those early losses, she began to express rage at the assailants for willfully threatening her life, body, and future. The psychic threat of tapping into her underlying anger about the early losses contributed to her initial dissociation from the violence. While the treatment focused primarily on the rape crisis, it also gave her new insight into her fears of her anger as well as new compassion for the sources of that fear.

Mr. B.

Mr. B. and three colleagues were taken hostage after crossing the border of a Latin American country where there was civil war. They were held under armed guard for five days, listened to debates about how their lives or deaths could be most useful to the soldiers, and were eventually released to officials in a neighboring country. After several days of medical care, Mr. B. was brought to the city where his corporation's headquarters are located. He was referred to me for brief treatment.

In our first session, Mr. B. told me that he wished to head home as soon as possible. He seemed unaware of his hyperalert, agitated state. He denied that his experience of being held hostage had been traumatic. He described it saying, "The six-hour hike through the jungle was a little frightening, because it was so uncertain what would be done with us. But the only thing that really scared me was to have all those automatic weapons in the hands of 14-year-olds. You just couldn't tell what they would do next. Our lives were in their hands." In the second day of captivity, Mr. B. had found a familiar coping mechanism, taking care of one of the other hostages, a man newly arrived in the region and extremely anxious. It seemed clear this activity had helped Mr. B. defend against much of his own anxiety. I told Mr. B. that it would be better if he did not go home immediately, that it would be wise to spend at least a week exploring the impact of this experience. He agreed and we had a four-session crisis intervention.

In the third session, he reported that the night before, he had gone to see a movie with guns in it. During the film and later on the street, he had experienced intense anxiety with a powerful impulse to run as fast and as far as he could. He was surprised at the intensity of his fear and said that now he was much more aware of his feelings in general. He had not realized how much had been blocked out. He wondered why he had not cried in his sense of helplessness or at least in relief when he was released. Then he remembered two dreams which he thought had occurred a few days after his release.

My old girlfriend arrived and was holding me. I cried and cried, and she said, "It's good that you're crying." The weird thing was that when woke up I wasn't. It was as though I could cry only in a dream. In the other dream. I kept having to deal with authority figures, people in charge, the police, the customs officials who make you feel so worthless. There was this terrible feeling of anxiety.

In associating to these dreams, Mr. B. told me that the last time he had actually cried was when he was 11 years old. His father had suddenly died of a heart attack. He described how he, his two older brothers, and mother had learned to cope through the difficult months and years that followed. Mr. B. became helper and emotional supporter of their mother. The person who was the angriest and had the hardest time, he said, was his brother who was 14 at the time of the death. This added another dimension to his fear of the 14-year-olds and their guns.

He associated to the second dream, the one about the authority figures, with stories of the frustrating hassles of paperwork and officials with rubber stamps in the country where he had been working. These were situations he had mastered many times. This gave the dream the quality of an examination dream, anxiety about times when others were in charge of his comings and goings with reassurance upon waking that he had mastered those situations before. This could help him manage his anxiety about being forcefully held by those who literally took charge of whether he would live or die.

The feeling of being worthless in the dream was a repetition of the hostage situation. It also raised questions of underlying guilt and the wish to be demeaned by authority figures. Mr. B. expressed many worries about the people still there dealing with the civil war, while he was now safe and comfortable in the United States. At a conscious level, he was experiencing typical survivor guilt. Since the associations came in the same session with the discussion of his father's death, I wondered to myself about underlying oedipal guilt at taking his father's place as mother's support. I asked Mr. B. what it had been like for him to assume that role in the family. He said he used to worry about his brothers' jealousy, felt he was too important to his mother–that was one reason for his need to get home so fast–and realized that he sometimes imagined he could do almost anything. In our next and last session, Mr. B. said the one part of the crisis that felt unfinished was facing the risk he took in crossing the border. Earlier, he had denied this reality and had not been able to talk about the guilt he felt at taking such a risk for himself and others. He now realized he had felt a certain omnipotence and impunity in crossing the border. In hindsight, it seemed immature and grandiose to him. By talking about this and facing it, he said, he felt that he was growing up.

As in the work with Miss A. the timing of Mr. B.'s presentation of the dream material coincided with a shift in his defenses. The comforting girlfriend suggested an alliance had been established with me. The loosening of his denial and isolation of affect allowed him to experience his intense fear and his wish to run away. The exploration of his father's death led to new insight.

Miss C.

Miss C. and her boyfriend were stopped on a city street by two men who robbed and assaulted them. One had a handgun; the other dragged the boyfriend away, left him in an alley, and then returned with two younger men. The four men raped Miss C. until they were interrupted by her friend and the police. After four days of medical care in the hospital, she was referred for outpatient treatment. I saw her for six crisis intervention sessions.

In our first session, Miss C. appeared deeply shaken by this experience of violence but was able to express a wide range of feelings about it. Her most noticeable symptom was trembling throughout the session. She said she had so much anger at the men and the fact that they had told her they had done this before to other women that she hardly knew what to do with it. Very much of a take-charge person with considerable professional success, Miss C. seemed both appealing and controlling in her attempts to cope with this trauma. I was aware of a feeling of uneasiness about when and how her anger might come my way.

In the fourth of our six sessions, Miss C. reported a dream from which she had awakened screaming.

I was in my bedroom at home. It's been the same since I was 10, and my mother helped me decorate it all with green gingham. It was the same checked bedspread and the same stuffed gingham clown on a trapeze that my mother gave me to one side. There was a man dangling in the window. I screamed. He had a red tie–the kind with a flower pattern or little dots, you know–a power tie. Fortunately the window was closed but he was leering at me like he owned me. I woke up screaming; they told me I was screaming, "Mom!" I lay there crying and crying and feeling I am so afraid. I don't want to be this afraid.

She thought the setting of the dream represented her wish to return to a simpler time. She associated to childhood fears of being left, of being totally alone. She said those times of feeling so alone were the most afraid she had ever felt until this violent assault.

After this session, Miss C. began to feel much better. Her symptoms of shakiness, nausea, and exhaustion faded, and she began to plan for the future. She was apparently relieved by the telling and exploring of this dream and the catharsis of reliving her sense of helplessness at being alone. Her associations suggest the terror of being separated from the comfort and security of her mother. This confirms the theoretical view of trauma as an experience of separation–feeling cut off from predictability, safety, and even life itself. Miss C.'s unusually close relationship to her mother suggested that another aspect of her separation anxiety is represented in the dream by the leering man whose phallic tie could separate her emotionally from mother. The dream distorts some aspects of the recent trauma: the threat came from one man, not four. Her room was a space she could control and decorate in her own way. The protective boundary of the window kept the powerful man at bay. But neither that nor the dream work was enough to contain the terror that awoke her screaming.

During this phase of Miss C.'s treatment, I was discussing issues of treating survivors of violence with a colleague. I mentioned the countertransference to this patient, the uneasiness about when her anger would come my way, as an example of one of the clues I use to try to understand the core conflict for the person attempting to integrate trauma. My uneasiness suggested to me that Miss C. was frightened of losing control of her rage and the helplessness underlying it. The colleague asked if I ever used my artwork to express or understand my own or the patient's responses. I immediately had an association to Miss C.'s dream. It was an image of a multidimensional collage in a shallow box, with layers of wood, gingham, flesh, and blood framing the man. Over his face was a handy little window shade with a pull, to be raised or lowered at will. In my identification with Miss C. and my wish that her fear could be managed by a flexible defense, I had created a power box to contain the power tie.

Miss C. returned temporarily to the city where she had been raped to participate in the legal process of trying and sentencing her assailants. She called me to tell me her anxiety and nightmares had returned briefly during the lengthy process, which required considerable patience and courage on her part. She said she felt much better once the trial and sentencing were accomplished. She considered this the best channel available for her anger, sense of helplessness, and wish to protect others.

Miss D.

Miss D. was assaulted by a man while walking alone on a beach. Despite her struggling, he raped her several times in the course of an hour. When I first saw her two weeks later, she complained of anxiety, frequent nightmares, and sleep disruption. She most wanted to get over feeling so frightened. She thought she was too passive and if she had just been a more assertive person this never would have happened. It is usual for rape victims to blame themselves (McCombie 1980) but Miss D. seemed especially critical of herself, not just her behavior but her whole personality.

She told me the hardest thing she had coped with before this violence was her mother's death four years earlier. In our next session, Miss D. reported this dream with much hesitation.

Sister Bernadette was showing us around the convent. It is a mansion with beautiful rooms. There was a girl with long red hair. We were both aroused. It was in her mind too. It was like a wet dream. She was going to help me. I was really crying and crying. She was saying it's good to cry.

The convent was the place Miss D. had gone to stay because she did not feel safe in her own home after the rape. Sister Bernadette was a reassuring friend. The girl with the long red hair she associated to the movie, *Pretty Woman,* although she had trouble remembering what the story was about. She was embarrassed to tell me about being aroused. She thought the reassurance that it is good to cry must have something to do with her first session with me.

As she went on to talk about how much she had cried after the rape and how understanding her friends had been, I was wondering to myself about the arousal I had experienced with this patient, what it meant, how it related to the dream. I too felt embarrassed and spent some time analyzing my responses for sadistic or voyeuristic pleasure in the violent details of Miss D.'s story, reaction to her attractiveness or intrusion of some part of my own history. It finally occurred to me that Miss D. had used the vehicle of the dream to speak about sexual arousal, a dream with both a nun and a prostitute, albeit a very nice one. Perhaps she was trying to tell me about another aspect of her anxiety about the rape.

In the next session, I asked if she could tell me more about her experience with the assailant; since women are often confused and upset if their bodies respond during violence, I said, I wondered if there had been pleasure for her. She acknowledged there had been and that she was embarrassed when the forced intercourse was not more painful or physically damaging. She worried about what this meant about her sexuality and went on to explore aspects of her relationships with her mother and father and previous boyfriends. Over the next two weeks, she had several nightmares which disrupted her sleep and seemed to represent various aspects of the rape, such as a man's hand on her thigh or the feeling of the sand and sticks bruising her skin. These were being relived in distorted and more manageable doses.

In the last of our nine sessions, Miss D. reported that she had been sleeping well. She experienced occasional mild anxiety but had made plans to return to her work and to move to safe housing. She also reported this dream.

I was running a race. I was passing all these men. I was running with a woman up the hill; it was steep. Then I was climbing. I could get my nails in little fingerholds, inch by inch. A girl in front fell off. She almost knocked me over. I went to one side. She was out of the race. I'm not out of the race. I can't win but I'm still in the race.

She associated to the feeling of being back into things, of having really accomplished something during our brief work together. She felt proud of having made an assertive response to a man who offended her, and she realized she was not as passive as she feared. When I asked about the finger-holds, she wasn't sure what they meant. I asked if they could be related to what she had told me about seeing the rapist, when she was asked to identify him at the jail. She knew immediately that it was he, but she was astounded to see that his face and arms were covered with scratches. She had had no memory of scratching him so fiercely during her struggling. Now in the dream, her fingernails seemed an image of a painstaking process of using her power. She responded that she felt the dream climb had something to do with the issues she had been exploring in our sessions: was it all right to feel pleasure, was it all right to express anger, to cry, to depend on others, to surpass men, to survive her mother, to be herself. She realized now that she was not passive and that she had done a remarkable job of surviving a violent assault.

Overall, the dream seemed to be a positive statement about her hard work in this brief therapy, a remembering of her tough fight to survive her assailant's attack, and a lessening of her fear that she had been irreparably damaged. I wondered to myself if her conclusion, "I can't win but I'm still in the race" represented a compromise formation, with some superego punishment for her pleasure, her survival, her aggression against the assailant, and perhaps fantasies about her mother's death. The dream seemed to express the wish to compete with her dead mother, with me in the transference, and to leave behind the man who had disrupted her body, her life, and her psyche.

DISCUSSION

Each of these clinical vignettes describes working with dreams of survivors of violence in the context of brief treatment. Most of these dreams were not the repetitive reenactments often described in the literature on trauma. They involved some repetition and some distortion. Like many dreams presented in the course of treatment, they seem to be attempts at managing the affects and conflicts associated with the current stress and also reviving earlier issues. They express transference themes stirred up by the therapy. Each of the four patients dreamed of a transference figure who offered reassurance, comfort, or safety. In terms of dreamwork's function of containing anxiety, the nightmares of Miss C. and Miss D. were not successful, but they were important steps in the integration of the trauma.

In terms of clinical process, the presentation of dream material was one aspect of the establishing of an alliance of relative trust and safety in a short time. This is crucial in brief therapy. It suggests that the appearance of a positive transference theme in the patient's material can be a useful marker in moving ahead. All four of these patients were able to use a basically positive transference to facilitate a shift in defenses. This allowed increased tolerance for and fuller expression of threatening affects. Defense analysis along with the experiencing and working through of the threatening affects led to reduction in post-traumatic symptoms. It also yielded insight into personality defenses and patterns. Mr. B. with a new capacity to acknowledge his sense of omnipotence and Miss D. with her greater awareness of her conflicts around pleasure and aggression made real gains.

Attention to countertransference is as important in brief work as it is in long-term treatment. The time-limited situation encourages use of intuition and trial interpretations. In these examples, working with my inner responses to the patients helped me to understand better what both of us were trying to manage. This approach is informed by Racker (1968), whose discussion of the meanings and uses of countertransference continues to be especially useful. He describes the concordant type of countertransference as that in which the therapist is pulled by readiness in himself as well as by the dynamic forces in the patient to experience what the patient experiences. In the complementary type of countertransference, the therapist's responsiveness and the forces within the patient combine to create feelings in the therapist which represent those of an internalized object with whom the patient is struggling, such as a critical parent. My uneasiness about Miss C. attacking me with her anger and my arousal in listening to Miss D. can both be understood as concordant countertransferences which became clues to the patients' conflicts.

Each of these four patients was high-functioning, articulate, and intelligent, with a good degree of self-awareness and impulse control. These are some of the signs of ego strength which indicate the capacity to make good use of analytically oriented brief treatment. Patients with multiple diagnoses, chaotic lives prior to the trauma, or much acting out in response to the trauma might benefit from a more structured problem-solving approach. Whatever the approach, an ear to the themes represented in dream material can enhance understanding.

Brief psychotherapy can be very useful in facilitating the expression of painful affects, exploring the unique meanings of the current crisis, restoring equilibrium, and gaining the insight into previous crises and conflicts that leads to growth. However, it does not offer the benefits of the long-term therapeutic relationship: strengthened alliance for exploring more threatening issues, heightened transference for experiencing conflicts in the here-and-now, open-ended time for the emergence of material usually kept out of awareness, and the extended process of working through that leads to lasting change. These advantages to long-term treatment often become apparent to patients who have a successful experience in brief treatment. They sometimes want to continue working on a theme reawakened by the current crisis. Most importantly, a useful experience in brief treatment establishes a positive foundation for seeking help, if needed, in the future.

Brief treatment is enhanced by listening to the multiple levels of meaning in clinical phenomena, such as dreams. Even with the assessment questions and active stance usually necessary in crisis intervention, the patient establishes an associative process which often describes transference themes, earlier losses, and developmental conflicts. A psychoanalytic perspective, which respects the capacity of the individual to make use of treatment in his or her own unique way, as seen in the emergence of dream material, can make short-term work especially creative. Many patients, like these four, find ways to turn the disruption and disorganization following an experience of violence into an opportunity to learn about themselves.

REFERENCES

Adams-Silvan, A., and Silvan M. (1990). "A dream is fulfillment of a wish": traumatic dream, repetition compulsion, and the pleasure principle. *International Journal of Psycho-Analysis* 71:513–522.

Freud, S. (1900). The interpretation of dreams. *Standard Edition* 4, 5.

—— (1920). Beyond the pleasure principle. *Standard Edition* 18.

—— (1923). Remarks on the theory and practice of dream interpretation. *Standard Edition* 19.

Kafka, E. (1979). On examination dreams. *Psychoanalytic Quarterly* 34:426–447.

Levitan, H. (1965). A traumatic dream. *Psychoanalytic Quarterly* 34:265–267.

Loewenstein, R. M. (1949). A posttraumatic dream. *Psychoanalytic Quarterly* 18: 449–454.

McCombie, S. L., ed. (1980). *The Rape Crisis Intervention Handbook.* New York: Plenum.

Racker, H. (1968). The meanings and uses of countertransference. In *Transference and Countertransference,* pp. 127–173. New York: International Universities Press.

Renik, O. (1981). Typical examination dreams, superego dreams, traumatic dreams. *Psychoanalytic Quarterly* 50:158–189.

Rose, D. S. (1986). "Worse than death": psychodynamics of rape victims and the need for psychotherapy. *American Journal of Psychiatry* 143:817–824.

13 A Psychoeducational-Psychodynamic Approach to the Treatment of Drug Addicts

Julie R. Miller

INTRODUCTION

The placement of drug addicts in residential therapeutic communities, with two years as the minimal time requirement, is generally regarded as the most successful way of treating this population at the present time. This approach provides the addict with a sociotherapeutic culture of treatment (Kaufman and Kaufman 1975) and offers him or her an opportunity for an extraordinarily intense therapeutic immersion. The latter in most programs consists of a here-and-now, behavioral, confrontational reality therapy, which encompasses a system of rewards and punishments. The emphasis is on group and family encounter styles of treatment in various configurations. Individual insight therapy is usually not provided.

THE OUTPATIENT RECOVERING ADDICTS

Frequently, however, the "graduated," abstinent patient from such programs finds it necessary to seek long-term psychotherapy to work through personal, unresolved issues in order to prevent relapse. To the extent that such therapy involves an intimate, dyadic, clinical relationship, it constitutes a novel experience for many of these patients (Miller 1994) and not an easy one. Many recovering addicts find it difficult to feel entitled to such treatment, due to profound feelings of guilt and shame. Some are fearful of losing whatever it is that helps them maintain the tenuous equilibrium they feel they have and they dare not risk themselves until they are convinced that they can achieve something more worthwhile. Despite their frequently engaging, articulate, and cooperative manner, many recovering addicts suffer from an affect intolerance (Sashin 1985, Khantzian and Wilson 1992), which contributed to their addiction in the first place and which leads to a shallow participation in psychotherapy (Wurmser 1974 and Khantzian and Wilson 1992). Finally, though this by no means covers all of the problems such patients and their therapists encounter, many recovering addicts appear initially to lack the capacity for introspection which an insight-oriented treatment calls for.

As a result of these and other factors, it is necessary for the therapist to adopt approaches that will help meet these patients "where they are," that will take their unique needs into account. For many addicts this means a preparatory educational introduction into the world of dynamic psychotherapy (Fromm-Reichman 1957). Preparatory therapy is by no means a new concept. Ralph Greenson (1967) long ago noted the need of certain patients for a period of preparatory therapy prior to analysis. It is the purpose of this paper to delineate such a preparatory approach which I refer to as a *psychoeducational-psychodynamic* form of insight treatment. This paradigm has enabled certain addicts who are wary of entering the introspective world to achieve sufficient trust that they may engage more successfully in the "talking cure." In this approach the therapist addresses the patient's urgent need for concrete life skills in the first half of each treatment session and then moves, in the second half, to helping the patient understand and work through the intrapsychic issues that contribute to his or her difficulties. While this approach draws on familiar case management and psychoanalytic psychotherapeutic techniques, it is the provision of both approaches and the way they are connected within each treatment hour that gives this paradigm its particular value for certain patients. This technique can best be illustrated by drawing directly from the treatment of a recovering addict who was seen by me for one and a half years, twice a week, in an agency setting.

ANNIE

Annie, a 30-year-old, single black woman who was an HIV-positive heroin addict in recovery, had been abstinent for three years following two years of rehabilitation in a residential therapeutic community. She was eager for individual therapy, insisting that she was "up to her eyeballs" in endless encounter groups. Annie's presenting complaint was her chronic depression, which she began to experience following her departure from the therapeutic community. Despite her fifteen years of heroin addiction, Annie, at that time, had found a job as an administrative assistant to a professor at a nearby local black community college, a testimony to her fine innate intelligence and certain well-developed ego capacities.

TREATMENT ISSUES

Annie described, at the beginning of our work, episodes of derealization and a feeling that every achievement of hers was inherently fraudulent. She explained that her external progress did nothing to alter her image of herself as a "bad" person. She was overwhelmed by guilt related to her life as a heroin addict. With great difficulty, she told of a life of street prostitution, in which she often played masochistic roles requested by her "johns." She submitted to their demands for agonizing anal intercourse and described jumping into cars to perform oral sex on her customers. Annie wept over time spent in the rat-infested squalor of shooting galleries, behaving like a "crazed animal," engaging in transient lesbian sex and dancing in topless bars to support her habit. Her sense of pervasive guilt tainted every achievement, and she repeatedly labelled herself as a "criminal" who deserved to die of AIDS because of her past "sins."

THE ROLE OF GUILT AND SHAME IN THE TREATMENT

The primary clinical goal of our work, as I saw it, was to help reduce Annie's overwhelming sense of guilt and self-condemnation. This meant addressing both her rational and irrational guilt and helping her to see that at certain times what she described as guilt and felt as guilt was in fact deep shame over her past behaviors. Often the guilt served as a defense against the shame.

As Somers (1990) writes, "Shame is perhaps the single most powerful human feeling state. . . . Guilt pertains to doing; to inflicting harm upon another. Shame pertains to being. If I am guilty of a bad deed, I have recourse. I can apologize. A reparative course of action is usually open to me. Shame is a much more archaic reaction than guilt, so primitive, that even higher primates and vertebrates can succumb to it" (p. 218). In Annie's case, guilt often served as a defense against "wanting to die from shame, wanting to disappear in the cracks of a sidewalk" (Somers 1990, p. 218).

Annie was chronically haunted by her "guilt list." Under the influence of magical thinking, Annie saw herself guilty of an endless array of transgressions. After exhaustive analysis, at times she would grudgingly acknowledge that certain self-reproaches were unrealistic. However, to the degree that her "terrible guilt" served as a defense against the more painful affect of shame, such a realization often led to the emergence of powerful feelings of shame associated with flashbacks of shame-evoking experiences. Annie herself referred to such occurrences as "cruel and unusual punishment." "Doctor Miller, don't laugh, I know I heard that phrase somewhere," she would say, to which I would respond, "Annie, do you see me laughing? You seem to find every reason to put yourself down. This is not an isolated example. I wonder where that comes from?"

Annie said, "Yeah, it's just one fucked-up reason why I'm here." It appeared that she was not ready to cope openly with accepting the catastrophic state of helplessness endemic to shame. She preferred to embrace guilt as her primary sense of misery, for it made it possible for her to temporarily envision a means of absolving herself. Later, in a position of greater relief and strength, she would be able to confront the deeper level of shame.

I tried at first to deal with her guilt directly. For example, at a time when she was reiterating the bad things she had done, there was this interchange between Annie and me:

Therapist: Maybe we can take a load of guilt off your back. Our job is not to get "ballistic" with you, but to find a way to do something constructive with the guilt you are carrying. Ain't no way that I, your Bible study group, or even your mother can convince you of your innocence, so let's try to find a way to help you act that will make you feel that there is something you can do to repair some of the damage you insist that you've caused. Can you boogey on down that, Annie?"*

Annie: Yeah, I could try to step out to that.

PSYCHOEDUCATIONAL-PSYCHODYNAMIC THERAPY

During the first few months of therapy in which the above exchange took place, Annie floundered, talking exclusively in repetitive narratives about serious concrete problems she was having in her adjustment to a separate, drug-free life. I waited for her to return to a discussion of her emotional life and to her depressive, shame-related ideation. Finally Annie became exasperated and complained that she was unable to work in what was a relatively unstructured format. She needed more practical help with her transition from the therapeutic community to "separate life." She spoke of her lack of interpersonal skills on the simplest level. She needed assistance with how to apply to college, how to deal with her slum landlord, how to find a new apartment, and how to deal with a host of obstacles in living with which she felt unequipped to deal. It appeared essential that we deal with both the outer and the inner world, a challenge long familiar to social workers. Annie needed assistance in managing her external life and a therapist who could serve her as a "structural anchor," to hold her so that she could eventually explore the role of shame in her life. Moreover, she needed temporarily some kind of direction to enable her to feel effective in the treatment if that experience were not itself to stimulate feelings of shame. Alexander (1924) has noted that shame is a "reaction to feeling weak, ineffective or inferior to others . . ." (p. 370). It became increasingly clear that I, as her therapist, would have to actively promote Annie's cognitive and interpersonal skills and a more consistent, mature affective life (Gaylin 1976) if I were gradually to help her gain a more profound understanding of the forces of early traumas and the addictive disease that led to her profound shame.

Taking into account Annie's ignorance and her still battered ego, a dy-

---

* From the outset I made a conscious decision to speak in the patient's language. It helped convey my involvement in her world and fostered what I term a *linguistic alliance*. Let me say that the use of Annie's vocabulary came very easily to me. Had it not, I would have been concerned lest I seem false.

namic therapy soon became transformed into a *twofold interaction*, which can best be described as a form of *psychoeducational-psychodynamic therapy*. Each session operated on two distinct but overlapping levels. The first half of a 60-minute session (I take an "hour" literally) consisted of ego-supportive, psychoeducational interventions. I took Annie's current concrete problems seriously in and of themselves. This attitude helped to create that "good enough" (Winnicott 1965) environment so essential for ongoing treatment. As therapist, I oscillated among a number of roles: that of counselor, educator, referral source, cognitive problem solver, and general resource object.

When I originally outlined this approach to Annie, I indicated that the structure of the hour was negotiable. I did not want to impose this approach or any other on her. I let her know I would welcome her reactions. Initially she expressed enthusiasm about including both parts of her life in sessions—problem-solving around the logistics of adjusting to being independent and drug-free, and having the opportunity to understand the felt inner conflicts and deficits that impaired her functioning. There were times, however, when she resisted the plan. Her resistance to what she called our "contract" tended to surface at the beginning of sessions when we were discussing, in our psychoeducational mode, necessary life skills. Usually, Annie's manifest reluctance was transient. It took the form of narrating every single event of the week with no indication of which were disturbing to her. I would then attempt to explore psychodynamically those blocks. I asked questions and made comments in an attempt to clarify her reasons for not selecting particular areas with which we might work.

Keeping in mind the desirability of maintaining this boundary between both parts of the session, I would merely raise the possibility that there were conscious and/or unconscious emotional forces that were inhibiting her from exercising her usual facility at pinpointing concrete difficulties in starting a new life. Eventually, Annie would agree. She would insist, nevertheless, on keeping the first thirty minutes of the session exclusively centered on the mechanics of her life as evidence of my unconditional support and to exercise her option to work on how to "TCB" (take care of business). Even if her mind was "blank," she savored having thirty minutes of time to just "ease on in," without having to deal with the "heavy psychological shit" which she often anticipated with dread in the second part of the sessions. The first half of the session seemed to serve as a non-threatening transition period, readying her to consider the more upsetting material that would invariably arise in the second half of the session. Annie often referred to me with pleasure as "my caseworker–therapist rolled up in one." Once having been assured of her therapist's alliance with her, it was possible for her to then deal with affective experiences not fully addressed in the first phase of the session. It was as if the first half of the session prepared her to deal with affect-laden experiences and to work in a more analytically oriented fashion the second half. What emerged seemed less threatening after our engagement around "real" problems and conflicts of daily life. After the first half hour, during which I took on an activist role, helping Annie with more immediate, "solvable" problems associated with acquiring adult, external living skills, she, like most patients involved in this approach, would feel fortified enough to say, "Okay, I'm ready, let's move on to the 'nitty gritty' therapy." During the remainder of the session both of us would assume more traditional psychoanalytically oriented roles. My verbal and non-verbal signals would unmistakably shift to a more exploratory, thoughtful, open-ended listening mode. I strove to concentrate on the spectrum of her emotional life, focusing on conscious and unconscious dynamic forces rooted in the past and in the present. The concept that feelings, memories, and behavior were "over-determined," indicating multiple causality of symptoms or emotional reactions, was introduced in order to highlight the notion of unconscious drives, needs, and simultaneous defenses against them. I directed my efforts toward eliciting her conscious and unconscious fears, fantasies, transference manifestations, resistances, and last but not least, the struggle to remain abstinent (drug-free).

THE USE OF DENIAL

Annie's dependence on denial during these sessions was repeatedly identified in the context of current and historical affective material. She consistently refused to speak about her HIV status, with all its traumatic ramifications. Denial was for her a means of mastering her environment and of controlling an extremely fragile intrapsychic equilibrium. Denial in Annie's external life operated like a galloping metastatic cancer, and it was automatically coupled with resistance in the therapy. As a defense mechanism, it was so powerful that, as a resident at the drug free therapeutic community, she had earned a reputation for having "skated" through the most humiliating verbal assaults, which exposed her pathology with a vengeance rarely seen from clinical staff in any setting. Once, when I asked her how she managed that, she replied "I kept on smiling and pretended that it was not me they were cutting. I was so good that I never had to really hit rock-bottom pain that was inside of me, so here I am getting real for the first time."

PSYCHOEDUCATIONAL THERAPY

I should like now to offer a picture of the approach I am detailing by citing the exchanges that occurred between Annie and me in two sessions. The first will focus on the psychoeducational component of the treatment hour.

Before the session to be described, I had spent several sessions educating Annie on the necessity of condom use, pointing out all the technical aspects involved. I discussed issues of responsibility, desired brands of condoms, how to avoid leakage, and every facet of the use of condoms for safe sex. Annie admitted her total ignorance of the use of condoms. She listened very carefully and asked questions. After this portion of the session we then proceeded to analyze her anxieties, fears, and unwillingness to "mess with that stuff" until she appeared sufficiently comfortable with making an emotional commitment to guaranteeing their use. Following this session, however, she arrived for her hour beaming. She had had a sexually exciting weekend binge. She had slept with five men in two days and casually mentioned that they had not used condoms, though all of them were HIV-positive. She explained, "Since we're all in the same boat, it didn't matter"; her partners "hated to deal with that shit" because it wasn't as good for them to "dick her that way." She also admitted that, even though she remembered sessions when I had meticulously taught her about HIV-positive partners reinfecting each other, she got "carried away." She had forgotten to register my suggestion that when she knew she was going to be sexually involved, she was to cognitively halt her libido, count to ten, and think "condom, condom." This had been helpful in the past but on that particular weekend she was more fearful of sexual abandonment than focused on her right to survival. She did not want to risk her partners' resentment by insisting they use condoms. Annie spoke in this session with giddy speed about her euphoria over having been "dicked so great after starving so long." It did not bother her that each man "fucked her and left her alone in the middle of the night," because her "righteous orgasms" (she said laughingly) were all that mattered to her. Here is a brief transcript of our exchange:

Therapist: Annie, I can see by your expressions and your tone of voice that you are very excited by finally "getting the sex you deserve" as you've told me many times. Can you tell me if you had any other feelings on the morning after when you woke up all alone?

Annie: Nope, I was just chilled out and satisfied. I can't think of anything else.

Therapist: Annie, let me run by you another version of other feelings you might have had, and you tell me what you think. I'm going to pretend it was me, okay? Because this is your life we're talking about, and nothing is more important. First, I'd be in a panic about the condoms. No condoms make you sicker and could shorten your life span. I'd be anxious and humiliated that I'd slept with strangers who could have carved me into chopped Julie. I'd feel lonely and scared that I had let myself go so out of control. Forget me if you want. That doesn't matter. All that matters is "keeping your eye on the tiger," your favorite quote from *Rocky*. Keeping you alive, helping you deal with hassles in the world, and understanding your inner problems so you don't burden yourself with depression and shame. We agreed on that, Annie, when you first came to therapy and you wanted me to teach you about therapy goals. Are you with me on that?

Annie: Right on.

Therapist: Annie, I promise you that most women would be as freaked out as I if they put themselves in your place that night. If you're going to live longer than shorter, it might be educational for both of us to find out why you didn't identify those feelings.

Annie: I can dig where you're coming from, my guts are moving with your rap. You've taught me about right HIV behaviors and the feelings I have to hold on to if I'm going to stay alive. And it's been a hip guide which I've always followed since I started here. But damn, last weekend I just couldn't think of myself as HIV and that I was going to die. It was too fuckin' much, and since I was physically healthy, I could tell myself I was well and cut loose my big problems. I just needed to pretend, like deny everything you've taught me to know.

Therapist: Annie, I realize it took a lot for you to say that but we've both learned something now. Together, you and I have been putting a kind of educational map on our table about unsafe sex and appropriate feelings, facts, and behaviors. It's so important that you tell me when you feel yourself slipping *before* the shit hits the fan instead of after the damage has been done. We both have to follow our contract that you call me any time you feel yourself slipping so we can put the package together again. You put it beautifully every time you tell me that I educate your guts and your mind.

Annie: You sure can preach! I gotta hold on tight that I'm like a student/patient and I gotta take them both real seriously since you always set it up that way with me and I liked your movin' back and forth with me.

Therapist: I'm hip, Annie, so let's keep on truckin'.

During this exchange there were shifting nuances in my style, but I remained sufficiently interpersonally related so that Annie never felt abandoned and was able to tolerate my responses to her. Her capacity to work in this fashion was due in part, I felt, to the fact that I had from the beginning of the treatment painstakingly provided her with a graphic description of how we would work and invited her to ask questions, express anger at "feeling deprived," or give expression to any other reaction she might have.

PSYCHODYNAMIC THERAPY

As an example of how we shifted from a more educational approach to a more psychodynamic approach, I offer an account of a session which occurred about two months into the treatment. It took place during an unbearably humid hot summer day, when the temperature had reached 95 degrees. Annie was wearing a heavy long dress, dark tights and a long-sleeved turtle-necked cotton blouse. I wondered to myself as she sat down whether she might be needing to cover up her heroin-related scars for some particular reasons at this session. I had observed the scars on many occasions when she had been dressed in sleeveless clothing. However, I had not brought up my observations nor had we explored the meanings of the scars to her. I was waiting for Annie to indicate her readiness to approach this topic. She immediately began the session by relating a conversation she had had with her landlord, admitting to her ignorance about how to conduct herself. At the age of 30, she was for the first time in her life living in her own apartment, having spent her adult life as a "junkie working and living in the streets." After talking and seemingly successfully considering some of her problems with the apartment, she began to complain about how cold the office was. Up to now she had found the office "deliciously cool" and had often complained about how hot her apartment in the projects was.

Annie: Damn, its so fuckin' cold in here. I'm freezing today and these are the warmest summer clothes I have. [She walks over to the air conditioner, inspects it, and sits down.] Julie, I can't stand being in this office, can we go to another one that doesn't have A/C? This is really a bitch! [She is sounding increasingly stressed.]

Therapist: Annie, you've just lost me. All summer long, you've complained about the heat, and thanked God that my office is so cool. You've been doing an angry about-face today. What's going on?

Annie: Nothing, I'm chilly. [This word is also meant to denote feeling "fine."] Everything's cool but for some reason, I feel like I have to cover myself up from the cold today and I can't afford to be sick from my job. Damn, I can't think about fuckin' shit today. This fucked-up office is messin' with my head.

Therapist: What was *in* your head before my office took it over?

Annie: [Sighing] I don't know, I'm up for a promotion to be assistant to the Dean of Student Affairs and I have an interview with him today. It's a great job, Julie, you have a lot of responsibility and power, yeah me. They'd raise me from 25 to 30 grand, more vacation time, my own office, me—a low life junkie. Ain't no one would believe it.

Therapist: No one would believe it especially since they don't know anything about your drugs, or *you* can't believe it? I ask because we both know that you often project your own harsh judgments about yourself on to others.

Annie: That's a hip question. You get a high five for that. It's me that thinks this is all just a fuckin' dream and I'll wake with a needle in my arm. Everybody has been really great to me and tells me I'm doing a great job. They invite me out after work and shit and my boss says I have great potential. But today, I'm uptight about the interviewer. He's white, tightass, but everyone says he's fair. Okay, time to cut to the chase, I'm scared shitless. He'll think I'm just another "nigger" no matter what I say. I'm still a fuckin' "nigger" who can do word processing but too dumb to run the office of the department.

Therapist: So far you've used the weather as a substitute for talking about how anxious and undeserving you are. Am I hearing that you're so scared that you'll mess everything up, not because *you* and only *you* know your history of sick behavior, but that they will find out and knock your ass out of the college for good? Is that what the session is really about for starters? Was your tantrum about the A/C your unconscious way of running for the hills and denying the real source of your pain?

Bearing in mind that clarification and confrontation are, for her, necessary precursors to interpretation, I am slowly, in gradual steps, trying for both of us to clarify her use of denial in the session (Loewenstein 1951, Dewald 1971).

Annie: Yeah, I was trying to deny my reaction to heat because I knew that the truth would get me started on something too intense for me.

Therapist: Tell me more about what it would be.

Annie: Let's get real, I'm a mother-fuckin' fake when you peel my onion.

Therapist: [Initiating a low-keyed confrontation] Annie, you've identified how you stayed with the A/C to avoid getting with it. But you also chose to stay with this need to cover yourself up from head to toe in this oppressive heat. I think there may be something in that you haven't copped to before. I don't think this was just accidental.

Annie: I think I'm getting your drift. I've told you before what a fake I think I am. That ain't news and we've talked about it before. But the A/C clothes shit, I think I know where you're going with that. I could have picked any way in the world to jive my way out, but in this weather, we both know I ain't that dumb.

Therapist: [Nods and smiles.]

Annie: Well, let's put it this way. By now I know that when the shit hits the fan I've always denied my way out. But I know I'm not going to skate my way out any more. Not out of your office, I can tell. You're on to me. Your mind is always going.

Therapist: While you're on the subject of my powers, how about staying with yours and go back a few steps where you left off?

Annie: [She smiles, laughs, and claps her hands.] You don't miss a beat. Okay, I know there's lots of layers but right now, I'll just say this, for the first time. I know you've been waiting until I'm ready. Damn, Julie, I got the most disgusting dope scars all over my body. They freak me out for a lot of reasons but I can't let anyone at work see them. They'll know in a minute. I mean this is heavy shit, Julie.

Therapist: Yes, Annie, it is and I'm glad that you know that there are *many* layers of pain here. We have a lot of time, Annie, but how do you feel about making the emotional connections that get you through this interview? Like some fast forward insight and then we can really go as deep as you need and are ready for.

Annie: I like that. Right now, even though I'm clean, all I have to do is see these scars all over my body and shit, they are grotesque, and I get reminded that fuck, all my rehab, I am a junkie. That's me, the real me, and it makes me have these flashbacks that won't stop. They take me back to the ugly, low-down junkie I was, and I can't shake that image of myself. It's like my recovery is just a jive-ass fairy tale. I can strut through the right motions, but I am one ugly, like, mutilated dope fiend. I'm an animal.

We spent the rest of the session talking about her scars, her fears, and fantasies of exposure in the interview and supplying enough reality-testing to make her feel more comfortable approaching the interview. Finally, we agreed that in just this one session, we were identifying some of the most basic, still unspoken material that defines her self-esteem. This hour also had afforded us a preview of the work that lay ahead of us.

TREATMENT REVIEW

Over time, Annie began to perceive me as her committed advocate, a role that helped to build trust and promote a positive transference. This developing relationship, in turn, enabled her to be more open and more responsive to a dynamic approach. My use of "generative empathy" (Schafer 1959), that is to say, "the experience of others not like our own but as our own" (p. 343), helped to foster a useful therapeutic partnership.

Annie told me on several occasions that if I had not "fed her belly and then her soul" (a quote her drug counselor used, citing Bertold Brecht), our therapy would have collapsed. This encouraged her to painfully and courageously reveal sources of her shame that were traumatizing and had a disorganizing effect on her. She desperately wanted to give shape to wordless shame in spite of her understandable fright. That her therapist could slowly integrate these forces into a comprehensive matrix of her heroin addiction and depression, without judging her, was a "luxury," according to Annie. She was "flattered" by my active stance, which she took as an absorption in and a valuing of her life. Under conditions of safety, she relived past traumas related to early maternal abuse and neglect, and her own past behaviors that had led to unbearable humiliation.

While I did make useful observations and interpretations in the course of this treatment, it was, I think, my "developmental empathy" (Emde 1990) or, as Stern (1985) put it, my "affect attunement" to the patient that contributed most to her therapeutic gains. Both Emde (1990) and Stern (1985) describe the instinctual, visceral response pattern of the mother and even the therapist to the developmentally determined requirements of the infant/patient's use of non-verbal cues to express a range of needs. There was an immediate chemistry between us, carefully boundaried, and a source of enormous, longed-for security for Annie.

I assumed the posture of a "nurturant authority" (Mitchell 1961). I encouraged Annie's cognitive and affective steps toward initial autonomy.

I was there for her, however, when she needed to return and touch base. This was somewhat similar to the way in which the mother of the practicing period in the separation-individuation progression, as described by Mahler (1965) appreciates the child's steps away from her but remains available for him or her to return for "refueling" when the need arises. Here again, I fulfilled two roles: that of an educating, supportive "coach," and that of an exploring therapist to whom she could return and examine all her attendant dependency needs. Annie herself designated me as her "cheerleading shrink," a combination which satisfied her. By the end of her treatment she no longer depicted our hours as sessions, but as "dialogues." This term underscored her perception of the therapy as an educational, object-relational base. Annie's use of the word "dialogues" was entirely her own and reflected her growth during treatment.

This positive therapeutic relationship made it possible for Annie to make useful identifications with me. Her eventual ability to mourn trauma, loss, physical illness, and shame bore testimony to her identification with me as a collaborator in the working alliance and as a positive transference object. Schafer (1968) describes the process of identification, which he proposes is the highest level of internalization, in a way that best describes Annie's major therapeutic achievement:

> The subject modifies his motives and behavioral patterns, and the self-representations corresponding to them, in such a way as to experience being like, the same as, and merged with one or more representations of that object; through identification, the subject both represents as his own one or more regulatory influences or characteristics of the object that have become important to him and continues his tie to the object. [p. 110]

DISCUSSION

By the time Annie terminated treatment, she had experienced a therapeutic relationship which was an adult version of the reparative experience for which she had always longed. This deepened her as a person and reinforced a gradual desire to expand her horizons culturally, professionally, and emotionally. Her vocational and social life had greatly improved. She had developed substantial interpersonal skills.

As was mentioned earlier, the successful outcome of this therapy can primarily be seen as the result of the powerful impact of the therapeutic relationship itself. Ours was a collaborative effort which served as a vehicle for promoting growth.

Despite her problems, it is clear that Annie herself brought much of facilitating value to this encounter. To begin with, from our very first handshake, she manifested a friendly warmth and enthusiasm that was truly heartwarming, knowing her drug history and her advanced HIV positive status. She was sincerely motivated to immerse herself in a dynamic therapeutic encounter. She wanted to learn and benefit from a treatment that emphasized introspection versus the purely externalized, "brutal" encounter approach used in her residential therapeutic community. While it was evident within the first fifteen minutes that she could with great charm express her resistance through a variety of means (e.g., lateness, purposely racing glibly through important material, seductively concerning herself with my welfare whenever a difficult subject arose), she was receptive to recognizing her resistance and working on understanding its sources.

The positive exchange between Annie and me was, I believe, facilitated by my ease and relaxed ability to understand and speak the same language as she did and yet at appropriate times to express myself in the more "educated," professional form of communication that Annie was eager to emulate and internalize. As she often said to me, with smiling admiration, "Hey, you walk the walk, and talk the talk at just the right times and you talk without apologizing. That's cool, you don't try to pretend you're black but go back and forth at the right time. You're okay, it's like you're comfortable in both worlds. I gotta say, I respect you for that. Now don't let it get to your head or nothin'," she would jokingly warn me. In spite of our linguistic differences at times, I cannot overemphasize that Annie was an extraordinarily bright, quick, sharp young woman with a tremendous intellectual potential that proved to be an invaluable asset in the work.

Annie's inner life was dominated not only by shame, but also by fears of relapse, social contempt for her drug use, defectiveness, and abandonment. Having failed to achieve sufficient object constancy, she experienced profound separation anxiety when parted from a needed person. She saw all relationships as inherently tenuous, unreliable, and destructive to her.

Annie's fears were more implied than articulated by her. Instead, as noted earlier, she denied them, and we continuously had to recognize her use of this defense and to name those fears she was avoiding. Ultimately, it meant a great deal to see all of her different avoidance behaviors as actually having a name, or a "label," as she put it. Understanding these phenomena made her feel important, "like a person with a real psychological life," and not just another nameless junkie who was processed through drug counseling in the identical fashion as all of her peers. In her treatment she felt as though her life was deemed worthy of many different narrative perceptions and configurations. She was a patient who was valued enough to be the object of long-term investigation and interest. Annie was gratified to be regarded as a patient with her very own life signature.

SUMMARY

In this chapter I have shown that motivated addicts in recovery are often able to engage in a psychodynamic form of therapy when it is especially fitted to their unique needs. Such an approach is the psychoeducational-psychodynamic technique elaborated upon here. This approach addresses concrete stresses of readjustment in the larger community and simultaneously offers an opportunity to explore affect and intrapsychic content through psychodynamic inquiry. For many recovering addicts, particularly those unfamiliar with the workings of individual psychotherapy, it is necessary initially to provide a kind of case-managing structure, which recognizes their urgent need for help in adjusting to the mechanics of living outside of therapeutic communities. Engagement in working on such concrete problems allows these patients time to ready themselves to make use of a dyadic relationship with their therapist and gain from insight-oriented work.

REFERENCES

Alexander, I. (1966). *The History of Psychiatry*. New York: New American Library.

Dewald, P. A. (1971). *Psychotherapy: A Dynamic Approach*. New York: Basic Books.

Emde, R. (1980). Mobilizing fundamental modes of development: empathic availability and therapeutic action. *Journal of the American Psychoanalytic Association* 38:881–913.

Fromm-Reichman, F. (1957). *Principles of Intensive Psychotherapy*. Chicago: University of Chicago Press.

Gaylin, W. (1976). *Carina.* New York: Knopf.

Greenson, R. (1967). *The Technique and Practice of Psychoanalysis.* New York: International Universities Press.

Herman, J. (1972). *Trauma and Recovery.* New York: Basic Books.

Kaufman, E., and Kaufman, P., eds. (1979). *Family Therapy of Drug and Alcohol Abuse.* New York: Gardner.

Khanztian, E. J., and Wilson, A. (1992). Substance abuse repetition and the nature of suffering. In *Hierarchical Concepts in Psychoanalysis: Theory, Research and Practice,* ed. A. Wilson, and G. G. Gedo, pp. 263–283. New York: Guilford.

Loewenstein, R. M. (1951). The problem of interpretation. *Psychoanalytic Quarterly* 20(1).

Mahler, M. (1968). *On Human Symbiosis and the Vicissitudes of Individuation.* New York: International Universities Press.

Miller, J. (1994). Substance abuse: the role of depression and trauma: a case report. *Journal of the American Academy of Psychoanalysis* 22:758–764.

Mitchell, C. (1967). A case work approach to disturbed families. In *Exploring the Base for Family Therapy*, ed. N. Ackerman, F. L. Bratman, and S. Sherman. New York: Jewish Family Service.

Sashin, J. I. (1985). Affect tolerance: a model of affect-response using catastrophe theory. *Journal of Social and Biological Structures* 8:175–202.

Schafer, R. (1959). Generative empathy in the treatment situation. *Psychoanalytic Quarterly* 28:347–373.

—— (1968). *Aspects of Internalization.* New York: International Universities Press.

Somers, S. P. S. (1990). *On Mood Swings: The Psychobiology of Elation and Depression.* New York: Plenum.

Stern, D. N. (1985). *The Interpersonal World of the Infant.* New York: Basic Books.

Winnicott, D. W. (1965). *The Maturational Processes and the Facilitating Environment: Studies in the Theory of Emotional Development.* New York: International Universities Press.

Wurmser, L. (1974). Psychoanalytic considerations of the etiology of compulsive drug use. *Journal of the American Psychoanalytic Association* 22:820–843.

14 Psychoanalytically Oriented Psychotherapy with the HIV-Infected Person

Sheila Felberbaum

Tired

I am tired of being asked, How long do I think I'll be
alive, I am tired of the fear, the awareness of
the fear, being the object of the fear, of being
afraid
I am tired of taking pills, keeping track of medicines,
having my life reduced to survival
I am tired of people who assume I am gay, assume I
still shoot dope, assume I feel fine when I'm not
hospitalized
I am sick and tired of the idea that AIDS has made
anyone a better person, tired of the notion that
anyone is paying for their sins, angry at this
twisted "blaming the victim" thinking
I am tired of the self-centered new age response of
meditation, introversion, and orchestrated denial of
the horror show I am living every moment of every
day
I am tired of all the people who believe that a cure
lies around the corner, who think that everything
will be ok just fine back to normal just as soon
as that magic bullet arrives
I am bored with the healing powers of crystals
I am tired of hearing of the evils of AZT and the
wonders of wheatgrass

> I am sick and tired of the treatment of the month club:
> vitamin therapy, ozone, good attitude
> I am really tired of AIDS activists who believe drug
> addiction is not their problem
> I am sick and tired of reading about AIDS in the style
> section of the *Village Voice*, of being a victim in
> the human interest section of the *New York Times*,
> of reading about innocent victims everywhere I
> turn
> I am tired of fighting and I am tired of hanging in
> there and the skin of my teeth is stretched very
> tight. [pp. 29–30]

The preceding is an abbreviated version of a poem written by Gary Mackler (1988) from the *Newsline*, a publication of the People with AIDS Coalition. In his moving words, Gary Mackler conveys something of the world he and other AIDS patients live in, a world that psychotherapists are increasingly entering. As diagnostic advances and more effective medical treatments are extending the life span of HIV-positive individuals, an increasing number of these patients are availing themselves of psychotherapy. As they do, therapists who are serving this population are discovering that, perhaps more than any other client population, these patients test a therapist's ability to negotiate the patient's shifting psychodynamics in treatment with pressing reality demands.

There is no general treatment approach indicated for this group of patients any more than for any other patient population. Rather, the clinician is called upon to vary his or her approach according to the stage of illness, the patient's personality configuration, including his or her ego capacities, and the unique meanings the illness has assumed for the patient.

In work with these men and women, somatic diagnosis should not supersede and overshadow psychodynamic formulations (Felberbaum 1993). As psyche collides with soma, the therapist walks a tightrope, balancing fantasy with fact. Preconceived constructs of the division of mind and body are demolished. Just as with other patients, the physical symptom can become a mode of expressing the verbally unexpressed, with the body serving as a battleground. Thus, the clinician needs to explore the specific meanings this particular disease process has for each individual. The therapist must guard against focusing *exclusively* on supportive efforts, for this may limit the person's chance to gain an understanding of the unique significance the illness has taken on, as well as deprive the patient of the opportunity to exercise whatever autonomy remains possible.

This chapter explores the incorporation of psychoanalytically oriented psychotherapy with compatible adjunctive techniques. Particular attention will be paid to the separation issues which are unique to this group of patients and to the inherent countertransference difficulties that work with them evokes in the clinician. I will share clinical material regarding two patients, the early stages of therapy with a newly HIV-infected young adult, and a more lengthy treatment of a person with AIDS. Concluding remarks will contain an example of the reparative and developmental opportunities available for the therapist who works with a patient who is dying.

COUNTERTRANSFERENCE ISSUES

The effects of this work on the therapist are powerful and varied. Fear of contagion, of the unknown, of an early, painful death, and the terror of abandonment intrude upon even the most carefully intellectualized defense. Increased education regarding modes of transmission resulting in AIDS does not eliminate the proliferation of irrational reactions to this dreaded disease. Our fantasy life is laid bare; our countertransference reactions are intense and demanding. To speak of AIDS is to evoke the specter of death; it must be dealt with head-on by patient and practitioner alike. Susan Sontag (1989) vividly illustrates this in *AIDS and Its Metaphors*, revealing the ways in which AIDS has supplanted all other illnesses from past plagues to current cancers in the hierarchy of horrific images. Therapists are often deeply shaken even when they contemplate the termination of a patient who will continue to live; small wonder that the ultimate, final separation, death, stirs up more than most wish to handle.

Lawrence and Eda LeShan (1961) address this in the following way:

> The fear of the therapist of his own hurt . . . seems to be a major factor in the reluctance to work with the dying patient. The feeling that a therapist develops for his patient consists of more than countertransference. When the patient dies during the process of therapy, it is a severe blow. Not only are the therapist's feelings of omnipotence damaged and his narcissism wounded, but also he has lost a person about whom he feels very deeply. [p. 332]

The anger patients feel and express evokes wide variations of reaction in therapists—rescue fantasies, anger at the medical profession for not treating effectively enough, or even fury at the patient himself for not doing enough, for not recovering. The frustration and despair often experienced by the medical profession, which views death as a failure, can infiltrate the psychotherapist's session and sap it of its vitality and meaning. Stephanie Atchley-Simonton (1985), a therapist who specializes in the treatment of patients who have cancer, cautions us against this. She states, "Success must not be tied to the continuance of life."

In the wake of the powerful and complex reactions stirred up in the therapist by high-risk patients, therapists often find themselves unwittingly led to adopt certain protective maneuvers. Among them may be a strong need to maintain a sense of difference from the patient. One way to do so is to rigidly categorize and stereotype the high-risk patient—homosexuals, IV drug users—and to classify themselves as the "helping professional." As long as we identify strongly only with our role as therapist and deny the possibility that we too could be the patient, we can, it seems, entertain the illusion of a magical immunity, an omnipotence earned through knowledge and service. This pseudo-sense of protection appears to diminish when the practitioner is faced with the stark, unyielding reality of the finiteness of time embodied in the patient who is referred to as "terminal." While difficult, this is therapeutically advantageous. To deny our own fears of becoming like the patient by a defensive need to maintain difference would interfere with our ability to temporarily merge with the patient for purposes of achieving empathic understanding, a matter that will be taken up more fully later in the chapter.

CASE EXAMPLES

Larry

Nelther my previous years of academic learning nor my clinical experience prepared me for the first session I had with a patient I will call Larry. He was 22 years old when he found out that his blood test was HIV positive. Two days later he sat in my office, a handsome, healthy-looking young man, a preppie dresser, in severe crisis. "I can't believe this," he said. "I should be worrying about what college courses to take, not what medical symptoms I will wake up with." His was the most difficult intake I have ever done. Larry was the same age as my son. His fear and panic flooded the room as he imagined his life destroyed before he had lived it. Each sore throat or pimple or freckle was an omen of death to him. His initial abhorrence of sex erupted into an I-don't-care attitude as he toyed with doing to others what had been done to him, not inform his partners of his HIV status while having unprotected sex. He wondered how could he have allowed himself to become infected when he had seen the tell-tale skin lesions on the body of the older man he'd spent the night with. "I took the class on this . . . I knew better–yet I believed him when he said it was nothing . . . he was so nice to me, giving me presents . . . I feel like dirt, how could he have done that to me?"

This theme of non-protection emerged from the experiences of his childhood and adolescence. Father abandoned him, his younger brother, and mother when he was 6, leaving him to be the "little man" of the house. A verbally and at times physically abusive alcoholic, his father resurfaced in Larry's life periodically, promising him vacations, closeness, and money but rarely providing anything but cruelty. During late adolescence, he experienced his mother's moving out of state to live with her second husband as another abandonment.

Larry created a script: he is seduced by an older man who lies to him. He knows (when he sees the lesions) yet suspends his knowing. He recreates a childhood scenario in which a man he loves betrays, damages, and leaves him. His most pervasive fantasy was to be taken care of by a man. This is the way in which an individual unknowingly tends to repeat in the present a pattern of relatedness with which he has struggled in the past. In Larry's case it seemed as if this endless repetition was in the interest of making the story turn out more favorably than it had with his father. This is in keeping with Patrick Casement's (1991) notion that the repetition compulsion can be understood in some instances as an expression of "unconscious hope," as an attempt, albeit unsuccessful, to solve past unconscious conflicts (p. 301).

During the brief time Larry spent in once-a-week treatment, he told me of his passion for motorcycles and the dangerous accidents he'd had. I had begun to see him as a young man "living on the edge," playing Russian roulette with his life. His relationships were intense and usually of limited duration. He moved frequently and left no forwarding address. Larry had only sporadic contact with his parents and brother. He felt unable to tell them of his HIV status because in doing so he would also have to inform them of his homosexual relationships.

He also left a short-term therapy experience without warning, informing me that the therapist was only interested in his telling her about his gay lifestyle. He felt she was excited by his behavior but assured me that it was different with me, I wasn't like that, he could talk about what he really felt.

Transference issues often centered on how I would respond to his acting out behavior: non-payment of fees, missed sessions, and his use of alcohol and cocaine–doubly dangerous in light of his knowledge that these were risky co-factors in precipitating the progression of HIV to full-blown AIDS. If I cared about him, he felt, I would not charge him for his sessions. (His fee was set according to his income level by the clinic.) Once he told me he only had enough money for a can of soup. I remember wanting to take him home, to feed him, to comfort him, to parent him. His attendance was irregular–would I notice if he were there or not? I worried: had he been in another accident, was he in a hospital? Would I confront him about his self-harming behaviors, or just ignore every thing as his parents had?

Larry was ashamed of his homosexuality and had such a paucity of trusted object relationships that his HIV status was known only to other members of the support group he attended.

After seven months he left treatment, just drifted away, no forwarding address, phone number, no goodbye. He had moved past his initial overwhelming sense of panic, worked through homicidal feelings toward the man he thought infected him, and had obtained a full-time job. The compulsion to repeat a lifelong pattern of short-term involvements reappeared, however, in his treatment.

As I reflect upon the treatment, I continue to wonder what I might have done that would have enabled Larry to continue. I could hear the threat of his premature termination in the material he presented, his short-term relationships and abrupt treatment ending. I think it would have been more helpful if I had explored Larry's assurance that I was different from his previous therapist rather than simply accepting his comment. I could have helped him consider the possibility that he feared that I would indeed have similar traits as the rejected clinician, as well as his hopes that I would not. When he raised this issue we might have been able to understand, together, what had transpired in the current treatment that brought this to mind. In retrospect, I believe my own grandiosity prevented me from analyzing this with him, I longed to be the "better therapist," the one who would not be left. Also inadequately explored was his relationship with his mother. A great deal of anger at his father was expressed, while mother was curiously left out, as if she were simply a bystander. Perhaps the determinants of his male rescue fantasies originated from unmet needs in his earliest relationship, the mother–infant dyad. In wanting to help preserve whatever good object representations Larry had of his mother, I may have been drawn into a reenactment of the past. In this new edition, I am the one who is left instead of him, he identifies with the one who leaves (the aggressor) rather than being left (a passive position). He therefore continued to repeat these patterns from the past and left treatment without significant resolution of this issue. I am reminded of how frequently unanalyzed transference issues can precipitate "acting out" in patients. Gill (1982) explains acting out as "the patient . . . [carries] out some action in the external world as a displacement of the transference" (p. 67). He stresses an emphasis on the analysis of the here-and-now situation of the therapist–patient interaction as most helpful in illustrating how previous modes of relating are enacted in the present. Thus, instead of being able to speak about and analyze his reactions and feelings about me, my patient acted—he left treatment.

I believe that another contributing factor to his premature termination was that he associated his therapist and his therapy with the HIV diagnosis. Once his basic functioning improved and he was better able to concentrate, socialize, and work, he wanted to sever a relationship that reminded him of an illness he wished to forget and deny. Establishing a therapeutic alliance based on issues beyond the impact of the physical condition may mitigate this common defense.

Separating characterological patterns and reactions from those that are crisis-related is also of ongoing importance. The patient is ideally made aware of those conflicts and detrimental modes of operating that existed prior to diagnosis (pre-morbid functioning). A therapeutic task is to render these modes ego-dystonic (no longer acceptable to the ego-self). Failure on the part of the therapist to isolate these aspects may impede the treatment and contribute to the ways in which the diagnosis can be used as a resistance. Examples of this would be canceling a session because of discomfort about the material being explored, but using a physical symptom as the reason.

Tom

Tom was diagnosed with AIDS two years before he began treatment with me. In the early months of our work he would saunter down the long hall to my office at the community mental health center, each week wearing a new outfit reflective of his artistic and creative flair for the unusual. He never lost this talent. In his final week of life he managed to have a Christmas ribbon tied around his neck, a last bit of panache. Tall, slender, with wavy blond hair, he was 28 years old, a master's-educated health-care professional with a love of what he called "black humor." What was at first weekly outpatient individual treatment became sporadic hospital visits, then weekly home sessions. At times his family members, parents and sisters, were included. The only son in a family of six children, his homosexuality was a humiliation and a sin to his deeply religious parents, especially his father. In spite of ambivalent feelings, his family was willing to be part of a home care support system. Tom continued to explore his conflicts about the church, God, and his sexuality until he died. He had frequent visits from a priest who offered him compassion and friendship. "I'm attempting to integrate his goodness within my trash-can mouth and mind," he told me jokingly.

During one of our sessions, Tom spoke of a suicide hot-line in the hospital and his own belief that people aren't punished if they commit suicide. I asked him if he had been thinking of killing himself. He responded,

> I won't. I came so close to dying, they put a mask on me and I couldn't talk. The doctor says, "Do you want to go on a respirator if we are unable to get enough air to you?" I'm thinking I've still got a brain, you can say oxygen to me, and all these people are around my bed staring at me. I don't know if any of these doctors are any good. And then the physician's assistant that I know comes in and stands at my bedside and just looks at me like "What's up?" and I'm thinking she wouldn't want me to go on the respirator, and I write, "Put me on the respirator if I need it." That didn't come from me. It was a spiritual reaction–not how I would have expected it.

I remember my own struggle about initiating home visits when Tom was no longer able to come to the Center for his sessions. I had left home health care nursing to become a clinical social worker, a psychotherapist, and had envisioned my work in the safety of an office. Instead I was to see the value in "social casework [that] . . . emphasize[s] the interdependence of people and their environment" (Hollis 1981, p. 218), of meeting the patient where he lives. Within this framework, Hamilton describes "the person-in-his-situation, which consists of the person, the situation, and the interaction between them" (Hollis 1981, p. 27). Once I entered Tom's bedroom, with its Judy Garland posters and a fishtank filled with fish who had names, I knew that I would somehow manage to see him through to the end. Utilizing my own support network of personal analysis, a bimonthly peer oncology supervision group, and individual supervision at the clinic helped me to work through my issues and reactions.

In his last year of life he was admitted to the hospital sixteen times, had a Broviac catheter for antibiotic administration, and fought multiple battles with opportunistic infections. I visited him frequently during a particularity difficult period in which he had pneumonia and was coughing productively. When I came down with pneumonia myself, the first time in my life that I had been so ill even though I had worked for years with patients in hospitals with all manner of infections, my immediate image was of sitting next to his bedside with the door closed and the oxygen running and no air circulating. My own terror rose up and I imagined that I had somehow contracted AIDS from him. The mystery surrounding AIDS, the fear that we don't know enough, negated all the workshops I had attended about AIDS transmission.

Over the fifteen months that I worked with Tom I grew to admire his spunkiness, his ability to say no to all types of mental and physical health care practitioners. He denied procedures he felt were unnecessary, stating, "I exercise my rights as a human being to refuse these painful tests." He withheld permission for the exchange of information between the hospital and the center for which I worked. I got to know him apart from lab values and grim predictors of his probable life span. He was for me a lively, sarcastic, provocative, and vulnerable man/child.

Toward the end of his life Tom agreed to permit the information exchange needed to facilitate his final hospital discharge. He wanted to die at home on the warm and comforting waterbed his parents bought him. He did not want to die in a hospital bed with the young nurses with whom he had joked, while they were cleaning his incontinent body. The hospital social worker saw his previous efforts to deny this permission as "manipulative," and viewed Tom's behavior as "difficult." I understood Tom, on the other hand, as seeking to exercise control and striving to keep his fighting spirit alive. His ability to extract from his environment and to use "No" to help orchestrate his life were, in my view, evidence of his strengths. I regarded my advocacy on his behalf with the hospital staff as in the interest of safeguarding and promoting Tom's autonomy. I was fortunately able to share this reframing of a negative to a positive with the hospital social worker, as I stressed the needs that all patients have who are confronting a life-threatening illness to maintain autonomy in the face of regressive pulls from both inner and outer worlds.

In my work with Tom I sought to enter his world, even as I maintained a degree of separateness from it. Initially I joined him by showing a comfort with his sarcastic and, at times, colorful humor and language. It was not only Tom who needed the protection of the jokes. We both needed to hide together from the dark days we could see just around the bend. We would laugh at a world less sophisticated and witty than we. This did not, incidentally, stop me from analyzing his desire and need to entertain me. "Who wants to be with me if I'm not funny?" he said.

In maintaining an empathic stance, I tried to keep Arlow's (1991) advice in mind. While we need to feel *with* the patient temporarily, we must be able to appreciate that what we have felt is *about* the patient and make use of that understanding. An excessive lingering at identification with the patient "implies merging and can be detrimental to the therapeutic work" (p. 222).

Sanville (1990), too, indicates that a merger occurs momentarily, but that in order to be helpful a return to one's own boundaries is in order: "empathy, like play, involves make-believe, an immersion into the psyche of the other, and then a defusion" (p. 5). Referring to Bakhtin, Sanville (1991) explores his concept that human understanding takes place when there is a "responsive dialogue" which is comprised of "empathy and alterity." Alterity is defined as otherness or difference. "If we were to stop with empathy or merging, we would, he claimed, only deepen the tragic character of the other's life or of our own" (p. 126).

RELAXATION EXERCISES AND IMAGERY

Later on, Tom's fear of death emerged each time he insisted his parents bring him to the hospital to be "checked out." Anxious breathing was followed by multiple crowding images of physical deterioration. He was propelled toward technology with a desire to be connected to machines and professionals who might alleviate his terror. My associative image at that time was of a safe, peaceful, pre-born state in which the mother, through the umbilical cord, provides all nourishment and removes all toxic substances. It was at this juncture that he allowed me to guide him to a place of comfort, to change some of the negative images. The person with AIDS suffers extreme psychic and somatic pain as he or she experiences varying levels of physical deterioration. Learning relaxation exercises and imagery techniques can result in feelings of increased self-mastery. This process has the potential to be ego-enhancing at a time when everything inside (somatic functioning) and outside (usual way of being in the world) seems to be disintegrating. The person who learns and can do something autonomously still has a modicum of control and "self-agency" a term coined by Stern (1985) which means "authorship of one's own actions" (Sanville 1991, p. 10).

Hartmann (1958) proposed that our ability to withdraw from the external world enabled us to return to it with improved mastery. He noted both the "regulating role in human action" that images have, as well as the organizing aspect that artistic activity promotes. In discussing fantasy, he stated that "there are fantasies which, while they remove man from external reality, open up for him his internal reality" (pp. 18–19). In other words, the journey away from the usual to a place of stillness, the quieting of the external. He continues, in the same vein, "that the normal ego must be able to suspend, temporarily, even its most essential functions" (p. 94). He cited as examples of "ego loss" the sexual excitement of orgasm and the "ego's abandoning itself to free associations in the course of psychoanalysis" (p. 94). I add the imagery process to this most abbreviated list.

I can think of no other situation more filled with incentives to alter the usual than the unremittingly painful psychophysiological reality encountered by the person with AIDS. Rather than construe the encouragement of fantasy and imagery as the use of denial in a negative context, the process may be apprehended in the spirit in which Hartmann (1958) proposed the following:

> Though fantasy always implies an initial turning away from a real situation, it can also be a preparation for reality and may lead to a better mastery of it.

> Fantasy may fulfill a synthetic function by provisionally connecting our needs and goals with possible ways of relaxing them . . . avoidance of the environment in which difficulties are encountered–and its positive correlate, the search for one which offers easier and better possibilities for action–is also a most effective adaptation process. . . . The search for a favorable environment among those available should probably be given a far more central position among adaptation processes–in the broader sense–than customary. [pp. 19–20]

I introduced this idea very gently. When we first began treatment he relished being the rebel in the AIDS support group he attended. When they discussed the use of imagery and relaxation exercises he told the other members, "That stuff is bullshit." He thrived on this feeling of being different and superior but, in actuality, he was using this aspect of the aggressive "no" to deprive rather than to enhance self-nurturing. One afternoon, when he was still able to come in to the Center, he told me of how dirty he felt in the middle of the night when he had severe night sweats and was too exhausted to do more than change his pajama shirt. He wished he could step into a whirlpool bath.

I said, "So wouldn't it be nice to have a hot-tub next to your bed . . . and what would you like in it?" "Some Obsession," he replied, "just the right touch." "What would it look like?" I asked. "A round, pink tub with mermaid handles, filled with rainbow-colored beads that dissolve." "How about some bubbles?" I asked. "And then you simply slide right in, into the warm, bubbly water so gently supported, just drifting away, the smell and the softness and the bubbles, a feeling of being held, and of peace." He managed to close his eyes and relax completely.

Winnicott (1971) describes the shared space between the therapist and the patient as the "third area of potential space" (p. 53), somewhat replicative of mother–infant interactions. He envisioned the emergence of psychotherapy from an "overlap of . . . two play areas, that of the patient and that of the therapist" (p. 54). The responsibility for enabling the patient to play (to engage in creative work) lies with the therapist, who must also be capable of play. Sanville (1991) expands Winnicott's description of "psychoanalysis as a subspecies of play" when she states that "much of the work [in psychoanalysis] consists of building the playground in which playfulness can occur" (p. 2).

Relaxation exercises and imagery became an integral part of our weekly sessions. The places and images changed over time; the audio cassettes of my voice guiding him to his favorite places functioned as "a transitional object" (Winnicott 1953) to soothe him. Much as a child might use a soft blanket to remind him or her of mother's soft breast and smell, so too did the sound of my voice embody an aspect of my presence. He regulated the IV administration of his pain medication with a pump-like device and turned my voice on and off at will. Thus, the imaging tapes became the method by which a primary goal of treatment was met: to empower the patient by helping him to master pain, anxiety, and fear, to enable him to self-soothe. Omin (1989) expresses this concept as having a patient "practice internalizing the comfort he feels [when the therapist is present]. . . . Through imagining the already taken in experiences of . . . [the therapist's] soothing, he was able to self soothe when alone" (p. 334).

Edward and colleagues (1991) describe ways in which infants and toddlers deal with anxiety associated with the loss of mother. "Fantasies are one source of protection they develop to relieve the pain of loss. The formation of fantasies and the ongoing use of symbols are employed by toddlers to calm themselves and help them retain the maternal object" (p. 69). They define imaging as

> the inferred activity of the mental work of the child who in the absence of the mother turns his psychic energy inward in search of an inner world that will bring back the perfect state of self that was lost when the mother left. The child is holding onto the sensations of well-being and safety that come from communing with the inner world. [Edward et al. 1991, p. 337]

An adult may also attempt to create a place of safety when using imagery. I realize now that the imagery work (imagery play, as Sanville would say) was also soothing to me. At times, when I felt there was nothing I could do, when ordinary words failed and sitting with him was not enough, I created a holding space, an "artistic arena" in our shared imagination. It helped decrease my feelings of being powerless.

One day he told me how angry he was that everyone, including his therapist, could walk out the door and get away. He longed for one last trip to New York City. This wish was followed by his relating a frightening recurring experience. "Sometimes I feel as if I'm separate from myself, as if I'm on the outside looking in . . . looking at me but not feeling like it's me. I think, this can't be who I am, what I look like." He was experiencing a loss of the familiar, an altered body image. We were both seeing a body wasted by disease. I responded:

> This isn't all of you, your body is only one part of you. Your ability to separate from your body can be used to great advantage. You can leave your body behind, like a coat on a chair, and drift off to the excitement of the city. Listen to the rumble of the subway as you move toward West 4th Street and fill your lungs with that smell of city air permeated with every kind of person, food, and activity. You're dressed to kill and ready to howl.

His episodes of dissociation had changed from moments of terror to a friendly respite from his boredom, anger, and pain. I reinforced the usefulness of his natural ability to disconnect from discomfort and to use his creative imagination and memories to enrich his days. This form of disconnection is a positive rendition of the painful disconnections that Patrick Haney (1988) explored in his article "Providing Empowerment to the Person with AIDS." He saw "many of the potential consequences of AIDS as disconnections: disconnections from the past, present, future, from loved ones, and ways of defining one's self, such as job activities, capabilities, skills and physical appearance" (p. 252).

The crisis of a life-threatening illness can potentiate symptoms related to previously poorly negotiated phases of separation-individuation, or it may offer the opportunity for change.

> Much as the 15-month-old child as described by Spitz (1965) shifts from primary to secondary process with the acquisition of the "No" gesture, so can the patient who, experiencing regressive pulls associated with illness and dependence on others, asserts him or herself as a separate being. As Gertrude and Rubin Blanck (1979) put it, "Perhaps beginning with the severing of the umbilical connection, undoing of connections serves constructive, life-promoting, developmental processes" (p. 45). I believe that the therapist's efforts are ego-enhancing when rightful claims to decision making are supported without sacrificing the need to discriminate between self-assertion and self-punishing behavior. [Felberbaum 1993, p. 19]

Self-punishing behaviors, actions that were not intended to be so but were born out of efforts to avoid pain, were evident with both of my patients. Larry left others rather than risk being the one who was left, and

Tom initially rejected helpful relaxation and imagery techniques in order to maintain his role as a rebel in his support group.

I visited Tom the day before he died. It was two weeks before Christmas but his parents had broken their life-long rule of waiting to put up the tree until Christmas Eve. They wanted him to see it one last time. It was a strange visit. He was in a semi-comatose state but I sat with him anyway and just talked about the decorations on the tree and places he loved and about letting go when suddenly he opened his eyes and just said goodbye.

CONCLUDING REMARKS

It was odd, the way he said goodbye in the middle of the session. It seemed to me that we both knew, that day, that the session, our work, and his life were ending, much too soon. Although this premature ending was painful, I strongly agree with Lawrence and Eda LeShan (1961) that a patient's limited life-span should not prevent a therapist from investing time and energy in his psychotherapy. Hattie Rosenthal (1957) eloquently captures the essence of this belief.

> Why should a dying patient have psychotherapy, when his time is so irrevocably limited? All psychotherapy is designed to help the patient cope with the contingencies of life; but in a broader sense it is also preparation for the acceptance of death. If it makes it easier for the living to live, it can also make it easier for the dying to die. For the therapist this is a great challenge. [p. 633]

Psychotherapy with the dying patient, as with all patients, affords the therapist opportunity as well as challenge. Loewald (1970) stated that

> we can analyze others only as far as we have been analyzed ourselves and understand ourselves. To this there is the corollary: we understand ourselves phychoanalytically [*sic*] by seeing ourselves as others (objectivating introspection), and our self-understanding is greatly enhanced by analyzing others. [p. 48]

He continues, adding that "to discover truth about the patient is always discovering it with him and for him as well as for ourselves and about ourselves" (p. 65). Thus, the therapist may also be able to begin to accept death and in the process have a new appreciation and reverence for life. To be truly present with another as he negotiates life's final terrain, the process of dying, is to dismantle a universal fear. The fear of being alone as we die is ubiquitous, as is the fear of being alone as we live. Our presence with the other affirms and validates the life that has been lived. The patients who determine who will surround them, and where they will die, continue to exercise control and mastery even as they die.

All endings and deaths remind us of those we have experienced in the past; each instance of separation and loss is replayed throughout our lives. When opportunities for resolution are available we can mourn loss yet continue to celebrate connection. Therapists are afforded the chance to rework their own personal themes, not at the expense of the patient, but through the space of inter-relatedness, the overlap of a shared space, in the artistic arena of psychoanalytic psychotherapy.

For this therapist, whose father died of a cerebral vascular accident, alone, unable to speak and surrounded by strangers in a hospital, opportunities to experience and be part of the environment of "a good death" have truly been reparative.

REFERENCES

Arlow, J. A. (1991). *Psychoanalysis: Clinical Theory and Practice.* Madison, CT: International Universities Press.

Atchley-Simonton, S. (1985). *The family within the healing context.* Paper presented at the meeting of the American Cancer Society and Adelphi School of Social Work, Huntington, NY, June.

Blanck, G., and Blanck, R. (1979). *Ego Psychology II: Theory and Practice.* New York: Columbia University Press.

Casement, P. (1991). *Learning from the Patient.* New York: Guilford.

Edward, J., Ruskin, N., and Turrini, P. (1991). *Separation Individuation,* 2nd ed. New York: Gardner.

Felberbaum, S. (1993). Individuation issues with HIV-infected and affected patients. Committee on Psychoanalysis *Newsletter.* Spring, pp. 19–20.

Gill, M. (1982). *Analysis of Transference,* vol. 1. Madison, CT: International Universities Press.

Haney, P. (1988). Providing empowerment to the person with AIDS. *Social Work Journal* 33:251–253.

Hartmann, H. (1958). *Ego Psychology and the Problem of Adaptation.* New York: International Universities Press.

Hollis, F., and Woods, M. (1981). *Casework.* New York: Random House.

LeShan, L., and LeShan, E. (1961). Psychotherapy and the patient with a limited lifespan. *Psychiatry Journal for the Study of Interpersonal Processes* 24: 318–323.

Loewald, H. (1970). Psychoanalytic theory and the psychoanalytic process. In *Psychoanalytic Study of the Child* 25:45–68. New York: International Universities Press.

Mackler, G. (1988). Tired. *People With Aids Coalition Newsline* 33:29–30.

Omin, R. (1989). To die in treatment: an opportunity for growth, consolidation and healing. *Clinical Social Work Journal* 17:325–336.

Rosenthal, H. (1957). Psychotherapy for the dying. *American Journal of Psychotherapy* 11:626–633.

Sanville, J. (1990). Editorial. *Clinical Social Work Journal* 18:3–7.

—— (1991). *The Playground of Psychoanalytic Therapy.* New York: Analytic Press.

Sontag, S. (1989). *AIDS and Its Metaphors.* New York: Farrar, Straus and Giroux.

Spitz, R. A. (1965). *The First Year of Life.* Madison, CT: International Universities Press.

Winnicott, D. W. (1953). Transitional objects and transitional phenomena. *International Journal of Psycho-Analysis* 34:89–97.

—— (1971). *Playing and Reality.* New York: Routledge, 1990.

15 Leaking Walls—A Tale of the Unconscious: A Psychoanalytic Reading of a Case of Post-Partum Depression as Seen through the Perspective of Ignacio Matte-Blanco[1]

Gail Sisson Steger

> Life which seeks its own continuance tends to repair itself without our help, it mends its spiders' webs when they have been torn; it reestablishes in us the conditions of health and itself heals the injuries inflicted upon it: It binds the bandage again upon our eyes, brings back hope into our ears, breathes health once more into our organs and regilds the dream of our imagination. . . . The wise part of us then is that which is unconscious of itself; and what is most reasonable in man are those elements in him which do not reason. . . . Our greatest illusion is to believe that we are what we think ourselves to be.
>
> Henri Frederic Amiel, from his *Journal* in *The Discovery of the Unconscious*, by Henri Ellenberger

We listen to our clients' stories in order to help them. The assistance, comfort, relief, or support we choose to offer depends on the way we organize what we have heard and rephrase it for the client. How do we pick and choose, how do we best understand the rush of language that cascades from the patient and threatens, at times, to engulf us by its seem-

1. In addition to a discussion of theoretical issues in the work of Matte-Blanco that are relevant to the specific clinical material, I have offered an appendix at the end of this chapter, an overview of Matte-Blanco's ideas.

ingly endless and immense range; alternatively, how do we best aid the patient to return to that rich well of personal language when he or she becomes choked up, mired, clogged? The task of listening, guiding, interpreting, facilitating, reopening areas that become blocked seems, at times, not simply immense, but overwhelming.

One dramatic way to clarify our own understanding and ability to mirror the richness of such a patient's associations is to keep reminding ourselves that there are only two basic ways of thinking, however complex the variations —*conscious* and *unconscious.* Conscious refers to thoughts that are easily available for us to think about and remember. Unconscious refers to thoughts that are not available, either because they are in a form that is not like usual thinking or because they are forcibly kept out of consciousness, usually because they are too painful to endure as part of one's emerging sense of self.

Dreams offer us one of the most directly useful ways to share, with the client, a skill in revealing the unconscious thoughts beneath their conscious representations. As much as any aspect of our therapeutic work, we are here perhaps best able to help clients to help themselves, to understand and know themselves and the ways they have habitually come to organize their experience. Interestingly, once the most important differences between conscious and unconscious thinking are grasped, it is far easier for the therapist to aid the client in beginning to interpret together, to share in their hearing the subtle movement between these two modes of thinking. In this sense, dreams are truly, as Freud (1900) claimed, "the royal road to the unconscious."

In conscious thinking, ideas which do not logically belong together are kept apart. Another word for this type of thinking is *asymmetrical* thinking, a key term in the approach to psychoanalysis by the Italian psychoanalyst Ignacio Matte-Blanco, who finds asymmetrical thinking occurring both consciously and unconsciously. When the mind puts ideas together that are not overtly logical (which is typical of Freud's description of the unconscious), the thinking is called by Matte-Blanco *symmetrical* thinking. Once again, Matte-Blanco finds this thinking ubiquitous on both the conscious and unconscious levels.

With her permission, I offer an account of a woman who I believe has been helped by our developing a mutual capacity to understand the various forms of her thinking (conscious and unconscious, asymmetrical and symmetrical), which were represented in pictures, language, emotion, and physical symptoms.

Almost unendurable sensations, thoughts, and emotions emerged in Mrs. L. when her baby was born. Possession by a dybbuk would have been the description in the middle ages. Unlike the expulsion of exorcism, however, analytic therapy released new worlds of genuine inner understanding and a full range of feelings for her baby.

Mrs. L. first came to see me for help because of her post-partum depression and palpitations of the heart that had existed since the birth of her daughter. Meeting the baby's "overwhelming needs" consumed and exhausted her. She had been to another therapist, who told her that she, the mother, was in danger of committing child abuse because she visualized acts such as cutting off the top of her baby's head, sticking a pencil or meat thermometer from one ear to the other, and putting the 2-month-old infant away in a drawer. These pictures would appear without warning as she was feeding and diapering her baby. They terrified her. Did the pictures mean she wanted to perform such terrible acts? She simply could not believe that, but she also had no way to account for these unacceptable images, which arrived unbidden.

Mrs. L., age 26, is an accountant, who had eagerly looked forward to the birth of her baby. When her daughter was born, she was shocked and revolted by the horrific imagery which plagued her. In every other way, her thinking seemed rational, lucid, and sane.

After listening for several sessions, I told Mrs. L. that I was not worried about her committing child abuse, just as in her heart she wasn't worried either. How was it that one therapist could be so frightened of Mrs. L.'s potential for child abuse based on what Mrs. L. told her and I wasn't, even though I heard the same information? My lack of concern about child abuse was supported in part by listening very closely to Mrs. L.'s language and feelings, so closely in fact that that at times I felt that I walked in her shoes. The kind of listening to which I refer goes beyond empathy. Matte-Blanco calls it symmetrical thinking. My lack of apprehension was also founded on a theory based on ego-psychological concepts. From the beginning, Mrs. L. never reported a dissociative (trance-like) state, even during periods of horrific fantasies. On the contrary, she was deeply concerned that she had these fantasies about her baby, whom she found so beautiful and whom she loved with so much tenderness. But she also needed to know why these other images continued, and with so much power. The fantasies were always accompanied by palpitations and at once an immense, continuous desire to be rid of them and also to understand (and, implicitly, to integrate) them. Mrs. L. envisioned with great clarity the forms of abuse and felt a loathing and fear about them. She *never* was consciously tempted to enact them.

The pictures, the dread she felt for them, and the physical symptoms of palpitations represented what in psychoanalytic theory is called a *compromise formation*, which consists of an unconscious wish, a defense against the wish, and the behavior, which is actually a compromise of the wish and the defense. Mrs. L. had some destructive fantasy pictures about her baby. I would call these "the wish," but it is essential to know that Mrs. L. never consciously wished anything bad to happen to her baby—the pictures simply appeared in her mind. The idea, or wish, was totally cut off from what she felt, which was love for her baby. In fact, she dreaded the vivid pictures when they appeared. I would call her dread "the defense" against the wish. Mrs. L.'s actual behavior was expressed by palpitations, terrible anxiety, and the utmost gentleness and competence with her daughter while, at the same time, she desperately searched for psychological assistance and relief. We agreed to work together to understand the meaning of these frightening visions so that Mrs. L. could fully enjoy her baby girl.

Psychological deprivation and abuse by mother and father and some physical abuse on the part of her father, who was often away on business, colored Mrs. L.'s childhood. Of the two, she much preferred and loved her father. He was powerful and intensely involved in the socialization of his nine children, whereas her mother seemed burdened and disinterested. Even though her father's method of rearing was based on taunting and goading, attention was being paid and intermittently and unpredictably he praised behavior. Throughout her life, Mrs. L. kept trying to re-find an emotional caring mother, testimony to the possibility that good mothering had been available at some point in Mrs. L.'s prehistory (before memory). Perhaps it was the maid who was present during her first two years of life. Throughout her life, Mrs. L. sought praise from her father. Both parents were alcoholic. By the time Mrs. L. graduated from high school, they had moved twelve times due to her father's occupation, a factor which increased her dependence on her nuclear family and, therefore, the intensity of her negative pictures of herself. Since they were her only consistent authority figures, their responses to her were her only source of reality about herself and about the world. A child who does not feel valued and loved feels she is unvaluable, unlovable, useless, ugly. In adolescence, Mrs. L. had a breakdown, which was dismissed by her parents. It was manifested by obsessive somatizations, which led her to experience herself as hideous.

I was deeply moved by Mrs. L.'s despair. In spite of the fact that she spoke in a monotone, her delivery expressionless, she bravely threw herself into therapy. I learned that her mild manner reflected the fact that she rarely consciously experienced emotions, although at the time of the request for help a doctor had told her that her palpitations were due to anxiety, not to a heart condition. It is not unusual that children who are traumatized suppress their feelings so successfully that by the time they are adults, they do not believe they have feelings. Mrs. L. expressed feelings through the metaphor of her body and the body of her child. Examples of this are the heart palpitations and the envisioned assaults against the body of her child, which, as a part of her own body, were also assaults against herself. The primary problem was what she was doing to herself and to her child in her nightmare fantasies. Fantasy is not abuse. The therapeutic work was to help her find a way to express her feelings rather than attack her body and the mental image she had of her child (or to save a baby). At this time, she did not have an emotional and symbolically meaningful language with which to convey her thoughts and feelings. I knew that the assaultive imagery she was having was related to aspects of her experience of her own early relationships.

Mrs. L., her baby, and I began to meet twice weekly. Her belief that I would help her allowed her to attend to the realistically difficult needs, as opposed to the "overwhelming needs," of her baby with the love and devotion with which she normally experienced her child. I saw the baby as an individual in her own right, enabling Mrs. L. to create anew her feelings about her baby and develop what we would consider the more familiar mother–infant bond. My presence and my way of relating to her and to the baby freed Mrs. L. Gradually she stopped experiencing the baby as an overwhelming multitude of negative old relationships and former ugly, needy pictures of herself. Thus, I was first used to enlarge her internal space and allow her to put aside her concerns and feel safe, and second, I offered her a temporary model through which she could experience her daughter in a new way. She stopped bringing the baby regularly after a few months.

Social workers utilize an understanding of unconscious or symmetrical thinking intuitively in their work with clients. It is impossible to conduct any kind of therapy without knowingly, or unknowingly, acknowledging these different forms of thinking both in the patient and in the clinician. For instance, a client regularly comes late to her appointment. She has a different reason each time. Clinicians are often dismayed, aggrieved, hurt, angry at this behavior. We recognize that the reasons given are not completely explanatory. The client insists that she is very upset about her lateness. She really wants the help. We believe that she is telling the truth, but how can this be true and untrue at the same time? We think that she doesn't altogether want to be with us. We may respond to her based on how we feel. If we are aggrieved and hurt, we may become more gentle in our approach so that the client may prefer to come. If we are dismayed or angry, we may become more confrontive. Perhaps more astonishing is that our emotional response is so often parallel to the client's unconscious reason for being late. She is dismayed, aggrieved, hurt, or angered by us and the therapy, just as we experience similar emotions in response to her behavior. It is much easier to do the work if we develop a clear systematic understanding of the varieties of the thought patterns we ourselves engage in.

FREUD AND THE UNCONSCIOUS

Hypotheses about the unconscious have existed since 130 A.D. Lancelot Law Whyte and Henri Ellenberger cogently discuss the history of the idea of the unconscious before Freud. Though the subject of the unconscious repeatedly appeared and disappeared throughout intellectual history, disappearing perhaps because man's omnipotence could not tolerate acknowledging so much of the unknown and bizarre within, some notion of the idea of the unconscious surfaced in each historical period, its definitions reflecting the language and culture of its time. The subject has again disappeared, buried beneath our current focus on a variety of competing theoretical systems such as ego psychology, object relations, and self psychology and intersubjectivity.

At the beginning of this century, Freud synthesized various hypotheses about the unconscious. His language bears the imprint of his own cultural background and training. While his overall theory is complex and emerged piecemeal in a process of constant revision and additions, his brilliant contributions regarding the *processes* of the unconscious unfolded early in his writings and were largely completed by 1900 in *The Interpretation of Dreams*. According to Freud, the unconscious is a form of thought governed by certain mechanisms. We shall consider five of them.

1. The Absence of Mutual Contradiction and Negation

There is no negation, no doubt, no degrees of certainty. For instance, a client dreamed that he was in Washington, DC, where he used to live, or in the house of his early childhood. The window in his dream looked out on a tree, like the one he looks on during therapy. "Maybe it was your office," he said. We found that it was all three (emotional memory of relationships in Washington, in the house of his childhood, and with me in my office.) The client identified above as "late" unconsciously does not want to come to therapy but obviously also wants to come. She wants it *and* she doesn't want it. If she were merely conflicted she would be aware of her ambivalence. The same may be said about Mrs. L., who loves her baby *and* has pictures of hurting her.

2. Displacement

An idea's emotional intensity is *detached* from its original source and *superimposed* onto other ideas or objects. Many children develop imaginary friends upon whom they may displace unwanted emotions and actions. "It was Johnny [imaginary friend] who did it, not me." Anyone who has tried to talk a child out of believing in his imaginary friend will be greeted with the greatest protestation and tears. Our "late" client really believes in the reasons (the displacements) that "prevent" her from timely attendance; she has no awareness that she prevents herself and displaces the causes of lateness on to uncontrollable events. Mrs. L. really believes that the baby has overwhelming needs. Her own overwhelming needs are unconsciously displaced onto the baby.

3. Condensation

Several ideas derived from different times in the life of the client or different relationships over time are expressed through a *single* object or idea. A patient dreamed he was in my office but it had an old-fashioned bar in it. He associated the bar to his former lover, an alcoholic (his parents were also alcoholics). Thus he condenses some aspect of our relationship in my office with the relationships with his lover and his parents. The horrific pictures described by Mrs. L. are prototypical condensations.

4. Timelessness

The processes of the unconscious are timeless; they are not ordered temporally, nor are they altered by the passage of time. This is often seen in dreams when the dreamer is himself at his own age and experiences himself living in the house in which he grew up, which, in fact, he left long before. Nothing is altered, there is no recognition of the passage of time, nor of any contradiction. It is generally impossible for people to imagine themselves old or dead. Mostly, we *feel* we go on forever even though we *know* that is not true. Mrs. L.'s feelings about the baby were a timeless repetition of what she believed her mother thought about her. In this situation, she experienced herself as both the unwanted baby and the burdened mother. It may be noted that although Mrs. L.'s mother had many children, Mrs. L. never saw her mother rock, feed, or kiss any of them at any age.

5. Replacement of External Reality by Psychical Reality

They become one and the same. The unconscious pays little regard to outside reality in dreams, where imaginary events appear at first as having equal validity with so-called real events. A woman aged 65 talked with me (I was 22 at the time and in my first social work placement) about how difficult life was for *us* during the depression. In order to feel understood she thought of me as having the same life experiences as she had, whereas her awareness of external reality would have acknowledged that impossibility due to my youth. When Mrs. L. first came for treatment, she and her daughter were playing out historical roles, repetitions of Mrs. L.'s psychic reality. It took therapy for her to envision herself as different from her mother, and her baby as a completely different individual from the babies of her childhood (herself included).

MATTE-BLANCO AND THE UNCONSCIOUS

Matte-Blanco is a well-known Italian mathematician and psychoanalyst who has taken up the study of the unconscious as a form of thought where Freud initially left off. In his two books *The Unconscious as Infinite Sets* and *Thinking, Feeling, and Being,* and in several articles, he has deepened our understanding of what Freud has identified as the basic characteristics of the unconscious. Unconscious thinking unites that which is usually kept apart. Freud's five basic mechanisms of the unconscious, absence of negation, displacement, condensation, timelessness, and replacement of external reality by psychical reality demonstrate how things are put together that are usually separated.

But, according to Matte-Blanco, the uniting of people and events that are usually kept apart is not always unconscious. It is apparent in metaphor, allegory, fables, parables, and poetry. It happens when we are highly emotional. When we mourn someone's death, we often re-experience *all* painful losses. When we are in love, the whole world and everyone in it seems beautiful and wonderful. He claims that human experience may be conceived as structured by the experience of an infinite series of strata. These strata range from the most indivisible mode of thinking (which, although generally unconscious, may occur consciously, as when someone dies or someone is in love) to the most abstract mode of thought. Matte-Blanco calls this indivisible model *symmetrical* thinking. The abstract, logical, differentiated mode, that which we tend to call thinking or concept formation, he calls *asymmetrical* thinking.

We may define asymmetrical thinking as that mode of thought in which the human mind discriminates or classifies. Early infant studies confirm that such thinking begins at the start of human life. Awake or asleep, the human mind is constantly carrying out classificatory activities. Asymmetrical thinking deals with things which may be distinguished from one another and the relationship between such things. It is ordered by categories of space, time, and differentiation into classes or sets. In asymmetrical thinking, a boy is a boy and is a subset of the class of children–he is different from a girl, who is also a subset of the class of children. My office is always my office, it is not Washington, DC, or the house someone lives in, as in the dream reported above. A cigar is always a cigar and not a penis, even though it might have the same shape and thus be similar in one way. If June is the mother of Spencer, then Spencer is never the mother of June.

Asymmetrical thinking seems so obvious to us as a basis for logic and communication that it is striking that all thinking incorporates what Matte-Blanco calls symmetrical thinking. In symmetrical thinking, the converse of any relation is identical to it. In a simple example, if Jane is the sister of Margaret, Margaret is the sister of Jane. The symmetry between the two is obvious; they are both female and sisters. However, the fact described would be true in asymmetrical thinking as well. In purely symmetrical thinking, however, if a boy is a child then a child (all children) is a boy. Is this ever possible? As adults we know that it is never possible. However, 2- to 4-year-old boys are dismayed, shocked, fearful when they see a girl. Where is her penis? After all, a 2-year-old boy thinks that all children are like him: a child is a boy. If June is the mother of Spencer, Spencer is the mother of June. Nothing is absolutely certain: my office might *be* Washington, DC, *and* the home of my patient's childhood. There are no sequences of time points. That is why symmetrical thinking is mostly unconscious. We would constantly feel confused if symmetrical thinking were conscious.

Matte-Blanco states that symmetrical thinking rests on the mathematical rule that unconscious logic is similar to mathematical infinity; when we are dealing with the symbolic logic of infinity, *parts are equal to and the same as* the whole. In symmetrical thinking, therefore, a cigar, a penis, a pencil are the same as each other in *all* ways and equivalent to a man's whole body and to the self. Logically, a part is not equivalent to a whole but we have often heard of a worker referred to as a hand, such as a factory hand, or a spotter referred to as an eye. In these cases, hand or eye stands for a person. We also acknowledge symmetrical thinking in emotional relations, where the converse of any relation is experienced as identical to it. If a mother is loving to her child, the child assumes he is a loving person, just as when a mother is abusive–does bad things to her child–the child believes he is a bad person. Much of our treatment of child abuse is based on our awareness of the fact that emotions arising from two different people may be experienced as identical, particularly when one person is highly dependent on the other as in a parent–child, boss–employee, or dictator–populace relationship. We have seen how negligent or abusive care fostered feelings of worthlessness and ugliness in Mrs. L.

Surprising as it sounds, according to Matte-Blanco, the only way we understand each other is by automatically utilizing symmetrical thinking. Empathy and intuition exist because of indivisible thinking. I am you and/or you are me, you are my father, my mother, and so on. This does not occur as a process evolving through time or in space; it simply is. We understand our "late" patient because we consciously or unconsciously put ourselves in her shoes, thus allowing the process of symmetrical thinking to occur. Matte-Blanco states that on the deepest level man does not simply understand his fellow man, he *is* his fellow man. On that level, there is a oneness between ourselves and everybody and everything else. He believes that this is the background to all thinking. It is there all the time while we unfold different forms of asymmetrical thinking. By the use of symmetrical thinking, I knew that Mrs. L. would not hurt her baby. By the tone of her voice, the language of her body, and a myriad of other sensations and symmetrical connections as well as what she said, I could imagine and empathize with the frightened, angry, overwhelmed, loving, caring young woman who she was. I then supported my convictions through a knowledge of ego psychology.

There are therefore two forms of logic: asymmetrical logic (abstract reasoning) and symmetrical logic (the indivisible logic of the unconscious, of infinity.) Normal thinking is always a mixture of the two; when thinking breaks the bounds of classical bivalent logic,[2] Matte-Blanco refers to *bi-logic*. Bi-logical thinking is seen in various ways of conceiving and living *all* aspects of human life, politics, religion, art, and even science. Bi-logical thinking is the basis of all disagreement, all relationships, all feeling, and, in fact, our whole sense of reality. Once one gets used to seeing this, one cannot avoid the surprising conclusion that we *live* in the world as though it were unitary, with no distinction between persons or things, between parts and the whole. On the other hand, we *think* of the

2. Bivalent logic includes the following concepts: " (a) the principle of identity –A is identical to A; (b) the concept of two-valued or bivalent logic–either A or not A (either proposition A is true or it is not true); (c) the principle of formal contradiction—two contradictory assertions cannot both be true at the same time; (d) the principle of incompatibility–A cannot be different than and totally equal to B; for example, A cannot be liquid and solid at the same time under the same conditions; (e) the operation of subtraction–if a part is subtracted from a given, positive quantity, the result is a smaller quantity" (Matte-Blanco 1988, p. 7).

world in terms of abstract, classical logic, in terms of the distinction between things and their division.

Bi-logic is particularly evident when emotions are involved. Love is experienced as unbounded, forever, infinite. A man may see his beloved as separate and individual (an aspect of asymmetrical thinking) and at the same time attribute to her *all* beauty, intelligence, and gentleness, of the class of flawless, archetypal, beloved women (symmetrical thinking). At moments of great intensity, one sometimes fears being overwhelmed by emotion. The emotion has a seemingly infinite intensity; nothing is left but the emotion–the emotion is the person. Once again I refer to the experience of mourning. The pain is unbounded, unending, seemingly unendurable. It spreads to everything and everybody. The world and people seem empty, gray, sad. No relief seems possible. This overwhelming feeling occurs even while we are aware that the unendurable sadness is related to the loss of a specific person or thing. Behind even the mildest emotion, there is the possibility of its being experienced on the most intense level and spreading to everything else. Other examples of infinite experiences are omniscience, omnipotence, impotence, idealization.

As Matte-Blanco points out, the one trait common to all five characteristics of the unconscious that Freud mentioned is that they unite or unify things which for ordinary thinking are discrete and separate. This union leads to blurring, timelessness, a lack of distinction between one instant and the next, between inner and outer reality, between cause and effect, and ultimately between thinking and not thinking. In schizophrenic thought, the profound disorder of the structure of thinking leads to a confusion of everything with everything else. For example, inanimate objects may seem alive and capable of communication. People who are alive may be experienced as if they were dead.

So many concepts, perceptions and misperceptions are usefully explained by Matte-Blanco's theories: prejudice, for instance, combines differentiated thinking and indivisibility, asymmetry, and symmetry. At various times in history (under the Nazis, during the Spanish Inquisition), all Jews were treated the same way as all other Jews (whether they were educated or non-educated, kind or cruel, just or criminal, fat or thin), as found in symmetrical thinking, but different from non-Jews, asymmetrical thinking. For centuries, all men were treated the same as all other men (allowed the voting right whether educated or non-educated, kind or cruel, just or criminal, fat or thin) but different from women. Both of these examples reflect bi-logic (two forms) thinking: differences exist (asymmetrical thinking), for example, between Jew and non-Jew, between men and women, but the classes lacking differentiation (symmetrical thinking) become larger and larger. Thus in every relationship there are multiple relationships depending upon the way the relationship is being experienced at a given time. A boss may be an individual, he may stand for all authority figures, all fathers, all men, even mankind in general.

In the normal course of development, the individual experiences a continuity between indivisible thinking and differentiated thinking. Each stratum is meaningful in its own right and in relation to the others. In psychic disturbance, dysfunctional thinking, the strata become increasingly jumbled. Thus, if we are treating a person describing a relationship with a boss, it is helpful to be aware of how much symmetrical thinking exists. We would call a person psychotic, for instance, if he "thought that plants, animals, and humans are equally evil because they are alive and all living things are greedy, hence evil" (Matte-Blanco 1988, p. 39).

Like our patients, we function on different levels at different times. The vocabulary used to express this fact has included a high level of functioning versus levels of regression, spaced out, borderline or psychotic features, hysterical and obsessional styles, concrete childlike thinking. *The capacity for bi-logical thinking is the essence of the therapeutic endeavor.* It is vital to be able to move flexibly between different levels of thinking in order emotionally to understand our clients and, equally, to convey our understanding of them at the level at which it can be heard. It is equally important to realize that they are attempting to do the same with us. In graduate school, we are taught "to begin where the client is." Freud said we must attune our unconscious to the unconscious of our patients, for through this understanding will develop. What I now understand both social work training and Freud to mean is that we clinicians must be comfortable with our own symmetrical thinking, with disorder and apparent illogic, with the rich parallels and fused experiences of that mode, in order to be able to hear multiple meanings in the expressions and actions of our clients, in order for them to hear themselves. I believe that being intuitive is the capacity to be comfortable with symmetrical thinking.

Mrs. L. talked to me about whatever came into her mind; we had no agenda. In the beginning, she told many anecdotes of her childhood. I often experienced shock or horror at her descriptions of negligence and abuse. She, on the other hand, seemed detached from awareness of any feelings related to these stories and, more important, that these feelings had been present, had affected her and her actions and reactions, throughout her life. She spoke more vividly to me through her fantasies about the baby, through the sudden appearance and departure of somatic symptoms, through dreams, and, beginning after two years of treatment, through writing. By listening closely to the symmetrical aspects of her thinking we gradually became acquainted with the vigorous, impassioned, injured, outraged, humiliated person who is also Mrs. L. We came to know not only the repressed or unconscious world but much of the world of her being, of her personhood. I have divided our work into five themes, which, like the musical themes of a fantasy, weaved in and out of our work, sometimes in harmony and other times in sharp, painful discord or flat, unrelenting suffering. Significant dreams related to each theme will be presented.

Theme A: Dissolution, Fear, Hope and Ambivalence

Mrs. L.'s palpitations were unremitting. The thunderous, thudding beats drowned out awareness of everything outside and in. She was frightened to the core, though repeatedly told by her physician that she was not having a heart attack. Early dreams spilled over with fear. Would she be crushed, completely lose herself, dissolve? Could she find in me and in herself a relationship she might trust, or would I repeat the indifference and hostility of the past? Dreams inundated the hours, rupturing a lifetime of muteness. Dozens of dreams showed subtle permutations of this opening theme of dissolution.

> A1 A tidal wave was coming. I said, "Should we stay in the car and see if it floats?" The guy I was with said, "No, we've got to get out!" We got out. There was water and I was swimming. Waves would wash over me and I'd think, "Okay I'm still here." But then I'd look and a huge wave would still be coming. Somehow we were following the route of the green line. A woman and her friend thought they would have time to stop at a restaurant and eat before going on. I was afraid and I just wanted to get to higher ground to be safe.

> A2 I worried about how I would get to you, to my appointment. My husband suggested a route through a liquor store. In the

dream I became angry and thought, "I will never give up going to treatment. This is important to me. This is my life." I was on foot. I was running.

A3 I am being taken to the hospital. There they asked for ninety dollars [my fee] and would not take my insurance [assurance]. The only treatment provided was to take a picture of me.

A4 A waitress told me to write my name on the bill. I said to the waitress, "I write my name? What the hell are *you* going to do?"

A5 I said to a woman, "I'm not going to take care of your snot-nosed brat."

My premise when working with a client on his or her dreams is that ultimately every element of a dream is a more or less recognized aspect of himself or herself, even if it *also* refers to important early figures, mother, father, siblings, and to the relationship with me (transference). My assumptions regarding dream interpretation are derived directly from my understanding of symmetrical thinking in which everything may stand for everything else and at bedrock is understood as a part of the self. Emotions in dreams mirror an important component of the client's internal state no matter how disavowed. While I do not share my perspective on dream interpretation with my clients, those who are interested in their own dreams quickly surmise my method and identify with my way of working with their dreams.

I approach the work with dreams in various ways, depending upon the client's openness to hermeneutical thinking. If he or she has a penchant for interpreting meanings, as Mrs. L. did, the work is immediately collaborative and productive. However, neither Mrs. L. nor I interpreted her first dreams. They flooded the hour and I listened. I saw my primary role as creating a safe space (external, internal), an environment that made Mrs. L. feel contained and affirmed. Simultaneously, a new psychic space inside me designated as Mrs. L. unfolded. In it, I registered, consciously and unconsciously, innumerable details, elements that together would compose an ever larger and more specific picture of Mrs. L. Her repetitive symbols and metaphors and distinctive images became as important to me in developing my portrait of her as her style of communicating, her range of affects, the content of the hours, and my own affective responses.

When I thought it was timely to begin to interpret a dream (refer to A1), I began in a very general way, and focused on her affect.

Analyst: The dream seems so reflective of your life.

Mrs. L.: I'm always waiting for the next wave of palpitations to come. They scare me so much. I like coming here a lot but I do not know whether you will be able to make them stop.

Analyst: You have been so frightened. At this time, your main aim *is* to "get to higher ground to be safe" and you want to be sure you are in the right place to help you get there.

I affirmed Mrs. L.'s fear and wish and said no more about the dream in this session, even though she brought the dream into our relationship. I noted for myself her conflict about me. She thinks of stopping for food (basic nurturance) but at present is afraid. She cannot attend to her deep hunger, her primary unfulfilled orality, while she is not safe. I do not address her conflict at this time as I believe she would feel criticized. It is too early in the treatment.

Between dreams A1 and A4 there were numerous dreams over many months. When Mrs. L. dreamed A4, and the symbol of the restaurant reappeared, I mentioned the repetition to her and asked her what thoughts she might have. By this time, we had worked together on her conflicting feelings about therapy, which I began to address shortly after she broached her concerns as to whether I could help her. She began to talk, this time with affect, about her longings to have had more attention, love, and care from her mother without having to do anything in return (I thought that she wants this from me, too).

As we worked in synchrony with her dreams by having her associate to (express thoughts about) different elements in her dreams, such as the symbols (e.g., the restaurant), the feelings, and the apparent conflicts, our talks led to an awakening of memory and, even more importantly, an eruption of increasingly intense affects. Sometimes Mrs. L. would begin by musing about the dream(s) as a whole. These thoughts might lead her far away from the content of the dream, more deeply into areas previously mentioned or never mentioned. That is what she did with many dreams. Often she followed her initial thoughts with associations to specific symbols or ideas. Sometimes I asked her about a particular symbol or metaphor, even a seemingly insignificant one. On many occasions, I connected her associations to things she had told me previously or interpretations to which we both had come, whether from dreams or otherwise. She would add her own links to my comments. In this way we worked in concert. A major outcome was that Mrs. L. became much more comfortable with wishes and feelings she had long disowned. By the time she dreamed C1, she was able to address far more directly her ravenous, aggressive appetite, an aspect of herself that had previously been cut off from conscious awareness along with so many of her affects.

If Mrs. L. had not been so eager and able to engage in the mutual process of dream interpretation, I would have attempted to facilitate her production of associations by offering my own. I would have suggested to her that she is the script writer, the actress, the director, and the producer of her dreams and my associations to her dream might be entirely different from what would eventually be her response to her own creation. Nevertheless, I have found that a client is often able to begin the flow of associations once she or he has permission to think freely and has had some examples from the therapist.

Although the description of the way I work with dreams sounds relatively straightforward, almost simple, the quality of affect of Mrs. L.'s dreams frequently arrested both of us. Additional associations and connections–hers or mine–came the next day or weeks or months later. Work with clients is never linear or static and the unfolding dream interpretations which I will now describe are unable to account for the unbelievably inventive capacities of each client to originate significant symbols and, with the help of the therapist, to use these derivatively to unfold personal meaning.

The overwhelming force of Mrs. L.'s tidal wave emotions (A1) leaves her feeling able and unable to keep herself alive and safe–stay in the car and/or get out, swim and/or be washed away, disappearing completely. In discussing her thoughts about the dreams as we would refer back to them at different times during the treatment, I learned that Mrs. L. had previously conceived of herself as already dead; she had used suicidal fantasies to calm herself in earlier years. The image of death by tidal wave is both horrific and relieving, at least in that death (in fantasy) offers a way out. Representations of old relationships emerge both to help and to hinder her, a male who tells her what to do and a woman who offers what should be nurturing (restaurant) and friendship but in this context is very dangerous, as the woman is oblivious to the fact that Mrs. L. will be inundated. Who is the man? Who is the woman? They represent her father, her mother, two sides of herself and of me. She has begun the journey we will take together in therapy and feels the road is green, meaning go. But she is tempted to avoid the pain of treatment (A2) by turning to alcohol, something she has used in the past, an identification with her parents. Her husband represents himself, herself, and, in tempting her towards management of her emotions by liquor, her parents, while being on foot lets us know that she is out of the safety/nonsafety of her usual means of transport, is more exposed and has to run to escape from being pulled in by the familiar "route through the liquor store." The running is identified with another aspect of her husband, who is, himself, a runner. The regression in time (change from being the driver of her car to being on foot) is also a potential for positive change (a husband who as runner is in disciplined control of himself just as she is now more grounded).

As in the former dream, the male is the active force within and the danger of the female/mother, therapist, self unfolds in dreams A3 through A5. Associations to the picture in dream A3 are to the photograph that the first therapist took of her in their first meeting. That same therapist had accused her of potential child abuse. This extremely damaging treatment that, though brief, she had difficulty ending led in this dream to numerous associations to images of her hideous self, as if the damaging treatment were now internalized. She must truly be a bad person, as she believed the first therapist thought. She wondered whether we would find the child abuser, the killer within (also D1 through D5). By the time she dreams A4 and A5, anger emerges about mothers who do not wish to mother, that is, her mother, herself, and, in some aspects me, the therapist, all unwilling to mother the more needy aspects of her hungry, dirty/sick ("snot-nosed") self (also C1 through C3) and daughter. The "snot-nosed brat"(s) also represent the numerous siblings who followed her birth for whom she was mother number two. It is important to notice that I am included in the group of non-mothering mothers because symmetrical thinking is increasingly inclusive when feelings are intense. What might appear like illogical feelings towards the therapist are actually one very important means of helping us to understand our clients. These feelings, derived from symmetrical thinking, are called transference.

THEME B. LEAKING WALLS—THE TEARS

As her negative feelings towards me began to emerge in dreams, Mrs. L. dreamed of me with children and patients she imagined I preferred, neglecting her. Consciously, she had not been aware of any anger toward me and had previously only the most superficial acknowledgment of her anger at family members. Mrs. L. was fascinated with her dreams. She could hardly believe all of this was going on inside. One day she said, "I often feel in dreams 'connected' to previous dreams—as if I've had them before." This verbalization is an acknowledgment of a new feeling of some control through the capacity to connect her dream (feeling) world.

About seven months into our work the dreams changed. The content was filled with walls and roofs that leaked from rain and pipes that broke, allowing water to bubble up through the floor. Everything was wet. Liquids soaked through the curtains, it left fungus growing on the baseboards. When these dreams began, the uncried tears of the unending infinite pain of her life began to flow. She was still inundated but could walk on the water of her tears. These dreams demonstrated a step in the direction of containment. She is surrounded by at least some structure (not tidal waves), and the structure, the walls, had never been there before, however leaky they are now in their initial appearance. The pipes, however broken, symbolize a new conduit to her flood of feeling. There was a multitude of dreams.

B1 . . . in an old house with people who were friends or family. It was raining outside and water was running down the inside of all the walls. The house was filled with old furniture. I was looking for mementos, even pulling out desk drawers and looking to see if anything was taped to their bottomside. . . . Mom was talking about trying to get her mother on the phone but Grandmother didn't have a phone. Mom was trying to get through to her neighbor but she, the neighbor was "dead drunk" and the operator wouldn't ring long enough.

B2 It was raining and I tried to call you. I didn't have your number and when I tried Information, the city you were in had been disbanded. When I told the operator it was L.A., there was no listing for you. When I came to the office I was too late to catch you between appointments.

B3 I was dying and trying to write to my daughter to tell her it would be okay that I didn't get to see her children. I would see them from heaven. My daughter was grown up at that point but I could also see her cheek as a baby and I was stroking it. In the dream, I thought about going to see you and just crying and crying.

Her anguish, the overwhelming sadness and depression of Mrs L.'s feelings of early abandonment, now came clearly into focus. The abandonment was of such early origin that it is represented as something between her mother and her grandmother; it was so intense that a whole city is "disbanded" (abandoned, the bands or ties removed). The symbols of the abandoners are numerous: a mother, grandmother, neighbor, operator, city, therapist, her own child.

Theme C: Terror of the Pig and the Rat—Cravings and Attacks that Can be Acknowledged

Fear of pre-genital (infantile types of) aggression had been present from the beginning and she experienced such aggression as coming from outside herself. In the early dreams: the hospital wanted money, the waitress wanted Mrs. L.'s name on the bill but seemed to be doing nothing (A3 and A4) and the "snot-nosed brat" (A5) was rejected. Now in numerous dreams, these aggressive fantasies were acknowledged as part of herself ("my house," which was also her house).

C1 There was a wild pig running through my house, which sank its teeth into me and there were papers that the KGB wanted, which I hid in a teddy bear.

C2 My brother showed his burn scars from kung fu. He reported getting to a certain level. There was a higher level but he couldn't stand the pain required to get to that level. [In the same night she dreamt that she moved without telling me.]

C3 I was in an old house, in the bathroom, trying to turn on the lights so I could see myself in the mirror, but the lights wouldn't come on. The house had two parts and when it rained

> a rat would go from one part to the other. It was raining and I felt like the rat was there. I had a dog with me who sensed him too and was scared.

We understood these dreams to mean that Mrs. L. feared she would die of her own intense hungers, that she feared the KGB gang, the omnipotent destructive narcissistic aspects of herself, would get after her for revealing her infantile desires and truths, for believing she could depend (teddy bear) on someone. This was an "old" part of herself. Now she felt divided into "two parts": the rat, a vicious and attacking self, and a self who longed to be dependent but might also be a more attacking Russian bear. The rat became most attacking when it rained (when she cried her mournful, sad, and longing tears). There is no mention of the rain being inside in this dream. There is a duality of self-representation in these dreams which reveals both the self-destructiveness (KGB–perhaps Kill Gail [therapist]; move without telling Gail) and the containment that is originating in the positive feelings towards the therapy that produces a new potentiality, "trying to turn on the lights so I could see myself in the mirror."

Theme D: The Killer Comes Forward–Someone Must Die

Just as neither one of us had been afraid that she would abuse her child, neither one of us was afraid that she would interrupt treatment (C2 and D6). Mrs. L.'s capacity to hold on to asymmetrical (logical) thinking while on this emotional roller coaster (symmetrical thinking) was remarkable. Through her dreams, she continued to be able to use me as both a good and bad person to understand and experience her feelings about old and deep wounds. I am no longer the container of her emotions; she has taken it over. It is leaky but it is hers. In D2, she is inside and "lots of water [is] outside of an old house." I was at the same time the person to whom she came to cry and the neglectful, unavailable, indifferent killer parent. What I saw that she feared, however, was the further loosening along with unbearable feelings (D7) of her historical internal bond with her mother and father. Could she begin to experience herself as different from the way that they experienced her? The next set of dreams contained the fantasy about how this would happen. This could only come about by someone getting killed, but who? Numerous dreams of killing and dying unfolded with a profound impact on both of us.

D1 Then a figure rose up at the top of the stairs with a white cloth over his head. I shot him over and over.

D2 There was lots of water outside of an old house. It had been raining. The rocks were filled with moss. My mother and father were fighting over the death of a child. They were fighting over why the child had died and who was to blame.

D3 I was trying to climb to the top of the mountain to get away from all of the water. [Associated the top of the mountain to a way of committing suicide. Reaching a high place meant both safety and lack of safety. It is noticeable that no container is required–she contains herself. High connoted alcohol (lack of safety) and alternatively, being emotionally high in her new capacities to mother and to write without being swept away. The danger of these new "high" positive self-representations leads her to an old defense, the association to suicide.]

D4 I told my mother that I am going to kill myself and that I wanted her to put a yellow rose on my chest in the coffin. My mother said, "That's fine. I have a nice blouse you can wear."

D5 I tell you that I will be leaving several months from now. You shake hands with me and say goodbye. I say with great upset, "Not now! I'm not leaving now!" You don't hear. In the dream, you turn from me–same gesture as my mom–and you call a colleague and say to her, "[the patient] is *la grande dragonness*," meaning she [the patient] is making it up. [*La grande dragonness* is a made-up word, not really French, of a made-up, frightening, bestially incorporating, fiery animal.]

D6 I dreamed I lost my clearance [security], that I was moving backwards in my car and could not stop. Finally in the dream I said, "I give up" and I let go. I felt things were taking me over. I was giving up my grip on sanity. I felt like I was going crazy and somehow I became resigned to that.

D7 Two women had been murdered, and their bodies stuffed into furniture–a couch and a chair. [I sit on a chair and she sits

> on a couch.] I was concerned that they remain hidden. I felt responsible like I'd been involved in their murder. I was more concerned with the body in the chair. Then I had a flashback, I was one of the women about to be murdered by a man at a river. I was trying to escape. I felt like I was trying to undo what had happened.

By the end of this series, Mrs. L., her mother, and I, had been united as in symmetrical thinking. Mrs. L. is the container of her own emotions and she has murdered the self that was merged with me and the historical mother of her childhood. She will begin to replace that old self with new images of herself and a clearer recognition of me as myself.

DISCUSSION

Mrs. L. intuitively understood her dreams. The abundance of her associations and her comfort in creating asymmetrical relationships between an idea in a dream and a multitude of thoughts that related to her past and present was remarkable, given the paucity of her conscious fantasy life prior to the birth of her daughter (a fantasy life which had been narrowly focused on bodily issues). "My dreams and my body pains are communicating with me," she said one day. "It's as if I call myself up and say, 'Listen, this is what is going on inside.'" When she reported a sad dream, it was easy for her to cry. When she reported a frightening dream, she was in the moment. That wasn't the case when she talked about her conscious emotional experiences, but when it came to the dreams, there was an immediacy to her reactions. She could be very angry at me through her dreams but her defenses did not allow such feelings to emerge more directly. She called me the fortune teller. She had created in me a strong, good, idealized individual who could contain and unfold the magic of the dream worlds. She believed her dreams sent messages and she did much of the interpreting herself. She used me to create alternate pathways (perhaps new "pipes") to her emotions. As she began to increasingly experience her thoughts accompanied by feelings, the frequency of her reported dreams abated. She still commented, however, that she could experience her negative feelings most powerfully through her dreams and in her writing.

Ella Freeman Sharpe (1930) said that every symbol is at root related to the body. It is from our experience of our body, and our body in relation to parents and siblings that our understanding of the world is derived. The dreams above are replete with symbols. One particularly forceful and omnipresent symbol is water. From the first dream's tidal wave to the last dream's river, the symbol of water is repeated numerous times. We might first speculate that the feelings of being overwhelmed (tidal wave, walls and floors that leak, rain that doesn't let up) originates in the infant's experience of urinating, drooling, crying without comfort, diarrhea, being potty-trained, being bathed, and perhaps even an intrauterine experience in the womb of her mother and in the delivery of her own child. I might have then anticipated, based on Mrs. L.'s descriptions of her relationship with her parents, that there was minimal comfort offered to her in these situations, in which she was submerged not only by her own liquid discomforts but by her parents' alcoholism, and that early training was rigid and bordered on cruelty. I took the position that encouraging associations that would delve into specific historical referents would be a mistake and might lead to highly sterile, intellectualized searches, even though numerous connections to history emerged in associations. In the therapeutic interaction, this symbol–water (like so many others, e.g., a restaurant for being fed and nurtured)–is understood on the symmetrical level by therapist and client alike. It is understood as the representation of a feeling that has been infinitized. It is a profound encapsulation of her overwhelming feelings about her life and herself. A process implying increasing control may be noted in the changing symbols of water. The movement is from tidal wave (theme A), to leaking walls (theme B), to rain outside (theme C), to a river (theme D). It is important to note that at no time did either Mrs. L. or I take her words too literally, one symbol equal to one meaning, as in allegory. The symmetrical thinking of dreaming is similar to poetic economy, rich in deliberate ambiguity and multiple meaning.

Once we utilize the explanatory power of symmetrical thinking to understand psychological phenomena, we notice that in these dreams we find much larger classes of things than we usually find in ordinary discourse. The displacements in the dreams abound. It is her brother who "couldn't stand the pain required to get to that level," a harder level (C3). But here, in her obvious displacement she and her brother are one. Kung fu represents a form of aggression. Facing her own aggression is very painful, particularly if she has murdered her mother/therapist (D7). The therapy (elsewhere described as a "restaurant" (A1), a "hospital" (A3), and a "city which has been disbanded" (abandoned, a band of . . .) (B2) represents in this dream training in kung fu (C2).

The "KGB" (C1), which is after her papers, is the destructive part of herself. There are condensations, that is, a grown daughter (B3), whose cheek remains that of herself as a baby. This soft baby cheek contains within its imagery ugly self-representations now made beautiful through the love and increasing acceptance of her own growth (from and including infancy). Certainly one might consider the displacement upwards from the cheek of her buttocks. This cheek was loved; her own buttocks were beaten. This condensation incorporates past, present, and future (potential change).

Mrs. L.'s dreams are replete with identifications. She dreams of herself as a pig (C1), a rat (C3), and a dog (C3). The first two animals often symbolize the hungers and messiness of early childhood. Both the pig and the rat are oral and anal, the pig representing principally the orality of hunger and greed (however, pigs love to roll in mud and are known for their messiness and sloppiness) and the rat, representing primarily the anality of dirt, filth, and viciousness (however, the dangerous biting of rats is also a common symbol of oral aggressiveness). One might ask how I know that these represent her. I return to the world of symmetry with its descending strata of increasingly unified objects; on the deepest level everything is equal to everything else, and as she is the only creator, director, and producer of her dreams, on the deepest level, she is also the only actor.

Representations of herself, her physical and emotional states, and vital former relationships are the constituents of all of her dreams. The rat, the pig, and *la grande dragonness* (D5) also represent internalized aspects of parents and siblings. The dog is the hope of the future. The dog is known as man's best friend. She had a dog who was her best friend. Perhaps she will finally befriend herself.

A NOTE ON THE SYMPTOM

The horrific visions of cutting off the top of her baby's head and putting a pencil or meat thermometer through one ear to the next disappeared within three months after treatment began. In themselves, these symptoms have never been directly analyzed because of the value of not taking them too directly and literally. The sources from which they were constituted, however, have become very clear to both Mrs. L. and me. This symptom demonstrates the brilliant creative organization of the logic of symmetrical thinking and how the mind relieves itself of the painful tensions within. It contains condensations of the parenting of mother and father along with pictures of herself as parent and as needy infant, representations of her siblings, and so on.

The top of the head represents the brain, all that was most valued by Mrs. L.'s father. In fantasy, she cuts this off in the baby, who is also herself (she is both herself and her baby). In so doing, she does not give her father what he wants; she becomes brainless and does not have to think about what she wants and how she feels. The ears listen. In putting a meat thermometer through them (actually through her own ears, which have been placed on the child), she is the mother who shuts her ears to her child's overwhelming needs. She numbs herself to what she otherwise must know and feel. She is also the baby who cannot hear what is going on around her and she is most immediately and most helpfully the adult woman, the client who will not hear her thoughts misread, misheard, or taken too literally as with the first therapist, whom she had the courage to leave. It is interesting to note that during one of our separations due to my vacation, Mrs. L. began to hear a buzzing in her ear. It continued to come and go at different intervals. The instrument of death, the meat thermometer, condenses her earliest feeding and toileting experiences. It is an invasive instrument constantly present, around, and used on children. It is, as well, the positive and specific pencil with which she is now writing.

On yet another level, the head represents the entire body, a part for the whole. In cutting off the top of the head, Mrs. L. demonstrates an act of castrative abandonment, which she experienced psychologically as a child (cut off at birth from loving surroundings) and which she fears she may perpetuate as a parent. The ears are every orifice and she plugs up what might come out: urine, feces, bad words. The meat thermometer penetrates an orifice as in the first sexual fantasies about parents. There were so many babies who followed her and who took her mother away. She is the baby and her siblings, with all their overwhelming needs. She is the baby whose parents are so rejecting. Her sadness over having such fantasies related to her baby girl was always present behind the horror. Thus the entire range of horrific fantasies, displacements and condensations of the history of her childhood, becomes the images of hurting her own child that torture and terrify her as she had been psychologically tortured and terrified when she was a child. These are from the past and never were predictive.

CONCLUSION

Freud's theory of thinking, including *conscious* and *unconscious* thinking and Matte-Blanco's expansion of this theory, *asymmetrical* and *symmetrical* thinking may act as an organizer for all psychological theory, general and clinical. It has the simplicity and clarity of a mathematical formula and the potential of illuminating the entire map of human relationships. It has been the aim of this chapter to present a brief overview of Freud's theory and Matte-Blanco's expansion, and to provide clinical material to demonstrate its usefulness to social workers doing any form of therapy. The main points Matte-Blanco developed are as follows: human experience, *thinking, feeling,* and *being,* may be conceived as structured by the experience of a series of strata in combination, which range from the deepest, most indivisible mode of thinking (mostly unconscious, with an emphasis on symmetrical thinking) to the most abstract mode (conscious and unconscious, with an emphasis on asymmetrical thinking). On the deeper levels, there is no such thing as contradiction and negation; time, cause and effect, internal and external, and people and things are increasingly melded. Some psychological experiences such as omnipotence, impotence, omniscience, idealization, grief, and in fact all emotions may become infinite and expand from something specific to include everything and everybody. In order to demonstrate the clinical usefulness of these concepts, I have presented a patient in whom the structure of thinking, particularly the unconscious symmetrical thinking, was emphasized.

The most often repeated question that I have been asked by students is what is really supposed to happen in the therapeutic endeavor. This question is not easy to answer. My best response to them is that a client first seeks to be understood by the therapist and then to understand him/herself. This understanding must come at the level the patient is ready to utilize, which for me ranges throughout the spectrum from the symmetrical to the asymmetrical thinking and experience. The more comfortable a patient or therapist is with symmetrical thinking, the more enabled s/he is to develop asymmetrical relationships (new possibilities) and that means the potential for more choices in life.

APPENDIX

Overview of the Work of Matte-Blanco[3]

Sigmund Freud named his discovery *depth psychology*. His emphasis on a specific spatial metaphor for the mental "agencies" or "systems," however, has both framed and limited clinical perceptions of analysts for almost a century. It suggests that mental operations, at least those that concern clinicians, may be understood through the normal tools of logic, time, and three-dimensional space. Frequently, Freud emphasized that what is unconscious may become conscious ". . . as a result of which the two records are brought to coincide," (1938, p. 160). Until the end of his life he believed "the one can be changed into the other" (p. 164) and that "thinking must aim at freeing itself more and more from exclusive regulation by the unpleasure principle . . ." (1900b, p. 602).

The evidently severe obstacles of making unconscious ideas/affects conscious, of making the two records *coincide*, had to be explained; this explanation has preoccupied and frustrated psychoanalysts and their theoretical assumptions since Freud's first definitions of depth psychology. Ignacio Matte-Blanco's utilization of symbolic logic, the mathematics of infinite sets, and the physics of space–time to understand the structure of thinking and, more important, of being, has not only catapulted us from a nineteenth-century model of the mind which focuses on instinct, energy, three-dimensional space, and a conscious/unconscious polarity, but has immeasurably widened the scope of our sense of the mind: its poetry and science; its health and pathology; its creative potential and inertia; and, inevitably, its capacity to foster a transition towards action and a way of being in the world.

In his two books, *The Unconscious as Infinite Sets* and *Thinking, Feeling, and Being*, Matte-Blanco presents a revision of Freud by substituting for the topography, the dynamics, and the economics of Freud's metapsychological concepts a view of the mind as both "discriminator" and "classifier." And for the systems *Ucs.* and *Cs.*, and primary and secondary processes (terms which are related to an energy metaphor and

3. An excellent summary of Matte-Blanco's work may be found in Rayner and Tuckett's introduction to Matte-Blanco's book, *Thinking, Feeling, and Being*. Most of the following overview has been taken directly from Rayner and Tuckett's introduction and from my dissertation.

which refer to a slow or rapid release of energy), Matte-Blanco substitutes symmetrical and bi-logical thinking and a mathematical metaphor called *infinite sets*. His most revolutionary idea is that not only thought, but *human experience* itself, may be structured by an infinite series of strata. These strata range from the most indivisible modes of thought to the most abstract. The ideas are not "transposed" (from unconscious to conscious). It is not true that "one can be changed into another." They are symmetrized or asymmetrized; they are translated or unfolded. These different modes of thinking occur simultaneously. At any given time, a person may experience herself as herself, as a clinical social worker, as a mother, as all mothers, as mankind, as a mammal, as a life form.

According to Matte-Blanco, the two basic principles of symmetry that characterize the unconscious are:

> I The system Ucs. treats an individual thing (person, object, concept) as if it were an element of a set or class which contains other members; it treats this class as a subclass of a more general class, and this more general class as a subclass or subset of a still more general class, and so on. . . .
>
> In the choice of classes and of higher and higher classes the system Ucs. shows a preference for those propositional functions which in one aspect constitute increasing generality and in others keep particular characteristics of the individual thing from which they started. . . .
>
> II The system Ucs. treats the converse of any relation as identical with the relation. In other words it treats asymmetrical relations as if they were symmetrical. [Matte-Blanco 1975, pp. 37–38]

These two principles eloquently encompass all of Freud's theories of the unconscious by utilizing the concept of mathematical set theory and the mathematics of infinity. In the symbolic logic of infinity, as in an infinite set, parts are equal to, and the same as, the whole; all parts are the same as, and equal to, all other parts. The property that links the thirteen characteristics of the unconscious that Matte-Blanco has identified is that they unite things which for ordinary thinking are discrete and distinctive. The symbolic logic of infinite sets is an undynamic, unconscious mode of being.

The mental world as defined by Matte-Blanco is ruled by two sets of behavior: ordinary logic and a special admixture, which Matte-Blanco calls *bi-logic*. By conceptualizing the mind according to mathematical set theory and the mathematics of infinity, as opposed to discrete agencies spacially or temporally connected through dynamics and energic concepts, as Freud had done, Matte-Blanco offers a metaphor that both encompasses all human thought, feeling, and behavior and explains the continuous subtle changes between different states of experience, explained as different organizations of symmetrical and asymmetrical (bi-logical) modes of being.

For Matte-Blanco, all thinking incorporates symmetry. It is a hidden aspect of normal thinking. When symmetrical thinking breaks the bounds of asymmetrical thinking, we slip into bi-logic, or what Freud terms the unconscious. According to Matte-Blanco, the only way we understand one another is by utilizing symmetrical thinking. Empathy, projections, identification, projective identifications, transference, or countertransference may exist because of indivisible thinking. Timelessness and spacelessness exist because in symmetrical thinking they are parts of an infinite set. The concepts of self and object take on new meanings when examined along the lines Matte-Blanco suggests. Human experience is structured by the existence of an infinite series of strata in which our capacity to recognize difference declines as the amount of symmetrization increases. In extreme symmetrization, the individual elements, which share something in common, become the same in all respects; ". . . towards the deepest levels, where there is 'pure symmetry,' hence, no space–time notions (that is, the level of *being* in contrast to the level of *happening*), there can be no aggression in the sense of destruction" (Matte-Blanco 1975, p. 17). Matte-Blanco calls the deepest level the indivisible mode. This mode is the background of all thinking. It is there all of the time while we unfold different forms of asymmetrical logic. According to Matte-Blanco, much of our work consists of unfolding meaning as opposed to analyzing resistances and making the unconscious conscious.

> When repression is lifted or the unfolding process occurs, there is enlargement of self-awareness. The unconscious is not diminished by this process any more than the size of an object is diminished by being reflected in a mirror or in a million mirrors. The translating function of psycho-analysis draws an inexhaustible supply of asymmetrical relationships from the unconscious to enrich the ego. Because the unconscious is infinite, it is not diminished by this process. [Matte-Blanco 1975, p. 302]

REFERENCES

Arden, M. (1984). Infinite sets and double binds. *International Jounal of Psycho-Analysis* 65:443.

Breger, L. (1980). The manifest dream and its latent meaning. In *The Dream in Clinical Practice*, ed. Joseph M. Natterson, pp. 3–27. Northvale, NJ: Jason Aronson.

Ellenberger, H. F. (1970). *The Discovery of the Unconscious.* New York: Basic Books.

Etchegoyen, R. H., and Ahumada, J. L. (1990). Bateson and Matte-Blanco: bio-logic and bi-logic. *International Review of Psycho-Analysis* 17:493–502.

Freud, S. (1900a). The interpretation of dreams. *Standard Edition* 4.

—— (1900b). The interpretation of dreams. *Standard Edition* 5.

—— (1905). Jokes and their relation to the unconscious. *Standard Edition* 8.

—— (1911). Formulations regarding the two principles of mental functioning. *Standard Edition* 12:213–226.

—— (1915a). Instincts and their vicissitudes. *Standard Edition* 14:109–140.

—— (1915b). The unconscious. *Standard Edition* 14:159–215.

—— (1916–17). Introductory lectures on psycho-analysis. *Standard Edition* 16.

—— (1917a). Mourning and melancholia. *Standard Edition* 4:237–258.

—— (1917b). A metapsychological supplement to the theory of dreams. *Standard Edition* 14:217–235.

—— (1921). Group psychology and the analysis of the ego. *Standard Edition* 18:67–143.

—— (1923). The ego and the id. *Standard Edition* 19:3–66.

—— (1933). New introductory lectures on psycho-analysis. *Standard Edition* 22:3–157.

—— (1938). An outline of psycho-analysis. *Standard Edition* 23:141–207.

Jimenez, J. P. (1990). Some technical aspects of Matte-Blanco's theory of dreaming. *International Review of Psycho-Analysis* 17:455–469.

Jordan, J. F. (1990). Inner space and the interior of the maternal body: unfolding in the psychoanalytical process. *International Review of Psycho-Analysis* 17:433–444.

Laplanche, J., and Pontalis, J. B. (1973). *The Language of Psycho-Analysis.* London: Hogarth.

Matte-Blanco, I. (1959). Expressions in symbolic logic of the characteristics of the system unconscious or the logic of the system unconscious. *International Journal of Psycho-Analysis* 40:1–5.

—— (1975). *The Unconscious as Infinite Sets: An Essay in Bi-Logic.* London: Duckworth.

—— (1984). Reply to Ross Skelton's paper "Understanding Matte-Blanco." *International Journal of Psycho-Analysis* 65(4):445–460.

—— (1988). *Thinking, Feeling, and Being.* London: Routledge.

Maw, J. (1990). Symmetry and asymmetry in language. *International Review of Psycho-Analysis* 17:481–484.

McIntosh, D. (1979). The empirical bearing of psychoanalytic theory. *International Journal of Psycho-Analysis* 60(4):405–431.

Mordant, I. (1990). Using attribute-memories to resolve a contradiction in the work of Matte-Blanco. *International Review of Psycho-Analysis* 17:475–480.

Racker, H. (1957). The meaning and uses of countertransference. *Psychoanalytic Quarterly* 26:303–357.

Rayner, E. (1981). Infinite experiences, affects and the characteristics of the unconscious. *International Journal of Psycho-Analysis* 62:403–412.

Rayner, E., and Tuckett, D. (1988). Introduction to *Thinking, Feeling, and Being.* London and New York: Routledge.

Rayner, E., and Wooster, G. (1990). Bi-logic in psychoanalysis and other disciplines: an introduction. *International Review of Psycho-Analysis.* 17: 425–431.

Rosenfeld, H. (1987). Destructive narcissism and the death instinct. In *Impasse and Interpretation,* pp. 105–132. London and New York: Tavistock.

Sanville, J. (1992). *Imagining the other: alterity in psychoanalysis.* Keynote address, Fourth Annual Conference of the Committee on Psychoanalysis. Los Angeles, October.

—— (1994). *Affect attunement in primary illusion and in psychoanalytic space.* Lecture for Institute for Psychoanalytic Training and Research. New York, March.

Sharpe, E. (1930). The technique of psycho-analysis. In *Collected Papers on Psycho-Analysis,* pp. 9–106. London: Hogarth, 1958.

Skelton, R. (1990). Generalization from Freud to Matte-Blanco. *International Review of Psycho-Analysis 17:471–474.*

Steger, G. (1994). *The Cosmology of the Mind and the Bi-Logic of the Kabbalah: Theoretical Isomorphy Across the Ages and Its Clinical Relevance.* Unpublished Dissertation.

Whyte, L. L. (1960). *The Unconscious Before Freud.* New York: Basic Books.

Williams, O., ed. (1961). *The Golden Treasury of the Best Songs and Lyrical Poems.* New York: New American Library.

Wooster, G., Hutchinson, D., and Evans, D. (1990). Two examples of supervised weekly psychotherapy, illustrating bilogic in relation to birth. *International Review of Psycho-Analysis* 17:445–454.

16 THE CHILD THERAPIST AND THE CHILD'S PARENTS: A PRECARIOUS ALLIANCE VIEWED FROM A PSYCHOANALYTIC PERSPECTIVE

Diana Siskind

Working with parents is often the most difficult aspect of child psychotherapy. This is so for child therapists at all levels of experience, including those who have devoted many years to the study, practice, and teaching of child treatment. Despite the many pleasures and challenges in this work, and the satisfaction in facilitating the growth and development of their young patients, many child therapists eventually limit, reduce, and even give up the practice of child psychotherapy. The cumulative frustrations encountered in contacts with the child's parents sometimes grow to be too taxing and impose conditions that defeat even the most committed practitioners. Why do so many professionals have such difficulty in this area? This chapter will explore this question, with the hope that the insights gained may transform some of our collective frustration into a more constructive form of energy.

While there is some written material on work with parents, this topic has attracted little attention and is sparsely represented in the literature. Equally surprising is the dearth of seminars on work with parents. This breach of attention only attests to the fact that the lack of popularity of a topic in no way reflects its clinical importance or degree of complexity. Perhaps the frustrations encountered in working with parents might even extend to an avoidance of this topic as subject for articles and seminars.

Confusion about the child therapist's role in regard to the child's parents invariably comes up at seminars on child treatment and I would like to list some of the questions that arise to convey the complexity of this therapeutic role and of the dilemmas it creates. Here is a sampling of the sorts of questions that arise:

Should the child's therapist also work with the parents, or should the parents be seen by a different therapist as a couple, or should they each be seen in individual treatment by separate therapists? If other therapists are involved in treating the parents, how much communication, if any, should take place among the various therapists?

When the parent of a child in treatment is seen by his or her child's therapist, is the parent to be viewed as a patient or is that parent something other than a patient?

Should parents be given direct advice regarding their children or would this represent the therapist as an authority figure who might undermine parental prerogative?

At what age should we consider the child too old for us to continue to maintain regular contact with his or her parents?

What is the child's right to confidentiality and what is the parents' right to know what is going on in their child's treatment?

Should the parent's participation in treatment be mandatory or voluntary?

What happens when the parents are divorced, in regard to confidentiality, contact with both parents, with step-parents, the therapist's role in custody disputes, and so on?

This sampling of typical questions facing the child therapist demonstrates the exponential growth of factors to be considered when so many people are involved in the treatment situation. Since no two situations are the same, there are no simple answers. What we do need is a mode of thinking that allows clinical decisions to have a sound and unifying base.

Psychoanalysis is both a treatment modality and a scientific theory. As a theory of human development it imposes a discipline and method of looking at human behavior that allows enormous scope and applicability.

The question posed earlier regarding the widespread difficulty encountered by child therapists in working with the parents of their patients will be explored using a psychoanalytic developmental framework. This exploration will, in a general way, examine the play of factors contributed by the parent *and* those contributed by the therapist, that is, the vicissitudes of transference and countertransference.

Let us begin by examining the assumptions generally made about parents. The very words: parent, mother, father, are rarely heard dispassionately. They set off an associative clang, rich with affect. When this visceral reaction is quieted and we speak objectively, most of us would agree that parents are two adults, a mother and a father who together have a child, care for that child, and take care of that child. This basic, simple, and general definition would probably be agreed upon by a wide range of people including mental health professionals, correction officers, teachers, doctors, judges, and so on. It appears that on this subject our expectations remain curiously impervious to our daily experience and *parent* is and continues to be equated with care and caring. In other words, *parent,* the noun, is not distinguished from *to parent,* the verb. Furthermore, despite the high incidence of one-parent households and the growing number of single-gender parent couples, many of us retain an old-fashioned image of parents. I believe that here lies the beginning of insight into the root of our problem. Since most of us hold on to our ego ideal of parent, then of course we are going to have difficulty in maintaining our customary neutrality when the parent in our consulting room does not fit our expectations. This shift from our usual therapeutic attitude of interest and curiosity combined with objectivity is certain to cause some professional disequilibrium, and affect the way we work.

For our purposes let us set down a definition of parent that is bare and realistic. A parent is a person biologically involved in producing a child, or a parent is a person who plays no role in the biological production of a child but adopts a child. There are no adjectives in these definitions, and no promises either. In fact, such definitions are hard to accept because an almost universal sense of protectiveness about children causes us to wish parents to have those characteristics that we associate with parenting: love, devotion, patience, and guidance. When these are seriously lacking, we become uncomfortable, and in fact anxious. This is not surprising since the severe mistreatment of children is bound to elicit sadness and pain in everyone, and disciplined mental health professionals are not exempt from having this reaction. But even among those parents who love their children and take care of them reasonably well, their shortcomings often arouse our criticism and disapproval. We tend to get angry at their lateness in bringing their child to therapy appointments, at vacations taken just as the child's treatment deepens, at home rules too lax or perhaps too strict, at bills paid late and demands that treatment be hurried along, and so on. When we feel our annoyance at these "infractions," when we are angered that these parents do not fit our ego ideal of "parent," we must recognize that our therapeutic role risks being compromised unless we analyze our negative reactions and deal with them to deepen our insight into what is going on between us and that parent. This is sometimes difficult to accomplish, but unless we succeed we are as much a saboteur of treatment as is the "uncooperative" parent.

Whether we consider the child's parent a patient or not a patient, that parent must still be viewed from a professional perspective. In fact, it is essential that parents be assessed with the same care and thoroughness that we apply to the assessment of any of our primary patients. A careful assessment of the strengths and vulnerabilities of the parent is our tool for understanding, but it is more than that. It is also an action on our part that delineates and formalizes the professional nature of our relationship with that person. Some therapists might find this objectionable on the grounds of the parent not being a "real" patient, and on the grounds that to assess is to classify, distance, and perhaps even take a superior position. I propose that it is rare for a therapist to be able to treat a child without having a working alliance (Greenson 1967) with at least one of the child's parents (Siskind 1992), and that in order to bring that about, an assessment is an indispensable safeguard. We must understand how our child patient's parents perceive themselves, their child, each other, our role in their lives; how they perceive their past and its impact on the present and so on. If we consider these questions with care and make no assumptions, we will have a better chance of understanding their difficulties in parenting and might, for instance, gain insight into their lack of "cooperation" regarding their child's treatment. This in turn could enable us to work constructively with parental ambivalence as well as our own. Not only is it our right to assess all family members, it is our job to do so and this action on our part helps us to transform "parent" into a person in their own right, and that is an invaluable shift of focus for the child therapist.

Parenthood, in the full sense of the word, is a developmental stage (Benedek 1959) that can only be attained if the development that precedes it has produced a reasonably reliable level of psychic equilibrium. From birth on, the human infant passes through stage after stage of growth and reorganization. For instance, Mahler (1975) discusses in exquisite detail the infant's journey through the parallel and interconnected processes of separation and individuation. Her timetable describes the infant's passage from the stages of autism, and symbiosis, to differentiation, practicing, rapprochement, arriving by about age 3 at a point where both his sense of specificity and awareness of separateness has been established. One of the most dramatic achievements of this process is the "attainment of unified whole self and object representations" (Edward et al., 1991, p. 344), a state wherein the child can retain mental representations of self and object regardless of the object's physical presence. This developmental landmark is referred to by Mahler as *psychological birth*. Simultaneous to and inextricably intertwined with the separation-individuation process is the child's passage through the psychosexual stages. As with all development, the more adequate the resolution of one phase, the better the foundation for the next. Conversely, the greater the difficulty at each pivotal point of development, the more likelihood for skewed development in the next stage. The state of parenthood places enormous demands on psychic resources and if the adult has reached the stage of "generativity" (Erikson 1950) all levels of development have converged to form a readiness to meet these demands. This fortunate synchronicity of developmental attainment with developmental challenge bodes well for both parent and child. When the demands of caring for a child can be reasonably well met, this experience affords renewed opportunities for furthering the parent's development. But when these demands exceed the emotional resources of an individual, the sense of failure can be devastating.

The following vignette will illustrate the frustration and sense of failure of a mother who feels unequal to her job. The mother is talking to her social worker psychotherapist. The social worker works in an agency for children located in a working-class urban neighborhood. The children are generally referred by someone in their schools. Although the child is the primary patient, parents are expected to participate by attending weekly sessions. In this agency it is generally mothers who attend these sessions. Fathers very rarely are willing to participate. The purpose of the sessions with parents is to help them better understand their child and learn improved ways of handling his or her problems. In other words, this is a pretty typical situation.

> This mother is young, pretty, and overwhelmed at having two children. Her older child, a first-grader, is the primary patient, a child whose rebelliousness precipitated the referral. The mother is fairly constant in her attendance at the "child guidance" sessions. However she spends her sessions in agitated complaining. She complains that her daughter does not listen to her at home any more than she listens to her teacher at school. She complains that she brings her to her social worker every week and nothing changes because her daughter is bad, was born bad, has always been bad, and will always be bad. Now her 2-year-old son is getting to be the same way. She told him to clean up his room six times and he didn't listen. She asked him with a "please" the first two times. She took a sharper tone the next two times, and finally she yelled and threw him into his room, slammed the door and left him there for an hour. When she opened the door she found the room the same mess it had been earlier. None of her efforts worked; they never do. There he was, fast asleep on the floor, the room as messy as ever. She stated with despair and anger that no matter how hard she tries nothing ever helps, not with him, not with her daughter, and not with her husband, who is as messy as the children. What was she to do, clean up everybody's messes? Why was it her job to clean up other people's messes? And what was her social worker doing to help her? Nothing at all![1]

This young woman is a mother. She has two young children and she is responsible for them and she takes care of them as best she can, but when that evocative word *mother* comes up, she doesn't fit our picture too well. In order to be useful to this young woman we will have to put away our idealized notion of mother and get to know the person in that chair facing us, how to listen and hear what she has to say, and how to work towards helping her.

---

1. I thank Ellen Wald for allowing me to use this material provided during her supervision.

This woman, let us call her Mrs. Kay, probably does not sound unusual to people who work in child guidance clinics. There are many young women who become mothers even though emotional development lags behind biological maturation. This is not to suggest that Mrs. Kay would necessarily have been ready to mother children ten or even twenty years later. Some people are not equipped for parenthood at any age because their early history was too stunting to allow adequate development of parenting abilities. What happened along the way to hamper the development of so many of the parents we meet, and limit their ability to care for their children? We know that many of them had terrible home situations and were themselves abused and neglected children, and while that knowledge might make us more sympathetic, it won't help us know how to work with them. Only through the thorough study of human development do we, as psychotherapists, begin to equip ourselves with the theoretical tools needed to unravel and understand the early failures that derailed the development of our patient population. This, of course, includes the parents of the children we treat. We need to know what went wrong in their psychological development: where they got stuck, how that impeded their ego development, their object relationships, and their mode of dealing with anxiety. Furthermore we need to understand what form of pathological adaptation took place, and what their internal life is like now. What I am describing does not necessarily require lengthy and intensive interviews with these parents.

When psychoanalytic developmental theory is well understood, the listening mode becomes fine-tuned and the therapist is alert to recognizing key communications. This aids the process of selection and affords the therapist some clarity regarding what to explore and what to leave alone, what expectations are appropriate, or might be beyond that person's psychological capacity. For instance, if a mother reveals that she cannot say "no" to her 3-year-old, two possibilities immediately come to mind. One possibility is that this mother is so undifferentiated from her child that to say "no" would feel too separate and cause unbearable anxiety over loss and abandonment. Another possibility would be that this mother is very angry at her child and that her indulgence is a reaction formation over this unwelcome affect. With these two possibilities in mind, the therapist would be in a position to explore with some focus and it would be relatively easy to discover whether either of these possibilities had merit, and if so which of the two fit the situation. The approach to the undifferentiated mother would differ from the approach to the mother whose anxiety stemmed from fear of loss of love, that is, anger at her child. In this example of typical parental overpermissiveness, some of Freud's theoretical formulations are used for the purpose of assessment. Freud (1905, 1926, 1933) speculated that each psychosexual stage had a corresponding anxiety level: the anxiety of the oral phase is fear of loss of the object; at the anal phase it is fear of the object's love; at the phallic, fear of castration; at the oedipal, fear of the superego. The above is a small example of how by combining this bit of Freud with Mahler's separation-individuation schema, and Spitz's (1959) seminal work regarding the three organizers of the psyche with particular attention to the importance of the "no" in development, and A. Freud's (1946) contribution to understanding defense mechanisms, our ability to listen is enriched, expanded, and given focus. Then our intervention can reach a level of depth and impact capable of bringing about change of an enduring nature.

If we return to Mrs. Kay for a minute, concentrate on the vignette about her little boy presented earlier in this chapter, and gather together the information she gives us about herself in this brief encounter, we will find that we can learn quite a lot about her on every level. For instance, it is startling that a mother would expect her 2-year-old to go into his messy room and clean it up all by himself. It tells us that Mrs. Kay's perception of her 2-year-old is not based on what she sees but on some quite unrealistic notion about her son's capabilities. When he fails to comply she does not question her expectation of him. Rather, she experiences his non-compliance as intentional and as an indicator of "badness." She has made up a story about her little boy and she believes her story with angry passion. Not even the sight of her child asleep on the floor of his still messy room evokes any feeling in her other than despair and hopelessness at her position in the family, as the one who is not heard. He went to sleep on her, he turned a deaf ear, more evidence that no matter what she does, *nobody* listens and *nobody* hears.

Imagine the futility of telling Mrs. Kay that 2-year-old children are not capable of cleaning their rooms by themselves and that her expectation that her little boy do so is unrealistic, and that she needs to match her expectations to his capabilities. No matter how kindly stated, this intervention would probably result in Mrs. Kay feeling criticized. She would experience the therapist as being more concerned with her 2-year-old son than with her. Most likely this would confirm that the therapist is part of that omnipresent *nobody*, no different from all the other people who don't listen and don't hear. She would be quite right in her perception because the therapist's "educational" information about 2-year-olds would have been offered at the wrong time in Mrs. Kay's psychic development. The therapist would not be seeing and addressing this adult as she is but as she should be to fit the therapist's image of parental behavior. Thus while much less obvious in its inappropriateness, an educational intervention at this point would be analogous to Mrs. Kay's misplaced expectation that her 2-year-old clean up his room. If really listening, the therapist would have learned that Mrs. Kay needs the experience of being heard. She said so, and a response directed at anything other than her urgent need to be heard would confirm that even the therapist has unattuned ears.

To understand Mrs. Kay's communication more fully, let us go back to the beginning of life, to early infancy, that time when some of us are lucky and some of us are not and the consequence of our luck, or lack of it, is more profound and irreversible than at any other time of life. At the beginning of life, an infant has very limited resources for communicating need. Crying generally is the signal for all uncomfortable states which include hunger, cold, indigestion, and all those states of unpleasure that most mothers and fathers try to allay and transform into states of well-being. When the infant's caretaker is good at giving care and the infant has repeated experiences of crying bringing about the relief of discomfort, then eventually that infant's unfolding ego lays down memory traces of states of satisfaction. Gradually the satisfaction becomes linked to what at first is only a hazy perception of a force outside the self that provides comfort. In the early months the infant cannot yet form an image of a person. That will come later. At this early stage the lucky infant perceives a vague presence that provides food and well-being. These repeated good experiences of being responded to build in the infant an affective state that Terese Benedek (1938) calls *confident expectation*. These infants expect to be listened to because over and over again they were, and being heard and satisfied becomes something they remember and learn to count on. By 3 or 4 months they already remember that footsteps in response to their cry will be followed by a greeting, a face, a way of being held, a familiar smell, food, warmth—whatever is needed. Because good memories allow them to anticipate a response to their cry, footsteps and a familiar voice grow to be enough to stop their cry. These sounds are recognized as a signal that help is on its way. Gradually the infant's cry will lose urgency and become a sort of calling, something purposeful, the beginning of a dialogue with the caretaking "other."

Here I am talking about something that happens, or fails to happen, at the earliest stage of life and sets down an immutable mark on all that is to follow in the development of a person. This earliest preverbal (Blanck and Blanck 1994) time can obviously not be remembered consciously, nor can it be forgotten, as it is preserved in the unconscious. Not knowing this unrememberable piece of history the patient cannot tell us in words, but does tell us in other ways. For instance, Mrs. Kay reveals her expectation that nobody will listen and nobody will hear her. She conveys her repeated experience that no matter how hard she tries it's all in vain. In listening to the vignette about her little boy, it is easy to be distracted by her unrealistic expectations and her lack of empathy for her son. It is difficult not to focus one's concern on that little boy who fell asleep on the floor after being yelled at and thrown into his room. Furthermore, Mrs. Kay's diatribe against her 6-year-old daughter whom she dismisses and condemns to "badness" has the quality of a bizarre tale, a horror story about a bad seed with a will of its own. This, of course, can be very off-putting, but as professionals we can derive a great deal of diagnostic[2] information from these extreme communications. Understanding and putting to use this information is the first step towards forming a working relationship with Mrs. Kay, and opens the path to helping her and ultimately helping her children.

The application of psychoanalytic concepts adds scope and depth to our work, and this is equally true whether the patient is viewed as primary or adjunct. There is no doubt that some exceptionally gifted practitioners who do not have any psychoanalytic training might find a way of working with Mrs. Kay and help her and her children. Some people are profoundly talented and are able to hear, behind the manifest content of a patient's statements, themes of their other story. By hearing these other themes, even in their vague, incomplete state, a very creative and intuitive therapist might find a way to connect with Mrs. Kay, but most of us are simply earnest, hard-working people and we need a theoretical framework to give us the tools to combine creativity with professional discipline.

---

2. The term diagnostic is being used to denote an assessment of development. It is not used in the *DSM-IV* (1994) sense of listing symptoms for purposes of categorization.

As mentioned earlier, the infant develops "confident expectation" out of repeated experiences of being heard and responded to by the caretaking person. This good early experience affects all developmental lines. Such early ego functions as memory and anticipation become operative and spark secondary process thinking in the infant, for example, cry > footsteps > caretake > feeding > satisfaction. This ego activity paves the way for the next ego function, intentionality. An indicator that this has taken place could be that change in the infant's signal, a call rather than a cry to summon the caretaker. This in turn sets off a *reciprocal dialogue* (Hartmann 1939), since the caretaker will register the alteration in the infant's way of communicating and will be likely to respond with warm affect to this friendly call. The infant who feels heard, and who can with intentionality summon his or her caretaker, does not experience the unimaginable anxieties of those infants whose cries go unheeded and who consequently are not able to develop, in the same straightforward way, the ego functioning, secondary process thinking, or "confident expectation" in their caretakers. Furthermore, the lucky baby with a mental representation of a good presence outside the self also experiences a good something inside. The baby is not yet sufficiently formed and differentiated to have a mental representation of a whole person outside the self or of a representation of a whole self. Edith Jacobson (1964) suggested using the terms *object representation* and *self representation* to find a precise way of discussing these theoretical constructs.[3] She distinguishes self representation from self, and object representation from object, self and object both being more concrete concepts that refer to the actual self and the actual object as located in time and in space. Jacobson's contribution is helpful in understanding the evolution of object relations and identity formation. For an illustration of how this might work, let us return to the satisfied infant mentioned above. The affect of satisfaction becomes stored in the infant's memory as an embryonic representation of satisfied self and satisfying part object. This psychobiological experience fuels and is fuelled by ego development. Simultaneously the mother's[4] experiences

3. Jacobson (1964) defines self representation as the "unconscious, preconscious, and conscious endopsychic representation of the bodily and mental self in the system ego" (p. 19). Object representation is defined the same way with the word object replacing the word self.

4. Mother is used to denote the primary caretaker.

of satisfying her infant are stored as representations of good-mother, good-infant, and good-mother–infant pair. These self-enhancing experiences fuel her confidence in her mothering ability, in the "excellence" of the infant she produced, and further promote her capacity to "fit together" (Hartmann 1939) with her infant. The experiences of "fitting together," a form of primary adaptation, are also stored in memory as aspects of self and object representations.

It is useful to the clinician to think of psychic structures building out of these minuscule experiences. It allows us to understand that when our patients speak of Mother, Father, Sister, Brother, and so on, they are talking about representations of these important "others." These representations are aggregates of images and experiences that date back to infancy. In other words, it cautions us to allow for a measure of distortion in our patient's description of members of their primary family, and in the picture presented of themselves as a child and adult.

This leads right into one of Freud's (1912a, 1915) fundamental psychoanalytic discoveries, that of transference and its corollary, countertransference. Freud observed that patients re-experience with the analyst many of the feelings, fantasies, and attitudes they experienced with their early caretakers, and that the repetition of these affects is largely unconscious. Through the analysis of the transference, much of the past is rediscovered and some of the infantile distortions are uncovered and revised. The concepts of self and object representation are again useful in understanding the aggregate nature of these affective experiences with significant objects dating back far into childhood, and the re-enactment of these in the psychoanalytic or psychotherapeutic situation. In turn, the psychotherapist also has unconscious responses to the patient and these countertransferential responses date back to early experiences in the life of the psychotherapist. Since these are also largely unconscious, the therapist might remain unaware of them.

Freud saw countertransference as an obstruction to the treatment process because it caused the analyst to have blind spots in regard to the patient. The combination of sound training and personal psychoanalysis has been viewed as essential in helping clinicians observe in themselves countertransferential manifestations through the derivative signals they produce. For instance, we might find ourselves consistently sleepy with a particular patient, or feeling very protective, angry, filled with rescue fantasies, highly critical, and so on. If we analyze these reactions we often find that the patient evoked in us something in our own past, and unless we analyze it we risk allowing a major obstacle to block the treatment. While this view of countertransference is still considered fundamental to psychoanalytic theory and technique, the concept of countertransference has passed through a gradual evolutionary enrichment and expansion. In the process of change, the former, strictly negative view has given way to one that considers analyzed countertransference to have the potential of communicating a dimension not accessible in any other way. This expansion is part of a trend to distinguish between different kinds of countertransference. For instance, Casement (1985) states that we should "distinguish that part of a therapist's responses which offer clues to the patient's unconscious communications from that which is personal to the therapist" (p. 67).

He goes on to suggest that we call the first "a diagnostic response" and the second "a personal countertransference." Along similar lines, Sandler (1976) suggested that among the many facets of transference is the patient's casting of the analyst into a particular role. When the analyst unconsciously complies and accepts the role assigned to him he aids the patient in "actualizing" some element of an infantile relationship. Sandler suggests that in some of these situations the countertransferential response can, when examined by the analyst, yield important information about the patient's unconscious communications, as well as information about the analyst's unconscious compliance to the role-casting imposed by the patient. In short, when we succeed in analyzing our countertransference we stand to learn something illuminating about ourselves, our patients, and the interaction.

A woman like Mrs. Kay is bound to evoke countertransference. She sits and complains about her little children. There is nothing motherly in her tone. Many a therapist listening to her would at times feel frustration, hopelessness, indignation, identification with her children, and the wish to rescue them from this condemning and unattuned mother. Furthermore, despite our best efforts, her insistence that we are useless to her, not listening, not hearing, and not helping when we were quite certain that we were in fact trying very hard to find a way to help, would perhaps make us begin to doubt our efforts. In fact, we might begin to feel similar to the way Mrs. Kay feels: helpless, hopeless, and unheard. The drama in the room may shift with this insight. Yes, this young woman is supposed to be here to find improved ways of mothering her children, but she can't do it, at least not yet. How do we bring her closer to this goal?

We could begin by examining our reaction to Mrs. Kay's complaints that nobody listens. As mentioned before, we are beginning to feel a bit the way Mrs. Kay feels; after all, we are listening, we are doing our best, and to no avail. But are we? Obviously not, since nothing has changed for her. Could it be that we have been cast into a particular role and have accepted that role? One problem is that despite all that she has said to us we are still viewing her as a 26-year-old woman with two children who is here to refine her mothering skills but is not letting us do our job. It's time to analyze our countertransference. Does Mrs. Kay evoke some archaic object representation in our own past, one of an unattuned and uncaring parental figure? If that is so, who are we? Are we the whiny child who isn't listened to, or the unlistening adult who feels reproached by the whining child, or both? Something countertransferential must be serving as a serious obstruction because otherwise we would hear the distress behind the complaining and feel empathy.

The tragic consequence of being one of the unfortunate infants who repeatedly waited too long for food, who received little comfort, who had no basis for establishing confident expectation, is that the very lack of expectation often generates defeat. Think of the difference between Mrs. Kay's quest for help and that of Mrs. Jones, who arrives in our office and says: "I feel nervous about being here, but I also feel a sense of relief. I've run into a situation I can't deal with and I'm very upset. Now that I'm here I at last feel the hope that you can help sort things out. That will make me feel less anxious and confused." Both women are revealing something of their preverbal experience, and clearly Mrs. Jones expects the therapist to continue a familiar pattern of being heard and helped, while Mrs. Kay's pessimism is an expression of a world deaf to her needs. The problem is that it is easy to be drawn to Mrs. Jones, who will probably make good use of our help, and to be put off by Mrs. Kay who relegates us to an unhelpful role. Mrs. Jones creates the satisfied baby = good mother equation transposed into satisfied patient = good therapist; Mrs. Kay is the opposite: frustrated baby = bad mother, updated to frustrated patient = bad therapist. Here is another good reason why we need to do careful assessments. Mrs. Kay's ability to adapt to another person is impaired. We see this in her inability to "fit together" with her 2-year-old. She is unable to adapt to his needs and developmental level as demonstrated in the vignette about the cleaning of his room. This rigidity, this lack of accommodation to another person, will be felt in the therapeutic situation as well. It will mean that the therapist will have to do most of the work for now because Mrs. Kay cannot communicate adequately. A person who is not accustomed to being heard naturally has difficulty communicating, in recognizing her own affective states, and in recognizing when she is listened to and heard. Hopefully, this therapeutic opportunity and the empathy it may tap in the therapist will, in time, spark Mrs. Kay's growth. Hopefully, Mrs. Kay will be able to travel developmentally and arrive at a point where, no longer the frustrated child, she can stop being the frustrator of her children. She will need to become a patient in her own right to achieve this goal. She has a long way to go and the main thing that she has going for her is her consistent attendance at her sessions. That too can be viewed as a preverbal communication; she has not completely given up hope.

For Mrs. Kay and many other mothers and fathers, nothing in their lives prepared them for parenthood, and if our expectations for this patient population take this into account, and if we are given the time and training we need, we can have an impact. Then, with no other agenda in mind, we can demonstrate to Mrs. Kay that we are ready to listen and mean it. Sometimes this is difficult to accomplish because, as mentioned, Mrs. Kay's expectation of being unheard makes it difficult for her to recognize when she *is* being listened too. However, once we understand what we are dealing with in our patients and in ourselves, it is amazing how attuned we become to even the smallest therapeutic opportunities.

I will now give a brief description of how the initially futile sessions with Mrs. Kay were transformed into something meaningful. To begin with, the therapist became consciously aware of her apprehension prior to and during her appointments with Mrs. Kay and of generally feeling useless to this parent. The analysis of this insight and a careful assessment of Mrs. Kay made it clear that "child guidance" was an unrealistic treatment plan and that Mrs. Kay needed to be viewed as a patient in her own right. With increased sensitivity to this patient, the therapist recognized that Mrs. Kay began many sessions by complaining about how hard it was to get to the agency on time: there was traffic, weather, chores at home, the phone rang, and so on. This litany of complaints, presented in a whiny tone of voice, had, in the past, caused the kind of role-responsive "actualization" in the countertransference described by Sandler: the therapist had accepted the assigned role of listening without hearing. Now the therapist responded to the scheduling complaint with interest. After some discussion she offered to move the appointment to 15 minutes later, allowing for the leeway this patient felt was lacking. Mrs. Kay responded with relief and appreciation, which rapidly gave way to concern that she was too much trouble and worry that her complaints had been offensive. This then became the theme of the therapeutic work: that being heard and responded to could cause such relief and worry at the same time. Mrs. Kay responded to this shift in focus with unexpected ease and spontaneously began to talk about herself, her past, and her childhood. Over time, and with her therapist's help, she began to see connections between her past and present difficulties. At around the same time, she for the first time reported some positive behavior on the part of her children as well as some nice interaction with them, and seemed pleased to able to share this with her therapist. The therapist noted this sign that the working alliance was stabilizing, an indicator of the important psychic growth that now allowed her patient to have a measure of trust, and a glimmer of hope that help was possible.

While Mrs. Kay has been presented as an example of a mother unprepared for her mothering role, we see many parents whose abilities in this area are well developed and who consult us about their children for a variety of reasons ranging from consultation about a mild, transient developmental disturbance to a request for help in dealing with such serious conditions as childhood autism. The more-intact parent is not necessarily easier to work with than a woman like Mrs. Kay. Regardless of diagnosis, the fact remains that the child's treatment depends on the parent's willingness to bring that child to sessions and pay for his or her treatment. This places manifold burdens on the treatment situation that are not present in work with adult patients.

Our relationship with most parents differs from our relationship with our primary adult patients and restricts the use of our knowledge in several ways. Because parents do not usually see us about themselves but come to consult us about their children, they expect our comments, observations, and interpretations to be in regard to their child and not about them. Their view of our role is reasonable but it places limitations on our customary therapeutic technique, and forces us to find other approaches for difficulties encountered. For instance, it is not appropriate to interpret the parent's transference manifestations and "acting out" of unconscious fantasies. Consequently, the revival of childhood rivalry that is experienced by many parents upon realizing that their child really values the therapist and the treatment situation cannot be interpreted directly. It becomes imperative that the rivalry not be allowed to develop to the point where the parents might discontinue their child's treatment. One approach to dealing with this difficulty is for the therapist to pay scrupulous attention to countertransferential manifestations. We must assess whether the parents' rivalry evokes retaliatory rivalry in us, and if it does, it is crucial that we analyze this piece of countertransference by locating its source in our own past. When we succeed in this self-analysis, the parents' rivalry can be responded to with empathy rather than with a critical attitude.

Another important complication lies in the interdependence of therapist and parent, a condition that further intensifies transference and countertransference manifestations. Many parents feel that their need for a therapist's help with their child places the therapist in a position of greater stature and authority than theirs as adults and parents. This reduced status is experienced as humiliation by some parents, and combines with narcissistic mortification at having a child in need of treatment. Consequently, parents sometimes feel antagonistic to the very help they seek. A regressive state of "badness" is then replayed, with the parent becoming the bad child of the bad therapist. In this state of negativity, the parents often undermine the treatment by such "acting out" as missing appointments, arriving late, and so on. In turn, the therapist's resentment at dependence on parental cooperation may heighten identification with the child whose treatment is now in jeopardy. This, combined with growing frustration with parental hostility, can also cause regression in the therapist to a state of feeling like the bad child of the bad, frustrating parent. Unless the therapist can resolve this countertransference and take charge of the situation the case will either limp along or collapse.

It takes a great deal of maturity, tact, and determination to establish and maintain a reasonable working alliance with hostile parents. Sometimes parental pathology is such that the case is doomed no matter how wise and skilled the therapist. We need to have working conditions that allow us to make full use of our skills and knowledge. If parental hostility invades the therapeutic climate and is impervious to our interventions, then we sometimes have to accept defeat and not subject ourselves to destructive conditions. Our commitment to our patients need not eclipse our concern for our own comfort and well-being. Perhaps some of the therapists who limit or give up working with children do so because they did not sufficiently protect the climate in which they work.

CONCLUSION

The relationship between the child therapist and the child's parents imposes conditions that can greatly heighten the potential for transference and countertransference. Because the parent is usually not the patient, the parent's transference remains uninterpretable, thus eliminating one of the therapist's most effective therapeutic tools. In order to deal with this deficit and with the general difficulties imposed by this complex relationship, it is imperative that therapists have thorough knowledge of psychoanalytic developmental theory. This knowledge brings depth and scope to the assessment of strengths and vulnerabilities of parents (as well as all patients), and leads to a mode of thinking that allows us to carefully match expectations to fit the development level of the parents in the consulting room. Clarity in understanding these parents is one safeguard to not allowing countertransferential problems to obstruct the professional neutrality and empathy that is fundamental to our work. Of equal importance is the therapist's self-knowledge. Only when this is highly developed is early recognition of countertransference, and the self-analysis this requires, possible. The best way to achieve self-knowledge is through the therapist's own treatment. Finally, knowledge, insight, and empathy are the vital factors that will allow the precarious alliance between parents and child therapist to stabilize, and in this situation the therapist will often have to do the lion's share of the work.

REFERENCES

Benedek, T. (1938). Adaptation to reality in early infancy. *Psychoanalytic Quarterly* 7:200–214.

—— (1959). Parenthood as a developmental phase. *Journal of the American Psychological Association* 7:389–341.

Blanck, G., and Blanck, R. (1994). *Ego Psychology, Theory and Practice.* New York: Columbia University Press.

Casement, P. (1991). *Learning from the Patient.* New York: Guilford.

DSM-IV (1994). Washington, DC: American Psychiatric Association.

Edward, J., Ruskin, N., and Turrini, P. (1991). *Separation Individuation: Theory and Application.* New York: Gardner.

Freud, A. (1946). *The Ego and Mechanisms of Defense.* New York: International Universities Press.

Freud, S. (1905). Three essays on the theory of sexuality. *Standard Edition* 7:130–243.

—— (1912a). The dynamics of transference. *Standard Edition* 12:97–108.

—— (1915). Further recommendations on the technique of psychoanalysis—observations on transference love. *Standard Edition* 12:157–171.

—— (1926). Inhibition, symptoms, and anxiety. *Standard Edition* 20:75–174.

—— (1933). New introductory lectures on psychoanalysis. *Standard Edition* 22:1–182.

Greenson, R. (1967). *The Technique and Practice of Psychoanalysis.* New York: Hallmark.

Hartmann, H. (1939). *Ego Psychology and the Problem of Adaptation.* New York: International Universities Press.

Jacobson, E. (1964). *The Self and the Object World.* New York: International Universities Press.

Mahler, M., Pine, F., and Bergman, A. (1975). *The Psychological Birth of the Human Infant.* New York: Basic Books.

Sandler, J. (1976). Countertransference and role-responsiveness. *International Review of Psycho-Analysis.* 3:43–47.

Siskind, D. (1992). *The Child Patient and the Therapeutic Process: A Psychoanalytic, Developmental, Object Relations Approach.* Northvale, NJ: Jason Aronson.

Spitz, R. (1959). A *Genetic Field Theory of Ego Formation.* New York: International Universities Press.

17 From Parental Failure to Foster Parent: Facilitating Development in the Life Cycle

Cecily G. Weintraub

INTRODUCTION

This case report focuses on an innovative treatment approach with a handicapped, paraplegic 45-year-old woman who was unable to care for her own son, but was nonetheless able to become a successful foster parent to an infant. In work with the mother, it became clear that there were few satisfactions for her as a woman. The sense of loss at her son's placement was profound, as was her loss of her role as a mother, both of which resonated for her with the emotional experience of an earlier accident. As she became more productive as a woman and as a mother, her own feelings of self-worth increased and her depressions ebbed proportionately. Her identification with her son's foster mother helped achieve a separation between her and her son and a dimunition of competitive struggles with her son's placement.

The theoretical formulations of Erikson (1953), critical issues at life stages; Colarusso and Nemiroff (1979), development continues throughout the life cycle; Benedek (1953), parenthood as a developmental phase; White (1963), mastery competence and ego effectance; Edward, Ruskin, and Turrini (1991), narcissistic development throughout life; and Mahler (1975), separation-individuation theory informed the diagnostic assessment and treatment which, capitalizing on ego strengths to overcome deficits, provided an opportunity for continued growth for the mother, her son, and the foster care infant.

A CLINICAL EXAMPLE

Let me start by telling a story. It begins on a hot summer day in Washington, DC, about twenty-five years ago, at a time when I was a case aide placing prospective adoptive children in temporary foster homes.

A supervisor from the special foster care unit for emotionally disturbed children approached me about the possibility of a temporary placement of an adoptive infant with one of the natural mothers with whom she worked. She explained that Mrs. Moran was a 43-year-old caucasian wheelchair-bound widow and amputee who had an 11-year-old son in foster care. Mrs. Moran was able to care for her son, Tony, as an infant. She became unable to handle his aggressive and demanding behavior, which had increased as he developed and matured. The case history revealed she had infantilized him and behaved overindulgently with him, which led Tony to behave in an overstimulated fashion. Several day treatment programs were utilized initially. However, full-time foster placement was urgently required in Tony's eighth year, when he kicked his mother's one remaining leg and set fire to her mattress.

Mrs. Moran became a wheelchair amputee of the left leg at the age of 20 as the result of an automobile accident. Recovery from this near-fatal tragedy had been further complicated by several strokes during the recuperation, which left her with muscle weakness on the right side, as well as speech difficulties. At the time of the accident, Mrs. Moran had been a young, attractive, and capable registered nurse in charge of the newborn nursery of a large city hospital. The crippling event cut off all hopes of professional achievement and advancement, and left her physically incapacitated. Years of physical therapy and other rehabilitative efforts had served to make her independent in regard to her own personal needs and capable of managing a household without outside help. She had married, though her incurably alcoholic husband had died when Tony was just 3 years old.

Since that time she had been known to the family agency, as she required a variety of family services. She had no relatives on whom to draw, and her own physical prowess diminished with advancing years. Five years after her husband died, her son's placement occurred when all other efforts failed to permit Tony to continue living with his mother.

In her role as Tony's mother, Mrs. Moran felt she had direction and importance. He was her connection to the world. Her physical infirmity was her focus of difficulties, and she denied and externalized problems with Tony until he became completely unmanageable. Vocational, volunteer, and casework services were offered to her, but Mrs. Moran was unreceptive even as she became more depressed.

One day in the course of speaking with the worker about her frustration over her son's placement, Mrs. Moran recalled how vital she had felt as Tony's mother when she cared for him as an infant and she had been able to meet all his needs. She felt she could do the same for other babies. She had heard the agency was in urgent need of foster mothers for infants awaiting adoption. Would the agency consider using her? Following this discussion, the worker approached me, asking whether I would undertake working with such an unusual prospective foster mother. The agency's need for temporary infant homes was indeed critical and the worker felt that Mrs. Moran had something valuable to offer a baby.

It was in this context that I first met with Mrs. Moran in a home visit to her one-bedroom apartment in an interracial housing project for disabled persons. We had first talked in an initial introductory phone conversation, in which I presented the idea of a meeting to discuss her becoming a short-term adoptive foster care parent for the agency. She was enthusiastically receptive to my call.

When Mrs. Moran opened her door, I was immediately struck by her Van Gogh-like, Madame Roulin appearance—long dark hair, braided, surrounded her head as she sat in a stately but stiff fashion in her wheelchair. She had a warm, though half-drooped, paralyzed smile. When she spoke, her words were slurred and garbled and I had to concentrate on understanding her.

She saw my perspiration and offered me iced tea. In the innocent acceptance of a kind gesture, I found my first understanding, on a simultaneously simple and profound level, of the task before us. Each movement is as clear now in my mind as I watched it then.

Mrs. Moran slowly wheeled her chair to the cupboard, removed a glass, put it into her lap, shut the cupboard and wheeled to the refrigerator. There, she opened the freezer, removed ice, and put it into the glass, retaining it in her weakened arm pressed against her body, closed the refrigerator, and wheeled her chair with one hand to the counter. She placed the glass on the counter and returned to the refrigerator, removed a pitcher of tea, changing positions and hands, and returned to the counter. Slowly and exactly, she poured a glass of tea and returned to the refrigerator once more to store the remaining tea. She retrieved the glass from the counter and painstakingly arranged the glass in her arm and hand, wheeling the chair and tea back to the sofa where I sat. She locked her chair in place, took the tea from the weakened hand, and extended it to me. I thanked her, telling her it "hit the spot." Casting her eyes downward, she said that it took her longer to do things than it used to.

I responded by noting her concern about what I might think about her, but what struck me was the effort she had displayed and her determination. I simply suggested that things took as long as they needed to accomplish, and her timetable seemed right for her. I understood that she was sharing both her wish and her concern about the job she hoped us to accomplish together.

Mrs. Moran responded with her thoughts about the task she wished, feared, and hoped to successfully undertake. We agreed that we didn't know one another and that this made our work of placement exploration more involved. Mrs. Moran was able to say that she worried if she was still as able to care for an infant. Was she still as physically strong and as capable as she had been when Tony was a baby some twelve years ago? She was older–was she weaker?–and how much so she could not realize.

Despite the complications, Mrs. Moran's sensitivity and resourcefulness were remarkable. I could see she would be a valuable foster mother. Toward the close of the first session, we both agreed to move ahead.

She told me about her son, also wondering how much I knew. I made an agreement with her: I told her I would tell her what I knew, and then what she wished to offer was her decision. I also suggested that when we had questions or concerns, we would each try to voice them with one another. I tried to leave her with the impression that I was willing to deal with her as an equal, that I in essence viewed her as any foster mother with whom we worked. My respect for her openness was more than rewarded. Many of Mrs. Moran's anxieties matched my own, and when aired gave us a common ground.

Together we went over every situation we could think of: the crib had to be on wheels, so a portacrib was purchased and we assembled it together. We had to fix the level of the mattress for safety for the baby and accessibility for Mrs. Moran. We practiced height and weight and spatial arrangements using household pots, containers, and wadded towels as simulators of shapes, sizes, and weights we needed to surmount. Often I was her "nurse," providing the necessary instruments as she tried to experiment. We agreed to use bottled formula and water initially to circumvent sterilizing issues, but that still left pacifiers, which had to be boiled.

And then in my mind came a stumbling block–the laundry. When I guardedly approached the subject during one of our twice-weekly meetings, Mrs. Moran smiled and said she had already thought of that and it was going to be no problem. She had ingeniously developed a hand washing system over the years, which she demonstrated to me by doing some of her own hand washables. The agency provided a diaper service. One by one, a check-list inventory of anxieties met with negotiation.

Though I was overtly empathic to her anxieties, I found myself anxious at the undertaking we outlined together. How would a crying baby be reached, and how long would it take to retrieve a bottle, no less to warm it? (Remember these were the days before microwave ovens!) What would happen in a crisis?

Over a period of about six weeks, we became well acquainted. Since I was not yet a mother myself and depended on the foster mothers to have established their own child-care routines in other placements, I found myself asking Mrs. Moran's expertise in issues about infant care. She was forthcoming with helpfulness. We made lists of needed equipment. She was the one who mentioned a thermometer. Next, we contracted with a local pharmacy to make deliveries.

The first time Mrs. Moran held Annalise, her 10-day-old African-American female foster child, remains a memory of shared pleasure and gratification. We maintained set contact in the morning, afternoon, and evening of the first weeks. Mrs. Moran knew how to reach me or the agency at any time. Our check-in phone calls diminished in length and frequency as Annalise's care evolved into a routine.

The fact that this placement was also an interracial one brought some criticism–after all, Washington was still very much a southern city in the 1960s–but we persevered. In fact, the opposite reaction occurred. One morning I arrived for a periodic home visit, and a black man was sitting in the apartment talking with Mrs. Moran. He introduced himself to me and said that he had heard about the baby and had stopped by to "offer his services" to pick up any groceries for Mrs. Moran and the baby.

This was the first of many such experiences. The baby, who was nicknamed "Cupcake," became the mascot of the housing project. Mrs. Moran's apartment became the center for residents who stopped by to see how things were going. Around her apartment coalesced a network to address concerns at the housing facility in general. Two seemingly segregated populations began to come together. Some days, residents would help Mrs. Moran into the benched courtyard with the baby where, before Cupcake's placement, Mrs. Moran had never ventured out.

As it was the policy for each foster mother to bring an infant to the pediatrician for monthly well-baby visits, we arranged appointments where we took Mrs. Moran, wheelchair, baby, and all on such check-ups. This helped her feel "like everyone else again." We enlisted the aid of several volunteers to have contact with her and to provide outings for shopping and errands for the baby as well.

When she received her first month's foster parent's check, Mrs. Moran asked me if she could donate the monthly fee money to the agency to pay her part toward her own son's care, something that was very meaningful to her in light of the fact that she was supported by aid to the disabled and local social service benefits.

And her son, Tony, who had been rocky in his foster placement, began to speak about the baby and his visits with his mother to his foster mother and worker. One time, when he was at his mother's, he was able to fix a broken wheel on the crib. From then on, each visit to his mother included asking if he could do anything to help her with the baby, and ultimately anything to help her in the house. Though Tony was only 11 at this time, he felt very proud of his mother's accomplishment. As he saw his own mother more favorably in the present with Cupcake, Tony was able to imagine that his mother had shown him the same love and caring when he was a little boy. His foster parents supported his positive feelings toward his mother, allaying loyalty conflicts. His schoolwork and placement progressed. For the first time he expressed interest in a group activity: he became a Boy Scout, and had his picture taken in uniform with Cupcake.

A particularly complex crisis, though ultimately emotionally enhancing, arose during the third month of Cupcake's placement. Early one morning I received a call from Mrs. Moran, who described symptoms of a seizure she had observed in Cupcake. Quickly, we took the infant to the doctor for care. Mrs. Moran was able to follow the course of the seizures, help determine the correct dosage of anti-seizure medication, and follow the course of symptoms in a homemade chart.

Cupcake's medical condition was worrisome in respect to her immediate health as well as future adoptive placement. Additionally, the event was fraught with meaning for Mrs. Moran. On one hand, she felt she had been able to be effective and helpful to the infant baby at a critical time. On the other hand, the fact that Cupcake developed seizures, and she herself had had seizures during her recuperation from the accident, caused intrusive, primitive fears to surface. Was she a noxious person who had, in her handling, caused this infant to have difficulties, too? How had she contributed to her son's mental instability? And would the agency feel this about her?

While I was driving her to a monthly medical appointment, Mrs. Moran offered a dream/nightmare which had awakened her from sleep. (If you will, this might be viewed as the first dream of treatment.) She was somewhat embarrassed at telling it, but thought she'd like to share it with me. In the dream she was preparing to go to a dance. She was putting on a gown of rainbow colored chiffon and swirled around only to awaken before she got to the dance. I listened as she told me that this dream was the way she had felt about her life. Her amputated leg had left her unable to dance. Now with Cupcake, she had felt she was "dancing" in another way. She feared that the "dance" (placement) would be over before it began. I suggested that the rainbow chiffon gown sounded very beautiful and she looked forward to wearing it, as she looked forward to "wearing" her role as a foster mother. She became tearful explaining that for the first time in many years she had enjoyed satisfaction as a woman, nurse, and mother in her work with us at the agency. She and Tony were getting on so much better. She and Tony's foster mother had been exchanging collegial foster-motherly calls together where previously there had been quiet animosity on her part.

Six months after the placement, Cupcake was transferred to an adoptive home. Another infant was placed with Mrs. Moran, much to her satisfaction. At the time I left the agency at the end of a year, Mrs. Moran's status as a temporary foster parent was secure.

Unfortunately, the story does not have an altogether happy ending. Later that fall, Mrs. Moran developed a severe infection in her foot and toes for which she had to be hospitalized. Her condition weakened dramatically, and several subsequent hospitalizations over the next several months were required before her untimely death occurred for reasons the doctors were never completely able to understand.

Of course, the ramifications for Tony were profound. Because her body and speech had so deteriorated, there was only one final visit to the hospital for him, a meeting which was anxiety-provoking for all. Mrs. Moran now feared upsetting Tony with the visit. All agreed that Tony needed to see her; Mrs. Moran, in a final and loving act of mothering, did manage to have a brief nonthreatening visit with Tony with his worker and foster parents accompanying him and simultaneously supporting her.

Though Tony is not the focus per se of this story, his ability to mourn his mother's death, his asking his worker to obtain his mother's permission to call his foster parents Mom and Dad, too, and Mrs. Moran's granting permission before her final hospitalization were critical for his continuing development. The pride he experienced when his mother was recognized in a newspaper article was yet another growth-promoting outcome of Cupcake's placement for him.

DISCUSSION

Many readers might have been surprised that I talk at length about an environmental manipulation; however, my interest in this case was piqued when all concerned observed the reverberating effect of this intervention. Thus, my final intention is to highlight three aspects of the situation that have particular relevance to clinical social work practice; first, briefly, the factors that help us assess ego strength and the capacity for development despite the seemingly overwhelming pathology which has been cited; next, the promotion of self-esteem and narcissistic enhancement as developmental phenomena throughout the life cycle are addressed; finally, the nature of the multi-faceted relationship, the "transference," of particular long-term client populations to community agencies is investigated.

Ego Assessment

Readers may have wondered why I dwelled on an initial glass of iced tea and the first moments of our meeting, but I hoped it set the focus, as it did mine, not only to the size and complexity of the physical and emotional aspects of planning a nursery on wheels, but also to that initial interchange as diagnostically important to me as background history. In a situation where a carefully drawn anamnesis could not detail the questions I found myself having to address, this first interchange provided me with observations which were crucial in the assessment of this plan in terms of hunches about what Mrs. Moran's capacities were.

That Mrs. Moran noticed I was warm meant that she was attuned to me. Likewise, if she was aware of my discomfort, I had reason to believe she could be attuned to an infant. Her care in doing the task at hand—however long it took—showed both her desire for and anticipated pleasure in mastery and ego competence despite the odds against her due to physical disability.

Additionally, whatever Mrs. Moran's difficulties, we do know certain facts from this incomplete history. Especially in the area of child placement, we must draw critically on what we know and operationalize that knowledge for best effect.

Prior to her traumatic accident, Mrs. Moran was a successful newborn-baby nurse/supervisor. Inasmuch as she had been able to meet, marry, have a sexual relationship, give birth to a child, and nurture her own infant, even after her debilitating injuries, we do know she had a certain level of functional competence indicative of significant ego strengths.

Classical psychoanalysis might reveal underlying oral-dependent needs of the mother vis-à-vis the mother's affect hunger, her need for love and affection, her wish to reunite with her baby, to "overprotect" and "overpossess" him. Nonetheless, as Benedek (1959) clearly pointed out, these factors are an exaggeration of the normal process of mothering. Thus, rather than overpathologizing the past, in this case intervention was aimed to buoy Mrs. Moran's strengths.

Benedek (1959, p. 393) points to the reciprocal ego developments between mother and child. She says that through introjection of good mother = good self the infant develops confidence. In the mother a reciprocal process takes place. For her it is the introjection of good-thriving-infant = good-mother-self whereby the mother achieves a new integration in her personality.

When Mrs. Moran was unable to handle Tony, the failure echoed with loss, not only of the parental role but of her own bodily competence as well. Her ego capacities seemingly diminished with loss of self-esteem (effectance). As a client she actually told this to the worker directly, when she asked to be allowed to be a foster mother for the agency. What she was saying was that she wanted and needed "direction," the same kind of feeling she had had when her son had been little. To my mind this was a perfectly normal, appropriate, and understandable desire—the wish to feel competent.

Such achievements with Mrs. Moran suggest that, as with issues of conflict, ego assessment should be viewed as part of a dynamic process rather than as a static quality judged at any one stage of life. Implicit in such an idea is the dimension of time. Thus, when we think of ego assessment, we must consider the meaning of the strengths or weaknesses (deficits) we are encountering as they have existed throughout the life cycle—especially understanding these factors in the context of the present.

Narcissistic Enhancement

Erikson (1953) is credited with the initial observation that development continues throughout the life span, particularly the issues to be negotiated at the different "stages of man." Through his insights, he made us aware that development can be enhanced or compromised by crises and life-tasks at all ages. For Erikson, the experience of generativity found in parenting, teaching, and caretaking provided new avenues for identification, opportunities for expansion of a maternal role, and feelings of mutuality.

That development continues throughout the life cycle (in childhood and adulthood) is significantly reaffirmed by Nemiroff and Colorusso (1979). Shane (1977) further emphasizes the distinction between the historical perspectives of the genetic and of the developmental view of the life cycle, the genetic being more deterministic, the developmental allowing for the epigenetic or later influences.

Note that as late as 1965 Anna Freud and her colleagues of the genetic persuasion referred to the adult as a "finished product" (p. 10) rather than an individual in the process of ongoing change. With the developmental perspective, one considers not only the past as a cause, as proponents of the Anna Freud developmental profile suggest, but the potentialities of the present and future. Among the hypotheses advanced by the developmentally oriented authors, adulthood continues a dynamic process influenced by interaction with the environment, physical and bodily change, and the consequent altered form of issues of childhood.

Narcissistic evolution, too, continues to be shaped throughout the life cycle, as pointed out by Edward and colleagues (1991). Mrs. Moran's case material highlights three developmental nutrients critical to the evolution of self-esteem: effectance, mirroring, and the illusion of power. Though each aspect is altered, and appears in different ways, the point which bears emphasis is that mirroring, effectance, and the illusion of power promote the development of healthy narcissism and can emerge with new experiences in adulthood.

The interaction between the innate givens, the environment, and the service offered was facilitating for Mrs. Moran. In this situation the foster baby was the developmental catalyst. If you will, the agency (and the worker as representative of the agency) was the admiring "mother" and Mrs. Moran was the "practicing toddler baby." The placement permitted her to return to a more gratifying time of life and simultaneously helped her to renegotiate narcissistic issues. The experience offered to Mrs. Moran encouraged new levels of narcissistic adaptation and development. Mahler delineates two concurrent strands of self-esteem development. First, mirroring admiration, being able to do and to accomplish, is recognized from external achievement. Simultaneously, a second essential component, the sense of effectance, is generated from within. Hand in hand, these two critical facets of the separation-individuation practicing phase so critical to the development of sound secondary narcissism could be appreciated in Mrs. Moran's current experience.

Afforded an opportunity to change her interaction with the environment, to see herself more "powerful" (a derivative of the illusion of omnipotence) her self-esteem increased and led her to utilize her capacities, compromised as they were by her disability. As she was encouraged, acknowledged, and competent, there was a reinstatement of a needed sense of power. Perhaps we might say that this case registers a plea for acceptance of a measure of grandiosity!

Before the placement, she had been unwilling and unable to discuss any aspects of her behavior that impinged on her sense of failing self-esteem. When her own sense of self was buttressed by her fine performance as a "helper" herself, she was able to consider her own anxieties with us.

As a successful foster parent, Mrs. Moran could also speak to her limitations as a natural parent in the past. She could forgive herself her limitations, recognizing the reality that had beset her. Her success as a foster parent relieved her guilt over parental failure. Once the ongoing potentials of development were accessible to her, she was able to participate with her son's foster mother, and encourage his separateness.

Mastery in parental function promoted expansion and self-regard. Mrs. Moran was able, for the first time, to send a holiday card signed Mrs. Anna Moran and Tony versus Anna and Tony Moran. Such action may be understood to denote a greater sense of self–object differentiation in her role as a mother. She no longer needed to rely on Tony as a fantasied partner. Inasmuch as she felt like more of a woman in charge, as Cupcake's foster mother, she was able to assert herself to the community as a competent mother of her own child.

In the foregoing material, I hope to have illustrated that while a parent may have difficulty with a child at one age, it does not necessarily mean that a mother or father will have trouble with children of all ages. Inasmuch as child care is in such chaos, with many of our children of color institutionalized from very early periods, assaying the potential effects of placing infants with the city's Mrs. Moran, or seniors who express such interest, might remedy more than the child's need. Such a view follows Mahler, who suggested that different mothers may vary in their ability to mother children of different ages.

Transference

As Mrs. Moran's situation demonstrated the force for development throughout the life cycle, it also led us to consider the relationship to the worker, the transference, in such situations. On one level this case is far from the clinical casework practice as we know it today. In another facet, it is closer to historical/traditional "social casework" and is perhaps relevant to a larger population in our cities than we now identify. This case is about people who will, for one reason or another, need to maintain contact with an agency or hospital for extended periods of time, the "lifers" we find in our practices and community agencies.

Because of the lengthy contacts, the relationship to the worker must be thought of as part of a larger bond (transference) with the agency or hospital, rather than just to the worker involved with a particular segment of work. The importance of this phenomenon when working with people who will have a long relationship with an agency or hospital cannot be overlooked.

Reider (1953) introduced the term *institutional transference* to refer to chronic populations who had minimal ability to form a relationship with a therapist, the kind of population comprising many chronic facilities, such as VA hospitals. Martin (1989) reviewed and elaborated the concept, suggesting that transference to an institution and transference to a therapist are not mutually exclusive. He has suggested that when the bond to the institution (agency) is secured, the aspects of loss so devastating for such populations may be mitigated. In such cases Martin understands the institutional transference to be akin to Winnicott's holding environment, one that provides the illusion of safety and protection from dangers without and within the self. In a case described by Gage and Gillian (1991), permitting the institutional transference to develop facilitated the development of a more trusting relationship between the patient and the staff and the individual therapist.

The clinical agency work with Mrs. Moran involving several workers adds to the understanding of institutional transference in a family service agency setting. The efforts of each component caseworker (and with Mrs. Moran there were three: her worker, her son's worker, and myself as foster care worker) occurred simultaneously. The transference (relationship) was greater than the sum of its parts and, inasmuch as the agency provided a holding environment, it potentiated developmental expansion.

This is neither to say that Mrs. Moran did not have a strong and positive feeling for me nor to detract from that fact, but it is to argue that she did have significant relationships with and transference to the two other workers involved with this case as well. All of us together were components to a broader "agency/ institutional transference." This transference is understood by me as unique, not "split," rather distinct and adaptive.

The fact is that Mrs. Moran was able to share aspects of her thinking with me that might have been shared with her "worker" per se in therapy, but, because of the transference to the agency and the sense of trust which existed between her worker (me) and herself, she was comfortable to bring her anxiety for us to discuss. It should be clear that Mrs. Moran's confidentiality and her right to share some things with either of us was always clearly understood and respected. In actual practice, because of the trusting relationship among the caseworkers and between them and Mrs. Moran, this did not present any difficulties. (Note, if you will, the seeds for countertransference development.)

Rather than viewing this situation as a field for the splitting of the transference, it might well be conceptualized as understanding that a new and particular type of casework relationship is called forth with such populations. In passing, it was especially interesting to observe the change in functioning of this woman as a "patient" in her own right while simultaneously an "employee" of the agency.

CONCLUSION

In this unusual case, a handicapped woman, unable to handle her own latency-aged son, was nevertheless able to become a successful foster parent to an infant. In this role she began to experience herself as more productive as a woman and as a mother. Her feelings of self worth increased and her depressions ebbed proportionately. Her identification with her son's foster mother helped her to achieve greater separation from her son. As she felt better about herself, she became less competitive with her son's foster parents and they developed a more positive relationship with one another.

The work in this case demonstrates how psychoanalytic theory, particularly recent findings regarding narcissistic development, may be drawn upon to promote a client's personal growth. As a psychoanalytically informed social worker, aware of the developmental importance of empowerment, effectance, and mirroring in fostering self value, I was privileged to be in a position to enable both infant and foster mother to grow in this mutually enhancing experience. At the same time, this was a growth experience for me as a social worker, strengthening my conviction regarding the potential for development in each human being and encouraging me to be more open and more creative in the use of myself and my theoretical knowledge.

REFERENCES

Benedek, T. (1959). Parenthood as a developmental phase. *Journal of the American Psychoanalytic Association* 7:389–417.

Colarusso, C., and Nemiroff, R. (1979). Some observations and hypotheses about the psychoanalytic theory of adult development. *International Journal of Psycho-Analysis* 60:59–71.

Edward, J., Ruskin, N., and Turrini, P. (1991). *Separation Individuation: Theory and Application.* New York: Gardner.

Erikson, E. (1950). *Childhood and Society*. New York: Norton.

Freud, A. (1965). *Psychoanalytic Psychology of Normal Development*. New York: International Universities Press.

Gage, K., and Gillins, L. (1991). Institutional transference: a new look at an old concept. *Journal of Psychosocial Nursing and Mental Health Services* 29(4):24–6.

Mahler, M., Pine, F., and Bergman, A. (1975). *The Psychological Birth of the Human Infant*. New York: Basic Books.

Martin, H. (1989). Types of institutional transference. *Bulletin of the Menninger Clinic* 53(1):58–62.

Shane, M. (1977). A rationale for teaching analytic technique based on a developmental orientation and approach. In *Journal of the American Psychoanalytic Association* 58:95–108.

White, R. (1963). *Ego and Reality In Psychoanalytic Theory: A Proposal Regarding Independent Ego Energies*. New York: International Universities Press.

18 Psychoanalysis and the World of Two: Object Relations Couple Therapy

Ellyn Freedman

Can psychoanalysis, with its telescopic lens on individual development in the conscious and unconscious dimension, provide a map of a two-person psychology? Is it possible through psychoanalysis, with its emphasis on individual intrapsychic development, to explain how interpersonal attachment is reached and sustained for "better or worse"? Can intimacy and the study of the couple's shared unconscious come to light in an interpersonal field with continued consideration of the rich, complex interior of each member's identity, defenses, and developmental struggles?

Can the principles of psychoanalytic treatment be adapted for therapeutic intervention and "cure" of the painful entanglements and systematic suffering often inflicted mutually within a couple's life? How can the psychoanalytically oriented psychotherapist enter this interpersonal field, often one of emotional contact, open or insidious? How can she and the couple survive the assaults on self-preservation within such an encounter and help change the quality of the field, often inaccessible, rocky, and explosive. In what manner can the therapist allow the myriad of evocative reactions from the couple to enter her conscious and subconscious as a window in the process of understanding their self and object representations without joining in as persecutor, rescuer, or depriver?

It is the intent of this chapter to illustrate how a relational perspective, mainly stemming from the British object relations school and their theoretical and clinical development of the concept of projective identification, can extend the applicability of psychoanalysis to the world of the couple.[1] The mechanism of projective identification, to be elaborated upon in the paper, will serve as a bridge concept between psychoanalysis as a one-person psychology and psychoanalysis as a two-person psychology. The value of an object relations perspective will be demonstrated through the detailed process account of the treatment of a homosexual couple. The influence of the AIDS epidemic and homophobia on the self and object representations of the couple and their effect on the nature of their interpersonal exchanges will be highlighted.

Projective identification can be understood as a process which ideally helps foster the development of consistent object relations. However, this same process can also be employed in ways that will adversely affect the relationship of a couple, as will be seen in the case material to be presented. In its broadest terms, projective identification will be defined as the manner in which painful or idealized images of the self are placed in another, re-enacted or modified by the other, and re-processed by the self.

The developmental spectrum of projective identification (Zinner 1989) ranges from its primitive form, as primarily a necessary defense that initially serves to rid internal threats, to the capacity to experience empathy. In locating the projective identifications on this spectrum, the solidity of self–object boundaries, that is, the ability of the individual to distinguish internal from external affective stimuli, becomes crucial. Borderline and severe narcissistic character pathology are reflective of diffused boundary states. In couples, these projective identifications are manifested in rigid control and stereotyped role construction. In more neurotic individuals, projective identifications are based on some degree of distortion of the object, mainly stemming from oedipal issues. Competition, triangulation, and unprocessed guilt are major themes demonstrated at this level of projective identification. Empathy, the highest level of projective identification, is the ability to loosen well-established boundaries in an attempt to discover a resonance of the self in the other for shared understanding and support.

1. Although not within the scope of this chapter, object relations theory has also expanded into the realm of family treatment through identification and modifications of parental defensive systems (Shapiro 1979, Slipp 1988).

OBJECT RELATIONS THEORY AND THE COUPLE

In accord with the theory of object relations being summarized here, the mind is understood as being formed primarily as a result of intricate processes of internalization derived from ongoing interactional patterns. The emphasis in object relations theory is on how internal object representations are sculpted and how they intermingle within the psyche, forming the self out of the exchange (Mitchell 1988).

Object relationists (Kernberg 1976, Mitchell 1983) examine the earliest forms of internalization, called introjection (the taking in of parts of objects) and projection (the placing onto the object parts of the self or fragments of an emerging self). Internal experiences to be kept over time are based on affect-generating components producing memories of good or bad images of objects, shaping prototypes for further modes of attachment. The capacity to develop boundaries of self and other, the integration of good and bad object parts with the desire to regain the lost parts of the self, are developmental markers which consolidate the essence of the self in relationships (Ogden 1986, Siegel 1992, Steiner 1993).

In adult love relationships, we observe the constant search for the completion of and complement to the self within the interpersonal field of the relationship. If the self and object representations are composed of damaging or inconsistent internal figures, the love relationship becomes a desperate channel in which to communicate the past injuries that are split off or remain only partially conscious. The spouse becomes the carrier of past emotional assaults and deprivations or the actual injurer or omnipotent figure of perfection. Often, loyalty in the couple is a masked martyrdom for a shared configuration of self and object representations equating attachment with sacrifice.

The British object relations school, although by no means homogeneous in their development, placed paramount importance on the intrinsic nature of attachment. The evolution from classical psychoanalysis is seen over fifty years, beginning with Klein's premise that drives cannot be defined apart from objects (Stein 1990) to Fairbairn's (1941) metapsychological shift to considering libido not as pleasure-seeking but object-seeking. Klein (1935) was greatly influenced by the death instinct as it relates to aggression. However, her concept of reparation strivings to the damaged object and gratitude to the nurturing object provided the basis for considering the central need of the individual as one of establishing and sustaining intimate bonds (Mitchell 1988).

Although internalized objects were not simply considered replicas of the real parents, increasing attention was given to differentiating caregiving situations. Fairbairn (1943) contended that deleterious parenting was internalized as systems of bad part objects, the ties bound by the intrinsic need to remain in contact with the parent, thus leading to internalization of a bad self in situations of child abuse. Winnicott (1962) described the concept of the "good enough mother" who can promote spontaneity and initial feelings of grandiosity. Disappointments follow but can be mastered within the protective environment of "holding." Balint's (1968) "basic fault" was attributed to failure in the provision of primary love combined with possible constitutional deficiencies, leading to a self bereft of good objects for internalization.

Bion (1967), in expanding on Kleinian theory, described that early in life the mother helps to promote the infant's development by "containment" of the unwanted parts of the infant's emerging self. These early projective identifications of the infant rooted in emotional and physiological need are received by the mother, metabolized, and given back to the infant in a more manageable form, often through responsive feeding and touch. This reprocessing of unpleasurable sensations and feeling states helps the infant to utilize the mother for further self-definition.

PROJECTIVE IDENTIFICATION AND THE COUPLE

Let us now look closer at the development of the concept of projective identification within the framework of its function as an early defensive process that optimally leads to the development of soothing positive object representations and object constancy in normal development. In contrast, the manifestations the mechanism takes when containment or holding was not provided will also be explained as it relates to couple interaction.

The term was originally coined by Klein (1946) through her work with young children. She defines it as a rudimentary process by which the infant attempts to deal with transient episodes of hunger and thirst by splitting off rageful reactions and projecting them into mother. When the infant then perceives the rage as coming from the mother, and not the self, it can serve as protection against self-annihilation. Depending on the ability of the mother to partialize the rage, the baby identifies with the dispelled part as being bound or unbound. This process marks the beginning of the paranoid-schizoid position, where the major developmental striving is toward the ability to distinguish good maternal experiences (introjects) from bad. The differentiation of self from mother occurs in the depressive position phase, characterized by fear of loss of the object and by laying of the groundwork for the capacity for empathy, the ability to distinguish the "me from not-me" experience. The object is felt as relatively whole, with the major anxiety residing in the possibility of injuring the object. Desire to establish reparation to the injured object is crucial, as well as the mourning of the imperfection of the parent. The projection of the fantasied ideal onto the object may be prevalent in this period.

Although Klein chronologically placed these developmental stages within the first twelve months, throughout life there is somewhat of a vacillation between the paranoid-schizoid and depressive positions. Usually a preponderance of one is established. Stein (1990) states that an internal sense of powerlessness, persecution, isolation, and envy colors the stagnation of the paranoid-schizoid position in adult life. The achievement of the depressive position serves as the foundation in which to view objects in their own right, with the potential of becoming the lost ideal of the parent. Here we can see the hallmark of a loving, often curative, couple relationship.

The paranoid-schizoid and depressive positions can be seen in couple interaction and the type of projective identifications expressed, also determined by the quality of the self–object boundaries. One or both members can habitually attempt to externalize harsh introjects by evoking self-punitive feelings in the partner.

> A son of one of the first settlers of Israel comes to couple treatment feeling rage and helplessness in regard to measuring up to the achievements of his father. He imposes an unbearably rigid regime on his wife, including demanding a strict "healthy diet" in order to help her unrelated neurological illness. His wife feels as though it is impossible to meet her husband's standards and becomes depressed, feeling inad-

equate and trapped, yet unable to separate. The husband's social isolation and general mistrust of the world represents his stasis in the paranoid-schizoid position. His desperate attempts at parenting his wife in an intensely controlling, demanding manner is the projective identification, making her feel the way he feels–ineffectual and small. The wife, who suffered from life-long feelings of unlovableness due to a critical, unattainable mother, accepts her husband's projection and resultant confinement. She expresses a continued fantasy in treatment that somehow she had injured her mother, persistently desiring a method of reparation. This unresolved yearning in the wife represents the beginning phase of the depressive position, the wish for a soothing mental image of mother. The challenge of the treatment, then, becomes helping the husband differentiate the "me–not-me experience," realizing the pain of his own denigration and how he has placed this in his vulnerable wife. If the wife can become aware of the limitations of her mother's capacity to love, she may effectively mourn and gradually build self-esteem.

Fairbairn (1944) describes projective identification in the child as determined by higher identifications with libidinal (exciting) or anti-libidinal (rejecting) part objects in the parent. The child, longing to have his needs met, identifies with the parents' similar fulfilled or unfulfilled needs. The rejecting experiences are subsequently split off from the "central ego." As painful experiences submerge, the individual is actively seeking compensatory treatment from others, as the force of the fantasy of the ideal object persists. Seinfeld (1993) contends that separate subpersonalities can form in the process and have a "life of their own" apart from the central ego, for example, a split-off addictive state.

Segal (1964), in elaborating on Klein's concept of projective identification as seen in adult relationships, posits that protective identification is the result of the projection of parts of the self into the object, whereby the object is misperceived as if it were like the self, and the object acts out the projected part of the self. It is this reliving in the mate of the self and object representations or fragments that distinguishes projective identification from the defense mechanism of projection. Ogden (1982b) outlines the phases of projective identification with interpersonal pressure and the "moves toward oneness" of psychological states as the core of the concept. Expelling parts of the self into the object, acceptance of the projections by the object across a continuum ranging from idealization to contempt, acting them out, and reidentification by the projector comprise the sequence. The final step, reidentification, determines whether the projector and his or her impact on the relationship is capable of change. Husbands and wives, then, are in constant interplay with each other in an effort to blend and fit their projective identifications with each other.

Scharff and Scharff (1991) utilize Bion's concept of valency, involuntary blending of one individual personality with another, and Racker's concordant identification (with self representations) and complimentary identifications (with object representations) to further understand the nature of the reception of the projection by the spouse. According to the Scharffs, the following steps comprise projective identification in marriage:

1. Projection
2. Object induction
3. Introjective identification by the object
4. Transformation by the object
5. Valency of the object to receive the projection
6. Complementary and concordant identification
7. Introjective identification by the self
8. Mutual projective identification

Zinner (1989) stresses the ubiquity of projective identification in the perception and behavior towards others. Emanating from Klein's view, his contention is that projective identification represents a developmental line covering a spectrum from primitive to mature forms. Kernberg (1981) and Meissner (1987), on the other hand, consider projective identification as a primitive or psychotic defense only, symptomatic of severe borderline pathology. This theoretical difference has direct bearing on treatment paradigms. According to a developmental perspective of projective identification, shared fantasies are not considered pathological in themselves. Projective identification occurs in all intimate relationships, the highest form serving as a complement to the self through recognition of a whole object. In its most primitive forms violence erupts (Williams 1976) or theft of emotional reactions take place (Bollas 1987). The innate need for blending of shared fantasy can occur in more restorative ways through achievement of higher levels of projective identification.

TREATMENT APPROACH

Dicks (1967), at the Tavistock Clinic in England, was the forerunner of the present object relations-based treatment of couples. He applied Fairbairn's terms of conscious and unconscious part–object systems to the study and therapy of spousal pairs. He explained the fit of marriage or change in fit through marital crisis as the result of mutual projective identifications.

Similar to psychoanalysis and psychoanalytic psychotherapy, in general there are no formulas or sets of prescribed techniques for the implementation of an object relations based therapy. As Slipp (1984) states, this differs markedly from other family therapy approaches, for example, strategic and structural, when change is thought to occur through the therapist's control and planned manipulations. McCormack (1989) states that the stance of the marital therapist within an object relations framework should center on encouraging the expression of internal experience, observing the distorted view each holds of the other through primitive projective identifications, and interpreting the distortions with allowance for the rejection of such interpretation. The therapist should be tolerant of regressions and not have superimposed goals for the couple.

Essential to the therapeutic progress is the provision of a holding environment, so that basic anxieties exposed in the systems of projective identifications can safely emerge. Scharff and Scharff (1991) identify two types of holding by the therapist conducting marital therapy. *Contextual holding* relates to the secure environment of the frame of the therapy, its consistency and provision of hope. *Centered holding* refers to the ability of the therapist to contain the intricate and intense series of projective identifications of the individuals within the couple. The anxieties involved with the expectation of the quality of the holding by the therapist is called the *contextual transference.* A major anxiety in the contextual transference is the concern over whether or not the therapist can hold the relationship together. The *focused transference* is made up of the various elements of the centered relating of the individuals within the couple, consisting of the exciting, rejecting part-objects and parts of the self observed in the projective identification with the therapist. The Scharffs caution against interpreting premature focused transferences rather than the contextual, as the primary preoccupation of the patient is with the expected deficit in holding rather than, for example, eroticized wishes of an oedipal nature. Transference that is reflective of the couple's joint difficulty with the holding situation is called the *shared contextual transference.*

One may ask how a focused transference comprised of a series of projective identifications differs from transference in general. Ogden considers projective identification as an aspect of transference, in that it involves not only the transferring of self and object representations onto the therapist but enlists the therapist in an "interpersonal actualization of them." Empathy in this type of therapeutic interaction is equated with the therapist's continual provision of containment (Ogden 1982a). It is only then that confronting basic anxiety and interpretation of defense can be implemented (Scharff 1991).

Corresponding countertransference states also form in the course of marital therapy as the therapist experiences the pushes and pulls of the couple striving for sustained attachment. This is called *contextual countertransference.* The *focused countertransference* emerges in the manner in which the therapist's object relation sets resonate with the individuals within the couple (Scharff 1991). The countertransference reactions are more than the concordant and complementary identifications of the therapist with the patient. The patient, and at times the couple unit, are consciously driving the therapist into a drama whereby the therapist, at times, is unable to prevent herself from being what the patient unconsciously wants her to be and act. It is the therapist's ability to recognize the part she is playing in the drama, experience it as a diagnostic tool, and gradually interpret it to the patient as his or her attempt to communicate painful experience that had previously been out of verbal reach. Rusczynski (1991) emphasizes that it is the therapist's capacity not to act out her given script that is the basis for a curative relationship.

CASE ILLUSTRATION

Case History

Lenny and Jim are a homosexual couple, in their early forties, whom I saw for fifteen months, generally on a weekly basis. They met in a large northeastern city in the '70s at a gay bar, at which time they were looking for "stability" after approximately ten years of homosexual activity and dating for Lenny, and about five for Jim. The couple have been monogamous, according to both, for thirteen years. Tension began to emerge in the relationship after three years, when Lenny's career as an actor seemed out of reach. He rarely auditioned, saying no part was good enough for him. Jim's career, on the other hand, was flourishing. At that time, first Lenny, then Jim pursued individual therapy with the same therapist. Lenny's motivation to seek therapy was "not knowing what to do with his life" followed by Jim, who viewed the therapist as a buffer to Lenny's outbursts and "emotional chaos." The therapist was described as supportive but communication between them remained problematic.

Ironically, it was Lenny's "ability to react" that seemed the initial magnet for Jim. "He made me feel alive, he would be funny and could easily connect with others." Jim felt that there was something in himself that was cut off. At times, feelings of being forced into rapid physical intimacy in the gay world in the initial stage of his coming out were especially difficult for him and eventually made him "shyer." Lenny felt that after therapy Jim remained a "stone," not revealing his thoughts or feelings. As a rule, Lenny felt that Jim would retreat in the face of emotional conflict and become engaged in long solitary pursuits.

Lenny was raised since birth by his maternal grandmother and step-grandfather. However, he was told that they were his natural mother and step-father. Just prior to her marriage Lenny's real mother revealed she had become a parent at age 16. Up to that time she was considered his sister. Following the marriage, Lenny went to live with his mother and new step-father. Within three months he was hospitalized for a suicidal gesture—placing a plastic bag over his head after blockading himself in his room for several weeks. Due to what he called the torture of living with strangers who were supposed to be his family, Lenny left the home and came to the large city.

Jim was the youngest of two sons of a southern working-class family. As long as Jim could remember, he cared for his mother, who had polio and was often bedridden or hospitalized. Jim's clearest memories of childhood were bringing his mother food and attending to her physical needs, like washing and later reading to her. Despite her illness and memories of her not being able to pick him up because of an inability to bend, Jim felt that mother provided him with "an aliveness, and once I got on her lap I felt safe and comforted." One of Jim's deepest regrets was not being present at his mother's death (five years prior), as he arrived at the hospital a few hours after she died. Jim's father was portrayed as stoical, racist, hard-working, and unapproachable. One of the few memories of his father and him together was venturing out into a field to shoot their sick dog. Jim felt forced to watch, trying to shelter his eyes under his father's arm.

The couple moved to a smaller southern city, where the treatment with me took place, to "get away" from the "chaos" of the larger metropolis. It was later revealed that Jim wanted to be near his dying mother. The move for both was also a way of "leaving all of the death behind," as forty percent of their friends had died from AIDS and another twenty percent were HIV positive. However, in this new city homosexuality was more closeted. It seemed as though whatever homophobic attitudes were reflected in Jim's and Lenny's self representations, these were heightened as they internalized the attitudes of those in the new community. Their sexual activity diminished and was "saved for the holidays."

Jim had made the initial call to me, as he felt desperate over what seemed to be inevitable in his case, impending morbidity. Jim had stated that Lenny had attempted to hang himself from a rafter in the basement the previous day. Jim found the rope with the noose still in place. Lenny had described to him that something came over him after Jim had left to visit his father for Father's Day. In Lenny's words, it was like "a deadness, an empty hole." Jim felt trapped and afraid to leave the house for fear that Lenny would try again. Jim's experience was described as "it was as if Lenny held me by the noose." Jim asked if Lenny could also come in for the session, but felt he wasn't going to agree.

Treatment Process

Jim came alone for the first session, as Lenny told Jim that he was going to leave the relationship. In the past, when Lenny had felt ignored, abandoned, or invalidated, he reacted by separating from Jim for several months to pursue vocational goals. However, they would continue to visit each other during these times. At present, Jim felt relieved that Lenny was going to leave; however, when Lenny actually left their home Jim felt anxious, "incomplete," and worried about Lenny's "staying alive." In many ways, Jim felt that his career as a graphic artist was thriving at Lenny's expense. "I give so much and he never gets better."

My initial contextual countertransference (feelings pertaining to the viability of their bonding), despite not meeting Lenny as yet, was mixed, from wondering if they could survive the effects of recurring death of friends, all under age 45, interfaced with the possibility of one or both dying. I was three months pregnant at the time of the first session and the treatment continued through the birth of my baby and after, in almost a parallel sequence to Lenny's becoming ill and the confirming of the HIV positive diagnosis. This led to many series of countertransference trends, including my anticipatory grief, which eventually I was able to utilize for therapeutic benefit.

After much coaxing, Lenny joined Jim for a conjoint session. I was impressed by Lenny's physical fit with his emotional history: pale, waif-like, and fragile, appearing as if a strong wind could knock him down. I could immediately feel Lenny's proclaimed vulnerability, although he was astonishingly verbally astute in describing his inner world. He seemed perpetually assaulted by bruises of non-recognition and abandonment by others, especially Jim. Interpersonally, he was a bottomless pit of grievances that he directed toward Jim, who was described as totally bad, mostly in the areas of withdrawing in face of his need to talk and "give."

Excerpt From First Session

Lenny: I needed to bash his things around and discard them after he left that day to see his father. If I can't have anything why should he? Jim has never wanted to know my needs—it was his decision to renovate another house. I wanted to move out of this city so I could get meaningful work. When I need to talk, Jim responds by withdrawing into one of his projects which is for him only. I guess I threw some of his stuff in the garbage after thinking it wasn't fair. I wanted to kill what he loves because I felt he was killing my needs.

Therapist: So you feel abandoned by Jim in your neediness.

Lenny: Yes. [He then looks at Jim who appears speechless, anxious and afraid to say anything, unable to contain Lenny's demands.]

[*Lenny keeps talking like a rambling engine terrified of running out of steam and the silence of perceived non-responsiveness.*]

Therapist: You feel you use words desperately to see if you can get a morsel of understanding, then you feel it is useless, endless. This painful longing to connect never happens fully and you are left with a sense of aloneness and hunger.

[I then develop an image of Lenny as a sea creature with tentacles always reaching out but never holding the found sustenance, the connection.]

Lenny: Yes, the need is so big I can't stand it.

Therapist: Like you're enveloped in it.

Lenny: It's like I'm suffocating by my own needs.

Therapist: And then do your needs feel bad?

Lenny: Yes, I then retreat and want to destroy myself but Jim can't see it. He deliberately turns away.

[I again turn to Jim, at this point appearing blank, unable to respond verbally though I desperately wanted him to. I wait, then turn to ask Lenny.]

Therapist: Lenny, I'm wondering if Jim's present stance is what you mean about non-responsiveness.

Lenny: Yes.

Jim: I don't know what to say, what to do. I asked you if you wanted to go to my father's–I thought you liked him–you said you didn't want to go. "

Lenny: You know I was feeling depressed. Why couldn't you delay it for another week?

Jim: OK–maybe I should have–but when I try to talk you always criticize me.

Lenny: (In a pleading voice) Well, if you were locked up in this house all day with nothing to do you would be irritable, too–and then when you left last weekend, that was it.

Therapist: What else was going on inside?

Lenny: That I never saw my father. I never had anything. I never had my real mother.

[I now have an image of Lenny as a skeleton, stripped of any possible chance of becoming alive again. I felt rather skeptical concerning my ability to create any possible reparation in the therapy for such massive deprivation.]

Jim: (Brings focus back to present.) I think you need to ask for more work. I'm sorry–I'm sorry your employment is so bad, I'm sorry about your life. I try to give you everything. I try to build you up.

Lenny: It's not worth it, the college pays so little and they actually want me to throw in some office hours.

Jim: [Long silence, looks dazed.]
Therapist: (to Jim) Is this what you mean by the multiple-edged sword?
Jim: [Cautiously] Yes, I feel trapped, bound.
Therapist: Helpless in helping Lenny.
Jim: Maybe there's another school.
Therapist: You keep trying.
Lenny: [Shrugs and continues to denigrate Jim's attempt at caregiving as a waste of time and reiterates he wants to move out of the city but Jim is holding him here penniless and unfulfilled.]

At this point, I experienced in my contextual countertransference a strong sense of being excluded from the circle of Lenny's arrows and Jim's vacant shield, their tense, unyielding centered holding. I sensed that Jim could not integrate Lenny's attacks into any type of conscious emotional response, which seemed to tease Lenny into increased verbal assaults while also barring me from any comments. Despite Jim's terror of Lenny's suicidality, I wanted to unleash Jim's real feelings about being bound by Lenny's noose, but felt that I was stuck in Jim's split-off rage, cementing benevolence as defense.

I drifted in and out of an urge to exclaim to Lenny that he is unrealistic in his demands and to "instruct" him on being less demanding. I began to realize, however, that Lenny was eliciting in me a rejecting stance which ultimately could also make me the depriver, the first projective identification. Instead of interpreting, I waited out my countertransferential hypothesis, and by the end of the second session I continued to feel Lenny was unconsciously trying to get me to treat him badly, like I wasn't doing enough. This was a parallel projective identification which Lenny was conducting with Jim, making us both feel guilty.

My focused countertransference (reaction to individual projective identifications of Lenny) was a combination of feeling bound in a noose he was holding around my neck, making it seem that I had to prove myself worthy enough to be his therapist for fear he may destroy himself, and an intermittent, strong maternal desire to care for him. The pinned-against-the-wall feeling of not knowing when I was good enough for Lenny I interpreted as a way of Lenny letting me emotionally know what it is like not to be worthy of having even parental acknowledgement, let alone parental care. It was at this point that it struck me that Lenny was replacing his fear of death by AIDS with suicidal gestures, although I had to consistently work on my denial of this possibility throughout the next several months. Lenny's ultimate schizoid retreat was death of his own making. However, his yearning for the libidinal object (as in Fairbairn 1944) was still alive, though expressed in denigration and attempted control of his objects.

I chose, in the beginning phase of the therapy, to provide a secure holding and containment for emerging split-off fragments of life-threatening self and object representations in Lenny, and dissociated rage developed by separation anxiety in Jim. I interpreted that I felt like everyone was "walking on eggshells," including me, because there was so much intense feeling underneath. I proposed that perhaps we were placing unspoken feelings into each other because they were so painful.

Excerpt From Sixth Session

Lenny: I have to act out in desperation.

Therapist: You mean you want to terrify Jim with abandonment by suicide because you feel you might be abandoned again?

Lenny: Yes, why can't he understand the prison I grew up in? It was like solitary confinement. My grandmother tried but she was helpless in terms of controlling my stepfather's rages. I was an albatross, another mouth to feed. I remember him shooting my dog when I was 4 because there wasn't enough food. What was I supposed to think about me?

Therapist: It was like you were always wondering if you had a right to live?

[*I was surprised that Jim, not Lenny, was the first to respond and express his self-evaluation as caregiver with mother.*]

Jim: Sometimes I feel like that–I guess behind it all I wanted to give my life so my mother could live.

Therapist: So you feel you worked hard to keep her alive and you work very hard to keep Lenny alive.

Jim: Yeah, but she wasn't sick all the time. Sometimes I forgot she was sick and she really could get a lot done. It wasn't bad at all. No, I don't think my mother has anything to do with this.

Lenny: I thought for a moment you understood how I feel, like I don't deserve to live, then you took back your feeling.

Jim: I did. I don't know why.

Therapist: How do you feel about how you were a caregiver to your mother?

Jim: I was good, I guess, I don't know. I acted more like a kid, or maybe I just wanted to be a kid. Maybe I shouldn't have wanted that all the time.

Therapist: So sometimes do you feel like you didn't do a good enough job?

Jim: I couldn't make her well.

Therapist: So sometimes when Lenny is hard on you, you believe you're bad, like a bad person, if you want your needs to be met as well.

[*I then observe in Lenny a speech modification after taking several deep breaths; his whiney, pleading tone changed to silence. For the first time, he looked into Jim's eyes as if he were able to tolerate the possible rejection of intimate contact.*]

Lenny: Let me tell you how I want you to understand. If we both are wondering if we should be living [sarcastically] then surely we can meet each other's needs a little better. I want you to buy more food at one time, I want you to hold me when we're sleeping, I want you to continue talking even if it gets rough.

Jim: I think I can work on those. But please give me some credit. Put some parameters on what I'm supposed to do, what you want of me.

By the eleventh session, I observed that Lenny was consistently taking in good introjects of Jim with less need to control him through insatiable standards of perfection. Jim seemed more able to modulate Lenny's requests into achievable action and thereby making Lenny's needs feel acknowledged. In the twelfth session Jim's projective identifications became clear, thanks to Lenny's emerging observations of him.

Lenny: I'm not just a bundle of wants. I help you out. I feel like I'm being pegged as a helpless, miserable infant. Jim never wanted to take a chance to get rejected socially. He puts me out front like a guinea pig

Therapist: He uses you to protect himself from bruises.

Jim: [Silence] Yeah–I use Lenny as a buffer. It's not fair. I want to be able to take chances.

This beginning awareness of the couple's mutual projective and introjective identifications generated much progress in healing splitting and overall communication. Lenny appeared less demanding, for example, giving Jim latitude on the "dinner curfew," and Jim made more efforts to connect, for example, sitting longer at dinner rather than retreating into one of his renovation projects. However, during the end of this phase of the treatment, I noticed that the dialogue the two of them had in the waiting room, usually about a friend calling from the north, continued about five minutes into the session. It seemed that I waited endlessly for them to acknowledge my presence.

I perceived that this exclusion was a shared transferential reaction to me as representing their internalized insular social position as probable HIV carriers. In addition, I felt their unconscious caution in expressing their massive grief reactions.

Excerpt From Thirteenth Session

Therapist: Sometimes I feel like it's hard to allow me to enter into parts of your world.
[*Instead of a shared transferential reaction, Lenny expressed a focus transference.*]

Lenny: Another friend is sick. Maybe I want you to know what it's like not to reach Jim–to feel alone and disconnected. He doesn't understand when my friends get sick.

Therapist: What happened to the connection?

Lenny: I don't know. Again I feel isolated, like my feelings don't exist. What about Jim? He got cut off again too.

Jim: I don't know, sometimes I feel that I'm sick of catering to Lenny all the time–what about my feeling of being fed up.

This led Jim, for the first time, to verbalize seedlings of ambivalence for mother, recalling a memory of feeling ashamed of her in the fourth grade because she was crippled and not like the other mothers. Jim began to explore that he must have had some mixed feelings about being so responsible for his mother, at the same time wondering if one of the diseases might kill her. I experienced in many subsequent sessions the stonewall, kind of blank, withholding responses that Lenny described about Jim ("he is like a goddamned statue") as Jim would rather consistently split off any awareness of his aggression toward mother as sole protective good object in face of father as retaliatory object. I felt tantalized by Jim's acknowledging "insight," then denying it, as though he had to keep a semblance of some type of autonomy, schizoidness, or retreat from Lenny or me taking him over.

Jim: [Silence] I don't know. I feel like I did when my mother would call to get me to do something for her, I wouldn't answer–I would run further and further into the woods.

Therapist: Were the requests sometimes like demands?

Jim: Yes, but I didn't mind doing them, but I guess I didn't know how to say no–I thought I would lose her.

Therapist: It was very frightening for you to feel anger toward mom.

Jim: Yes, but no, she was really quite strong most of the time. [Silence] She was really very good to me.

[*He seems to begin to unravel any reconstruction.*]

Jim: That's why I think I needed to run. When I was little, she had to tie me to a tree, because she couldn't chase me.

Therapist: Jim, your anger seems to get tied up with Lenny–all in knots–so tangled you can't get it out in any way that would make sense. It seems it's easier to place it in Lenny, so he can vicariously experience it, then there won't be any loss of your sense of balance or Lenny himself.

Lenny: Yes, he likes to make me suffer by carrying this around for him. I feel like a damn chameleon, and then he stays the sane one, and I get pegged as needing an individual therapist.

Jim: I guess I was attracted to Lenny because he could be like this, because I do feel like a stone. I just had no real outlet.

Lenny: Then you call me demanding.

Jim: Yes, I guess it feels like a tease.

Therapist: Perhaps this was the only way you could say no–teasing your mom when she was calling you and you didn't answer.

Jim: Maybe. I guess I admire Lenny for being able to express his emotions, but then I feel he's insatiable in his demands or that he gets out of control and he wants too much. Nobody can give that much.

Therapist: How do you experience being out of control?

Jim: Knowing that my mother might not come back from the hospital–knowing that Lenny could kill himself, even though I work hard at taking care of her–him. My relatives were out of control, drinking all the time, showing me guns. My aunt told me she shot a policeman who was trying to trespass on her property. My mother had to involuntarily commit her sister many times to state institutions. I was afraid of them, and that's all I saw growing up. We lived so far out from anyone. My mother was the only sane one. All she wanted to do was protect me. I guess my anger is buried. Maybe I feel guilty about it.

Therapist: So after you gave your anger to Lenny, you may want to punish him for it.

Jim: Maybe–God, that is cruel, I love Lenny. [*For the first time he is tearful.*]

In subsequent sessions, Jim began to become more able to articulate his inner feelings. Lenny's noose around him and his knotted emotions gradually seemed to be placed into words, as he attempted to empathize with Lenny, at the same time attempting to defend himself from global accusations. He became more comfortable, letting me and Lenny find his anger. Lenny's suicidality seemed to be contained by Jim's ability to confront him. This was the most difficult part of the treatment, detoxifying Jim as the bad object, and to a lesser extent, myself. Lenny was able, in a number of occasions, to express the seedlings of gratitude towards Jim. Jim was able to give examples of when he felt he actually was being taken advantage of by Lenny, for example, being stuck paying all the bills because of Lenny's minimal employment. Jim, still needing to somewhat rationalize Lenny's behavior, however, could state, "I want to help Lenny, not be exploited." Overall, he was able to tolerate more aggression in himself and gradually verbalize it as he confronted his lifelong defenses of denial, avoidance, and withdrawal.

Lenny's longing for the unconditional ideal mother, which, of course, as an adult is unattainable in its original form, seemed to mitigate to the point of introjecting the many pieces of psychological sustenance that Jim could offer. Jim's almost slavish devotion to Lenny as emotional invalid and his resultant nurse-like role became less and less gratifying to Jim. Jim became aware of this reenactment of his role as caregiver to mother who provided his connection to life and served to protect him against paternal deadness, inability to relate, and possible punishment for connection to mother. He likened his father to an empty emotional barrel; the only contents it possibly contained were unrelatedness bullets of envy. As he visited his father, who became ill, Jim began to view him instead as "pathetic," "tragic." He discovered that making Lenny the victim of his emotional distance was a way of working through the pain of never having father as a "real connection with concern if I lived or died."

The next few sessions seemed to slowly dismantle the brittleness of collusive rigidity of self–object representations, the manifest issue being whether they would move so Lenny could have a chance to develop his career. However, there still appeared to be little, if any, discussion of the paucity of sexual activity, although more affection was shown. No desire to change the isolationist position to the outside world was noticed, and I observed that Lenny, already slight in build, lost weight.

What was emerging was a new joint sadness, and I again commented that I felt they were sharing an extremely painful series of emotions and anticipations that centered around not just their emotional relationship, but their physical survival. I wondered, now that they were feeling more secure with each other, if they could articulate what they were experiencing and let me in. The issue of secrets, however, was actually occurring on both sides of the treatment, as my pregnancy was beginning to show and I remained confused about how to handle it. It occurred to me that the couple was unconsciously protecting me as they denied the pregnancy. As a result, I became to them less and less a potential container for the massive tragedies they experienced and were attempting to begin to grieve. I was also concerned about their feelings of my being so different from them as a child bearer and member of the heterosexual world that I would be considered unable to understand their world, thus damaging the positive contextual transference. In determining how and when to introduce the subject of my pregnancy into the treatment, I was concerned lest they might perceive my doing so as cruel. It seemed like rubbing salt into their emotional wounds. I thought how unfortunate it was that they should need to confront my bringing in life at a time that they were getting prepared to face a terminal illness. After much thought and growing awareness of my anticipated grief concerning the possible death of a patient within treatment, I decided to interpret what I perceived to be a denial of my pregnancy with the hope that this would unleash their repressed grief and fear of their own death.

EXCERPT FROM TWENTIETH SESSION

Therapist: For some reason I feel there is much less anger between you, but there is something shared by you both that is not being put into words. I'm wondering if it has to do with knowing on some level that I was having a baby.

Jim: No, this is a shock but a good one. It's nice to hear about life. I think we've pushed you back from all the death. It's almost impossible to describe the loss experience over and over. I feel there is no way you can understand. You're not gay. I don't think anyone our age who isn't gay has any emotional idea or parallel, but then again we don't talk about it. It's like Lenny supports his friends who've been sick, I support mine long distance, but we never acknowledge our own fears about how it would affect us if we got sick.

Lenny: It's a silent time bomb. We've never been tested. I don't want to know. Anyway, you're pregnant. I didn't want to destroy your happiness in bringing in life. I want to think about your baby. I think I would be an excellent parent. I think I have a lot to give. I wondered if I could ever have a child, but then again I don't know how long I'll be around.

Finally, the years of thwarted bereavement due to oversaturation and depletion caused by multiple trauma began to be processed. This split-off longing to mourn evolved in death story after death story, individuals' and couples' funerals, individuals and couples disappearing, as well as whole resorts and clubs dying. Lenny stated, "After a while, you just don't know who you were not going to see anymore." During this middle phase of the treatment, which involved building internalizations and mental memorials of friends deceased, much affect was displayed with sadness, disbelief, and anger, especially toward "homophobic society that had their dream come true." "They are wiping us out" (Jim's remark). "No one else dies from their sexuality" (Lenny's remark). Both were able to support each other when shameful childhood feelings concerning their homosexuality had re-emerged over the years of the deaths, emphasizing "not going into and taking in the hate" (Lenny).

Lenny, during this phase, was experiencing recurring dreams of being chased by wires and tubes, and calling a close friend who was HIV positive and never answered. As he described his symptoms of fatigue, what he called "thrush," he recalled an image of himself at age 16 walking out in the snow like an Eskimo, feeling that despite reuniting with his mother, he still was feeling unwanted. Now he'll just wither away slowly with this disease. "I'm not going to bring Jim down. I need to leave. I'm tired. Jim is tired of taking care of me and look at you–you're eight months pregnant. You are not up to this. Anyway, you will see the baby and forget about me and us." He wondered what it was like for his mother to give him up. Would that have been my choice? He pondered why it had to be such a secret, why even though she couldn't support him, why she couldn't have acknowledged her maternity, rather than sacrifice all the possible time together. Jim responded, "It was the time, the stigma." I reiterated at this point that there would be a month's break in the treatment but after the birth I would return. During the month I would be available by phone. Gradually, Lenny and Jim began to weave some type of meaning and continuity in themselves as gay men and as a gay couple whose loyalty persisted over many individual, couple, and community threats. Contextual transference seemed strongly held at this point. This new foundation allowed them both to be tested for HIV, results indicating that Lenny was positive with a very low T-cell count. Jim was negative.

Jim began again to be devoted to Lenny, both financially and through actual physical care, although Lenny's only persistent symptom was fatigue. Eventually, two weeks before the birth of my baby, Lenny refused to come to the sessions. Although disappointed, I gave Lenny this space as I felt that he needed to integrate this awesome development alone, although it represented old self-representations as an abandoned pariah. This provoked in me a feeling, once again, of not being a good enough therapist for Lenny and a return of the feeling that I was betraying him by my anticipated absence to have the baby (Lenny's mother had another child that she did raise from birth).

I began to experience at this point that I should relinquish my need to work with their object relations, considering the nature and severity of the crisis point including all the difficult decisions regarding Lenny's physical care. I soon realized, however, that this severing of the concrete, intrapsychic, and interpersonal was impossible, as the knowledge of at least one of them being positive had been held by them subconsciously for years, and has had a pervasive influence on the shaping of their relationship. Simultaneously, I respected Lenny's need to retreat at this point as he needed to integrate before communicating the anticipated loss or theft of a major part of his life. The holding of the therapy, I felt, was still present for Lenny, despite his physical absence from it.

As one might have anticipated, the HIV test results were a major stress for each of them and led to significant regression. However, during this period, Jim individually was able to work through survivor guilt, as he continued to shed his harshness in evaluating himself as a not-good-enough caregiver for mother and Lenny. Lenny, after an initial acceptance of Jim's support, was again projecting his rage and helplessness onto him as persecutor through insisting that Jim once more was holding him down in fulfilling his life. Jim decided, at that point, that he had to give Lenny a "chance to live." During subsequent individual sessions, Jim was able to work through his separation anxiety from Lenny by encouraging him to move to–Lenny's choice–the west coast, get started, and he would follow, thus allowing Lenny to design his future. Jim felt that both of them needed to be in a "gay-friendlier" place that could provide them with more support, as returning to the former city of residence would be like visiting a graveyard. I felt that Jim's decision was not based on the need to care for Lenny in order that Jim might survive emotionally. Rather, I saw it based on loyalty with room for open negative expression without guilt and separation anxiety. Despite a very painful leaving on both parts, Lenny did move–Jim allowing him to "make his own path without thinking I'm holding him down." Jim was able to withstand the possibility that Lenny would leave him permanently.

Lenny returned to treatment from the west coast during the crisis of having to put to sleep the dog given to them by their closest couple, friends who died eight years ago. He also wanted to see a picture of my baby. Through a series of individual, and then couple sessions, Lenny expressed the envy that he had towards my baby because of my "expected devotion" and, at the same time, began to realize the limits of a 16-year-old mother. He was able to express his terror of dying and the fact that he still did want to try to find a fulfilling vocation. He could express gratitude for Jim allowing him to "take the reins." His remaining friends in the north seemed to provide additional support to him, and he was able to take this in without distortion. Although he stated that he hadn't found a good job yet, he joined two support groups and saw that HIV-infected individuals can still "live." He was able to ask if Jim could join him, although he was very anxious about Jim's possible rejection of his needs.

Jim did agree and emphasized "it was his choice." Jim decided to look for a humanitarian interest in his new place of residence, in addition to his financially successful career.

As they move to the west coast, I do not feel that Lenny and Jim's intrapsychic, interpersonal struggles are over, as they deal with a terminal illness where Jim again is caregiver, Lenny the needy child and authentic victim. However, due to the modification in their internal self, object, and projective world, both are better able to provide for each other what they so deeply long for in a continuum of growth for themselves as individuals and their relationship.

SUMMARY

Object relations theory in psychoanalysis explores the link between real individuals and others' internal images of them molded by residues of relationships. The unconscious contracts issued in the formation of coupling can be attempts to undo past damages, or to maintain stifled images or glorified inner pictures of the other. Through the mechanism of projective identification one can evacuate one's undesired parts onto the mate, live out one's aspirations through them, or find in each other the longed-for understanding of past emotional pain and hope for interpersonal change. Projective identification and its counterpart, introjective identification, and their manifestations within the therapeutic relationship between the individuals of the couple, the individual and the therapist, and the couple and the therapist can provide a framework for the creation of a new synthesis of intrapsychic worlds. Through awareness of the split-off parts of their selves and their increased capacity for containment, the couple's shared inner life can become one of safety and an ever-growing arena for the expansion of inner needs. Ultimately, this can offer a solid anchor for the family in face of stressful environmental impingements, in the above case, a homosexual one facing an epidemic of mammoth proportions perceived as an emotional holocaust.

REFERENCES

Balint, M. (1968). Primary love. In *The Basic Fault: Therapeutic Aspects of Regression*, pp. 64–72. New York: Brunner/Mazel.

Bion, W. R. (1967). *Second Thoughts*. London: Heinemann.

Bollas, C. (1987). *The Shadow of the Object*. New York: Columbia University Press.

Dicks, H. V. (1967). *Marital Tensions: Clinical Studies Towards a Psychoanalytic Theory of Interaction*. London: Routledge and Kegan Paul.

Fairbairn W. R. D. (1941). A revised psychopathology of the psychoses and psychoneurosis. In *Psychoanalytic Studies of the Personality*, pp. 28–58. London: Routledge and Kegan Paul, 1952.

—— (1943). The repression and the return of bad objects. In *Psychoanalytic Studies of the Personality*, pp. 59–81. London: Routledge and Kegan Paul, 1952.

—— (1944). Endopsychic structure considered in terms of object relationships. In *Psychoanalytic Studies of the Personality*, pp. 82–136. London: Routledge and Kegan Paul, 1952.

Kernberg, O. T. (1976). *Object Relations Theory and Clinical Psychoanalysis*. Northvale, NJ: Jason Aronson.

—— (1987). Projection and projective identification: developmental and clinical aspects. In *Projection, Identification and Projective Identification*, ed. J. Sandler, pp. 93-115. Madison, CT: International Universities Press.

Klein, M. (1935). A contribution to the psychogenesis of manic depressive states. In *Love, Guilt, Reparation and Other Works, 1921–1945*, pp. 26–89. New York: Free Press.

—— (1946). Notes on some schizoid mechanisms. In *Envy and Gratitude and Other Works, 1946–1963*, pp. 1–24. New York: Delacorte, 1975.

McCormack, C. (1989). The borderline/schizoid marriage: the holding environment as essential therapeutic construct. In *Journal of Marital and Family Therapy*, 15(3)299–309.

Meissner, W. W. (1987). Projection and projective identification. In *Projection, Identification, Projective Identification*, ed. J. Sandler, pp. 27–49. Madison, CT: International Universities Press.

Mitchell, S. A. (1983). *Object Relations in Psychoanalytic Theory*. Cambridge, MA: Harvard University Press.

—— (1988). The relational matrix. In *Relational Concepts in Psychoanalysis*. Cambridge, MA: Harvard University Press.

Ogden, T. (1982a). Issues of technique. In *Projective Identification and Psychotherapeutic Technique*. Northvale, NJ: Jason Aronson.

—— (1982b). The concept of projective identification. In *Projective Identification and Psychotherapeutic Technique*, pp. 11–37. Northvale, NJ: Jason Aronson.

—— (1986). *The Matrix of the Mind*. Northvale, NJ: Jason Aronson.

Rusczynski, S. (1993). Working with couples. In *Psychotherapy with Couples: Theory and Practice at the Tavistock Institute of Marital Studies*, ed. S. Rusczynski, pp. 197–219. London: Karnac.

Scharff, D. E., and Scharff, J. S. (1991). *Object Relations Couple Therapy*. Northvale, NJ: Jason Aronson.

Segal, H. (1964). *Introduction to the Work of Melanie Klein*. London: Heinemann and the Institute of Psycho-Analysis.

Seinfeld, J. (1993). Melanie Klein and the interpretation of primitive phantasy. In *Interpreting and Holding: The Paternal and Maternal Functions of the Therapist*. Northvale, NJ: Jason Aronson.

Shapiro, R. L. (1979). Family dynamics and object relations theory: an analytic group–interpretive approach. In *Foundations of Object Relations Family Therapy*, ed. J. S. Scharff, pp. 225–258. Northvale, NJ: Jason Aronson.

Siegel, J. (1992). Investing resources in the new object. In *Repairing Intimacy: an Object Relations Approach to Couples Therapy*, pp. 27–35. Northvale, NJ: Jason Aronson.

Slipp, S. (1984). *Object Relations: A Dynamic Bridge between Individual and Family Treatment*. New York: Jason Aronson.

Stein, R. (1990). A new look at *the* theory of Melanie Klein. *International Journal of Psycho-Analysis* 71(3):499–511.

Steiner, J. (1993). The recovery of parts of the self lost through projective identification: the role of mourning. In *Psychic Retreats*, pp. 54–63. London: New Library of Psychoanalysis, Karnac.

William, H. A. (1976). *Violence in the Family*. Unpublished paper.

Winnicott, D. W. (1962). The aims of psychoanalytic treatment. In *The Maturational Processes and the Facilitating Environment*, pp. 166–170. New York: International Universities Press.

Zinner, J. (1989). *Developmental Spectrum of Projective Identification*. Unpublished paper.

19 Ending Where the Client Is: A Psychodynamic Approach to Forced Terminations

Margaret Coker

INTRODUCTION

Traditionally, the process of termination has been presented as a separate stage within the course of treatment, carrying special considerations and practice techniques. At the same time, however, termination is recognized as part of the ongoing process of treatment and preparation for it may be viewed as commencing in the first hour. Like parents who, even as they are ministering to their child, bear in mind that they must also prepare him or her to eventually "leave the nest," so are therapists mindful of the need to help their patients achieve sufficient autonomy to leave their treatment. In the case of the more disturbed patients, this can be a challenging task, for to varying degrees they tend to lack those capacities that are requisite for autonomy, such as the capacity to tolerate themselves as more separate individuals, the ability to relate to others in a give-and-take fashion as persons in their own right, and a wide range of ego functions that enable an individual to more comfortably cope with the inner and outer demands of everyday life.

Thus, developmentally oriented therapists treating such individuals try first and foremost to safeguard, support, and encourage whatever autonomous capacities a patient already possesses. At the same time, they seek to promote, to whatever extent possible, an extension of these capacities. The patient is encouraged to participate as actively as possible in the treatment process itself. Forward strivings, both in and out of treatment, are acknowledged and supported. By temporarily performing certain needed ego functions that the patient cannot perform himself or herself, such as setting boundaries, helping the patient calm down, enabling him or her to try to think before acting, and so on, the therapist tries to serve as a temporary auxiliary ego for the patient and as an object for purposes of identification. In time it is hoped that the patient will take in certain functions of the therapist that have proven useful. What has transpired between the two of them becomes a resource in the mind. To the degree this process is successful, the person of the therapist becomes less and less needed (Blanck and Blanck 1979).

The achievement of such an autonomous state is, at best, only an approximation. Many patients, however, feel better when they have reached a comfortable degree of autonomy and seek to terminate at that point. Other patients, for varying reasons, are never able to reach a point where they can function with sufficient autonomy and require some kind of care or external supports throughout life. Still others could, perhaps, proceed further, but their treatment is interrupted by the fact that their therapist cannot continue to work with them for a sufficient period of time. Situations such as employment changes, agency restructuring, funding reallocations, and the training of student interns whose commitment to the patient is circumvented by the academic year often precipitate such premature endings to therapy.

In this chapter, I will consider the kind of premature ending that is caused when the intern–practitioner must conclude treatment in accord with his or her schedule rather than when the patient is ready to end. It is these interns who frequently are assigned the more disturbed patients, such as those suffering from severe characterological problems (i.e., borderline pathology) or patients who manifest severe chronic mental illness such as schizophrenia. These patients are unlikely to make significant therapeutic progress over the course of an academic year. As a result, the intern working with them may view their contribution as limited to helping them avoid a crisis. Frequently, however, interns experience a sense of futility in these circumstances, asking, "What difference does the treatment make?"

I will demonstrate here, however, that even in the case of a severely impaired individual, some significant progress can be made in this necessarily time-limited treatment. I shall show how, by drawing on the contributions of contemporary developmental ego psychology and making full use of the relationship between patient and therapist, it was possible for me, as a student, to utilize the inevitable parting between a deeply disturbed patient and myself to help him move some steps forward in his development and to continue to use the further treatment he required advantageously. I will present here an approach to dealing with forced termination that will help prepare both the intern and the client for the inevitable parting.

LITERATURE REVIEW

Ideally, it is the patient who broaches the subject of termination. When therapy must end due to the therapist's leaving and before explicit or implicit goals have been reached, the therapist must, of course, bring up the topic. How the ending is addressed must, in turn, take into account the problems raised by this particular ending. Fortunately, there are many analytic writings that help us to think of the issues that may be involved and of ways of addressing them (Alexander et al. 1989, Beatrice 1982–83, Glenn 1971, Keith 1966, Mikkelson and Gutheil 1979, Pumpian-Mindlin 1958, Schafer 1973, Smith 1982–83, Weiner 1975). Among the writers on the subject that have also been particularly helpful to me have been Blanck and Blanck (1987), Gavazzi and Anderson (1987), Glick (1987), Penn (1990), and Seibold (1991).

Glick (1987) points out that in forced terminations there may be heightened transferences and countertransferences, since "both the unconscious fantasies with their associated affects and the defenses against them are heightened" (p. 450). Some patients, for example, may feel that it is their badness, their negative and hostile feelings, that have led the therapist to wish to abandon them. The present prospect of loss may also evoke past experiences with renunciation, so that the pain is intensified. The facilitation of positive transference is particularly important at this time.

Drawing on anticipatory grief theory, Seibold (1991) proposes ways to assist patients to deal with their feelings of bereavement when the therapist must leave. Each person will, of course, react in his or her own unique way, and the human environment in which the loss occurs will also exert an effect on how the event is processed. Seibold recommends the provision both of ample time (at least six weeks) and of discussion of the facts that render termination necessary. Some therapists, she suggests, may deny their importance to their patients, and thus fail to anticipate the significance of the pending loss.

These recommendations are echoed by Penn (1990), who proposes four steps: (1) informing the patient before the start of treatment, (2) leaving time for discussion (she too mentions six weeks), (3) facilitating the expression of feelings, and (4) recognizing indirect expressions of reactions, as perhaps in dreams, memories, or other themes of separation. Both therapist and patient need to recognize that something good has resulted from therapy and from the meaningfulness of their relationship.

Forced termination frequently necessitates preparation for transfer of the patient to another therapist. While Wapner and colleagues (1986, p. 384) question the value of such transfers, and recommend that interns and residents be assigned only those patients who are likely to achieve their goals within a specific time frame, others have suggested ways in which such transfers can be carried out with greater effectiveness. Gavazzi and Anderson (1987), for example, focus on the importance of adequate preparation in transferring a patient to another therapist. Pitfalls may be avoided, they propose, if the parting therapist provides sufficient information to the new therapist, including a description of the therapeutic approach found to be most helpful. The process should include: (1) preparing the client for termination and transfer; (2) orienting the client and incoming therapist to one another; (3) bringing the client and incoming therapist together; and (4) facilitating the continuation of the therapeutic process. Sufficient preparation may often be neglected by student-interns because of time constraints, inadequate staff, or the academic calendar, which may allow no overlap from one intern to the next. I would agree with Gavazzi and Anderson that preparation for transfer is an integral part of the termination process when further treatment is indicated.

STARTING WHERE THE CLIENT IS

I first met John, the patient to be considered here, during my social work internship in a state-operated outpatient clinic that serves persons diagnosed with a chronic mental illness. John was a white, divorced male in his fifties who had been diagnosed as a chronic paranoid schizophrenic, in accord with the diagnostic criteria elaborated in the *DSM-IV* (1994). His initial psychotic break occurred after his first wife left him. His first hospitalization had occurred in his early twenties and it was followed by numerous courses of treatment and several lengthy stays in state-run institutions. During his early episodes, John was so violent that he had required restraints. Over the years, however, he had gained greater control of his impulses and became better able to express his anger verbally.

Prior to being assigned to me, John had a history of noncompliance with treatment and, at one point, was assigned to an Intensive Case Manager (ICM) who followed up on him in the community. When his ICM was moved to another position and was not to be replaced, John was dropped from that program and referred to the clinic. At the time our work commenced, he was residing in a community-supported apartment and was required to participate in some form of outpatient treatment.

It was not expected, however, that outpatient treatment would be sufficient to provide the holding experiences that such a deeply disturbed individual as John required. The treatment of most schizophrenic patients, as Lidz and Lidz (1971) have stressed, must encompass more than psychotherapy. John received medication, participated in a sheltered workshop program, and was in contact with other professionals. I served as his case manager as well as his therapist, and had the task of coordinating these services.

After an initial screening, a plan was worked out that I would see John weekly. In our first session, I informed John of my status as a student–intern who would be working with him until the end of the academic year (the following May). John received this information with no discernible affect or comment. He made no eye contact. A slight shrug of his shoulders said it all . . . "And I should care?"

Explicitly, we were offering John psychiatric care and a place to get his prescriptions. This fulfilled his residence requirement. Implicitly, I was offering him a therapeutic relationship, which did not seem to interest him at the time.

I essentially joined John's resistance at the start. John was not a voluntary client, and he and I both knew it. My message to him was a simple one, "Look John, just show up and we'll see what happens. You don't have to like it. That's not a requirement. I know you don't want to be here and that's okay with me. It's not my job to make you miserable." By uncritically acknowledging my understanding of his resistance to coming to treatment, I was able to get him to agree to come weekly for at least two months.

Developmental Diagnosis

When one knows one has such a limited amount of time to work with a patient, it is important to ascertain as quickly as possible, the nature of the patient's intrapsychic deficits and strengths. Both A. Freud (1981), who has carefully delineated the many developmental lines that must be negotiated in normal developmental to enable an individual to reach psychological maturity, and Gertrude and Rubin Blanck (1994), who draw on Margaret Mahler's (Mahler et al. 1975) conceptualizations of the separation-individuation progression and its role in promoting both object and self-constancy, have provided the clinician with useful guides for such a developmental assessment. Broadly speaking, these assessment guides encourage the clinician to consider treatment goals and a treatment approach that takes into account the state of the patient's drives, the strengths and weakness of his or her ego, the defenses he or she employs, the nature of the affective repertoire available to the patient, the degree of self–object differentiation the patient has acquired, and the quality of the patient's self and object relations.

As I sat with John in the beginning sessions, I had these schemas in mind and tried to identify where John's development had faltered and why. At our first meeting, John made no eye contact and refused to shake my hand. When we first met, I had asked him whether he would prefer me to call him John or Mr. R. He angrily replied that he did not care what I called him. In the following sessions, he utilized vulgar, highly sexualized terminology in his conversations and was as disrespectful and hostile towards me as he was towards others.

What did this suggest? I questioned first the level of his object relations, an important area for diagnostic assessment. Was his hostility a displacement from past persons towards whom he was angry? Had he failed to develop sufficient basic trust in others so that he used his anger to fend off contact? In observing when he was angry, I noted that this occurred most when he was upset or anxious. This led me to think that perhaps his anger was a way of protecting himself. I began to consider that it might, at least some of the time, be serving to protect him from close contact with others whom, for one reason or another, he feared.

As I came to understand John, I could see many of the developmental deficits that are associated with psychosis. As noted earlier, his first psychotic break occurred with the loss of his wife. Such a reaction is suggestive of significant problems in self–object differentiation, of a lack of a sufficient sense of self to tolerate separation, and a profound fear of abandonment. Lacking a stable, relatively autonomous inner structure, the poorly differentiated individual is highly dependent upon outside supportive structures. When these are lost, disorganization is likely to follow. I began to see John's hostility as his way of warding off the closeness he sought in the face of his great need for it. He experienced what Burnham and colleagues (1969) have referred to as an "object need–fear dilemma" (p. 27) and which they regard as a central problem in schizophrenic pathology. Needing an outside source to provide external structure and control, the schizophrenic individual is desperate for another. However, according to these clinicians, the very excessiveness of this need makes others appear dangerous and frightening since they are perceived as capable of destroying the individual through abandonment. This dilemma leads to profound fear and distrust of others. Because of a lack of separateness and autonomy, schizophrenics also fear that their need for the other will dissolve their own fragile self–nonself boundaries and lead to the collapse of whatever sense of self they possess. Along the same lines, Sanville (1994) has noted that in the cases of some schizophrenic patients, there is a profound fear of being "swallowed up" by another who is perceived to be more powerful.

These factors, as well as other developmental deficits that became apparent, such as his reliance on primitive defenses including splitting, dissociation, idealization, devaluation, and projection, his limited repertoire of affects, his inability to bring together good and bad aspects of self and other, suggested that his development had gone off-track very early in life.

In light of this and other considerations, I felt that what John needed in the treatment was for me to become a constant enough object who could offer him a chance for a reparative experience. I saw myself as adopting a stance whereby I would receive and contain John's negative, hostile, and rejecting "approach" behavior. He could express verbally his anger, as well other negative affects, and learn that I would not be destroyed, leave him, or retaliate. Winnicott (1982) has emphasized the need on the part of such patients for a therapist who can endure their unconscious wish to destroy the other (the therapist), in order that they may internalize the constancy of the object.

What I sought to provide for John was a holding environment (Winnicott 1965) akin to what caretakers offer to a developing child. Of course, adult patients are not children and what a therapist can provide is of a different order than what parents provide. However, we can and do offer, to varying degrees and in accord with the needs of the patient, such functions and attitudes as interest in him or her, empathy, attunement, soothing, acceptance, and containment, responsiveness to fluctuating needs, and mirroring, all of which Winnicott has identified as aspects of "good enough mothering" (Winnicott, 1965).

At the same time that I kept these and other matters in mind, I was cognizant of the limited time in which I had to work with John and the fact that he would be confronted in the treatment itself with a separation and loss experience to which he was particularly vulnerable. How, I wondered, could I help to use this time-limited opportunity to help promote in him a sense of autonomy, even in a situation over which he had no control?

Treatment Progress: Discernible Differences

John made remarkable strides in the treatment. Initially, his ability to engage in a session was limited to 10 to 15 minutes. In time, he came to leave reluctantly after the scheduled 50 minutes. In our sessions, he began to show a deep sensitivity to others and revealed a wry sense of humor. It was clear that he was forming a relationship with me. From a person to be avoided, I became someone to idealize. In his eyes, I became someone who could do no wrong. John began to express his wish for closeness directly, as evidenced in the following dialogue:

John: You know what?
Margaret: What, John?
John: I was thinking about you the other day.
Margaret: Oh?
John: Yes, I was thinking how it would be if you were in bed with me . . . not for sex, but just to be able to be close to you.

While I was aware that this exchange might well have sexual implications that John was defending against by his disavowal, I chose, on the basis of my developmental assessment of John, to focus on his wish for closeness. I was impressed that he had not apparently become frightened of such a wish, suggesting that closeness, at least in this instance, did not lead to fears of merger and loss of self. I also was struck by his ability to carry an image of me in his mind, perhaps to think about me. This suggested that he was acquiring some representation of me in his mind as a more separate person who had some value to him—a step on the way to object constancy (Mahler et al. 1975). I hypothesized that the fact that I neither abandoned nor "swallowed him," that I did not "take over," but respected his slender autonomy, had begun to have meaning to John.

As time went on, John's dependence upon me intensified and he began increasingly to idealize me. This led to a tendency towards overcompliance and a fear of offending me, which I understood as related to his fear of now losing me as a valued person. It was important to encourage John to be as honest as he could be. I carefully sought to show that he did not need to fear this would result in my abandoning him. I was also careful not to take advantage of his compliance, in the interests of promoting his autonomy. It was tempting, at times, to want to take advantage of it, especially in getting what I needed from him (e.g., signing releases). However, to the degree that our goal was to enable him to become as autonomous as possible while not shying away from connectedness with others, it was essential that he have the opportunity to decide matters for himself even though this, at times, proved frustrating to me. I viewed the treatment situation itself as an opportunity to help him extend his own decision-making abilities.

At the same time that I sought to promote John's ability to do things on his own when he could, to stretch his capacities, it was essential to perform some of those functions for him that he was, as yet, unable to master. His well-being clearly depended upon his maintaining contact with significant people, whether as individuals or as part of a social structure (Burnham 1969). He needed ongoing, constant reassurance and some form of external soothing. He smoked two to three packs of cigarettes per day and was known to check in with his workshop adviser several times a day. This emotional refueling was important to him.

John also required others to provide the organization and regulation which he was unable to provide for himself. Thus, it was important for me to establish clear rules and boundaries. For example, early on, John would sometimes arrive late to an appointment, or not show up at all. I encouraged him to call if he could not make the scheduled time, and offered to call him in the morning to remind him of our meeting time. This arrangement successfully brought consistency and reliability into the therapeutic relationship.

All of us who worked closely with John tried to lend him our ego capacities to serve as a conglomerate auxiliary ego (Burnham 1969). We hoped that in time he would begin to internalize those attitudes and functions that he found of value, which in turn would foster a greater degree of autonomy and a sense that others could be useful to him.

An important component in the achievement of this approach was a careful coordination of all the services he was involved with and a development of a more unified approach to John. It was my task as case manager to bring this about. This was not always easy to achieve. For example, in the workshop expectations were often geared towards what John could produce as opposed to what the workshop could provide for John. A high priority was placed on the number of pieces John could package in a day. The expectations were high and not individually tailored to meet his specific needs. Part of my role as John's therapist and social worker was to intervene and advocate for him. I was able to recognize the system's impingements upon him and help to adjust the environment to respond better to his psychological needs. Through consultations and conferences, personnel at these agencies became increasingly more amenable to altering John's program in ways that better fit his unique requirements. This contributed much to his dramatic improvement.

It is important to note that the working together of various professionals was not only essential for the purpose already mentioned, but had further ramifications. It extended the "holding environment" beyond myself, one person who, in fact, would be leaving John. It enabled John to begin to extend his sense of trust to others, an important step in his gaining greater comfort with people in general.

Countertransference Responses and Reactions

Working with John raised both countertransference reactions and responses. Reactions, according to Sanville (1994), are closer to the action level and are not experienced ordinarily as ego-syntonic. Responses, on the other hand, are more likely when there is a sense of reciprocity prevailing.

At times, John's verbalizations induced in me what I would consider to be countertransference reactions. What he had to say would not make sense. Unable to comprehend what he was saying, I would begin to feel inadequate and confused and became blocked in the work. Let me cite one exchange which went as follows:

John: Do you know what's in liverwurst?
Margaret: I don't think I do, John.
John: Pigs' lips.
Margaret: Really?
John: Yeah. Pigs' lips and pigs' tongues and . . . sounds good, doesn't it?
Margaret: It sounds disgusting, John.
John: Yeah, I hate liverwurst.
Margaret: But last week you said you loved liverwurst.
John: I did?
Margaret: Yes, you love liverwurst on rye with catsup. You said it was the best sandwich.
John: And mustard, too. No, I hate liverwurst. I like pigs though. I like animals.
Margaret: Uh huh. . . .

While my first reaction to this exchange was confusion, I then thought of something Joyce McDougall (1979) had said. Referring to some incomprehensible associations of certain patients, she proposed that these could be a "demand to be heard rather than listened to, a need for communion rather than communication" (p. 289). I began to consider that while there may have been unconscious meanings in such an exchange, such as John's wanting to induce in me his own feelings of confusion and inadequacy, he might have been primarily trying to engage me.

I had also had many responses to John, which, I believe, were a consequence to my attunement to his needs and wishes. For example, I developed a strong motherly urge to take care of him and to magically heal him. For the most part, I think this contributed positively to the treatment. At times though, when a therapeutic intervention proved successful, I was aware of the stirring of feelings of omnipotence within me. This sense of omnipotence eventually was replaced by its affective opposite, humility.

Termination and Transfer

As the time to begin the termination process came closer, I drew some support for what was to come from John himself. He did a remarkable thing one day. Somewhat late to our session, still wearing his winter coat on a beautiful spring day, John arrived clutching a brown paper bag which he promptly put down on the desk in front of me and said, "Here, I brought you a cup of coffee." I was touched by this. It symbolized his movement from using me as a need gratification object, to an increase in his capacity to love an object separate from himself. It is an experience that every mother knows when her toddler brings her his first gift of a dandelion. It is a time when both can share their joy for one another. That cup of coffee was the best I had had in a long time. I wondered whether he had some sense that we were getting close to the end.

We did not go into the matter of termination then, but some time afterwards, about four weeks prior to my leaving, I reminded John that our work together would soon be ending. (In retrospect, let me say I wished I had followed Seibold's [1991] recommendation of allowing at least six weeks for this process.) Here is an account of that session:

Margaret: John, do you remember when we first started working together, I told you that I was doing my internship here?

John: No. What does that mean?

Margaret: It means that I'm a student, and my work here will soon be finished.

John: When?

Margaret: In about four weeks.

John: Oh. [He is mulling it over.] Does that mean I won't see you anymore?

Margaret: Yes, John. I will be leaving here.

John: Oh. [pause] I like you.

Margaret: Thank you, John.

John: I like you very much.

Margaret: What do you like about me, John?

John: Your face.

Margaret: What about my face?

John: It's pretty.

Margaret: It is?
John: Yes. You have a pretty face and nice hair and a nice shape. I don't want to be disrespectful. I told myself that I would treat you with respect today.
Margaret: Thank you, John. Do you want to know what I think?
John: What?
Margaret: I think you like me because I treat you with respect.
John: Yes, that's right.
Margaret: And I care about you.
John: Yes.
Margaret: And I listen to you.
John: Yes. I think you're right.
Margaret: These are very important things to you–to be treated with respect. I don't think you were treated that way when you were young.
John: That's right . . . you know what my father did?
Margaret: What?
John: He threatened to kill me.
Margaret: He did? How?
John: One day I was in the kitchen doing the dishes. My father came into the room and said, "John, turn around." I didn't want to turn around, but I did. He was standing there with a .22 rifle and he was aiming it right at me. He said, "You know, John, I could kill you right now." I looked him right in the eye and said, "Go ahead." I didn't care if I lived or died. He didn't kill me, but I wished he had.
Margaret: [Silence, then] John, are you angry at me for leaving?
John: No, I like you. I was talking about my father. I hated him.

In referring to this painful exchange with his father, John was, of course, revealing something about the way in which his development came to be so seriously impaired. However, what was important at the moment was to appreciate the message he was conveying to me. My leaving him was threatening his very existence. Casement (1991) defines the use of derivative communication to mean "the indirect communication of thought or feelings unconsciously associated to, or derived from, whatever has previously provoked them" (p. 11). John was unable to accept my interpretation at that time, but I was able to let him know that I understood his anger and his fear. This affective attunement allowed him to later verbalize his sense of loss and abandonment.

This communication also did suggest that he was angry at me, as he had been angry at his father for treating him so badly. However, while I sought to help him feel he could express anger towards me throughout our work, I respected what seemed to be an important need, at this point, to maintain a positive feeling toward me. This, in keeping with Glick's (1987) notion that it is important to foster the positive transference in such situations. John's fears of abandonment and annihilation were reawakened at this point, evoking a variety of transference and countertransference reactions. The following is an excerpt from the sessions after I had reminded him that the time for our parting was drawing near.

John: I don't want you to leave. [He stares at me. He appears exhausted. He has not shaved in a couple of days which has never before happened. He is obviously distressed and in pain.]

Margaret: John, I know how hard this is for you. [Silence . . . necessary silence.]

Both Winnicott (1965) and Greene (1982–1983) emphasize the importance of the therapeutic use of silence. It is this "capacity to be alone in the presence of another" which helps to facilitate reparation of early object loss (Winnicott 1969). John continued to express his sadness:

John: What am I going to do without you? [He sounds so young.]

Margaret: It will be hard, John, but there are others who will help you. M. cares about you very much and so does D. They know how hard this is for you. I want you to talk to them about it, John. It will help you to do that. It will still hurt, but if you talk to them, they can help you with the hurt.

John: I love you. I do. I really love you. [At this point my heart feels wrenched. I deeply feel his sadness and mine, too. We are both near tears.]
[Long silence]

Margaret: John, I care about you very much. I want you to know that I am not leaving because of you. It's just that I will be graduating soon, and I will need to move on and find a job.

John: Why can't you work here?

Margaret: I would if there were a position open, but there are no positions here, so I have to look somewhere else. It's not because of you that I'm leaving. It's not because you are bad or evil or anything like that.

John: You've been so kind to me, more than I deserve.

Margaret: More than you deserve? [I wanted to cry.] John, you deserve to be treated kindly. You are a good person. You deserve to be treated with respect. John, I want you to know . . . that this is hard for me, too. You have touched me very deeply. You have touched my heart . . . it has been a privilege to work with you.

It was painful to watch John's decompensation and regression. His distress was noticeable. He was not sleeping well. He was expressing more hostility and he had been seen talking to himself at the workshop. Whereas three weeks prior to this, he had been joining in the recreational activities, he now isolated himself. His workshop advisor said she was seeing the John she first met. His sense of humor had disappeared. He had, as a result of our imminent termination, "retreated" and had "suspended" his attempt to relate to others (Sanville 1982, p. 124). John was in pain and I shared in that pain. However, the words I quoted above from Sanville to describe what can occur when a person feels denied of that which he needs and seeks reminded me of the task that was at hand for me at this point in the treatment. I needed to help reverse this retreat and enable John to regain the ability to make contact.

John was eventually able to verbalize his sadness and sense of loss. My sharing with John his intense sadness was a powerfully affective experience for him. I sought to acknowledge his feelings, understand them, and feel them with him. I tried to counteract his negative feelings about himself, which led him to interpret my departure as occasioned by what he perceived as his badness. In turn, I had to contend with my own guilt and feeling of badness for what I experienced as my abandoning him, as well as dealing with my desire that I could somehow rescue him from his pain.

I rallied his resident advisor and workshop advisor in an effort to provide maximal support for John during this time. I asked them to go out of their way to talk with him, be with him, and stay with him. They, too, had grown fond of him and were committed to provide him with the special holding he needed at this time. They had seen John's potential to grow and were keenly aware of the importance of their relationships with him.

Knowing that my leaving had the potential to undo John totally, I prepared him, other helpers, and myself in advance to insure the smoothest possible transition to his new therapist, Mary, in whom I had great confidence. I trusted this confidence showed when I introduced John to her. I informed Mary of where he had been so that she might know where they could go together. John seemed to be accepting of her and said to me, "I like Mary. She's a friend of yours. I will respect her because she is your friend."

My hope was that John would be able to transfer his trust and good feelings for me to Mary, and thus be better able to let go of me. Mary also was closely connected with the workshop and residence personnel. John was encouraged to talk with all of the helping professionals with whom he was involved. He was reminded that they were a team working together for him. In their contacts with John, other workers focused on his loss in their conversations with him. His feelings were heard and validated and each of those working together on John's behalf conveyed their deep caring for him. These joint efforts on the part of those connected with John did much to help him move forward during this period.

CONCLUDING COMMENTS

I have sought to show in this paper that even when treatment must, of necessity, be prematurely terminated, it can prove a meaningful experience for the client, even as seriously troubled a client as John. It was impressive how John was able to respond to the opportunity for a relationship and draw from it in a way that advanced his own capacities. He became, even in this brief time, better able to express a broader range of feelings, including those of joy. He acquired greater control of his impulses, achieved an increased capacity to delay gratification for longer periods of time, and became more aware of the needs of others. He also became more reality-focused and was able to stay in the present for longer periods of time. These and other gains helped to promote his ability to act autonomously, and at the same time they made it possible for him to connect with others in a more reciprocal way. Despite the regression that John manifested in response to the loss and separation attendant to our ending, he was able to hold onto what had proven of value to him in our work and to bring it into his new therapeutic relationship.

The positive outcome of this effort owed much to John, who, despite the severity of his difficulties, could move toward an ability to use an object (Winnicott 1969) who did not either retaliate or withdraw when he manifested his initial hostility. His gains also owed much to the efforts of those other auxiliary staff person and services that cooperated on John's behalf. As for my own efforts, I think my provision of a strong, dependable holding environment, my offerings of support, concern, interest, acknowledgment, and mirroring, and my affective engagement with John in this brief but important journey proved of value. Let me say in closing that the work I did with John owed much to the knowledge I drew from current findings in psychoanalytic developmental psychology. It was this body of theory that helped me assess John's needs and to consider ways that I might respond to them in a therapeutic way. Not only did the theory inform my technique, but it afforded me a kind of support that helped to hold me through the ups and downs of this challenging but rewarding work.

REFERENCES

Alexander, J., Kolodziejski, K., Sanville, J., and Shaw, R. (1989). On final terminations: consultation with a dying therapist. *Clinical Social Work Journal* 17(4):307–321.

Beatrice, J. (1983). Premature termination: a therapist's leaving. *International Journal of Psychoanalytic Psychotherapy* 9:313–352.

Blanck, G., and Blanck, R. (1979). *Ego Psychology II*. New York: Columbia University Press.

—— (1987). The contribution of ego psychology to understanding the process of termination in psychoanalysis and psychotherapy. *Journal of the American Psychoanalytic Association* 36:961–984.

—— (1994). *Ego Psychology: Theory and Practice*, 2nd ed. New York: Columbia University Press.

Burnham, D. L., Gladstone, A. J., and Gibson, R. W. (1969). *Schizophrenia and the Need-Fear Dilemma.* New York: International Universities Press.

Casement, P. (1991). *Learning from the Patient.* New York: Guilford.

Diagnostic and Statistical Manual of Mental Disorders (1994). 4th ed. Washington, DC: American Psychiatric Association.

Freud, A. (1981). The concept of developmental illness: their diagnostic significance. In *Psychoanalytic Study of the Child* 36:129–145. New Haven, CT: Yale University Press.

Gavazzi, S., and Anderson, S. (1987). The role of "translator" in the case of transfer process. *American Journal of Family Therapy* 15:145–157.

Glenn, M. (1971). Separation: when the therapist leaves the patient. *American Journal of Psychotherapy* 25(3):437–446

Glick, R. (1987). Forced terminations. *Journal of the American Academy of Psychoanalysis* 15:449–463.

Green, M. (1982–83). On the silence of the therapist and object loss. *International Journal of Psychoanalytic Psychotherapy* 9:183–200.

Keith, C. (1966). Multiple transfers of psychotherapy patients. *Archives of General Psychiatry* 14:185–189.

Lidz, T., and Lidz, R. W. (1982). Curative factors in psychotherapy of schizophrenic disorders. In *Curative Factors in Dynamic Psychotherapy*, ed. S. Slipp. New York: McGraw Hill.

Mahler, M. S., Pine, F., and Bergman, A. (1975). *The Psychological Birth of the Human Infant.* New York: Basic Books.

McDougall, J. (1979). Primitive communication and the use of countertransference. In *Countertransference,* ed. L. Epstein and A. H. Feiner. Northvale, NJ: Jason Aronson.

Mikkelson, E., and Gutheil, T. (1979). Stages of forced termination: uses of the death metaphor. *Psychiatric Quarterly* 5:15–27.

Penn, L. (1990). When the therapist must leave: forced termination of psychodynamic therapy. *Professional Psychology: Research and Practice* 21:379–384.

Pumpian-Mindlin, E. (1958). Comments on techniques of termination and transfer in a clinic setting. *American Journal of Psychotherapy* 12:455–464.

Sanville, J. (1982). Partings and impartings: toward a non-medical approach to interruptions and terminations. *Clinical Social Work Journal* 10(2):123ff.

—— (1994). Unpublished communication.

Schafer, R. (1973). The termination of brief psychoanalytic psychotherapy. *International Journal of Psychoanalytic Psychotherapy* 2:135–148.

Seibold, C. (1991). Termination: when the therapist leaves. *Clinical Social Work Journal* 19:191–204.

Smith, S. (1982–1983). Interrupted treatment and forced terminations. *International Journal of Psychoanalytic Psychotherapy* 9:337–352.

Wapner, J., Klein, J., Friedlander, M., and Andrasick, F. (1986). Transferring psychotherapy clients: state of the art. *Professional Psychology: Research and Practice* 17:492–496.

Weiner, I. (1975). *Principles of Psychotherapy*. New York: Wlley.

Winnicott, D. W. (1965). *The Maturational Processes and the Facilitating Environment.* New York: International Universities Press.

—— (1969). The use of an object and relating through identification. In *Playing and Reality*, pp. 86–94. New York: Basic Books, 1971.

—— (1982). The use of an object and relating through identification. In *Playing and Reality*. London: Tavistock.

20 In Defense of Long-Term Treatment: On the Vanishing Holding Environment

William S. Meyer

The mental health literature has long recognized the similarities between the role and functions of a good therapist and a good parent. Both the good therapist and the good parent are strengthened when they feel supported and they are diminished and made less good when their natural talents are undermined by external influences. Only recently have such impingements been inflicted on therapists; parents have been familiar with such pressures for generations.

In 1914, the U.S. Children's Bureau issued the first edition of the bulletin *Infant Care* (Wolfenstein 1953). It was a compendium of bad advice. Parents were instructed to have their babies potty-trained by 8 months of age. They were told that thumb sucking and masturbation, if not rigorously interfered with, would permanently damage their child. They were warned not to pick up their crying child and that such caretaking would turn the child into a tyrant.

Many parents, particularly mothers, were torn between their own instincts and the advice of the child-care experts of the day. We can sympathize and easily make allowances for those mothers who, in spite of misgivings, followed these instructions in hopes that their compliance with figures of authority would be in the best interest of their children. It is most difficult to maintain an unsupported position. It is difficult for mothers; it is difficult for clinicians.

The clinician of the 1990s is under relentless pressure to provide ever-briefer forms of treatment for *all* patients and clients, even though many such individuals have a compelling need for longer treatment. One recent author (Good 1987) states that such pressures are symptomatic of what he called the "age of Reagapeutics," in which "brief therapy is symbolic . . . of the modern age in which we do everything intensely and quickly" (p. 8).

These pressures abound. For instance, in a brief article titled "Finding the Right Psychotherapist" published in a widely sold consumer guide (Boardroom Classics 1989), the first item advises consumers to look for someone who does "short-term therapy" (p. 437). Professional clinicians are tantalized by articles with sensational titles like "Psychotherapy That Takes Weeks, Not Years" (Michaels 1989). It is telling that in my computer-generated literature review for this chapter, I found nearly 300 papers extolling the benefits of brief therapy and fewer than five specifically addressing its limitations.

This steady barrage of such communications cannot help but have an insidious impact on the confidence with which contemporary clinicians approach longer-term, slower-paced psychotherapy. As a consequence, clinicians are at risk for caving in to outside pressures, to becoming ever more involved in the treatment of symptoms rather than people.

How did we get to this point? The trend toward shorter relationships was noted over two decades ago in Alvin Toffler's popular book *Future Shock* (1970). He drew attention to the soaring acceleration of change in virtually all areas of contemporary society. One key symptom of this extraordinary pace, he noted, was the ascendancy of transience–the new "temporariness" in everyday life. In particular, relationships that once lasted for long periods of time had ever-decreasing life expectancies.

We can see clear evidence of such trends in mental health. In a simpler time the much-loved Harvard psychoanalyst Elvin Semrad used to tell his students, "If you want to learn about psychiatry get a good suit with two pairs of pants and be willing to sit with your patients until you have worn out the seats of both pairs of pants" (Castelnuevo-Tedesco 1990, p. 1258). How archaic this statement seems in today's fast-paced health care market!

Bruno Bettelheim (DeAngelis 1989) reported a seemingly minor personal incident that occurred during his training that had a profound impact on his thinking about treatment and time. At the time, Bettelheim was undergoing psychoanalysis. A disturbed young boy used to sit in the same waiting room as Bettelheim to see the wife of Bettelheim's analyst, who was one of the first child psychoanalysts. The boy, unresponsive and nearly mute, had the strange habit of plucking and chewing leaves from a cactus plant in the waiting room. As time went on Bettelheim eventually blurted out, "Johnny, I don't know how long you have been seeing Dr. X, but it must be at least two years and here you are still chewing these awful leaves" (p. 38). Then, in Bettelheim's words,

> I still do not know how he managed to give me the impression that at this moment he was looking down at me. But he did and spoke his first sentence to me saying disdainfully, "What are two years when compared with eternity?" Johnny's comment about time permitted me to grasp that neither I nor anybody else can put a limit on the amount of time one needs to become able to cope or to change, and that trying to hurry up the process has more to do with one's own anxieties than with anything else. Only people themselves can judge when they are ready to change. [p.38]

What has catapulted such thoughtful, patient approaches to therapeutic treatment into the hurry-up mentality of today's mental health practice? Among many factors, none has been so influential as third-party reimbursement, a relatively recent artifact, that now dominates decisions about the delivery of psychotherapeutic treatment.

From its inception, psychotherapy had been financed almost exclusively in a fee-for-service, two-party relationship. During the 1960s and early 1970s, however, there was rapid growth in both private and governmental medical health insurance plans covering treatment for psychological illnesses. As noted by Halpert in 1972,

> Many of these insurance plans include partial or total reimbursement, usually up to a certain limit, for treatment in the various psychotherapies, including psychoanalysis. If the trend continues, and all indications are that it will, then even greater numbers of people will be covered for ever greater total amounts for psychoanalytic treatment. [p.122]

Practitioners of that era faced therapeutic problems that we can only wish for. In the luxury of such third-party benevolence, "The anonymous third party, the insurance company, becomes like the anonymous therapist —a transference figure. But the insurance company, unlike the therapist, *gratifies transference wishes; it takes care of and protects the patient*"

(Halpert 1973, p. 67, emphasis added). Such *was* the case in the brief Camelot era of psychotherapy reimbursement.

Contrast this with a recent report by Zuckerman (1989) on the effects of managed care on his patient, a 36-year-old, twice-married, potentially abusive mother of two who presented with a long history of anxiety and depression. Zuckerman described the patient's perception of the case manager as a

> denying, ungiving mother, [and this] began to permeate her thinking. When the patient was feeling better she became afraid that the case manager, upon discovering her improvement, would feel that she was cured and withdraw his treatment authorization. When she was feeling depressed and hopeless, which was often, she felt that the case manager, upon sensing her lack of progress, would refuse to underwrite any further treatment. [p. 127]

SHORT-TERM PSYCHOTHERAPY

For decades, theories and methods of one or another form of brief treatment have been formulated, taught, published, and refined. And it has been repeatedly demonstrated that briefer therapies, *when used appropriately*, are effective.

Briefer therapies are especially useful for the basically intact person who possesses at least a modicum of ego strength, someone who, for instance, adapted reasonably well in life but became the victim of an unfortunate predicament that unduly taxed his or her endurance or rekindled a previously dormant internal conflict. Such treatment is then aimed at relieving a patient's most pressing symptoms and restoring the person to a state that existed before the acute difficulties (Castelnuevo-Tedesco 1971).

Longer or more intensive treatment should never be invoked for trivial reasons. As Stone (1954) once pointed out, "There is sometimes a loss of sense of proportion about the human situation, a forgetting or denial of the fact that few human beings are without some troubles, and that many must be met, if at all, by 'old-fashioned' methods: courage, or wisdom, or struggle, for instance" (p. 205). For many individuals, a few consultations or a more extended form of brief treatment *is* the clear treatment of choice.

Mackenzie (1991), in a comprehensive review of brief psychotherapy, defined four features requiring clinical assessment before considering a recommendation of brief psychotherapy: (1) a capacity to relate, (2) psychological mindedness, (3) motivation, and (4) evidence of adaptational strength. (For years, clinicians have acknowledged the irony that people possessing such strengths make the best use of virtually all therapeutic modalities.) Mackenzie stated that "while [the above] criteria do not in themselves constitute exclusion standards, when a patient is low on several of them, *caution should be used in recommending brief approaches*" (p. 401, emphasis added).

As more definitive *exclusion* criteria, Mackenzie (1991) listed an inability to attend to the process, major characterological features that preclude effective use of the treatment, and the possibility of the patient doing harm. Included here are patients with limited impulse control, a history of repeated suicide attempts, recurrent premature termination of therapy, or entrenched alcohol or substance abuse.

Other patient characteristics Mackenzie (1991) cited that should direct clinicians' thinking *away* from brief therapy include the use of defenses that block access to internal states, a dominance of primitive defenses such as projection and denial, major schizoid features, major antisocial characteristics of an enduring nature, and the presence of profound negativism and rigidity. Further, Mackenzie stated that patients with a history of easily triggered suicidal ideation

> may experience the confrontational qualities of brief psychotherapy as evidence of rejection, and respond with impulsive, self-destructive behavior. . . . *Indeed when any dysfunctional characterological style is deeply pervasive and influences adaptation in many spheres of the patient's life, rapid alteration is not likely and a course of brief psychotherapy may be viewed by the patient as a further failure.* [pp. 400–401 emphasis added]

Yet I recently received a postcard from an employee assistance program soliciting psychologists, social workers, and therapists to provide brief therapy for patients suffering from, among other maladies, alcoholism, chemical dependency, sequelae of sexual abuse, and eating disorders. Brief therapy, as defined by this company, was "up to four sessions."

D. W. WINNICOTT AND THE HOLDING ENVIRONMENT

Many elements of the therapeutic relationship, as we have known it, are reminiscent of the first relationship between infant and mother. This was first elaborated on in the eloquent writings of Donald W. Winnicott.

Winnicott studied and wrote extensively on the characteristics of healthy and unhealthy relationships, particularly early mother–child interactions. Winnicott was repeatedly struck by the parallels in the relationships provided by good-enough parents and those provided by successful analysts, psychotherapists, and social workers. These relationships contained common elements that facilitated development and were created by caregivers devoted to an individual's unique needs, whether the individual was a baby, a child, an analysand, a patient, or a client.

A central component of this relationship was encapsulated in Winnicott's (1965) familiar phrase, *the holding environment*. Briefly, the holding environment, as applied to a newborn, is one that is created by a maternal figure who can identify with a baby in a state of absolute dependence, and who, as needed, can provide whatever support is necessary—day and night—to meet the baby's most basic physical and psychological needs. As the infant matures, the caretaker providing the holding environment, while encouraging developmental growth, ensures that the infant is not expected to relinquish its dependent state prematurely.

A similar holding environment can be found in a therapeutic relationship. Modell (1976), while referencing psychoanalysis, makes comparisons. Like the good-enough parent, the therapist is constant and reliable, responds sensitively to the patient's affects, accepts the patient, uses judgment which is less critical and more benign, is there primarily for the patient's needs, does not retaliate, and does at times have a better grasp of the patient's inner psychic reality than does the patient and therefore can help clarify what is bewildering and confusing.

The holding environment helps to foster, and does not prematurely challenge, an illusion that the patient is protected from the dangers of the world, and that the therapist in some way stands as a shield between the patient and these dangers. The good-enough therapist, like the good-enough parent, allows for and tolerates phase-appropriate dependency, all the while looking for opportunities to support maturational thrusts.

HOLDING, MANAGEMENT, AND THE CLINICAL SOCIAL WORKER

The concept of holding at first may seem intended only for the patient suitable for analysis or insight-oriented psychotherapy. What, one may ask, of the more outwardly disturbed and challenging individual, whose treatment may require more than can be accomplished within a tidy 50-minute hour–the type of client or patient, for instance, who has traditionally been in the care of the clinical social worker?

Winnicott, who frequently lectured to social workers, expanded the concept of holding to encompass clinical management as performed by the trained psychiatric social worker. In a fine paper on case management, Kanter (1990) lamented the current perceptions of case management as an impersonal, administrative service more concerned with cutting costs than helping people in need. Winnicott, Kanter wrote, used the term *management* to describe direct interventions with the person and the environment that were aimed at facilitating the healing and maturation of even the most troubled individuals.

Winnicott elaborated on the issues of management in a personal letter (Rodman 1987). He wrote:

> In social work (as in psychoanalysis) certain factors such as reliability, dependability, and objectivity, provide a specialized environment *over a period of time* [note Winnicott's italics] in which the highly complex *internal* factors in the individual and between the various individuals in the client group may rearrange themselves. The "good" (or I would say "good enough") climate enables a client to review his or her relationship to climates that were not, or did not seem to be, good (or good enough). [p. 141]

CLINICAL EXAMPLE

I began seeing Sue nearly seven years ago. Sue was a 35-year-old who was proud of her steady employment for the past fifteen years at a nearby manufacturing plant. She was referred to me by her daughter's psychiatrist for adjunctive "parent work." Her daughter, Paula, a deeply troubled adolescent, was doing miserably in relationships at home and with peers and in her school work.

Sue had divorced Paula's father shortly after Paula's birth, and she and the girl had since resided with Sue's mother. The mother, a retired woman, seemed to enjoy the secondary gain she received by virtue of her continual state of seemingly poor health.

Our initial appointment was memorable, if only for Sue's severe level of agitation. In the session she avoided eye contact, was fidgety, chain-smoked, paced, and nonverbally conveyed her terrible anxiety. As she spoke, taking short quick gasps of air between phrases, she repeatedly attempted to assure me that she was not a bad mother. My attempts at gentle reassurance seemed to have only a minimal effect on her anxiety—anxiety which overwhelmed her, causing her to lose her train of thought every few minutes. This caused her great embarrassment, yet her apologies seemed only to make her more anxious. Never in her wildest dreams, she told me, would she have imagined herself speaking to a counselor!

No one had ever known her. To her acquaintances and co-workers she was the lighthearted clown who could inject humor into many situations, often making herself the butt of a self-denigrating joke.

Yet, as I was to discover, she had a private self with private symptoms. She suffered from periods of both debilitating depression and terrible anxiety. For some years, under the supervision of her internist, she had been taking an antidepressant medication for "nerves" and found it helpful. Although she always managed to function at work, frequently she felt unable to go anywhere there were people and she would spend long periods of time lying in bed in a darkened room. In time she would inform me of her fitful sleep and terrible dreams: ghoulish nightmares of blood, violence, and murder and killings involving almost everyone in her immediate family.

Given this situation, it was clear that we could not meaningfully discuss the problems of Sue's daughter without simultaneously attending to her own anxieties. And why this degree of anxiety? But, of course, the answer to this question would simply have to wait. Someone as frightened as Sue would have to be approached gently and carefully.

Sometimes I wonder what I would have reported to a third party had she been in one of the managed-care groups who required preauthorization for treatment. How many would have accepted my true assessment? I was working with what appeared to be a fragile, terribly anxious person who, while not without strengths, was someone with whom I needed to take whatever time necessary to establish an alliance.

What if after a first session or two I had been asked to spell out goals in behavioral terms? Would I have been clever enough to say something true, yet acceptable? And what if I said that my reading of the situation suggested that *if* an alliance was formed (a big "if" at the time) my sense was that treatment might very well involve years of work? What then? Fortunately, those were not issues I needed to address.

Over the ensuing weeks, Sue's anxiety lessened, we chatted more easily, and I was able to get a better sense of the overall situation in her household. Sue felt caught in the middle between her mother, who she felt manipulated her by playing on her guilt, and her troubled daughter, whose relentless sarcasm inflicted pain on everyone in the household. Sue felt she was an utter failure as daughter and mother and was unaware of any feelings of resentment toward her family.

Early on, I raised the issue with Sue that regardless of what might be troubling her daughter, she had her own share of troubles, and I indicated my willingness to talk with her about them. She did not warm to the idea.

"You're not strong enough," she said. "Neither am I. I look at things differently than anyone. I'll be a pain, hard to know. What's important to me is different than others. I have no dealings with anyone." Soon after she told me that she thought she could be divided into three parts: (1) a clown, (2) someone struggling for self-respect, and (3) someone who is crying and dying.

Six months into treatment Sue revealed that throughout her childhood, since the age of 2, she had been sexually abused by her alcoholic father. She related a terrible incident when, at age 9, her father called her elementary school to ask that she be sent home, ostensibly to provide care for her ill mother. She arrived home to find only her father, drunk as usual, who took this opportunity to beat and rape her.

During the following years of therapy, Sue began to talk about her early memories. Gradually, there emerged a terrible story of a child who, until mid-adolescence, was routinely beaten, invaded, and humiliated at the hands of a psychopathic father, while an ineffectual mother stood passively by. Each new memory seemed worse than the preceding one, and was accompanied by floods of affect which, until then, had been frozen for decades. Sue angrily told me, "The only positive thing I remember my father saying about me was that I was a good cocksucker."

Sue had a rocky time those first few years, as did our treatment relationship. She began to consider her upbringing and its consequences. "I used to think it was just the way things were," she said. "Now it seems so unfair. Not living, just existing, surviving. Never thought about how it affected me. I just said it did." Memories evoked grizzly flashbacks involving all five senses. Flashbacks of noxious odors induced marked sleeplessness and severe agitation.

And then came the full brunt of her depression, which in spite of medication increases and changes seemed untouchable. She refused hospitalization and, not unlike her worst pre-treatment periods of stress, her life narrowed to work, bedrest, and therapy appointments.

My weekly appointment hour with her, which was typically supplemented with a call or two, was far and away the most demanding hour of my week. Most of my interventions fell flat, and the key thrust of my therapeutic efforts was aimed at repeatedly telling her, trying to convince myself at the same time, that there *was* a light at the end of the tunnel, and that her depression would not go on forever, and that I would hang in there with her.

Finally things did get better. For most of the next year her mood was considerably brighter and her self-esteem much improved. To her family's dismay, she began asserting herself and setting limits on their manipulations. She began attending weekly outings at a neighborhood restaurant with friends she had made at work. She became involved in crafts, and began receiving recognition awards at local craft shows. Co-workers were delighted to see her return to better spirits, and her employer gave her increased responsibilities over a new project.

But this newfound emotional health was still too fragile to withstand the blow that was to come. Lisa, of whom Sue was especially fond, was the older daughter of Sue's former neighbor. Lisa, a young woman in her twenties, revealed to Sue that on several occasions she too had been sexually abused by her own father during her adolescence, and at times by her mother as well.

Sue became overcome with rage. The powerful identification she had with Lisa's trauma left her feeling that if she were anywhere near Lisa's parents she would kill them. She was unable to sleep for days. Reluctantly she agreed to be admitted to the hospital for what was to be the first of several brief hospital stays.

While in the hospital her flashbacks and night terrors became more severe. She began remembering in even more detail scenes of unimaginable degradation and father's threats that he would gut her like a fish or cut off her hands if she dared tell anyone. With the help of a treatment team and a devoted social work intern, she began to talk and write about her experiences and began avidly reading accounts of other trauma victims. She attended art therapy sessions and drew pictures of her memories, including one of a giant headless man wlth a grotesque erect penis.

The man towers over a small naked girl who cries from a face with no eyes. Within weeks Sue left the hospital remarkably stronger.

This is where an author is tempted to end a case report. I wish I could say that she lived happily ever after. But sometimes, in spite of our good work and our patients' best efforts, things do not go as we would wish.

Sometime the following year, during a family get-together, an argument became heated and a family member lost control and physically assaulted Sue. Once more she was briefly hospitalized, and once more the flashbacks and depressive symptoms returned.

Now, seven years since the start of therapy, I have grown accustomed to the fact that Sue will probably always be vulnerable to such setbacks. During the difficult times she tells me that she has no hope, that she wants to give up, and she insists that I should give up too. She tells me of her nightmares and haunting memories and her burdens of rage, guilt, and self-loathing.

I tell her that *I* will carry the hope until she feels stronger, and that I am not yet ready to throw in the towel. I extend myself a bit more during these times. Sometimes, at her request, we go outside and walk during our sessions and, when necessary, we arrange additional brief phone contacts through the week. Sue receives additional support and hope from the social work intern who has remained in contact with her, and from her psychiatrist, a devoted health care provider who closely monitors her medication. For the worst times, hospitalization remains an option.

I do not anticipate a change in the treatment plan in the foreseeable future.

DISCUSSION

In my attempt to defend and justify long-term treatment, I could have presented a dfferent kind of case for this article. I could have presented clinical material of someone healthier, of someone, for instance, who credited intensive clinical work with making a fundamental change in his or her life. I could have described someone, for instance, who claimed long-term treatment enabled him or her to save a failing marriage or to leave a hopeless one, to complete an education or change a dead-end career, to get over a developmental hurdle, or to stop the repetition of destructive patterns. There is no shortage of this type of clinical material. We have worked with many such individuals. Indeed, many of us count ourselves among them. A more successful case might have more generously supported the effectiveness of long-term treatment. After all, Sue is not a typical client. Yet I chose this case because, although it is not a typical case, it is not altogether rare.

I present this material to support those of us who work in clinical settings and can bear witness to the steady stream of individuals who come seeking help and whose developmental histories, although perhaps not as severe as Sue's, are nonetheless riddled with abuse, neglect, and deprivation. It seems their numbers are growing.

And many of us continue to hold fast to the belief that the ideal treatment for people who have been failed by human relationships is an enduring human relationship that does not fail. In the words of Winnicott (1987), "In a particular way we can actually alter the patient's past, so that a patient whose maternal environment was not good enough can change into a person who has a good-enough facilitating environment, and whose personal growth has therefore been able to take place, though late" (p. 102).

CONCLUSION

Winnicott stressed that mothers who have it in them to provide good-enough care can be enabled to do better by being cared for themselves in a way that acknowledges the essential nature of their task. Therapists have similar needs. Like the mothers of decades past, it becomes increasingly dfficult for clinicians to trust their own good instincts when their professional institutions, colleagues, and supervisors declare their devotion to long-term work with a suffering person is theoretically suspect or antiquated.

It is all the more difficult to lose this support when the third parties on whom we have–for better or worse–grown to rely for our living become withholding and punitive. Insurance companies that limit sessions to twelve per year, that insist on all-too-frequent case reports and case reviews, influence therapists to mistrust their skills and training and to adopt the insurance point of view in place of their own.

It is a battle for the mind of the therapist, in what Kramer (1990) referred to as the *sentinel effect*. If all goes well in the insurance world, therapists will internalize a hostile sentinel and become suspicious of their own good intentions. The internalized sentinel of the insurance company fans the flames of the therapist's doubts and uncertainty. A subliminal shift will occur in the mind of the therapist. The limits of treatment covered by an insurance company will gradually be registered in the mind of the therapist as, "This is all the patient needs."

It is frightening to see where we are allowing ourselves to be led. Kramer (1990) posed the question, "If sentinel effects and restrictions on care cause us to alter our thoughts and behavior–to starve our patients and then see their hunger pangs as whining–how will we act when these pressures are universal?" (p. 23).

What we will see is a naturalistic study of parallel process. As we clinicians feel supported, as we feel held, we can, in kind, support and hold our clientele. As we feel mistrusted, hurried, and pressured, so too will this be transmitted to the people under our care and to our trainees.

In *Future Shock,* Toffler (1970) acknowledged that change is essential but warned that change unguided and unrestrained can overwhelm our defenses and erode our decision-making processes. It is this sort of runaway change, I believe, that is occurring in the mental health practices of our day.

Increasingly, our clinical sensibilities are being molded by the whims and pressures of the marketplace. And the pressures mount. Today's clinician, interviewed as a prospective provider for an insurance company, is subjected to managed-care McCarthyism. Now it is not communism that must be disavowed, but beliefs in a long-term treatment relationship, even though we know, particularly because of our heritage as clinical social workers, that a reliable, enduring relationship is no less necessary for the tormented individual of today than it was for such individuals in days gone by.

We, and especially the next generation of clinicians, stand to lose the clinical wisdom that has been painstakingly accumulated, refined and passed down from our teachers and supervisors. We must work to insure that the legacy of this knowledge continues to be transmitted to our students and supervisees.

And finally, we clinicians must maintain and strengthen our connections with each other, individually and through our professional organizations, so that, especially in harried times like these–when so much of the health care world seems pressured, confusing, and reckless–we can find for ourselves, among kindred spirits, a holding.

REFERENCES

Boardroom Classics, ed. (1989). *The Book of Inside Information.* New York: Board Room Reports.

Castelnuevo-Tedesco, P. (1971). Decreasing the length of psychotherapy: theoretical and practical aspects of the problem. In *The World Biennial of Psychiatry and Psychotherapy,* ed. S. Arieti, pp. 55–71. New York: Basic Books.

—— (1990). Letter to the editor. *American Journal of Psychiatry* 147:1258.

DeAngelis, T. (1989). Personal events pave road to understanding. *American Psychological Association Monitor,* July, p. 38.

Good, P. R. (1987). Brief therapy in the age of Reagapeutics. *American Journal of Orthopsychiatry* 57:6–11.

Halpert, E. (1972). The effect of insurance on psychoanalytic treatment. *Journal of the American Psychoanalytic Association,* 20:122–33.

—— (1973). A meaning of insurance in psychotherapy. *International Journal of Psychoanalytic Psychotherapy,* 1:62–68.

Kanter, J. (1990). Community-based management of psychotic clients. *Clinical Social Work Journal* 18:23–42.

Kramer, P. D. (1990). Dino or dodo? *Psychiatric Times,* November, p. 23.

Mackenzie, K. R. (1991). Principles of brief intensive psychotherapy. *Psychiatric* Annals 21:398–404.

Michaels, E. (1989). BPP: psychotherapy that takes weeks, not years. *Canadian Medical Association Journal* 140:842–843.

Modell, A. (1976). "The holding environment" and the therapeutic action of psychoanalysis. *Journal of the American Psychoanalytic Association* 24:285–308.

Rodman, F. R. (1987). *The Spontaneous Gesture: Selected Letters of D. W. Winnicott.* Cambridge: Harvard University Press.

Stone, L. (1954). The widening scope of indications for psychoanalysis. *Journal of the American Psychoanalytic Association* 2:567–594.

Toffler, A. (1970). *Future Shock.* New York: Random House.

Winnicott, D. W. (1965). *The Maturational Processes and the Facilitating Environment.* New York: International Universities Press.

—— (1987). *Babies and Their Mothers.* Reading, PA: Addison-Wesley.

Wolfenstein, M. (1953). Trends in infant care. *American Journal of Orthopsychiatry* 23:120–130.

Zuckerman, R. L. (1989). Iatrogenic factors in "managed" psychotherapy. *American Journal of Psychotherapy* 63:118–131.

21 Clinical Supervision: Its Role in "Containing" Countertransference Responses to a Filicidal Patient

Linda A. Chernus
Paula Grote Livingston

THE EMPATHIC MODE AND THERAPIST COUNTERTRANSFERENCE[1]

With the growing influence of self psychology on clinical practice, many clinicians have increasingly recognized the importance and powerful impact of the use of the empathic mode of understanding in psychoanalytic psychotherapy. Empathy, or "vicarious introspection," is the therapist's primary tool for gathering data regarding the patient's subjective experience and communicating this data to him (Kohut 1959). Through the consistent use of the empathic mode, the therapist immerses himself in the patient's ongoing subjective experience, including the patient's experience of the therapist's verbal and nonverbal responses to him (Rowe and MacIsaac 1989). If the therapist is reasonably consistent in maintaining this empathic vantage point, the patient will gradually begin to make use of the therapist to serve needed psychological functions, including what Kohut initially described as mirroring and idealizing selfobject functions, later adding functions which served so-called "twinship" needs.

1. This chapter was developed from a presentation of the case of "Mrs. Jay" at Department of Psychiatry Grand Rounds, University of Cincinnati College of Medicine, on May 2, 1989.

Not only is the nature of our understanding of transference configurations different from a more traditional psychoanalytic formulation of transference as a repetition of early childhood relationships, but the consequences of the use of the empathic mode for what is regarded as curative in the treatment process are equally divergent from more traditional formulations. Classical analytic theory sees the curative process as consisting of re-experiencing and thereby understanding early childhood relationships, with their attendant internalized conflicts. This leads to eventual resolution of infantile conflicts. In contrast, the consistent use of the empathic mode seems to give rise to transference configurations which promote cure through the patient's being able to utilize the therapist, at least within the transference, in ways that he was unable to utilize earlier selfobjects of childhood. As a result, growth occurs through the filling in of internal deficits as selfobject functions of the therapist (not deliberately performed, but experienced as such by the patient within the transference) become a part of the patient's internal psychic structure.[2]

The consistent use of the empathic vantage point in psychotherapy seems to promote therapeutic change as a result of both the content of what is understood and communicated and the very process of feeling understood by the therapist. In this way, therapists utilizing the empathic mode are responding to an ongoing criticism of analytic psychotherapy, namely that cognitive understanding does not necessarily lead to internal change. From this frame of reference, although our understanding is certainly not irrelevent, it is also essential that the patient feel understood and thus begin to experience a remobilization of archaic needs and longings, as well as internal vulnerabilities and deficits. If the patient does not feel understood, this reactivation cannot occur and the basis for the utilization of the therapist's selfobject functions will be unavailable. Though the therapist does not directly or actively provide the patient with the missing or deficient selfobject experiences from early childhood, it appears that the consistent feeling of being deeply understood meets a powerful and fundamental selfobject need. In addition to this experience, the interpretive work around the mobilized transferential needs, be they needs for mirroring, idealization, or a sense of sameness, is helpful in

2. This process can be seen as parallel to the way the child initially acquires internal self-regulating psychological functions and structures within a reasonably good enough selfobject milieu (Chernus 1988).

cognitively understanding such needs and eventually transforming them internally into more mature forms which can be met through relationships with other people.

The clinical illustration presented here beautifully demonstrates growth of the patient's capacity to tolerate previously unacceptable affects and memories. However, the therapist's countertransference responses to the nature of Mrs. Jay's experiences, especially the murder of her son, threatened to interfere with her remaining empathic with this patient. Through supervision, the therapist was able to communicate to the supervisor her subjective responses to Mrs. Jay. This helped the therapist both understand what Mrs. Jay felt and see how her own reactions interfered with consistently hearing the patient from the patient's subjective vantage point. The supervisory focus on the therapist's responses in the clinical situation enabled her to become aware of her initial denial and subsequent negative responses to Mrs. Jay's repugnant and frightening feelings, memories, and experiences.

As a result of this empathic stance by the supervisor, though the therapist's negative responses were not completely removed, she became sufficiently aware of and able to contain them so that the empathic breaks could be repaired and the treatment process resumed. The empathic stance by the supervisor can be said to have enhanced the therapist's capacity for empathic responsiveness with the patient, so that the "therapeutic self" of the supervisee became more firmly integrated. This in turn enabled the patient to effectively utilize the therapist to serve various selfobject functions, which eventually led to internal growth.

THE PSYCHODYNAMICS OF FILICIDE

When we turn to the small but growing literature on filicide, and in particular the filicidal mother, we find that Mrs. Jay seems to fit, psychodynamically, with the findings of researchers exploring their personality traits and history through nonclinical approaches and methodologies. Literature describing the psychodynamics of the filicidal mother, however, is sparse.

Filicide has been defined as the murder of a child by a parent. Interestingly, it represents the largest subtype of child murders. Adelson (1961) reported in the *New England Journal of Medicine* that of forty-six child murders committed in Cuyahoga County (Cleveland), Ohio, thirty-seven were committed either by parents or persons functioning *in loco parentis*. He also found that the vast majority of these parents were acutely psychotic at the time of the murder. Another major study, published by Tavistock (Dale 1986), substantiated the finding that a very high percentage of murdered children are murdered by parents or other close family members. Yet little has been published on filicide in the clinical literature, and only slightly more in the legal literature. It appears that filicide has not been consciously seen as sufficiently prevalent to warrant study, though this may be largely due to our inherent repugnance to it.

In addition, the correlation or relationship between filicide and child abuse in general is unclear. One researcher (Resnick 1969) has found a definite subtype among filicides, in which the child's death is accidental and associated with chronic though not necessarily severe child abuse. Yet Campion (1988), who studied twelve psychiatrically hospitalized men charged with filicide, found that although eleven of the twelve men were seriously disturbed, few had any history of having abused these children prior to their murders. Campion believed that this contrasted sharply with a group of physically abusive fathers, among whom he thought psychosis and other serious psychiatric disorders were rare. Since so little has been written about filicide at all, it is not surprising that its connection with child abuse remains so controversial and unclear.

When we turn to the clinical literature, what we find is mostly descriptive, demographic, and concerned with diagnosis rather than psychodynamics. Furthermore, none of the studies reviewed gave serious consideration to the role of family dynamics in contributing to our understanding of the filicide.

Campion (1988) reports that three percent of all American homicides are filicides, and that mothers commit far more filicides than fathers. In his previously mentioned study of filicidal fathers, seven of the twelve were either acutely or chronically psychotic as well as intoxicated at the time of the murder. All had histories of physical and/or sexual abuse when they were children, early loss of parents, and chronic and often severe neglect during childhood. Campion concluded that rather than psychological motives being primarily involved, organic impulse disorders and the impact of substance abuse on poorly structured and often chronically fragmented men led to a break in their fragile sense of reality and their tenuous impulse control.

Resnick (1969) reviewed 131 cases of filicide and attempted to classify them by apparent motive. He discusses filicide within 24 hours after birth of the child, which he considers to have a unique and highly specific dynamic constellation. In addition, he defines a subgroup in which the parent was psychotic, another subgroup in which the child was unwanted and could not be cared for due to a variety of reasons, a third subgroup in which, as previously mentioned, the murder was accidental and associated with chronic child abuse, and a fourth category in which revenge against the spouse (the so-called Medea complex) was the primary motive behind the killing.

Resnick discusses in detail the psychodynamics of a fifth category, which he calls "altruistic." This includes cases in which the child was suffering from a physical illness which the parent intended to relieve through the murder, as well as those not so infrequent instances, such as Mrs. Jay's, in which the parent, usually the mother, is severely depressed and either projectively experiences her child as suffering as she is or cannot adequately differentiate between her own and her child's subjective experience. The description of the "suicidal/filicidal mother" seems to fit Mrs. Jay perfectly. This mother may kill her child because the child is experienced as a part of her "bad" self which needs punishing (as a result of her own unacceptable feelings) and/or to protect the child from experiencing the same sense of abandonment and motherlessness that she herself experienced as a child. Many of the patients in Resnick's study had felt abandoned by their mothers as children, and thus experienced their own children as once again abandoning them when any conflict arose between them. By killing the child, the suicidal/filicidal mother is symbolically acting out unconscious rage toward her own mother.

These dynamics are powerfully convincing, especially in light of the clinical material to be presented. They were also explored by Feinstein (1964), who described six mothers involved in a therapy group because of infanticidal impulses. All had a history of strong feelings of resentment toward their parents, "particularly their mothers, for not meeting their dependency needs during childhood. In every instance, the feeling that one had not 'gotten enough' as a child was repeatedly raised in the group" (Feinstein et al. 1964, p. 882). Also, all of the filicidal mothers had at least one parent or significant parental figure who had "uncontrolled outbursts of temper during which they were the object of or witness to acts of violence" (Feinstein et al. 1964, p. 882). They also tended to marry men who were feminine and motherly in their roles. Interestingly, this dynamic was so powerful that it superseded or cut through diagnosis on a characterologic basis, which ranged from the neurotic to the psychotic ends of the spectrum.

It appears that our clinical material, derived from an experience-near (empathic) mode, is consistent with the findings of experience-distant researchers regarding the psychodynamics of the mother who kills her child. The difficulty of a therapist remaining empathic with such a patient comes as no surprise, and appears to be a normal response to the threatening nature of the patient's communications, which deeply offend our internalized social norms. The therapist would tend to respond with either repugnance or a defense against such a reaction, namely a wish to exonerate Mrs. Jay from blame and thereby deny the seriousness of her crime.

TWO CONCURRENT CLINICAL PROCESSES

The therapist became involved with Mrs. Jay when she called the Children's Counseling Center to request help for her 12-year-old son, Tom, who was exhibiting minor vandalism, poor school performance, some oppositional behavior at home, and frequent nightmares about his mother being killed. During the intake interview, she noted that Mrs. Jay was tearful and expressed strong feelings of being overwhelmed by Tom's behavior, yet wanting desperately to find help for him.

The therapist felt sympathetic during the diagnostic phase, while Mrs. Jay's affect vacillated between anger at Tom for his behavior and crying when describing her own background. She movingly described a chaotic childhood filled with emotional deprivation. Her parents were alcoholic, physically abused her, and divorced when she was only 4 years of age. Then followed the typical pattern of moving several times between maternal and paternal homes, a one-year foster placement, and finally placement in a state school at the age of 14. The therapist noted how positive her experience at the school had been, primarily because a housemother took a personal interest in her. She told the therapist that she currently lives with Tom, his two sisters (ages 10 and 20), and their stepfather, to whom she has been married for two years. The therapist's impression was that, although her current marriage is problematic and both she and Tom are obviously symptomatic, the status quo is at least as stable as during any previous period of her life.

During the last ten minutes of an early session, in which Mrs. Jay had described her experiences growing up with an alcoholic mother, she spontaneously related she had another baby five years before her first child was born. Her affect changed, and she became increasingly agitated. As she began describing what happened to the baby, the therapist immediately thought of abortion or adoption. Amidst a flood of tears, Mrs. Jay said that when she was 18 years old, she had smothered her 1½-year-old son to death "just to get him to stop crying."

The therapist was still in shock when a moment later the fire alarm sounded for a drill, and everyone hurried out of the building. Mrs. Jay's face was stained with tears. Feeling completely unnerved, the therapist compensated with small talk and asked Mrs. Jay to return to the office, where she told her she appreciated how painful it was for her to share this information and apologized for the disruption.

For the next several days, the therapist was preoccupied with wondering how Mrs. Jay could live with herself after killing her own baby. She was curious for more details. What had the circumstances been? Did she go to jail? Did she receive treatment? How were Tom's symptoms connected to his mother's smothering his brother almost twenty-five years ago? At this point the therapist did not know what she felt about Mrs. Jay and was very uncertain about how to handle this new information. The therapist had never dealt with anything so far from the usual range of human experience. Because of her apprehension, she quickly consulted with her supervisor.

Mrs. Jay cried throughout the next session. She talked at length about being scapegoated as a child and identified with Tom and his acting out. She blamed the stress she experienced in her life on her emotionally unavailable parents. She made only a few brief references to her dead baby. At one point she did state that she felt Tom was her punishment for killing her first son. The therapist was reluctant to ask questions or make comments regarding the dead baby and reacted as if the tragedy were too horrible to talk about. She later learned that this had been Mrs. Jay's experience with numerous other professionals.

During the next session, the therapist recommended individual treatment with a male therapist for Tom (his preference) and continued sessions with Mrs. Jay, focusing on how her feelings about the death of her son affected her relationship with Tom. Again she was very tearful and stated no one could ever understand or accept her after she smothered her son. The therapist did not verbally reassure her but acknowledged how painful her situation was. Later in that session Mrs. Jay recalled that the court had placed some of the responsibility for the tragedy on the instability of her family life, and that her sentence had been five years probation and mandatory outpatient psychiatric treatment.

Mrs. Jay shared her overwhelming fear that if her children or husband found out about the dead baby, they would abandon her. She also revealed that when Tom was 5, her sister took him to the cemetery where the baby was buried and told him he had an older brother whom his father accidentally smothered. Tom had questioned Mrs. Jay about his brother, but she denied she ever had another son.

Mrs. Jay revealed how in the past, after telling her secret to other therapists, she would drop out of treatment before they could reject her. The therapist felt Mrs. Jay was forewarning her of the depth of her pain and was reluctant to make interpretations, fearful Mrs. Jay might take her own and/or Tom's life if she were unable to tolerate the pain which was surfacing. In spite of the intensity of Mrs. Jay's feelings, the therapist wanted to convey to her a feeling of acceptance and for the remainder of the session was fairly quiet. In retrospect, the therapist believed Mrs. Jay felt accepted through the silence, since she continued to share important memories of her life from the time she killed her son.

During the next two sessions, Mrs. Jay showed more control with fewer tears. She stated proudly: "I didn't cry much today. This was a good session." She related how successful she was in starting her own housecleaning business, how hard a worker she was, and how much her clients appreciated her services.

In the next session the therapist had to tell Mrs. Jay she was changing jobs but would like to continue with her in private practice. Mrs. Jay immediately agreed. The event was significant because the therapist let her know she would not abandon her for what she had done. Later in the treatment, Mrs. Jay expressed numerous times that she became more able to trust her because of the therapist's action of not abandoning her.

Mrs. Jay came to the next session very ambivalent. She exhibited concern about the expense of treatment for herself and Tom and stated her husband did not feel she needed to continue. The therapist's willingness to continue with her caused Mrs. Jay to question whether she deserved help. She also wished to back away from the painful affects beginning to surface. The therapist stayed with the manifest content, appreciated her concerns regarding her husband and the money, and made no further interpretations. She was becoming aware of the powerful sense of responsibility she felt to not say more than Mrs. Jay could tolerate, since Mrs. Jay could be truly capable of murder or suicide if she "fell apart" in the treatment.

The next content issue which arose was Tom's going to court after calling 911 with a false emergency. Mrs. Jay reported Tom had faked emergencies several times in the past, a not-so-subtle cry for help. Mrs. Jay vacillated between wanting Tom punished by the court and fearing that she would feel abandoned if he were removed from home. The therapist reassured her that since this was his first offense, it was highly unlikely he would be placed anywhere. The patient grew increasingly agitated following this comment. The therapist realized that Mrs. Jay's experiences with the courts colored the issue of Tom's punishment.

The therapist's unempathic response at this time reflected her countertransference feelings, which had begun to surface several days earlier. In a conversation with Tom's therapist, the father of a 2-year-old, he mentioned that at the time of the baby's death (age 18 months), the child would have been walking, talking, and moving into the toddler stage. It occurred to the therapist that she had been picturing the child as an infant, somehow less of a person, who was quietly smothered.

Following that conversation, the therapist began to have disturbing images of Mrs. Jay smothering her child and the child struggling against her. She felt disgusted by these thoughts and grew increasingly agitated with Mrs. Jay and protective of Tom. During this time Mrs. Jay's projection onto Tom was intensifying as she needed to rigidly defend against intolerable affects. Irritated by this projection, the therapist found herself wanting to cut through Mrs. Jay's defenses and connect her feelings to her dead child. What she did instead was to keep quiet, hoping to be less harmful to Mrs. Jay.

At this point, the therapist shared with her supervisor her disturbing image of Mrs. Jay smothering her child. The supervisor's understanding and acceptance of her feelings of disgust and anger with Mrs. Jay allowed the therapist to address her negative countertransference. She helped the therapist become in touch with how isolated and alone Mrs. Jay had felt for the last 24 years because no one could tolerate her overwhelming feelings of guilt, grief, and self-hatred. This was a turning point in the therapist's ability to empathize with Mrs. Jay. When she accepted that a human being suffering immense stress has a potential for unspeakable acts, the therapist was more able to remain empathic with Mrs. Jay.

During the next session, Mrs. Jay was intensely ambivalent, struggling with whether she could trust the therapist. The therapist was now able to interpret how alone and isolated Mrs. Jay must have felt when she could not trust people to understand or accept her feelings. She began crying softly, sighed several times, and appeared to experience a bit of relief. She spoke quietly and calmly, confirming the therapist's words by giving examples of how lonely and isolated she had felt. By the end of the hour, she became very global and talked about writing to the President regarding the pain of abused children in the United States. The therapist made no further interpretations as Mrs. Jay gradually began to distance herself from the pain.

Mrs. Jay canceled for the first time following that session. She told the therapist she did not feel like coming in and had not gone to work following the last hour because she felt so depressed. When asked if some of the feelings she had experienced seemed overwhelming, she replied, "I don't know what we talked about last week, but I know it does me a world of good to talk to you." The therapist supported her knowing when she needed a break, and they rescheduled for the following week.

At the next session, Mrs. Jay was angry, cried, and expressed great pain as she described seemingly minor trouble Tom had at school, for which he was suspended for one day. She stated that on the way down with Tom she wanted to crash the car, killing them both. Understanding how real that possibility was, the therapist wanted to help Mrs. Jay put a lid on her feelings and regain a sense of control as well as relief from the pain. Mrs. Jay expressed fears that Tom might one day kill her, including "I have failed him and he hates me." It appeared to the therapist that Mrs. Jay unconsciously projected onto Tom the painful affects she felt in order to regain control over them.

The therapist, despite much ambivalence, decided to call Mrs. Jay the next day to see how she had "survived" the evening. She was more controlled and expressed several times that she was pleased the therapist had called. She canceled the next session, however, stating she felt tired of "dragging up the past for Tom." When asked if staying home was a way to keep a lid on her own intense feelings, she agreed. The therapist validated how it seemed she could trust her instincts when she needed a break. Afterwards the therapist began questioning if she were losing Mrs. Jay and if she would drop out of treatment because her pain had become intolerable to both of them.

At the next session, Mrs. Jay was very anxious and talked excitedly about how Tom was impossible to handle. She didn't feel treatment was helping and cried every day because of him. The therapist interrupted her and gently told her she had seen her pain grow since they had talked about her feeling alone with the grief over her dead son. She began crying and stated, "I can't deal with both Tom and Peter (her dead son)." She thought about her dead son and feared she would go to hell for killing him. She feared that if she died, her sisters would tell her children she killed their brother. At this point, the therapist understood more clearly how intolerable her pain had been. Even in death, she anticipated no relief.

At the end of the session, the therapist asked if there was any way she could help Mrs. Jay keep her next appointment. She said there wasn't. The therapist said she could be counted on to be there no matter what Mrs. Jay decided and hoped to see her. She replied candidly and to the point, "I need this more than Tom does."

DISCUSSION OF PARALLEL CLINICAL PROCESSES

In order to examine the impact of supervision on the therapist's countertransference responses, we have chosen to conceptually organize this material into segments, with several pivotal or nodal points that significantly affect both the patient's subjective experience and the therapist's understanding of it, including both her countertransference-based reactions and her verbal interventions.

The use of the empathic mode first becomes quite obvious in the dramatic session when Mrs. Jay "confesses" to having murdered her 18-month-old son when she was 18 years of age. In supervision, it became clear that it was the therapist's initially empathic and nonjudgmental stance that allowed Mrs. Jay to be able to reveal the murder to her, without being intolerably overwhelmed by guilt, shame, and subsequent fears of abandonment. Her statement about appreciating how painful though important the confession was for Mrs. Jay strengthens the therapeutic engagement considerably and allows the affect that has become exposed to remain available, despite fluctuations in Mrs. Jay's capacity to tolerate it. Interestingly, the therapist does not initially feel negative in response to the confession, but rather is curious about the circumstances of the murder and its aftermath. Perhaps the traumatic nature of what Mrs. Jay reveals has resulted in an initial response of "psychic numbing" (Lifton and Olson 1974) within the therapist.

The confession can be seen as a nodal point in this treatment, because it enables Mrs. Jay to begin to experience not only her own feelings of grief and loss, but also the feelings that led to and were further reinforced by the murder of her child. She begins to be in touch with sadness over the neglect she experienced as a child. Physically and emotionally abused and deprived herself, perhaps the sound of her 18-month-old child crying was too painfully familiar and therefore had to be extinguished, along with the traumatic memories of her own childhood. Or perhaps the child's becoming more separate from her intensified chronic feelings of abandonment and isolation, which children who have experienced multiple foster placements, even with relatives, seem to feel. Though Mrs. Jay does not consciously link her inability to tolerate her child's crying to her own childhood, it seems that the "confession" enables a working-through process to begin in both areas, a working through of her own childhood depression and of the murder of her own child, which was both a symptom of it and further intensified her self-hatred and despair.

In the same session in which the working-through process begins, the therapist becomes aware of her own growing reluctance to empathize with the details of Mrs. Jay's experience at age 18. She realizes that, like Mrs. Jay, she too really wants to avoid talking about the death of the child and thereby diminish its importance. After discussing this in supervision, she was able to make a comprehensive interpretation of Mrs. Jay's need to resolve feelings about the murder and how they have affected both her and Tom. In response, Mrs. Jay says that the ways in which others (including legal and mental health professionals) have responded to her have made her feel misunderstood and unaccepted, because they could not tolerate the feelings she had about herself and what she had done. So they tried to make excuses for her behavior rather than hold her responsible, which would mean having to empathize with her feelings. As a result of her own unresolved feelings of guilt, grief, shame, and self-hatred, she feels continually "punished" by the fear that she will be abandoned if the truth is discovered by someone she needs (including her husband, son, and previous therapists), so she leaves them first.

Interestingly, as Mrs. Jay's affect becomes more available and memories and feelings are intensified, the therapist becomes more aware of her negative feelings in response to the murder and her own wishes to avoid empathizing with the intensity and nature of Mrs. Jay's pain. She dislikes having to imagine what it would feel like to be Mrs. Jay, to experience such total self-hatred and a strong sense of not being a member of the human family. Though her countertransference responses persist, with understanding of them she is able to consciously try to convey a degree of acceptance.

During the third and fourth sessions after the "confession," Mrs. Jay is very rigidly defended against affect. She is telling the therapist that she needs to slow down the process of recovering feelings about the trauma, and is even proud of her ability to be controlled, compulsive, and efficient, stating that, in effect, "my defenses are back and they are my source of self-esteem." If one understands these communications from a non-empathic vantage point, one might see such behaviors primarily as defensive evasions of her affect, resistances to the task of working through her powerful feelings of grief, guilt, and abandonment. From the empathic vantage point, however, these hours are indicative not only of Mrs. Jay's need to gain some control over her inner experience, but also of her desire to communicate that she is competent in other areas. Perhaps Mrs. Jay needs to feel secure that the therapist sees her as having good qualities, rather than as and only as a child murderer. By interpretively commenting on her need to communicate more about herself than just her "badness," the therapist is responding to Mrs. Jay as a complete person, which intensifies the patient's feeling of being accepted as well as more fully understood. Mrs. Jay can be said to be unconsciously "helping" the therapist to not be overwhelmed by her feelings of disgust and outrage.

In the next session, extratherapeutic issues emerge and complicate the treatment. The therapist is changing jobs, but will be working part-time at the Center and would like to continue with her. Although the situation stirred up the patient's fear of abandonment were she to be "found out," she is so engaged in treatment that she chooses to continue. Had she discontinued treatment, she would have protected herself against the abandonment threat and also against her difficulty tolerating the affects aroused in the sessions following the "confession." The affects have become particularly intense because of the meaning of the murder in light of Mrs. Jay's life-long feelings of unacceptability and fears of abandonment.

In the following session, there was indeed some intensification of Mrs. Jay's ambivalence about continuing in treatment. The crisis was dealt with in a characteristic way by Mrs. Jay–the locus of her fear shifted from the issue of possible abandonment by her therapist and guilt over receiving help that she did not feel she deserved to fear of abandonment by her husband and/or children if they learn the truth. And her concerns began to focus once again on Tom, who had a court appearance scheduled following another incident in which he called the 911 emergency number as a prank. Mrs. Jay's increasingly acute awareness of her fear of abandonment (both within the treatment and within her family) threatened to overwhelm her, when suddenly Tom's action and its meaning to Mrs. Jay abruptly intervened and consciously became far more compelling than the internal crisis over abandonment. Her need for punishment, to have her crime taken seriously, was vicariously met through her wish that Tom be punished with abandonment, but the defensive mode did not hold up and she herself also experienced guilt and her own sense of abandonment. She vacillated between wanting Tom punished and guilt over "causing" his behavior problems, along with fear that she cannot survive if she loses him.

As Mrs. Jay's efforts to cope with these conflicts within both the transference and her family reached a feverish pitch, a second interesting nodal point emerged in the therapeutic process. The therapist, unable at that moment to respond empathically to Mrs. Jay's pain and instead fearful of its intensity, made a statement designed to reassure the patient that Tom will probably get off lightly for his deed and will not be separated from her. Intended to calm Mrs. Jay, she instead responded with increasing agitation.

In retrospect, the therapist began to realize that the attempted reassurance was in response to her own wish to distance from the intensity and horror of the deed by sparing Mrs. Jay, symbolically through Tom, punishment. She next remembered a recent conversation with Tom's therapist, who mentioned that at 18 months of age a child is already walking and talking. He was a fully aware person with a developing sense of identity and a long history of attachment to the woman who struggled with and killed him. This marked another turning point in the treatment, because it enabled the therapist to empathize with Mrs. Jay's own traumatic reactions, including even more disturbing and intrusive images and affects of disgust and agitation. The therapist also became aware of feelings of anger at Mrs. Jay for her current need to use her son Tom as an object for a form of "projective identification."

In supervision, the therapist explored what her responses to Mrs. Jay suggested about how others probably responded to her and the murder. When she next met with the patient, the therapist was able to verbalize the chronic aloneness and isolation which Mrs. Jay had indeed felt since the murder. The patient responded with intense relief and an enhanced capacity to feel and communicate about these painful affects. This only lasted briefly, however, when the therapist again noticed a gradual but steady distancing from the feelings, which had once more threatened to become intolerable for her. Consistent with the use of the empathic mode, at this moment the therapist chose to make no further interpretations.

An interesting sequence of events ensued. During a phone conversation in which Mrs. Jay called to cancel the following session, the therapist asked her a direct question about whether she was overwhelmed by some of the feelings she had experienced the previous hour. Significantly, Mrs. Jay could not respond and did not even remember the content of the session. Yet she "reassured" the therapist about how important their work together is to her.

Mrs. Jay's becoming emotionally overwhelmed led her to regress once again, utilizing Tom as a "selfobject" around whom she can reorganize and thereby contain her anxiety. Her intense feelings of rage, including suicidal and homicidal thoughts, were focused on Tom and his misdeed. Instead of fearing that her husband will leave if he knows of the murder, she was now acutely fearful that he will leave because of the intensity of her anger and frustration with Tom. Her response the next day to news of the imminent closing of the Center was once again in terms of how upsetting this will be for Tom, with no conscious concern about the possible threat to her own psychotherapy.

Consistently, she canceled the next session, probably in part because it was too threatening for her to be the only patient, with Tom's therapist on vacation. She verbalized being tired of "dragging up the past for Tom" and the therapist commented on Mrs. Jay's need to keep a lid on her increasingly overwhelming feelings. She was so well engaged in treatment and successfully utilizing the therapist's selfobject functions to increase her capacity to tolerate painful affects, that she could openly agree with her about the need to keep a lid on her feelings but not feel criticized for doing so. She may also be closing off affect because of the actual possibility of losing the therapist if an alternative treatment arrangement cannot be made.

In response to this phone conversation, the therapist began to question her own motives in not wanting to threaten Mrs. Jay's defenses and being so accepting of her need to "keep a lid on her feelings." In supervision, it became apparent that her questioning of the possible countertransferential nature of her response stemmed from the relief that the therapist, too, felt at Mrs. Jay's backing away from the intensity of her affect. This was not, however, the primary motivation for her empathic acceptance of Mrs. Jay's need for defense and self-protection. In fact, the therapist increasingly recognized that her acceptance of Mrs. Jay's self-protective measures and understanding of the underlying reasons for them did not encourage or reinforce them, but rather promoted the opposite, namely an opening up of deeper and more intense affect.

Interestingly, in the next session the therapist learned that Mrs. Jay had not told Tom the news about the Center closing, just as she tried to "protect" him (as well as herself) from feelings regarding the earlier traumatic loss by manifestly not telling about it. She continued to focus on her concern about Tom and his loss of control. She felt she could not tolerate him, and her own intense feelings were becoming less well controlled outside of the treatment setting and interfering with her capacity to function at work. The therapist decided to again make a comprehensive interpretation. She skillfully lessened the risk of prematurely threatening Mrs. Jay's tenuous defenses by saying that she isn't sure if Mrs. Jay will be able to hear her, but she will give it a try. She gently went on to interpret Mrs. Jay's response to their discussion of the feeling of having been left alone all those years with the pain and grief. The sense of being abandoned by everyone had become a daily, continual, "punishment" for her, both because she felt emotionally exiled and could not talk with others in depth about her feelings of guilt and self-hatred, and because she therefore could not resolve them. Mrs. Jay cried, because she felt powerfully understood, and she confirmed this by further elaborating on the material. She shared with the therapist the daily presence of memories of her dead son, strong feelings of guilt, and fear that she will be punished by her live children if they know what she did. The session concluded with the therapist implicitly communicating her awareness that it would be difficult for Mrs. Jay to attend the next session both because of her intensity at the moment and a vacation planned by Tom's therapist. She asked if there is any way she can help Mrs. Jay to keep the appointment. The candor of Mrs. Jay's spontaneous response–that "there wasn't"–revealed the depth of her intuitive understanding of her internal states and the need to modulate her affect, despite a firm engagement in treatment.

SUMMARY

To look back for a moment and trace the contours of this very powerful treatment process, we can see that it began with the therapist's use of the empathic mode, which led to the revelation of the murder of Mrs. Jay's child and to a subsequent temporary break in the therapist's capacity to empathize with Mrs. Jay's subjective experience. The therapist's negative countertransference only emerged in the context of her effort to consistently immerse herself in the patient's subjective experience both before, during, and after the killing of her child. With the input of supervision, she became aware of her responses and their significance, which enabled her to become again more consistently empathic, on an even deeper level, with the grim reality of what Mrs. Jay's experience had been. As a result, richer and more meaningful material, containing more genuine affect, began to emerge and become available for therapeutic understanding and working through. Had it not been for the supervisory process, the therapist would have had even more difficulty than she did tolerating her feelings of disgust and horror in response to Mrs. Jay's affective states and the events giving rise to them. The supervision also enabled her to feel less overwhelmed with the responsibility to "keep" Mrs. Jay from becoming so distraught that she could commit murder once again.

The therapist's awareness of her negative feelings (following a vivid visual image of how the murder occurred) also enabled her to begin to reconstruct, first in supervision and eventually in a therapeutic dialogue with the patient, what had happened to Mrs. Jay following the event. She realized how others (including professionals) had distanced from Mrs. Jay by minimizing the severity of the crime. This invalidated her own feelings, led to increased guilt because no punishment ensued (she literally "got away with murder"), and resulted in chronic isolation and inability to work through the intense feelings of trauma and loss. The responses of others intensified her feeling of not being a member of the human race, as did the chronic isolation which was her response to it. As this gradual reconstruction took place, Mrs. Jay increasingly felt understood and accepted, which further strengthened the therapeutic engagement and enhanced her subsequent capacity to utilize the therapist's calming and soothing functions in order to tolerate affects which were previously too overwhelming to be allowed into consciousness. Not only could the meaning and repercussions of the murder become available for therapeutic intervention, but also the constellations from childhood giving rise to the event itself could become accessible on an affectively significant level.

REFERENCES

Adelson, L. (1961). Slaughter of the innocents: a study of forty-six homicides in which the victims were children. *New England Journal of Medicine* 264: 1345–1349.

Campion, J. F., Cravens, J. M., and Covan, F. (1988). A study of filicidal men. *American Journal of Psychiatry* 145(9):1141–1144.

Chernus, L. A. (1988). Why Kohut endures. *Clinical Social Work Journal* 16(4):336–354.

Dale, P. (1986). *Dangerous Families: Assessment and Treatment of Child Abuse.* New York: Tavistock.

Feinstein, H. M., Paul, N., and Pattison, E. (1964). Group therapy for mothers with infanticidal impulses. *American Journal of Psychiatry* 120:882–886.

Kohut, H. (1959). Introspection, empathy, and psychoanalysis: an examination of the relationship between mode of observation and theory. *Journal of the American Psychoanalytic Association* 7:459–483.

Lifton, R. J., and Olsen, E. (1974). *Living and Dying.* New York: Praeger.

Resnick, P. J. (1969). Child murder by parents: a psychiatric review of filicide. *American Journal of Psychiatry* 126:325–334.

Rowe, C. E., and MacIsaac, D. S. (1988). *Empathic Attunement: The "Technique" of Psychoanalytic Self Psychology.* Northvale, NJ: Jason Aronson.

22 Collaboration between Psychoanalysis and Social Work Education

Carolyn Saari

The question I was originally asked to answer in this chapter was "What can psychoanalysis contribute to social work education?" I acknowledge having taken the liberty to change this somewhat and instead to address the question "What can a collaboration between psychoanalysis and social work education contribute to today's world?" I prefer this question simply because I believe that our profession and our society currently have critical needs that will not be rectified by a piecemeal infusion of psychoanalytic theory into the curriculum in social work education, but which *might* be significantly altered through a true collaboration.

It is unfortunately true that, in the face of social, educational, and theoretical differences that have existed in the past twenty-five years, social work educators and clinicians interested in psychoanalytic theory have tended to forget how very much they have in common. Under these circumstances it seems worthwhile to begin this discussion by reminding us of the basic goals and values of our profession. Social work can be characterized by its beliefs in: (1) the inherent dignity of all persons, (2) the understanding of human beings as social creatures, and (3) the obligation of society to provide for all of its members, including equality of opportunity and justice. Social work's goals would include: (1) the provision of assistance to individuals, families and groups in the maximal development and utilization of their inherent potential as human beings; and (2) the achievement of a social order in which there is retention of maximal freedom regarding life choices within a system of shared responsibility for communal well-being (Saari 1986).

Clearly there is nothing inherent in these values and goals that would automatically lead to unbridgeable differences between social work and psychoanalytic theory. After all, Freud envisioned psychoanalysis as playing a major role in the creation of a better world. Yet clinical social workers have been in something of an adversarial position in relationship to the leadership of social work education since the late 1960s. There are a number of complex factors that originally led to this situation, many of which are changing significantly today. I will not have space to elaborate on all these factors, but do want to focus on some shifts in the intellectual context that are now influencing both social work education and psychoanalytic theory. What I hope to convey is the fact that there is increasingly a new base on which it ought to be possible for the two to meet.

The reason for focusing primarily on shifts in the intellectual context is that social work educators are generally more influenced by conditions within the university environments in which they function than they are by the demands of the practice community. Practitioners often experience this influence on social work academicians almost as if it were a betrayal of the profession. From my perspective this must be understood simply as a fact of life—the principle that everyone is highly influenced by the conditions of their immediate environment. This difference in the influences of the immediate contexts of practitioners and academicians probably will always mean the existence of some differences in the priorities of these two groups. It is a matter of some importance, then, whether these differences lead to unbridgeable chasms or creative tensions.

The chasm that developed in the 1960s was caused in part by the fact that faculty of social work schools, ordinarily units that exist somewhere on the periphery of influence in their academic environments, were looking for increased acceptance in the university setting and therefore began to pay allegiance to the tenets of American behaviorism and of the cognitive movement, both of which were then dominant in the social sciences. Attempts, originally motivated by the goal of legitimizing social work, to examine treatment in a scientific manner raised questions about treatment efficacy as well as about the validity of its theory base. Clinicians influenced by the traditions of psychoanalytic theory reacted negatively to these ideas, knowing that these presumably methodologically pure research efforts failed to capture the essence of the treatment process and that generally behaviorally oriented treatment interventions were conceptualized at such a concrete level as to miss the individuality of the client and the complexity of his or her problems.

The intellectual context of the 1990s, however, is altering this. I want, then, to demonstrate an increasing convergence of ideas by focusing on just a few areas.

THE SOCIAL MOTIVATION AND MEANING OF BEHAVIOR

Social work has traditionally seen the human being as a social animal, not only functioning within a social environment, but having characteristics that were basically determined through social interaction as well. This assumption was clearly in conflict with Freud's ideas about a genetically inherited intrapsychic life in which ontogeny recapitulated phylogeny. Because of this difference there was a long period of time during which psychoanalytic purists tended to see considerations about the interpersonal as "surface" and inevitably inferior.

Today, however, the Darwinian literalism of ontogeny recapitulating phylogeny has long since been discredited in mainstream science and psychoanalytic theory is increasingly moving toward a perspective involving an important relationship between the interpersonal and intrapsychic worlds. Examples of this are readily at hand–Stern's (1985) interpersonal world of the infant, Stolorow's (1988) intersubjectivity, Emde's (1989) notion of social referencing, the growing respectability of Bowlby's (1969) ideas of attachment.

CENTRALITY OF THE RELATIONSHIP IN TREATMENT

A second area is clearly related to the first. The psychosocial tradition within social work long hailed the client/worker relationship as central to any therapeutic effects (Biestek 1957, Perlman 1979). Since "relationship" could not readily be measured in objective and empirical terms, this factor in treatment was downplayed or ignored in much of the research that was influential in academic circles during the 1970s and '80s. The situation in psychoanalytic theory was not, however, much better. There it was presumed that the force of verbal interpretation, not the relationship, was curative.

Yet current linguistic theory is now positing that meaning is constituted through an interpersonal dialogue (Bruner 1983). This implies that treatment theory needs to consider interpersonal interactions and interpretations as resembling a seamless whole. The concepts related to this position are having an influence on both psychoanalysis and academia. Thus, for example, one finds theorists such as Daniel Stern (1989) who is now influential in both circles and who has noted that the essential difference between an interpersonal interaction and a relationship is that the relationship includes the meaning assigned to the interactions by the participants.

THE ROLE OF ACTION

Social workers have always been more willing to pay attention to client actions and to be more involved in action on behalf of their clients than psychoanalysts have. Freud assumed that reality was captured through the representational system in language and that action served to defend against or to distort that meaning (Litowitz and Litowitz 1977, Schimek 1975). Yet one tenet of the cognitive revolution of the past 30 or so years in psychology which does seem to have lasting significance is that meaning is constituted through action, ordinarily through action involving interpersonal interactions. Thus, psychoanalysts are paying attention to the fact that, as Schafer (1983) has clearly indicated, patients not only tell their stories but they show them to us. At the same time, current social work theory undoubtedly needs to redirect its attention to the fact that actions on behalf of clients in the forms of such things as concrete services will remain incompletely effective if not seen as housed within carefully constructed treatment relationships.

SCIENCE VERSUS MEANING

There is currently a heated debate among psychoanalytic theorists (Brenner 1982, Spence 1982) as to whether that discipline is essentially scientific or hermeneutic (that is, interpretive). The controversy in psychoanalysis seems in part to derive from Freud's failure to separate meaning, causation, and motivation in his explanatory scheme involving the instinctual drives (Saari 1991). This debate has often taken on an all-or-nothing cast, with claims that treatment is either scientific or hermeneutic. It is, however, becoming increasingly clear that it is both.

Bruner's work (1986) has made distinctions between two equally legitimate but quite different ways of thinking. Bruner described (1) the paradigmatic or scientific mode of thinking which involves causal propositions, and (2) the mode of thinking that involves meaning or the narrative construction of the possible. The paradigmatic way of thinking, which formulates generalizable rules that are context-free and utilizes statistical procedures of probability to achieve this, has traditionally been fundamental to the assumptions underpinning research formulations. In this scientific mode the aim is of being able to identify those conditions that are necessary and sufficient for a particular phenomenon to occur. An understanding of the necessary and sufficient causes is expected to provide the ability to predict that which will occur in other cases.

A symptom-based, medical-model approach to mental illness such as that which underlies the DSM classification system essentially relies on Bruner's paradigmatic way of thinking. Here treatment is presumed to work through the identification and removal or reversal of the causal factors underneath the illness or symptomatology. Such an approach frequently relies heavily on the identification of a precipitating event, which is then seen as the major causal factor in the illness. Treatment is directed at altering the existence, effects, or conditions surrounding this precipitating event. Treatment carried out within this model and its efficacy can be studied within the rules of research set out in the scientific mode of thinking.

However, much of clinical work, and particularly psychoanalytically oriented work, is more heavily influenced not by the scientific mode of thinking but rather by the mode more associated with meaning. In stark contrast to scientific thinking, the narrative construction of the possible not only has no predictive ability but in fact actually reasons backwards. Therapeutic interpretation is not predictive, but rather seeks to explain something that has already occurred in the client's life. Understanding meaning is fundamentally *ex post facto* (Edelson 1975). Whereas paradigmatic thinking aims at the formulation of context-free rules, meaning is always context-dependent (Mishler 1979). Furthermore, the narrative construction of the possible does not aim at generalizability, but rather at a detailed description of a single example. The construction of meaning is infinite. Since there is no single right answer but a limitless unknown of potential significance, one never arrives at a finished end product.

I have elsewhere (Saari 1991) proposed that treatment influenced by psychoanalytic theory ordinarily does not aim at the removal of pathogenic influences but rather at building on the strengths of the individual. This treatment approach generally falls more readily into the form of thinking characterized by the narrative construction of the possible. As therapists in this mode we accept the client's evaluation of how he or she is now and then help in the construction of a story of how he or she arrived at that end point. The therapeutic process thereby arrives at a more complete understanding of the client's identity and at an increased capacity to create meaning on the part of the client. This process, by its very nature, is poorly captured in the research designs formulated for the examination of scientific data. Instead new research methods designed to study the phenomena of meaning need to be created and implemented.

Although tensions between proponents of treatment based upon scientific thinking versus that based in meaning have existed for many years, it is only quite recently that there has been a beginning recognition of these as two distinctly different ways of thinking. They are indeed quite different and yet in reality probably all treatment relies on some mix of both. The recognition of the differences, however, now makes it possible to study their interrelated as well as their separate uses in theory and therapy with the prospect that we might not only learn how to reconcile old conceptual differences, but that we might also learn a great deal about treatment.

A more complete understanding of how science and meaning interrelate within the world of theory and therapy offers the possibility of finding better matches between therapy and the research methodologies designed to study it. Thus, not only is there considerable potential for healing the intellectual rift between social work academics and psychodynamic clinicians, but there also appears to be a potential basis for fruitful collaboration as well.

CONTEXT

Although social work has long considered its person-in-environment approach to be a defining characteristic of the profession, there has been a serious conceptual problem in understanding the person/environment relationship. Psychoanalytic theory has tended to posit an inner life for the individual and then proceed as if the nature of this inner life were more or less unaffected by environmental conditions. On the other hand, more scientifically oriented social work approaches have tended to posit a social environment and then assume that this external world should take precedence over considerations about inner meanings. Clearly neither approach is truly adequate.

As I have already noted, current theoretical revisions are now beginning to push the more research- and scientifically oriented social-work academicians toward a new recognition of the validity and significance of meaning and an inner life. At the same time, however, these revisions are moving psychoanalysis in the direction of a recognition that meaning is invariably context-dependent. (You read, for example, the very words that I am writing differently since I am writing for this particular book than you would if I were delivering an address on a street corner.) The inner life of an individual is not merely a genetic inheritance or drive derivative that evolves throughout life in a basic pattern relatively unaffected by the environment. Instead the content of one's identity as well as one's very ability to construct and understand that identity is highly influenced by patterns of social participation (Schafer 1992).

Thus, current revisions in linguistic and cognitive theories (Bruner 1990, Lakoff 1987, Nelson 1985, Saari 1991, Vygotsky 1962) are at long last making it possible for us to build bridges between the person and the environment.

FINDING COMMON GROUND

I have been talking about the importance of understanding contextual influences. We are living in a time of a huge gap between the rich and the poor, when millions of people are suffering from serious economic deprivation, when there is an insistent need for all of us to learn to live cooperatively with an ever more diverse population, when public services have been cut nearly into oblivion, and when adequate health care is rapidly becoming a privilege of the wealthy. We are living in a time when it seems increasingly important for all social workers to reaffirm the traditional goals and values of our profession.

Social work educators are now, understandably it seems to me, seeing issues of social justice as central to the curriculum. Thus, the current draft of the revised Curriculum Policy Statement lists the first premise underlying social work education as:

> The purpose of social work education is to prepare competent and effective social work professionals who are committed to practice that includes services to the poor and oppressed, and who work to alleviate poverty, oppression and discrimination. [Council on Social Work Education, "Curriculum Policy Statement," 3rd draft, 1991 p. 1]

In the 1960s many academicians decided that casework was dead and that therapy simply adjusted individuals to a sick society. After that many clinicians began to hear issues about social policy, including calls for social justice from academicians, as code words for criticism of clinical work. Yet twenty-five to thirty years later casework is far from dead; (90–95 percent of the students in most schools of social work want to study clinical work). What's more, the research that is generally accepted in academia no longer indicates that therapy is ineffective. The influence of behaviorist and/or logical empiricist theories is still present in many circles, but there is an increasing recognition that these ideas may be inadequate for an in-depth understanding of human processes and there is a related and growing movement for more qualitative methodology in research.

Slowly "clinical social work" is becoming more respectable in academic circles. True, the word clinical still does not appear in any of the Council on Social Work Education's accreditation documents. But, whereas for many years at the Annual Program Meetings of the Council on Social Work Education those of us who thought of ourselves as clinicians simply held meetings that we did not generally publicize and that served as a support group, in 1992 there was for the first time an accepted Symposium on Clinical Social Work which sponsored about six papers on the official program. The Symposium has continued to be successful at getting papers into the program and the list of educators interested in participating in the Symposium has been growing exponentially.

So clinical work is no longer automatically thought of within academia as dead, ineffective, or simply adjusting individuals to a sick society. It is nevertheless true that many of my colleagues in academia still think of "clinical" as equaling private practice and the purely intrapsychic concerns of the wealthy and the comfortable. For example, in a recent issue of the *Journal of Social Work Education* Barbara Shore (1991) argued against allowing a place for clinical education at the doctoral level on these grounds.

Educators and clinicians may now have less to argue about in relation to theoretical issues, but if there is to be a meeting of the minds, clinicians will need to make an extra effort to convey to educators the idea that they do have concerns about social justice issues and that their knowledge can be useful in this arena. Similarly, supporters of psychoanalytic theory should not assume that educators know what current psychoanalytic theory involves. In fact, it is true that many educators know little about psychoanalytic theory other than concepts of intrapsychic drives and the Oedipus conflict–ideas they can readily dismiss as outmoded and oppressive.

So we clinicians will need to help academics understand psychoanalytic ideas better. But it seems to me at least that this will not–and should not–be enough. Perhaps it is true that I have simply become contaminated by having lived too long within the context of academia, but I admit that I am myself sometimes dismayed these days by the number of programs now being sponsored by our professional organization on how to cooperate with managed care and/or restrictive governmental or insurance rulings in private practice. I do not want to give the impression that I am against private practice–in fact, I engage in it myself. Yet it seems that by trying to work within the restrictive codes being placed on clinical practice even we have now bought into the very same "effectiveness" code word of the logical empiricists to which we once objected.

I am not against legislative programs aimed at licensing or gaining more status for our profession. Yet I also wonder if we could not do more to protest the fact that managed health care and other such programs *are* actively undermining the availability of adequate treatment for most Americans. I know that many social workers have gone into private practice because they believed the quality of their work with clients was being compromised by working conditions in agencies. I understand that perfectly well, but could we not collectively work harder at changing those agency conditions? Conditions in agencies are a major concern to educators–after all, this is where students obtain their practice experience.

I know that many clinical social workers have been feeling powerless in the face of the professional and societal conditions brought about through the Reagan years, but I also think that if psychoanalytically oriented clinical social workers want to have an influence in schools of social work today, we will need to readdress the questions of how it is that our expertise relates to issues of social justice. I am personally convinced that we are now in a position to do this more convincingly–from both preventative and rehabilitative perspectives.

POTENTIAL CONTRIBUTIONS

With the wonderful idealism of youth, I once believed that something akin to a Utopian society was possible. I must acknowledge that I am no longer so optimistic. Yet it is true that, thanks to the work of psychoanalytic theorists and researchers such as Stern (1985), Emde (1989), Winnicott (1971), Bowlby (1969), and a whole host of others, we now have a much more adequate picture of child development than we have ever had before. Current theories of meaning are providing us with a newly enriched way of understanding the interrelationships between such things as culture, personality, and mental health. There are newly evolving research approaches and techniques which could be adapted to examining these issues in more depth. Conceiving that these new conceptual tools could be utilized to achieve greater understanding of human dilemmas does not strike me as being necessarily Utopian.

Thus, the outer limits of what might be achieved for our clinical students, our clients, society, and our world by a renewed collaboration between educators and clinical social workers will only become clear if we try to reach them. It does seem to me that the possibility of our working together is greater now than it has been in at least 15 years and that minimally such collaboration can produce better clinicians who are also committed to the profession of social work. I hope I don't sound too overly optimistic if I add that I would also hope we could find new ways of persuasively demonstrating for our fellow citizens the ways in which poverty, injustice, intolerance, and oppression lead to individual and social dysfunction.

REFERENCES

Biestek, F. P. (1957). *The Casework Relationship.* Chicago: Loyola University Press.

Bowlby, J. (1969). *Attachment.* Vol. 1 of *Attachment and Loss.* New York: Basic Books.

Brenner, C. (1982). *The Mind in Conflict.* New York: International Universities Press.

Bruner, J. S. (1983). *Child's Talk: Learning to Use Language.* New York: Norton.

—— (1986). *Actual Minds, Possible Worlds.* Cambridge, MA: Harvard University Press.

—— (1990). *Acts of Meaning.* Cambridge, MA: Harvard University Press.

Council on Social Work Education. (1991). *Curriculum policy statement,* 3rd draft.

Edelson, M. (1975). *Language and Interpretation in Psychoanalysis.* New Haven, CT: Yale University Press.

Emde, R. N. (1989). The infant's relationship experience: developmental and affective aspects. In *Relationship Disturbances in Early Childhood: A Developmental Approach,* ed. A. J. Sameroff and R. N. Emde, pp. 33–52. New York: Basic Books.

Lakoff, G. (1987). *Women, Fire and Dangerous Things: What Categories Reveal about the Mind.* Chicago University of Chicago Press.

Litowitz, B. E., and Litowitz, N. S. (1977). The influence of linguistic theory on psychoanalysis: a critical, historical survey. *International Review of Psychoanalysis,* 4:419–448.

Mishler, E. G. (1979). Meaning in context: Is there any other kind? *Harvard Educational Review,* 49:1–19.

Nelson, K. (1985). *Making Sense: The Acquisition of Shared Meaning.* New York: Academic Press.

Perlman, H. H. (1979). *Relationship: The Heart of Helping People.* Chicago: University of Chicago Press.

Saari, C. (1986). *Clinical Social Work Treatment: How Does it Work?* New York: Gardner.

—— (1991). *The Creation of Meaning in Clinical Social Work.* New York: Guilford.

Schafer, R. (1983). *The Analytic Attitude.* New York: Basic Books.

—— (1992). *Retelling a Life: Narration and Dialogue in Psychoanalysis.* New York: Basic Books.

Schimek, J. G. (1975) A critical re-examination of Freud's concept of unconscious mental representation. *International Review of Psycho-Analysis* 2:171–187.

Shore, B. K. (1991). Point/counterpoint: Is there a role for clinical doctoral education? *Journal of Social Work Education,* 27:231–240.

Spence, D. P. (1982). *Narrative Truth and Historical Truth: Meaning and Interpretation in Psychoanalysis.* New York: Norton.

Stern, D. N. (1985). *The Interpersonal World of the Infant.* New York: Basic Books.

——(1989). The representation of representational patterns: developmental considerations. In *Relationship Disturbances in Early Childhood,* ed. A. J. Sameroff and R. N. Emde, pp. 52–69. New York: Basic Books.

Stolorow, R. (1988). Intersubjectivity, psychoanalytic knowing and reality. *Contemporary Psychoanalysis* 24:331–338.

Vygotsky, L. S. (1962). *Thought and Language.* Cambridge, MA: M.I.T. Press.

Winnicott, D. W. (1971). *Playing and Reality.* New York: Basic Books.

Postlude

Jean B. Sanville

Social work and psychoanalysis have a long relationship with each other, sometimes loving, sometimes rejecting. Many of us who came into social work decades ago actually chose what was then called "psychiatric social work" as a profession precisely because MSW programs that trained in that specialty were psychoanalytic in their orientation. Our classroom teachers included both psychoanalysts and social workers, the latter enthusiastically working to adapt analytic theory to the job of the practitioner in our field. While our supervisors were social workers, they too were versed in analytic theory, and usually had been analyzed themselves. And the agencies and clinics and hospitals in which we had our field placements provided abundant psychoanalytic consultation. There was mutual learning in that collaboration as the consultants, largely male analysts, tried to impart their ideas to us, largely female social workers. They heard in detail about patients far more deprived, disadvantaged, and damaged than those then deemed suitable for psychoanalysis, and we discovered together both the value and shortcomings of the then existing theories about development and pathology for the understanding our clientele. We assumed that there were limits to psychoanalysis proper for the treatment of most of the patients we were seeing, that there would have to be some stretching of parameters. That conjoint learning, I suspect, has served psychoanalysis well in its "ever-widening scope," the gradual expansion and adaptation of its theories and methods for the treatment of those with more severe pathologies than were originally thought to benefit. And clearly it has benefitted several generations of clinical social workers who, like those who have contributed to this book, continue to think and write about adapting psychoanalytic theories to their clientele.

Both psychoanalysis and social work have developed and changed radically from those days, and this book is dramatic testimony to those changes. In it, we find a rich syllabus, affording a detailed view of how these clinicians in a variety of practice settings are drawing on psychoanalytic theory in their work. Many of their clients are persons whose lives have had inauspicious beginnings and who suffer therefore from developmental deficiencies and cumulative traumas. Their treatment calls for a greater focus on the preoedipal period, that is, the earliest years of life. This does not mean that they do not also suffer conflicts that are oedipal in nature; instead we would suspect that such conflicts would present for them infinitely greater difficulties because they lack the inner resources of the more neurotic person. Indeed, for them the oedipal stage is likely to be more pathogenic than for those with more fortunate experiences in infancy. So while earlier versions of psychoanalysis featured the father, who was presumed to come into focus somewhat later than the mother, today's theories tend to feature the mother, with whom the child experienced the first relationship. We note a "feminization of psychoanalysis" therefore, not only because of the increasing number of women entering psychoanalytic training but because today's practice demands that therapists of either sex be prepared for mother as well as for father transferences, and for the countertransferences that these will evoke. They may be assigned by their patients to play re-parenting roles, and sometimes to serve as collaborators in generating insights. The writers herein give us vivid pictures of the challenges presented by their clientele of today, and enable us to speculate on what factors in treatment are healing.

In the historical review with which Strean begins this book, he claims that he finds psychoanalysis easier to define than social work. There seem perhaps to be many "social works" today, and the view toward the inside may be somewhat harder to attain than the outward view at another, albeit related, profession. Psychoanalysts are having something of this problem too, struggling with the question of whether we can declare today that there is but one psychoanalysis, or if we must admit that there is considerable heterogeneity on the current scene. So many and diverse are the schools of thought that have evolved that there is an urgent search for common ground, for answers to questions of whether even core concepts can be consensually agreed upon. Such soul-searching can be painful, but it is one of the strengths of psychoanalysis–indeed of any profession–that it recurrently allows itself to re-think the premises from which it works.

Strean gives us his perspective on the "classical view." He declares that the major tenet of psychoanalysis is *determinism*. If by that we mean the doctrine that every event, act, and decision is the inevitable consequence of antecedents, such as physical, psychological, or environmental conditions that are independent of the human will, then how do we understand that psychoanalysis aims to restore a human sense of agency, the enjoyment of felt freedom of will? Even classical analysts have long noted this paradox (Brenner 1955). It could look as though we must become comfortable with the idea that seemingly incompatible statements may both be true. When we can enable the patient to comprehend the forces, inner and outer, that have both shaped him and *been shaped by him*, he will have a greater sense of freedom. The domain of freedom lies in the capacity of the person to claim the basic sense of self as agent, the sense that one can intend, act, and bring about an effect. There are those who would say that there may lurk a "determinism" even of that felt freedom. As one analyst put it some forty years ago, freedom ". . . is a subjective experience which is itself causally determined" (Knight 1954). I believe that many authors in this book are showing that when the patient can utilize or be enabled to utilize the ambiance and the relationship with the therapist to restore something of the play spirit, he will come to enjoy more the illusion (from *in ludere*, in play) of freedom. Play itself is hard to define, but the closest synonym may be freedom.

In his definition of psychoanalysis, Strean tells us that it is a theory of personality, a form of psychotherapy, and a method of research. In this book we have seen how all of the authors have drawn on the theory of personality, particularly on the developmental view, emphasizing the influences of early family relationships on the lives that people then make for themselves. None is reporting treatment via psychoanalysis per se, that is, with a frequency of four or five times a week or the use of couch and free association. But all aim to create an atmosphere that enables clients to talk freely, and all assume their task is to listen and understand. Not always do they assume that the person must fully understand wishes, defenses, superego admonitions, and memories, but in many cases the patient enjoys the illusion of spontaneous insight, based on internalizing the conjoint process of understanding. In some instances treatment is very extended, over years when necessary because of the nature of the psychopathology. All these therapists attend centrally to transference, countertransference, and resistance (although readers may have observed that the word resistance itself is seldom used)—the cornerstones of psychoanalytic therapy. When transferences makes for *distortion*, therapists attempt to enable their patients to attain a view closer to the actual. In some instances this involves interpretation, but usually conjointly arrived at rather than made by the therapist as authority. Again it would seem that the new relationship is so unlike the original ones on which the patient formed his premises that changes may take place without conscious cognitive measures. The case reports do not purport to be research, although we might propose that a collection of such studies might indeed be utilized for purposes of research. It is rare indeed to have data available such as these writers have generously provided.

About one issue there is no question: the existence of *unconscious* forces that interact at all times with conscious ones. It would be a great burden, if not an actually impossible one, were we to have to be at all moments conscious of all of the factors in any given situation. There is great advantage to doing some things unconsciously, but when our ways of seeing keep making problems for us, we try to dredge up our premises and generate new ones more in keeping with the present. When the repression of some experiences results in their influencing attitudes and behaviors in ways not open to conscious re-evaluation, there is obviously great advantage to being able to re-claim what has been denied or disavowed. In addition to the potentially conscious or *preconscious* components of thinking and feeling, those that are capable of being put into words, we have been introduced to a re-examination of Freud's *primary unconscious*, ubiquitous and containing potential for health or for pathology, depending upon how it combines with so-called rational thinking.

Strean traces broadly social work's relationship with analytic theory, and, to those of us who have lived that history, it evokes many memories, including affect-laden ones. Psychoanalysis had an original appeal when it replaced our early moralistic approach with a non-judgmental one. It was even more congenial for social workers when drive theory was replaced by ego psychology, helping us to work with the very disturbed clients who generally peopled our case loads. Then, in the '60s and '70s, there came a split of sorts, with some social workers abandoning analytic ideas as no longer "fashionable," as Strean says, and turning to crisis intervention and short-term models, allegedly for good reasons, to join the "War on Poverty." There was a "regression" to something like our early "manipulation of the environment." This author sees the establishment of the Federation of Societies for Clinical Social Work as preserving a domain for the assessment and treatment of individual clients, but so far not successfully stemming the tide in the other direction.

Ironically, at this time in the history of psychoanalysis, when that discipline is increasingly developing theories potentially more congenial to and enriching of social work even than ego psychology–theories that attend to the interpersonal and the intersubjective as well as the intrapsychic–schools of social work have virtually abandoned teaching those theories. And psychoanalysis is neglected as a subject of study also in schools of psychology and of psychiatry. It is the thesis of this book that all of the mental health professions would benefit by a "return of the repressed," a renewed relationship with psychoanalysis.

THE BASIC CONCEPTS OF PSYCHOANALYSIS AS SEEN IN THESE WRITINGS

The writers herein represent various schools of psychoanalytic theory, some fairly classical, some ego psychologists, some self psychologists, some object relationists, some intersubjectivists. And we often notice certain combinations of these, since over time most therapists probably draw on more than one schema. Can we find common ground among these clinicians? I think we can, although we will inevitably note differences. There are those that stem from the way in which each conceptualizes the problems the patients bring, that is, upon which of the existing analytic theories a given therapist is drawing. There are those determined by the particular patients with whom one is predominantly working. And of course there will always be the inevitable individual idiosyncrasies, born either of their own personalities or of the particular education and training to which they have been exposed. The uniqueness of each dyad is part of the reason for difficulty with quantitative research.

Looking back over the chapters in which case vignettes are reported, I would simply call attention to some themes and the variations on them, observing that, in spite of seeming dissimilarities, there are underlying commonalities that lead us to acknowledge that all are practicing psychoanalytically oriented psychotherapy. The hallmarks upon which I will comment are the ethic, transference, countertransference, the working relationship with its interplay of transferences and countertransferences, and the philosophy of healing.

THE ETHIC

I would like to start with the ethic of psychoanalysis, which is close to that which has characterized social work, at least from the time I entered the field over a half-century ago. It is respect for the individual's *self-determination* that shapes everything that these therapists do and try not to do. Although so long ago social workers were articulating that as a central value, it is not certain that we as yet grasped what was required to implement it. Edward has attempted to spell it out, an approach of non-imposition, use of "evenly suspended attention," rather than deciding in our own minds what the patient's focus should or should not be. To be capable of disclaiming the authority the patient sometimes seems to want to place in us, we have to be able to stay open to our own inner workings, to the aspects of us that might want to take charge. To the extent that such unconscious motives could be intruding, we would look for clues in the transference that the patient may not be coping just with the inevitable internal resistances, but feels some need to fight us off. Edward reminds us of Freud's Emmy von N., whose rebukes to Freud led to his development of the analytic method as one that would be minimally imposing, one that let him keep learning from his patients. Not all of our patients can be so bold and forthright, and not all therapists are as willing to re-think their approaches as was Freud. A main reason for the desirability that therapists themselves have experienced analysis or psychoanalytically oriented therapy is that they are rendered keener at detecting and containing their own wishes and tendencies, including those to control the action. Edward points up how neutrality, anonymity and abstinence make both for the patient's felt safety and for the therapist's freedom to oscillate between attunement and stepping back into her own psychic skin to think about what empathy has revealed. Neutrality has been very much misunderstood as meaning that the therapist is a kind of non-person with no investment in the patient's overcoming his problems, a virtual not caring. Instead it refers to the non-imposition that is described by this author, designed to free the patient's own design for and ability to implement self-repair.

Coleman makes this same point in a different way, asserting that the basic ethic of both psychoanalysis and clinical social work is not to change the person in a direction predetermined by us, but to enhance insight so that the patient will be equipped to modify patterns that have been unrewarding. Influenced by Winnicott, he advocates our accommodating to the patient, lest we, like the not-good-enough mother, foster false selves in the patient. We all know of clients who, in the attempt to please us, maintain a vigilance to detect clues from us as to what we want or expect, and would comply with our unspoken wishes, but then not own the changes in themselves.

One of the preconditions for an ability to take the ethical stance of neutrality is what Reik (1937) called the "capacity not to understand." That tends to puzzle young therapists who assume that they must be infinitely knowing and not be caught with areas of ignorance. Yet the advantage of not knowing is that the patient has an opportunity to educate us. This is, I would suggest, particularly important when the patient is of a race or culture different from out own. We can never be well informed about every race and subculture in this increasingly multi-racial and multi-cultural nation, but we can perhaps learn how to make an advantage of that very fact. One of the dangers of the emphasis in some schools today on teaching about minorities is that we could neglect the likelihood that no individual is typical, but that each will have absorbed or rejected or differently combined various aspects of that which she has been "carefully taught."

Applegate, after giving us a charming sketch of Winnicott, the man, informs us that this pediatrician/psychoanalyst was enlivened rather than disconcerted by not knowing. He assumed the patient to be a partner in the therapeutic endeavor, one who knew better than the therapist about his own internal workings. His squiggle technique with children was perhaps the equivalent of "evenly suspended attention" with adults, an openness to what the patient brings combined with a willingness to engage in dialogue about it. It is mutual collaboration that makes healing possible.

The therapist mirrors what he sees in the client, and via that mirror, the client discovers himself as a separate somebody. Winnicott wrote that he regretted the many times that he violated his own ethic, giving an interpretation when, had he waited, the patient might well have come upon it himself and have enjoyed the heady pleasure of arriving at his own insight.

TRANSFERENCE

One of the reasons for alertness to transference is precisely to protect the ethic of respect for the patient's selfhood. Transference can be seen as evidence of the patient's unconscious way of interpreting relationships. It is, as Frank says, the "vehicle of the repetition compulsion." Freud (1914) wrote of it as "a playground . . . an intermediate region between illness and real life through which the transition from the one to the other is made" (p. 154). He too was thinking of it as part of the compulsion to repeat, and he wanted to turn that inclination into a motive for remembering and an intention to repair. He affirmed that the transference should be allowed to expand freely, so that a new condition would be created, manifesting "all the features of the illness, but it represents an artificial illness at every point accessible to our intervention" (p. 154). How can that happen? Many of the case histories herein illustrate how the patient may come, in the therapeutic dialogue, to see his role in perpetuating that of which he complains. But some also show how problems may turn into artificial illness precisely because the therapist's responses are such that the person can no longer regard his attitudes and reactions as inevitable natural results of this context, but as unnecessary carry-overs from past experiences. I do not see these therapists assuming that the patient in any basic way wants to defeat them. Instead, although it is not always articulated, they would seem to believe with Freud that every symptom is an attempt at cure. If the patient seems stubbornly fixated in his thinking and feeling, the so-called "unconscious gratification" is that these ways represent the best he has been able to do to date to play the hand that life has dealt him. He is not likely to give this up easily; his resistance is self-preservative, not primarily opposition to the therapist. It requires time and the perseverance of therapists such as these who regularly respond in ways that ultimately tend to enable the patient to disconfirm his old schema.

The ever-present controversy about what is healing in psychotherapy centers around whether it is the experience of the new relationship or the insights that the person gains from new ways of interpreting past experience. Most therapists herein see roles for both, although perhaps generally regarding the former as the necessary preliminary in most of the clients they serve.

It would seem to be the schools of thought emanating from Kohutian writings who most take the view that it is the actual experience of the patient with the therapist that is the source of healing. Chernus and Livingston claim that self psychologists have a different way of understanding transference, not as a repetition of early childhood relationships but as serving needs for mirroring, idealizing, or twinship functions. Growth occurs, they say, through filling in deficits, rather than re-experiencing and understanding early childhood relationships and their attendant conflicts. Some will find themselves not quite understanding that way of putting it, perhaps noting that it confuses the phenomenon with the possible use that could be made of it. Many writings in psychoanalysis today acknowledge that the tendency to repeat is, as Freud was declaring, also an unconscious search for experiences that would disconfirm the person's worst expectations, so that their life stories could turn out better. But we should notice that therapists who think as do these two writers have strong faith in the reparative intent that motivates both the filicidal patient of whom they write and the therapist whose work is being supervised.

Those who embrace the thinking of the British independent tradition tend to regard the *process* of interpreting as more important than the knowledge being imparted. This is illustrated by Chescheir, who takes a Winnicottian approach. Her male patient was referred by his previous male therapist, who thought he needed to work with a woman. Chescheir was mindful that her patient's mother had been particularly impinging and she therefore avoided interpretations "from on high." In her view, if Mr. B. was to reclaim his true self, he would have to experience his own role in arriving at understanding. We see the workings of the repetition compulsion in this man nevertheless, for in spite of her non-authoritarian approach, he has "mixed feelings about coming" and reiterates how he "must comply." Chescheir must deal with her own feelings about his assertions that therapy is not making much difference. Yet there are hopeful signs. When he dreams of male/female toilets with mother and baby in one stall, she defers to his associations and he and she begin work on the male–female issues and the internalized mother–child relationship. I would say that their *playing* with the dream leads to a degree of freedom that lets this once very constricted patient remember it differently later and associate further. We could also see in his unfolding playfulness with his baby daughter some identification with the therapist/mother and modeling his role with his little girl according to experiences his baby/self has with her. The sheer pleasure he enjoys assures us that his gains are likely to continue. We can imagine, even perhaps in response to his complaints about therapy, commenting, "It must feel that the big difference in your life is Betsy and in your capacity to delight in playing with her." Such a comment would reveal the therapist as not one either to be hurt or to retaliate in reaction to his aggressive complaints, and could thus enable him to use her as a separate person (Winnicott 1971).

From her Masterson approach, Clark finds a role for interpretation of transference actings out, but her focus is on the function of safety rather than on what the defense covers up. She does not name and identify feelings for her patient but shows her how she, the patient, stops the verbal flow. Readers will appreciate her explicit examples of the language she uses to such ends. Her patient kept getting herself into painful and humiliating situations, but Clark persevered in interpretations of the wish for safety. It is, I would propose, as important to interpret the reparative intent as to interpret defenses. We could assume that, if the person knows what she is intending, she is in a better position to evaluate her own means of achieving it.

Even without history, and we do find some case reports among those in this book where history is meager, the person's way of relating to the therapist affords clues to probable qualities of experiences in earlier life. In Frank's chapter, we make the acquaintance of Terry, whose only way of telling his story was in action, language not yet being a tool of his ego. So he recreated his life scenario within the inpatient agency where he was being treated, prompting the environment to act as a disapproving parent. Drawing on transference clues, the sophisticated consultant could imaginatively construct a likely history—of this man's having had parents who did not talk with him about feelings or help him express them appropriately. The therapist, who had been making assumptions that Terry could reflect upon and control his behavior, had not clearly seen this developmental deficit. She now began to promote language and we see how she enabled her patient to attain some actual insight into his negative views of himself and even to understand the meaning of conflict! It is a case in which we see validation of hypotheses based on educated guess.

Although we no longer assume transference as distortion, in the beginning with some patients it may be manifest in states close to that. Whereas a "normal neurotic" can simultaneously *feel* a certain way toward the therapist and also recognize discrepancies between that feeling and the external reality of the other's attitudes and behavior, those who suffer borderline or psychotic states experience an equivalence between the internal feeling and the external fact. For example, Coker's paranoid schizophrenic man initially was an unwilling patient, sullen and hostile, employing highly sexualized terms with her. He was virtually appointing his would-be helper as enemy. She too had little history to fall back on, but inferred his needs from her knowledge of human development. She did not assume what was being called in the outpatient setting his noncompliance, and what some would call *resistance,* to be a reaction to her. In fact, she joined him in his resistance (perhaps feeling some of her own at treating a patient who began as he did). She saw his behavior as his way of protecting himself from anxieties and fears about close contact. Coker's ability gradually to engage him is such that he actually reclaims a capacity to feel love, and later to suffer profound grief when they must part.

In the days when transference was assumed, even in healthier persons, to be dangerous distortion, Coleman reminds us, social workers were advised to deal with it only as it pertained to outside persons, not to the here-and-now of the therapeutic relationship. Today we see each individual having developed her own theories, albeit mostly unconscious, out of life experiences as to what can be or cannot be expected of the other. Some patients are so exquisitely sensitive to us that they may sense certain reactions before we are consciously aware of them. Even a slight trace of an old familiar theme may be enough to resurrect strong feelings. So when we note that a client assumes that we will react with disgust, anger, or withdrawal, we first do some soul-searching to ascertain whether she may have detected signs of that in us. An example is offered by Frank, whose patient one day felt some remoteness in her. She responded by admitting some distraction, since to deny the patient's perceptions would have been doing her a disservice. But she kept a certain anonymity by not revealing the reasons, since these were not relevant for the patient's consideration and might well have felt a burden. Clearly, as the honest therapists writing here attest, we are human, and at times may find in our hearts affects that are not therapeutic. When we are also highly motivated by the basic ethic, we go off to a supervisor to see whether we can find a suitable place to express what has no place in the treatment sessions, and whether we can find ways to contain what could be a repetition of past pain for the patient. A good example of this is the therapist in the Chernus and Livingston chapter, whose capacities to "contain" were sorely tried by affects evoked by the mother who had murdered her own son. Her supervisor enables her to identify with the client's shame and anguish and to re-establish an empathic connection.

I have so far focused on transferences, but they cannot be fully understood without considering the countertransference of the therapist.

COUNTERTRANSFERENCE

There was a time when countertransference was defined as that which the therapist unconsciously carried over from her own past and projected upon the therapeutic encounter; it too was thought to be made up of distortions, to be a sign of her having been inadequately analyzed, not sufficiently acquainted with herself. It might be better, some of us think, for that to be called the therapist's transference. Certainly something of that system of beliefs construed from early life experience is quite likely present in all of us, no matter how thoroughly analyzed. An excellent analysis will not necessarily have eliminated this potential, but ideally it will have left us with the capacity for ongoing self-analysis. And indeed one of the advantages of being in this profession is that, in the course of pursuing the ethic, we put ourselves under obligation to exercise that capacity so long as we practice, and out of it comes both personal and professional growth and maturation.

Currently, with the attention being on the intersubjective domain, we are aware that the workings of what Matte-Blanco calls the *symmetrical* (as described by Steger) means that when we are intensely attuned to the patient, we may find in ourselves feelings that "belong" to that other. Steger's own illustration is of using this in her diagnostic thinking. She felt herself in a sort of "identicality" with her patient, beyond empathy, and out of this was convinced that Mrs. L. would not commit the horrendous abuse that she fantasied toward her infant daughter. We note however that, drawing also on ego psychology, she bolstered this intuitive clue with an observation that this patient never reported dissociative states. She did not just proceed on the basis of her deep resonance with her patient (the symmetrical) but supplemented this with a diagnostic perspective from theory (the asymmetrical). She saw Mrs. L. as loving her baby and wanting to be rid of the obsessive thoughts that she might harm her, a conclusion that probably also stemmed both from the therapist's internal feelings and from perceptions of the patient.

One of the ways we understand patients is via our own emotional reactions and responses. As Freud said, we lend our own unconscious like a receptive organ to the unconscious of the patient—descriptive perhaps more of communion than of communication. When we emerge from that state, we have the job of translating the experience into language, both to reassure ourselves of the validity of what we are making of the merger experience and to ascertain its significance for our interventions.

When Miller writes of her "immediate chemistry" with Annie, a black HIV-positive prostitute, we assume an instantaneous positive countertransference. Why does that sometimes happen, in spite of marked differences in the race, culture, life histories, and current ways of life of the two persons? Even Kohut recognized that when there are marked differences between therapist and patient, empathy may be harder to generate. Annie suffered from affect intolerance, from a deficient capacity for introspection, and she utilized a powerful defense of denial, all qualities promising to make her a most difficult patient. But her therapist could find her also charming, intelligent, and educable! More clearly than any of the other therapists in this book she deliberately employs educational measures along with psychodynamic treatment, and she does not hesitate at times to share her own feelings. She tells Annie that had she done what Annie had—slept with five men without use of protection, she would have been anxious, humiliated, lonely, scared, freaked out! It was a desperate attempt to generate in the patient the feelings she *should* feel. Annie rewards her by telling her, "My guts are moving with your rap!" And she rewards Annie by telling her that they have both learned something. We are tempted to posit, as some writers have about mothers and infants whose temperaments match, that Annie was like the good enough baby to this more than good enough therapist/mother. Miller astonished us in her facility with the street language of her patient, and we are moved deeply when Annie winds up using her therapist's words, even dialogue! If, as

Spitz (1964) hypothesized, all pathology can be understood as "derailment of dialogue," in this therapy it surely got re-railed.

Sometimes our countertransferences take on quite negative qualities in reaction to what the patient may be projecting on us. Clark's patient, for example, manifested transferences stemming from internalized representations of others who either savagely attacked and controlled her or ignored her when she reached out for connection. So she gave vent to explosive anger toward her therapist in her first therapy, and when she returned for further treatment Clark felt some fear and dread of the sessions. In the drama of transference and countertransference we see re-enactments of the patient's childhood, now with the roles reversed: Ruth the abuser, Clark the abused. With such dynamics the therapist has the difficult task of refraining from acting out herself. She is helped in containing possible reactions by several factors: she is glad that the patient has returned, for the second chance to deal with some unfinished tasks. Moreover, she is seeing the patient differently, either because Ruth presents patterns not quite like the original, or perhaps because Clark has herself in the meantime learned more.

Shechter is impressed with the resistance that can come from a certain kind of transference. From her classical perspective, she sees her patient, Maria, who is complaining of inability to find a man, as in an oedipal transference. Although seemingly asking help with this, she is simultaneously not talking about men to her therapist for long periods. One could have some negative countertransference feelings about being thus deprived of information, but Shechter turns to her theory for help, seeing herself through the patient's eyes as the oedipal mother, critical and competitive, from whom she must keep silent about her sexual interest in men. Later in the treatment the therapist becomes aware that the very pleasure the patient detected in her when she began seeing a man may have kept her in that relationship even when it began to seem not the one for her. Perhaps her identification with her woman patient led to this especially concordant countertransference. It is somewhat harder in face to face therapy to maintain that ideal version of neutrality, to manifest no personal investment in what the patient is doing or not doing but to enable her to plumb her own depths for data to guide ultimate decisions.

Even in brief treatment, the writers herein see value in attending both to concordant and complementary countertransferences—the former being identifications with the patient, and the latter being identifications with those in the person's life who seem to react in certain ways to him. Patients often are puzzled about why their friends or acquaintances behave toward them as they do. While it is rarely indicated that we share directly our complementary countertransference reactions with the patient, they do give us clues about the whys, and thus help us to formulate hypotheses for him to examine. We could wonder whether the sex and gender of therapist and of patient affect the general patterns of transference/countertransference.

SEX AND GENDER IN TRANSFERENCE AND COUNTERTRANSFERENCE

In the depths of the unconscious (Matte-Blanco's *symmetrical*) there is no discrimination between male and female. But the minds of therapist and of patient contain also the *asymmetrical*, that is, categories of thinking, feeling, and being that their respective cultures have decreed appropriate for a woman or a man. So at issue is the extent to which a therapist can imaginatively "regress" in such a way as to own both feminine and masculine aspects of self, and hence experience anything like that merger with the other out of which true empathy comes.

When Winnicott (1971) wrote of creativity, he found himself also discussing "male and female elements." He posited that each of us, regardless of sex, contains both, and that when they are dissociated from one another there are obstacles to creativity. It is probable that therapists like those in this volume, who deal with patients with the extensive deprivation and trauma seen in these cases, must be comfortable with the likely maternal transferences that will be aroused.

The two male writers herein who offer case reports, Coleman and Meyer, seem to me particularly at ease with what Winnicott describes as the female element, the experience of *being*, along with the male element of separateness. Coleman explicitly describes some of his work with Linda as *being with*, and, all in all, he appears undaunted by playing a motherly, supportive role. Meyer's patient, Sue, sexually abused by her father from the age of 2, and having had a mother felt to be ineffectual, needs re-parenting, especially re-mothering. Her therapist believes that the ideal treatment for those with failed human relationships is an enduring one that does not fail, and he certainly manifests the stamina and staying power of the very good mother. Although Applegate does not herein offer us a case, both he and Meyer are attracted to Winnicott's general philosophy and approach to therapy, which certainly emphasizes the maternal.

What of the female therapists herein, with their male patients? There is Frank's consultee with her patient, the sex offender Terry and his action orientation. In her countertransference before the consultation, the therapist was in danger of reacting with a punitive stance to his many provocations in the institution, that is, to be caught in a complementary countertransference, seeing him with a quality of "being not-me." Some of us have hypothesized that mothers generally, even in the so-called "lower" primates, have that sense of their male offspring as *not-me* (Shor and Sanville 1978), and that it makes for difficulties in male development that can be seen as more complicated than that for females. While the primary identification of both males and females is with mother, the boy child soon learns he must "dis-identify."

Chescheir's male patient manifests many longings to claim a female aspect of himself, including identifying with his wife's birthing experience, albeit also being frightened by that fantasy, perhaps lest he be feminized as was his injured father. His dreams demonstrate a split between his male and female aspects, and he is very little tuned in to inner life. One aspect of his transference is to see Chescheir as weak like his father, perhaps because she is minimally confrontive, not intrusive as his mother had been. She seems to contain whatever feelings she may have had about his projections, and he finds himself with a feeling of wanting to hold his father's hand, to be in touch with someone not tough but gentle. So, paradoxically, through a father transference to a woman, he begins to heal the split.

One of the patients about whom Austin writes is a male who complains of great anxiety and sexual dysfunction when with a woman. His own theory has been that he was sexually abused by his father, a theory that she neither confirms nor disconfirms. We do not know any details of her countertransference to him, only that she maintained sufficient neutrality about his theory that, as he took a fuller look at his developmental history, he discovered other factors to account for his symptoms, and he himself gave up his original notion.

Among her patients who were survivors of violence, Brunkow writes of Mr. B., who had been taken hostage in a foreign country at civil war.

In what we might regard as macho style, he at first denied that the experience had been traumatic. After what could seem a self-traumatization (Shor 1971), going to see a movie with guns in it, he had a dream of crying and crying, and his old girlfriend holding him and saying it was good that he could cry. He claimed not actually to have cried since he was 11, when his father died. So we assume the comforting woman is also the therapist. In contrast was a dream of authority figures, police, customs officials, who make one feel worthless. He admitted to having felt a certain bold omnipotence in crossing the dangerous border, and could experience some survivor guilt about that. Since he discussed that episode in the same interview with the story of his father's death, the therapist suspected oedipal guilt and inquired how he might have felt at assuming father's role. He recalled his brothers' jealousy, and his own fantasies that he could do anything. Brunkow's ability to thus imaginatively identify with the 11-year-old boy in her patient was, I suspect, her own ability to employ some regression to the symmetrical probably combined with her having assimilated oedipal theory (asymmetrical) into her responsiveness. So again we see theory as enhancing and extending empathy, even when the patient is *other*, male and not female.

There can be painful countertransferences for women, perhaps especially those who are mothers, working with young adult patients threatened with AIDS. Felberbaum describes therapy with two men, the first seen shortly after diagnosis of being HIV positive. With Larry, she became aware of fears of the dread disease and of death itself, and she was stunned to realize that the patient was the age of her own son. Sometimes there are aspects of our immediate personal lives that will exert impact upon our countertransferential feelings. Empathy demands a temporary abandonment of our boundaries, and when frightened, we may defend by maintaining a sense of difference from the patient, as by categorizing and stereotyping, which Felberbaum avoids. This man had, as in previous therapy, left without advance notice. Her hypothesis was that, having been abandoned by his father, he was "turning passive into active." But she also did the self-supervision that sophisticated clinicians attempt and realized that he had indeed warned her when he affirmed that she was different from his ex-therapist. She acknowledged the wish—perhaps present in us all in such circumstances—to be the better therapist, the better mother. She felt that, had she not been so busy fantasizing meeting Larry's old unmet needs, she might not have lost her patient. In that supercaretaking, we could guess that the countertransference was affected by some equating of Larry with her son. In the second case, that of Tom, she developed a very positive countertransference, admiring his creative flair, his sense of humor even about his plight. She knew that his humor was protecting them both, and she could indicate to him her awareness also of his desire to entertain her. Some separateness is as important as is empathy, but it may have a special role when we deal with patients toward whom we feel a lot of countertransference love, as did Felberbaum. Those of us who have lived with dying loved ones know the anguish we can suffer when the ill person turns to us in the vain hope that we, like the mother of infancy, could relieve the pain, take away the threat of non-being.

Countertransferences are complex when we see a couple, not just an individual patient, and especially so when the therapist is a woman and a pregnant one, working with two gay men, one of whom has AIDS. In her case report, we see Freedman sensitively using her specific concordant responses with each to understand the individual dynamics, her complementary responses to comprehend their problems with each other, and a combination of the two to see what is happening to their relationship. Her pregnancy lends special poignancy to the situation, exaggerating the otherness of therapist vis-à-vis both patients. She fears to hurt them by letting them know she is bringing to life while they are confronting death. Indeed Lenny, who had been an illegitimate baby, missed several weeks of sessions before the birth, but he then wanted to see a picture of the infant. And he somewhat remade his version of the past, reflecting on the difficulties for the 16-year-old who became his mother.

Coker's patient is a man, one suffering from schizophrenia. She needed to be particularly nurturing, to create the holding environment in which she could enable him to develop a workable, that is, positive transference. Her paper is about terminating with this patient, and we are moved by the sadness of both members of this dyad in their last hours together. Winnicottians might say that he emerged from his paranoid state into one characterized by the capacity for concern, or what the Kleinians call the depressive position. We find ourselves hoping with Coker that, when he sees the new therapist there will be something like a transference from a transference.

THE "WORKING" RELATIONSHIP: INTERPLAY OF TRANSFERENCE AND COUNTERTRANSFERENCE

Over the years, some analysts have declared that a necessary precondition for analysis was a certain amount of nurturing of the patient by the analyst, modeled after the original mother–child relationship. Others spoke of a *therapeutic alliance,* the analyst's role analogous to the parents' early caretaking of the infant in such a way as to establish basic trust and positive ego identification. A part of the process was thought to be the meeting of certain infantile needs, so that the mature aspects of the patient's personality could engage in transference regression. Such regression could then safely take place in the context of the analytic space, where the patient could suspend for the nonce something of his grown-up self with its array of character defenses, and its seemingly rational ways. The frame of the analytic situation marked off an area in which what transpired was tacitly acknowledged to be of a different nature than experiences in the outside world. It was, as Freud (1914) wrote, both real and artificial, actual and pretend. The analysand sensed this, and the regressive mode in which he could engage in sessions did not have to carry over to the rest of life. Although he probably did not think of his analysis as playful but as serious work, to do it—even to be accepted for analysis—he had to be capable of discerning the actual from the make-believe, of reflecting on the nature of psychic reality.

All of that was on the assumption that the patient had more or less successfully negotiated the earliest ages of life and was mainly beset by conflicts of the oedipal stage and their later derivatives. So there were voices advising that gratifications should be kept to a minimum, that it was deprivation and limitation which ultimately would render the transference neurosis possible. The therapeutic alliance, they averred, was between the analyst and the *healthy* part of the patient: empathy, caring, and compassion could be included in a scientific and objective attitude.

In the case stories told in this book, we see patients of many developmental levels, a few of whom manifest reflective and verbal capacities that suggest they might be able to use psychoanalysis itself, had they but the resources in money and time. Perhaps Edward's Mrs. Foster is one such, with her keen intelligence, fine sense of humor, sense of trust, capacity to reflect before acting, her psychological-mindedness. And indeed both therapist and patient worked very much in the analytic mode.

In many of the other stories, therapists feel it necessary and growth-promoting to modify details of conventional therapy–sometimes doing things for the patient, being flexible about the place and the time of session, educating.

For example, we encounter Coleman's patient, depressed, feeling worthless, considering suicide. He intervened with the social service system on her behalf, referred her to legal aid. But they also explored together the significance of these services, finding that she took them as evidence of his seeing her as worth helping.

Sometimes patients do not have the words to say what needs to be said. The therapist of Terry, in Frank's chapter, had to work on developing her client's use of language, help him to discern and manage feelings. Graziano experimented with giving her fragmented abuse survivor two-hour sessions, feeling this alexithymic woman's need to tell yet lacking the words for feelings. She let the patient choose the degree of physical closeness, even adding a small sofa to a room that had once only two chairs. She at times used physical touch, and, when asked by the patient, put an arm around her shoulder. She reassured, as when Eva overcame terror enough to talk, she said "There, you told me and you did not die!" The result of these responses by the therapist was an increase in trust so that the healing process could continue.

And in Frank's chapter, the therapist of the black adolescent girl who had witnessed the murders of her mother and brother takes walks with her on the city streets. Some of the dialogue that eventually enables the client to relinquish her belief that the bad things had happened because she herself was black, bad, and ugly took place in a scene away from the office. We could see Aronson's anorectic patient as creating also for herself a different space for connecting with her therapist–the telephone and the answering machine–and her therapist going along with that atypical mode, respecting Ms. K.'s compromise solution to her wish for, yet fear of intimacy–a conflict that seems often present in the patients reported herein.

In her work with drug addicts, Miller has designed a "psychoeducational-psychodynamic" approach, actually dividing the session into two parts, the first in which the patient narrates events and problems of daily life and the second dealing with what Annie calls "the heavy psychological shit." She too modifies the time span of a session: 60 minutes instead of the usual 50. Miller does succeed in instilling in this woman a previously nearly non-existent capacity for introspection and even a degree of psychological-mindedness. Certainly we experience an atmosphere of serious playfulness in their hours together.

In her chapter about the complications of working with the mothers of child patients, Siskind says she avoids educational methods, even with this mother who sees her children as "bad seeds," because of the likelihood they would fall on deaf ears. The mother's complaints include one about the time of her appointment, and the therapist responds by changing her hour by 15 minutes. This small "gratification" elicits some redoing of the initial transference, even catapulting the client into examining whether she had herself been offensive and eventually into introspection about her relationship with her children.

Weintraub shares with us the amazing tale of a woman whose own son had been removed and placed in a foster home because she could not handle him, and who was granted her request to become a foster mother. The caseworker made home visits, both prior to placing a baby there and while Mrs. K. was mothering the infant. The client made excellent use of what the author calls "environmental manipulation," and what some of us think deserves a more elegant term, maybe "implementing the client's image of repair." It allowed the patient to reclaim a sense of effectance or agency, to forgive herself for the past, to realize her reparative intent in the present.

In her work with AIDS patients, Felberbaum also made home visits and saw her patients in the hospital. She intervened with hospital personnel whom she saw as misunderstanding, interpreting Tom's behavior as manipulative. She reframed their negatives into a positive, enabling them to see the patient's urge to maintain some autonomy in spite of regressive pulls from outer and inner worlds. And she used guided imagery with Tom himself, gave him audio cassettes with her voice on them so he could use them as transitional objects for self-soothing when she was not present.

It is not exactly in the pure analytic mode to see both members of a couple, as did Freedman. But, as in that mode, the analytically oriented therapist stayed in touch with the transferences of both men to her and to each other, and with her reactive and responsive countertransferences. And, unlike many of the contemporary styles of conjoint therapy, she was not directing and manipulating their patterns but maintaining a respect for their inclinations, both individually and as a couple.

Coker's schizophrenic patient was forced to accept therapy as a condition of residing in a community-supported apartment. He was on medication, worked in a sheltered workshop, and so had ongoing contact with other professionals. She intervened for him, attempting to render the surround an "extended holding environment." She bore with his initial troubles with time, his being unable to stay more than 10 or 15 minutes, and later being unable to leave after 50 minutes. Toward the end, she accepts his gift of a cup of coffee, seeing it as evidence of his new capacity to love other than himself and to enjoy a sense of reciprocity.

Meyer too makes much of time, the sheer time needed to make a working alliance with such a frightened woman–some six months before she could even tell him of her sexual abuse by an alcoholic father. With such a patient, Meyer believes, there are no alternatives to very long-term treatment. Although there was evidence of growth, in that she became able to give words to her feelings, she also at times regressed so malignantly that she needed hospitalization.

In the case of the filicidal mother, presented by Chernus and Livingston, we have, as with Coker, a therapist leaving the agency, albeit in this instance she could invite the patient to go with her to her private practice. This seemed important therapeutically, since the patient might otherwise assume she was being abandoned, as she felt by the rest of the social world, for what she had confessed.

In all instances the permutations were introduced as aspects of a facilitating relationship. Often, if treatment were to procede at all, the patient had to be helped to develop at least some of those attributes already possessed by Edward's Mrs. Foster, and the how of that was dependent upon negotiations between therapist and patient in each instance.

SUMMARY: A PHILOSOPHY OF TREATMENT

Although, as we have noted, the therapist/writers herein do not all embrace the same school of psychoanalytic thought, there seem to this reader to be some commonalities in how they view treatment.

They nearly all rely on a developmental view in their assessment of their patients, and they draw upon psychoanalytic theory and on the burgeoning research, particularly into the very earliest stages of life. Very few of them seem to have much time for the *DSM-III* or *-IV*, and this to some of us is promising. There is an ever-present danger when we have labeled a patient that we may tend to keep looking for what confirms that designation, perhaps not perceiving the ways he/she does not quite fit the category. And we may discourage ourselves by the knowledge that some labels describe the difficult (if not impossible) to treat.

When they have sufficiently verbal persons with whom to work, therapists may hear narratives of the patient's life to date. They seem not to "take a history" as some of us were once trained to do. They do not, I think, assume the stories that the patient proffers to be objective reporting of facts, for they know that human beings perceive their experiences through the eyes of the personal "theories" they have at the time, and to see that these are mutable is to be aware of areas where change might occur. With further development, the stories may be altered, the past seen differently. So the tales are heard as clues to the patterns of thinking of the patient now.

Sometimes, with clients who lack the words to describe events and the emotions connected with them, therapists must make educated guesses on the basis of the action patterns that are manifested. Or they read the transference clues to comprehend the ways in which the person seems to interpret the other and the relationship. They also attend to their own countertransferences, and when they find no idiosyncratic reasons of their own to explain them, they explore the possibility that they are clues to what the patient is experiencing, now projected onto the therapist. They are conscientious about their own feelings, discerning differences, as I would describe it, between *reactions* (close to an involuntary action level) and *responses* (tempered by sensitivity to the other). When they find themselves with a predominance of the former, they tend to turn to supervision, and sometimes to some psychoanalytic therapy for themselves. They believe that it is not only the patient who sometimes behaves unconsciously.

Assessment is not seen as a process only at the beginning, but a continuing one. It is as essential to observe nuances of change as to observe continuities. To do otherwise risks our reinforcing the person's own inner obstacles to try on the new. Although these therapists notice *resistances,* these are not taken as resistances to them, but as the consequence of natural apprehension about abandoning a way of seeing things that is closely connected with a sense of self. Not until alteration of old patterns feels relatively safe should one rush to make them, and they see patients as making their own assessments as to when that safety can be assumed. Meanwhile, they attempt to provide a "holding environment," an ambiance in which the patient can feel supported in facing difficult and often painful aspects of self or of situation.

There is, all together, evidence in these stories of therapists' profound respect for their patients, even when the latter give them a very hard time. In the old social work terms, they "start where the patient is," and they stay close to that throughout. This does not prevent their alertness to the possibilities of fortifying the patient who is on the threshold of trying out a new way of thinking, feeling or being. But they certainly show themselves valuing and deferring to the patient's right to self-determination, his or her view of what would be helpful.

Being particularly interested in the reparative intent (Sanville 1991), I looked for signs in each story that the therapist took notice of that, whether or not they gave it a name. And there was much to suggest that they did. In the few cases in which an involuntary patient was involved, the relationship freed that ubiquitous wish to make things better. That wish/intent is the healthy part of the personality, our main ally in the treatment process. They also attended to the strengths and assets in their clients as much as to the problems and disabilities. So their mirroring, amounting at times to spontaneous admiration, could afford the patients a fresh look at themselves.

Often the gains made are seen as the result of the patient's experience of the *new relationship*, sometimes almost without explicit interpretation, sometimes combined with it. When *interpretation* is employed, we have the impression that it is not "made" by the therapist so much as it is constructed jointly by the two participants. So the patient is afforded an opportunity to reclaim an often lost sense of agency, the power of being able to intend and to carry out intentions.

We have the impression of a group of professionals who find pleasure in the ideas with which they work, and enjoy what they are doing. They learn from and with their patients. I tend to believe that if we do not grow in the course of treatment with a patient, it is unlikely that he/she will, either. I finished each chapter with a sense that not only the client but the clinician had grown and developed.

The goal of therapy is not seen as cure, as in the medical model. Instead it is to remove obstacles to on-going development, so that the person becomes able to take more charge of life in the future.

This is, as Saari writes, more a hermeneutic model, emphasizing meanings and narrative construction. Each narrative creates an individual story, context-dependent, not necessarily generalizable. So, psychoanalysis in recent years has not found much place in the academic world, the preferences there being for behaviorism and cognitive sciences, more easily quantifiable by research. She holds out some hope for a reintroduciton of psychodynamic content, in view of certain changing contexts in academia, especially the contributions of the analytically oriented researchers who are looking at the earliest stages of human life and seeing the crucial role of the interpersonal and the intersubjective in giving shape to the intrapsychic. It should not be hard to show the relevance of what they are describing for the societies and cultures in which we develop and live, as they are the contexts for all human development, whether benign or pathological.

Infant observation and research is demonstrating the serious role of playfulness in human life. Equipped with that knowledge, we may be better able to generate societal contexts that can afford more playgrounds in which creativity can flourish.

REFERENCES

Brenner, C. (1955). *An Elementary Textbook of Psychoanalysis*. New York: International Universities Press.

Freud, S. (1914). Remembering, repeating and working through. *Standard Edition* 12:143–153.

Knight, R. P. (1946). Determinism, 'freedom' and psychotherapy. *Psychiatry* 9:251–262.

Reik, T. (1937). *Surprise and the Psychoanalyst: On the Conjecture and Comprehension of Unconscious Processes*. New York: Dutton.

Sanville, J. (1991). *The Playground of Psychoanalytic Therapy*. Hillsdale, NJ: Analytic Press.

Shor, J. (1972). Two principles of reparative regression: self traumatization and self-provocation. *Psychoanalytic Review* 59 (2):259– 281.

Shor, J., and Sanville, J. (1978). *Illusion in Loving: A Psychoanalytic Approach to the Evolution of Intimacy and Autonomy*. New York: International Universities Press, Penguin Paperback, 1979.

Spitz, R. A. (1964). The derailment of dialogue. *Journal of the American Psychoanalytic Association* 12:752–755.

Winnicott, D. W. (1971). *Playing and Reality*. New York: Basic Books.

Glossary

Patsy Turrini

This glossary is made available for the convenience of the reader and is drawn from definitions that appear in the general analytic literature, psychoanalytic glossaries, and from those provided by the authors in this volume. For more complete definitions of these terms the reader is advised to consult the original sources. It is important to note that different theorists define psychoanalytic terms differently. We have tried to offer definitions that seem in keeping with our authors' use of the terms defined.

Acting out: Acting out occurs when an individual expresses through action rather than words a memory, an attitude, or a conflict. Acting out refers to behavior motivated by unconscious object-related fantasies (psychic content) that the ego has repressed (Blanck and Blanck 1974, Felberbaum, this volume, Moore and Fine 1990).

Action: A state or process of acting or doing; movement; the discharge of an impetus along motor pathways. The first interchanges between infant and mother take place in what Spitz (1965) has called *transactions*. In later life, however, if language development is inadequate, that can lead to the ego having minimal capacity to delay, to use words to channel affects and other psychic content. Action can offer clues to preverbal experience. Action is distinguished from acting out in that the latter is a reflection of some form of defense, while action may or may not have particular psychic content. (Blanck and Blanck 1974, Frank, this volume).

Affect attunement: The intersubjective sharing of feeling states between mother and infant, via non-verbal clues which express a wide range of affects (Miller, this volume, Stern 1985).

Alexithymia: Having no words for emotions or capability of distinguishing one emotion from another (Graziano, this volume, Krystal 1978, Sifneos 1967).

Affect differentiation: The capacity to identify, name, and discriminate different emotions so they may be brought under the control of the ego. When the patient is unable to do this, special therapeutic measures can be undertaken to provide the person with this ability (Blanck and Blanck 1974, Frank, this volume).

Affect intolerance: Emotions and feelings are felt to be too painful and/or shameful for the individual to bear.

Alterity: Otherness or difference. Since one cannot become self without the other, in the dialogue of psychotherapy both empathy and alterity will play a role (Sanville 1987).

Ambivalence: The simultaneous presence of contradictory tendencies and feelings in the relationship to a single object (Steger, this volume).

Anaclitic transference: The therapist is related to by the patient primarily as a caretaker, as someone to respond to needs and to provide protection (Freud 1914).

Assimilation: A mental activity whereby an external situation is so perceived or handled that it can be dealt with by an existing schema. For example, when the child has learned to move a rattle that is hung before it and then applies this motor action to a suspended doll, this generalization is an act of assimilation (Spitz 1965). As used by Paris and Lindauer, remembering requires assimilating, that is comprehending and encoding. The experience must be perceived and interpreted to make sense, and new features may be added to make the event comprehensible (Paris and Lindauer 1977, Steger, this volume).

Association: An idea that is linked to other ideas in a chain of thoughts indicating that it is relevant to the theme or dream in a session even though it may not appear to have a logical connection (Steger, this volume).

Asymmetrical thinking: Normal, everyday logical thinking that deals with things which may be distinguished from one another and with the relationship between such things (Matte-Blanco 1988, Steger, this volume).

Autonomy (autonomous self): The sense of being self governing. The individual's capacity to experience herself/himself as owner of her/his interest and unique personality, and to express this ownership in a variety of contexts, many of which involve relating to other people (Clark, this volume).

Average expectable environment: A concept designated by Hartmann that refers to the environment into which the child is born. First is the mother and the maternal care she gives the infant. Behind the mother is the father, the concept of the family, the entire social structure, and the generational cultural continuity. The infant born with innate potentials interacts with the average expectable environment (Edward et al. 1991, Hartmann 1939).

Basic fault: According to Michael Balint, this level is characterized by a two-person, more primitive relationship than that associated with the oedipal level. The patient's experience in this state is not that of conflict but of frustration and lack of attunement in the object, which in turn leads to severe symptoms. At this level, adult language is often useless or misleading in describing events because words do not always possess an agreed-upon conventional meaning. Balint compares this term to its use in geology and crystallography where the word *fault* is used to describe a sudden irregularity in the overall structure, an irregularity that in normal circumstances might lie hidden but, if strains and stresses occur, may lead to a break, profoundly disrupting to the overall structure (Balint 1968, Freedman, this volume).

Bi-logic: A form of thinking that combines asymmetrical thinking and symmetrical thinking but breaks the bounds of normal asymmetrical thinking, which always includes some symmetrical thinking–as in generalizations. This form of thinking ranges from poetry and emotional thinking to irrational or psychotic thinking, depending upon the nature of the combination of asymmetry and symmetry (Matte-Blanco 1988, Steger, this volume).

Bivalent thinking: A form of thinking that is considered scientific and in which the rules of classical Aristotelian logic are followed (Steger, this volume).

Capacity for holding: The therapist's capacity to listen, provide support, and convey a sense of safety through a patient's emotional crisis (Chescheir, this volume).

Centered holding: The ability of the therapist to contain the intense and intricate series of projective identifications of the individual couple (Freedman, this volume).

Compromise formation: An unconscious wish (repressed idea) is distorted by defense to the point of being unrecognizable. The entity, or compromise, that occurs is then permitted into consciousness as a symptom, a dream, a feeling or an action (Steger, this volume). An attempt at solving conflict between the psychic agencies and the outside world, by providing some acceptable degree of expression for the demands of each of the psychic agencies (id, ego, superego) as well as the demands of external reality (Moore and Fine 1990). For example, a person wishes to make a mess (an id impulse), which is unacceptable to the demands of the superego and the expectations of the outside world. Through a floor-cleaning compulsion the ego institutes a defense, reaction formation, which in disguised form allows the individual to be involved in the dirt. Such formations may take various forms: fantasies, symptoms, dreams, character traits, feelings or actions.

Condensation: A single idea represents several associative chains. In Freudian theory, the idea, represented as a condensation, has all of the energy that comes from the many different chains of associations which it represents (Steger, this volume).

Conflict: A struggle or clash of seemingly incompatible forces or structures. There can be intrasystemic conflict (within a given structure, ego, id, superego) or intersystemic conflict (between structures), or conflict with the outside world. An example of the former would be when different demands of the superego are in conflict (i.e., the child whose parents teach him to be honest but who he finds are not themselves honest, creating a conflict between two superego identifications). An example of the latter would be when what one wishes to do is in conflict with what one's conscience approves. Conflict is manifest in such observable phenomena as symptoms, actions, thought, and characters. Present theory sees the formation of conflict in terms of a sequence; instinctual wishes come into conflict with internal or external prohibitions. The ego is threatened and produces anxiety, which serves as a signal. Defenses are instituted and the conflict is then resolved by way of compromise formation and expressed through symptoms, character changes, or adaptive efforts (Moore and Fine 1990).

Constructivism: Underlying a constructivist approach is our understanding that there is no ultimate objective truth, that each person interprets experience in terms of his/her background, cultural and personal. In the therapeutic situation, each of the two participants will have different perspectives on the issues under discussion, and meanings will be negotiated together (Coleman, this volume), social constructionist perspective (Applegate, this volume).

Containment: Infants at times feel self-cohesion to be threatened by strong negative emotions; when the mother can "metabolize" those feelings–demonstrate by her own responses a reassurance that fragmentation will not result–the baby's own sense of being able to manage painful feelings is strengthened. Something analogous to that containment occurs between patient and therapist (Bion 1967, Freedman, this volume); a process essential in helping patients manage anxiety and intolerable physical or emotional pain (Chescheir, this volume).

Contextual holding: Refers to the secure environment of the frame of therapy, its consistency, and its offering of hope (Freedman, this volume, Scharff and Scharff 1971).

Contextual transference and countertransference: The major anxiety and content of both therapist and patient is concern over whether or not the therapist can hold the couple together (Freedman, this volume, Scharff 1991).

Countertransference: This refers to the therapist's own conscious or unconscious reactions to the patient. These may be derived from earlier situations in the therapist's life that have been displaced onto the patient (Moore and Fine 1990). They may be unconsciously evoked by the patient and as such become an important tool for learning about the patient (Frank, this volume). Casement (1990) has referred to such responses as *diagnostic responses* (Edward, this volume).

Defense: An unconscious mechanism designed to temper internal excitation (reflected in memories, affects, or fantasies) and maintain psychic equilibrium. Some well-known defenses are repression, reaction formation, denial, isolation of affect, negation, and intellectualization (Steger, this volume).

Depersonalization: A change in the perception of the self, whereby the usual sense of one's reality is temporarily lost or altered. One's perception of oneself is split into a detached observing self and a participating or experiencing self. There occurs a feeling of self estrangement or unreality about the latter (Graziano, this volume, Moore and Fine 1990).

Depressive position: With the recognition that the mother is a whole object and the source of both good and bad, the child begins to fear that his or her own aggressive impulses may destroy the object, now seen as needed, important and loved. The principal concern in the depressive position is for the object and its welfare (Klein 1940, Moore and Fine 1990). The predominant fear is the loss of the object. The major anxiety is the possibility of injuring the object. There is a desire to establish reparation to the injured object as well as a mourning of the imperfection of the parent. The projection of a fantasized ideal onto the object may be prevalent in this position (Freedman, this volume).

Developmental theory: According to the developmental point of view, a person, regardless of age, is in the process of development throughout the life cycle, as opposed to being only in possession of a past that influences his present conscious and unconscious life (Shane 1977).

Displacement: An idea's emphasis, interest, or intensity is detached from it and passed on to other ideas, originally of little intensity. In Freudian theory, the energy from the original idea has been detached and runs along associative pathways until it finds the new, or displaced, idea (Steger, this volume). The interest or intensity (cathexis) attached to one idea is shifted to another idea that is associatively related but is more acceptable to the ego (Moore and Fine 1990).

Ego-dystonic: When drives, affects, ideas, or behavior are experienced by the observing ego as foreign to the self they are termed ego-dystonic, or ego-alien (Moore and Fine 1990). When the therapist helps the person view an aspect of the self that is favored by the person but is detrimental to him or her, as unacceptable, we refer to this as rendering it ego-dystonic (Felberbaum, this volume).

Ego psychology: A psychoanalytic theory which concerns itself primarily with the ego and its relation to the other agencies of psychic structure, the id and the superego. The study of the ego includes the study of defenses, adaptation to reality, self and object representations, affects, and primitive ego states (Steger, this volume).

Ego-relatedness: One of the functions of the ego, an inborn propensity toward and ability for connectedness, rendering possible the important early relationship between mother and infant. The introduction of this concept into psychoanalysis makes for basic changes from the original idea of a "driven" infant. Some analysts see more evidence for "ego instincts" than for "id instincts" (Stern 1985). In therapy with adults, they regard ego-relatedness as facilitating a working and a playing relationship (Winnicott 1956, Applegate, this volume).

Empathy: Refers to a mode of perceiving by vicariously experiencing the psychological state of another person (Moore and Fine 1990).

Dynamic theory: Refers to the existence and interactions of psychological "forces" within the mind and the pressure of the instinctual drives and restraining influences (Moore and Fine 1990, Strean, this volume).

Economic theory: Refers to the disposition of psychological energy within the mental apparatus. Concerned with matters of excitation, discharge, and/or restraint. (Moore and Fine 1990, Strean, this volume).

Evenly suspended attention: A way of attending to the patient that calls for the avoidance of directing one's focus to anything in particular and instead remaining open to all that the patient does and says (Edward, this volume, Freud 1912).

False memories: A memory produced by suggestion that in reality is not true, but is believed to be true (Austin, this volume, Loftus 1992, Loftus and Ketchem 1991).

False self: A self developed in compliance to please the caregivers that appears real but hides the true self (Moore and Fine 1991).

False defensive self: a way of relating that appears acceptable to others; the genuine self is not expressed (Clark, this volume).

Fixation (fixation points): The continuation of early modes of achieving satisfaction, relating to objects, and/or reacting defensively to danger, as if modes of functioning associated with particular earlier stages of development have remained as they were in the psyche, ready to play a role in a later situation (Moore and Fine 1990); repressed memories that are invested with energy and constitute the vestigial remains of early trauma (Shechter, this volume).

Fragmentation: A sensed loss of cohesiveness of the self, leading to fear of regression or disintegration from which there may be no return (Winnicott 1952). The intellect may begin to operate as though it were distinct from the psyche (Winnicott 1949). There can be dread of estrangment of mind from body and a sense of loss of continuity in time (Graziano, this volume, Kohut 1977).

Fundamental rule: The patient is asked to express thoughts, feelings, wishes sensations, images, and memories, without reservation (Edward, this volume, Moore and Fine 1990).

Genetic theory: Theory about the origins and development of human beings from infancy through all ages. Psychoanalysis holds that one cannot understand an adult without some comprehension of the history of earlier stages of life (Moore and Fine 1990, Strean, this volume). In recent years, this theory has been supplemented with *epigenetic* theory, since it is clear that decisions and actions at later stages will also influence outcome.

Good enough mother: Refers to a mother who offers her infant an optimal amount of constancy, comfort, attunement, and care in accordance with the infant's needs (Applegate, this volume, Moore and Fine 1990, Winnicott 1965).

Healthy Narcissism (sound secondary narcissism): Healthy self regard, an affective state in which the self representation is invested with positive value (Blanck and Blanck 1979, Weintraub, this volume).

Hermeneutics: The science and methodology of interpretation (American Heritage Dictionary, 3rd. ed., Saari, this volume).

Holding environment: A metaphor derived by Winnicott from the literal holding of baby by mother, her presence felt by her offspring as available, reliable, consistent, empathic. He later uses the term to describe the importance of the same qualities in the therapist enabling the patient to feel safe and secure in this adult relationship. A holding environment can include not only the parental relationship, the home, the immediate and the extended family, but also the community with its protective services, and the country with its laws and provision for its citizens (Applegate, this volume, Austin, this volume, Meyer this volume, Winnicott 1971).

Holding: Denotes the actual physical holding of the infant as well as the total environmental provision. In the clinical situation it refers to psychological holding so that safety is experienced, and also to therapeutic help in managing experiences that are inherent in the process. Provision of context in which changes can take place (Chescheir, this volume).

Holding phase: A period where the mother and infant are experienced as one (one might think of a cocoon in connection with this), even though there may be some illusion of self-sufficiency. The infant is dependent on the caretaking functions of the mother (Chescheir, this volume).

Imaging: The inferred mental activity of the child who in the absence of the mother turns inward in an effort to hold on to a state of mind associated with the internal and physically experienced sensation of dual unity (oneness) with mother (Edward et al. 1992, Felberbaum, this volume, Kaplan 1978, Mahler 1979).

Interpretation: The evolving meaning that patient and therapist discover of the patient's patterns thoughts and emotions (Chescheir, this volume); what the analyst expresses in words that has come to be understood about the patient's mental life (Moore and Fine 1990).

Intersubjectivity: A concept that refers to an interaction between the psychic reality of two people in interaction (Stolorow and Atwood 1987); a term that emphasizes the reciprocal influence of the conscious and unconscious idiosyncratic aspects of two people in a relationship. The transference and countertransference are understood as contributed to by both participants and shaped by one another (Frank, this volume, Natterson and Friedman 1995).

Intersubjective knowing: Interpretations are open to correction and revision; understanding and meaning grow out of the shared experience and ideas are not imposed (Chescheir, this volume).

Introjection: A means by which aspects of the external world and interactions with it are taken into the individual and represented in its internal structure. Through introjection part properties and functions of the object, though not fully integrated into a cohesive and effective sense of self, do become part of the self-representation or of the mental structures, ego, superego, or ego ideal (Moore and Fine 1990).

Love (adult): The constant search for the completion of or complement of the self through the blending of internalized self- and object-representations within the interpersonal field (Freedman, this volume).

Limbic structures: These are a group of structures in the brain, including the hippocampus, cingulate gyrus, and amygdala, that are connected to and normally controlled by other parts of the brain (e.g., hypothalamus); the system is associated with emotions and feelings such as anger, fear, and sexual arousal (Austin, this volume, Dictionary of Medical Terms, Rothenberg and Chapman 1989).

Mirroring interactions: When the baby looks at the mother's face, what is seen is him- or herself (Chescheir, this volume, Winnicott 1971).

Memory: A function of the mental apparatus which makes it possible for impressions once perceived or learned to be retained and reproduced (Austin, this volume, Moore and Fine 1990).

Mirroring selfobjects: Objects (other persons who) accept and confirm the grandness, goodness and wholeness of the self. (Chernus and Livingston, this volume, Kohut 1971, Moore and Fine 1990).

Multiple determination (*principle of multiple function*): A construct that states a psychic event or aspect of behavior may be caused by more than one factor and serve more than one purpose in the psychic life (Edward, this volume, Moore and Fine 1990, Waelder 1936).

Narcissistic transference: The need to relate to the therapist as a part of or complement to the self (Edward, this volume, Freud 1914).

Negation: A defense mechanism by which a person disowns a formerly repressed wish and thus defends himself against acknowledging it as his or her own (Steger, this volume).

Neutrality: The therapist keeps his or her feelings in check, avoids imposing values, judgments, or desires and maintains respect for the patient's wishes and capacities (Edward, this volume, Freud 1911–1915).

Object relations: A term that refers to the relating of object-representations within the mind (Moore and Find 1991).

Object relations theory: A system of psychological explanations based on the premise that the mind is comprised of elements taken in from the outside, primarily aspects of the functioning of other persons. This model of the mind explains mental functions in terms of relations between the various elements internalized (Moore and Fine 1991). The mind is understood as being formed primarily as a result of intricate processes of internalization derived from ongoing interactional patterns. The emphasis in object relations theory is on how internal object-representations are sculpted and how they intermingle within the psyche, forming the self out of the exchange (Freedman, this volume, Mitchell 1988). A psychoanalytic theory which concerns itself with a person's unconscious internal relationship with more or less fantasied objects. The fantasies refer to specific pregenital developmental stages during which phase specific instincts or aims color the apperception of important objects (Steger, this volume).

Object-representation: An enduring schema of a particular person, other than the self, modeled by the ego from a multitude of impressions, images, and experiences with that person (Moore and Fine 1968).

Object use: According to Winnicott, there is a world of difference between relating to and using an object. When one relates to an object, the object is felt to be meaningful, but projective mechanisms and identifications are operative; that is, something of the subject is found in the object. To be able to *use* an object the other must be seen as a person separate from the self, not composed of projections. One can *relate* to a subjective object, but to use that other, the object has to be experienced as part of external reality (Applegate, this volume, Winnicott 1971).

Obsession: A mode of thinking characterized by ruminations, doubt, and scruples and which leads to inhibitions of thought and action (Steger, this volume).

Oedipus complex: A characteristic constellation (in both sexes) of instinctual drives, aims, object relations, fears, and identifications, manifest at the height of the phallic phase (2½ to 6 years), and persisting as an unconscious organizer through life. During the phallic period the child strives for a sexual union (conceived variously according to the child's cognitive capacities) with the parent of the opposite sex and with wishes for the death or disappearance of the parent of the same sex. The negative Oedipus coexists along side of the positive Oedipus such that the child wishes to unite sexually with the parent of the same sex, with wishes of death and disappearance for the parent of the opposite sex (Moore and Fine 1990, Schecter, this volume).

Certain analysts have been rethinking the oedipal myth and its significance for practice today. Among them are those who emphasize the intended filicide as much as the parricide in the tale and point out that Oedipus was middle-aged when we meet him, and that his troubles are not reducible to incestuous impulses but more attributable to his frustrated wish for ontological well-being in a world of careless caretakers, where he has had to search for truth among many lies (Ross 1995). We are also reminded that while Freud applied the Oedipus myth to the normal family, Oedipus was the child of parents who abandoned him, of a destructive father and of a mother who complied with her husband's plan to destroy their offspring (G. Blanck 1984).

Oedipal introject (*unconscious fantasy*): The mother or father for whom sexual strivings must be hidden (Schecter, this volume).

Mother of the oedipal Phase: The mother perceived of as critical and competitive, the result of the projection from the superego (Schecter, this volume).

Optimal distance: A description of the toddler's choice of that distance from the mother (physical distance) from which that child could function best (Edward et al. 1991, Mahler 1975); a safe distance between the self and object that is believed to prevent destruction (Clark, this volume).

Orbiting (*orbiting compromise*): a form of relating (both being there and not being there) in order to preserve the ties to the object, maintain safety, and prevent destruction (Clark, this volume).

Paranoid-schizoid position: The young infant projects love and hate onto the mother's breast, splitting it into a good gratifying, and a bad frustrating, object. The good object is perceived as capable of offering unlimited gratification and is thus idealized. As a result of the projected badness on the frustrating object, the infant fears being destroyed by the bad object. This position is therefore characterized by persecutory anxiety (Klein 1940, Moore and Fine 1990).

An internal sense of isolation, powerlessness, persecution and envy characterizes the paranoid–schizoid position in adult life (Freedman, this volume).

Phylogeny: The evolutionary development and history of a species or higher taxonomic grouping of organisms, as contrasted with ontogeny (the origin and development of an individual organism from embryo to adult (American Heritage, 3rd. ed).

Post-traumatic syndrome (*traumatic neurosis*): A specific form of neurosis resulting from exposure to the threat or actual experience of severe physical or psychic trauma (that is, intense and sudden stress) (Moore and Fine 1990). "The essential feature of Post-traumatic Stress Disorder is the development of characteristic symptoms following exposure to an extreme traumatic stressor involving direct personal experience of an event that involves actual or threatened death or serious injury, or other threat to one's physical integrity; or witnessing an event that involves death, injury, or a threat to the physical integrity of another person; or learning about unexpected or violent death, serious harm, or threat of death or injury experienced by a family member or other close association" (*DSM-IV*, p. 424).

Primary Process: A form of thinking that is characterized by a freely flowing psychical energy, passing unhindered by means of the mechanisms of condensation and displacement and able in ever new ways to reattach to the ideas rooted in primitive satisfying experiences (Sisson, this volume), a type of mental functioning characterized by specific patterns and organization. It is represented in wish fulfillments in images, symbols, specific memories, and sense impressions. It has distinct patterns: things that look alike are alike; things that sound alike are alike; ideas are represented by one another; and by their opposites (Edward et al. 1991).

Projective identification: Klein, who originated this term, defined it as a rudimentary process by which the infant attempts to deal with transient episodes of hunger and thirst by splitting off rageful reactions and projecting them into mother (Klein 1946). In its broadest terms, projective identification is the expression of painful or idealized states of the self placed in another, reenacted or modified by the other, and reprocessed by the self (Freedman, this volume).

Projective identification in its primitive form is thought of primarily as a necessary defense that initially serves to rid the person of internal threats. It involves the projection of parts of the self onto the object. The object is then misperceived as if it were the self, and the object acts out the projected parts of the self (Freedman, this volume, Segal, 1964). In its most developed form it is associated with the capacity to experience empathy. Empathy, the highest level of projective identification, is the ability to loosen well-established boundaries in an attempt to discover a "resonance" of the self in the other for shared understanding and support (Freedman, this volume).

Psychic reality: Because reality is never perceived directly but always through the psyche of the perceiver with its wishes, fears, and fantasies, Freud called this *inner reality*. In addition to external reality, this inner reality also influences perception and behavior. Since people often have a sense of conviction about their own perçeptions, they experience resistance when therapy raises doubts about the reliability of those perceptions.

Representations: Representations are constructed out of a multitude of impressions and constitute a more or less enduring existence as an organization or schema, (Sandler and Rosenblatt 1962); aggregates of images and experiences that date back to infancy (Siskind, this volume).

Representational world: The perceptual or inner world includes images and organizations of a person's internal and external environment. The construction of a representational world is one of the functions of the ego. It provides the "furniture" for the ego function of thinking (Sandler and Rosenblatt 1962).

Repetition compulsion: Recognized clinically as pressure on the part of certain individuals to repeat distressing, even painful situations during the course of their lives without recognizing the relationship of the current situations to the past or their own participation in bringing about such incidents of the relationship of current situations to past experiences (Moore and Fine 1991). Seen as an expression of unconscious hope, as an attempt, albeit unsuccessful, to solve past unconscious conflicts. (Casement 1991, Felberbaum, this volume). A convergence of psychic force which leads to the reenactment of past life scenarios (formed in the earliest period of development) in the present (Frank, this volume).

Repression: A defense mechanism whereby certain unacceptable thoughts, images and memories are repelled or confined to the unconscious (Steger, this volume).

Resistance: A special instance of the ego's efforts at defense. It is encountered regularly in the course of treatment. When treatment threatens to bring into awareness unacceptable wishes, fantasies, or impulses that would produce pain, the ego defends against this by opposing the treatment itself. (Moore and Fine 1991); The concept of resistance moves from being seated in the client to being a limit on the shared understanding possible between the therapist and the client (Coleman, this volume).

Schizoid disorder: The world schizoid refers to a defensive tendency to retreat from interpersonal reality to an inner world of objects (Moore and Fine 1990). The disorder is characterized by a defect in the capacity to form social relationships, evidenced by the absence of warm, tender feelings for others and an indifference to praise, criticism, and the feelings of others. It is a personality structure in which feelings, needs, and wishes, whether for autonomy or for connectedness, are anticipated as having disastrous consequences, associated with profound feelings of detachment and emptiness (Clark, this volume).

Secondary process: The logical, orderly, and primarily verbal thinking that dominates ordinary conscious mentation. In such thinking the reality principle is the main frame of reference. A form of thinking in which energy flows in a controlled manner. Ideas remain stable and repeatable and satisfaction is postponed. It is a form of thinking in which mental experiments test different paths leading to satisfaction (Steger, this volume).

Separation-Individuation phases:

Differentiation: This term is synonymous in Mahler's metaphorical language with "hatching from the mother–infant symbiotic common orbit" (Mahler 1972, p. 122).

Practicing: Characterized by the infant's beginning ability to move away physically from the mother by crawling, climbing, and righting himself, while still holding on. The practicing phase proper is characterized by free, upright locomotion. This is accompanied by an exhilarated mood, and the toddler is described as experiencing a "love affair with the world."

Rapprochement: As the toddler makes greater use of maturing physcial and cognitive abilities and becomes more aware of his or her physical separateness, there is a waning of an earlier imperviousness to frustration as well as a relative obliviousness to the mother's presence during the previous period. This is accompanied by an increase in separation anxiety and a fear of object loss. Now the toddler actively approaches the mother. The events of this phase often culminate in a more or less transient crisis.

Rapprochement crisis: The realization of separateness becomes acute. The child wants to be both separate from and united with the mother (ambitendency). Temper tantrums, whining, sad moods, and intense separation reactions are common during this period.

On-the-way to object and self constancy: The last of the four subphases is an open-ended phase, characterized by a unification of the good and bad object and self-images into differentiated, unified, predominantly positive object and self representations. Now the positive, cohesive inner representation of the mother can be retained, regardless of her presence or absence and irrespective of the child's need of her. A positive, cohesive self-representation also begins to form and remains more or less continuous in time and space despite alterations in the surround or in the intrapsychic world (Mahler et al. 1975, Siskind, this volume).

Screen memory: A memory that conceals other memories and their associated affects or drives. The screen memory is often a rigidly fixed, seemingly unimportant recollection of an affectively charged, traumatic early childhood experience. It represents a compromise between denial and memory. A painful experience is screened or covered by the benign recall of something less significant (Moore and Fine 1991).

Self-agency: A sense of owning one's actions and being able to bring aobut an intended result. One of the four core senses of self (Felberbaum, this volume, Sanville 1991, Stern 1985).

Selfobject: One's subjective experience of another person who is experienced as providing a sustaining function to the self (Moore and Fine 1990). According to Kohut such objects are experienced as if the subject has control over them as they would over their own body and mind (Kohut 1971).

Self-representations: Mental contents in the system ego that unconsciously, preconsciously, or consciously represent aspects of the bodily and mental self (Jacobson 1964).

Sentinel effect: An internalization of the hostile voice (sentinel) that causes a person to be suspicious of her or his own good intentions (Kramer 1990, Meyer, this volume).

Symmetrical thinking: Thinking which unites things which are usually kept apart, in which the converse of any relation is identical to it, and parts are equal to and the same as the whole. An understanding of thinking based on symbolic logic and the mathematics of infinite sets, as opposed to energy as in primary and secondary process. The mind puts together ideas that are not overtly logical. It unites people and events. In one stratum, an indivisible frame operates; everything may stand for everything else and at bedrock is understood as part of the self. (Matte-Blanco 1975, Steger, this volume).

Structural theory: The theory of three component "structures" in the mind. It describes the interaction of the id (which embodies the drives), the superego (composed of conscience, ideals, and ethical imperatives), and the ego (which mediates between the inner and outer world and contains functions such as thinking, judgment, frustration tolerance, the defenses, and the self- and object-representations) (Strean, this volume).

Therapeutic alliance (*working alliance*): Refers to the realistic cooperation and collaboration between patient and therapist in the therapeutic process (Moore and Fine 1990).

Topographic theory: Refers to the conscious, preconscious, and unconscious areas of the mind (Strean, this volume).

Tracking the triad: The triad is descriptive of the series of three states in the schizoid dilemma: (1) self expression that leads to (2) depression (shame, emptiness, sadness, insatiable longings for unavailable supplies, anxiety, and rage) and (3) defenses designed to stop the dysphoria by stopping the expression of the self (i.e., seeking safety). tracking the triad (Masterson 1981) involves the following components: (1) an aspect of self-activation or expression, which (2) triggers feelings concerning object loss or unavailability, which in turn triggers (3) a renewal of defensive behavior in order to avoid the painful feelings (Clark, this volume.).

Transference: The displacement of patterns of feelings, thoughts, and behavior originally experienced in relation to significant childhood figures onto a person involved in a current interpersonal relationship (Moore and Fine 1990).

Transference fantasies: Feelings and thoughts about the loving and/or frustrating figures from childhood that are displaced onto the therapist (Moore and Fine 1990).

Transference ideation: The relationship with the analyst is invested with wishes, fears, and core conflicts that are the result of early trauma and that have influenced the nature of psychic structure (Shechter, this volume). Some theorists extend this concept to refer to the thoughts, conceptions, and opinions that exist in the mind (or the psychic structure) as a result of early experiences, whether of deprivations, suppressions, or frustrations that sometimes were felt to be of traumatic proportions. In treatment, these attitudes affect the relationship with the therapist until they are well understood.

Transitional object: The infant's first "not-me" possession, something inanimate but treasured (usually a small soft blanket or toy) which the child uses in the course of emotional separation from the primary love object at times of stress, often when going to sleep (Winnicott 1953). The transitional object often must have a characteristic odor and feeling thought to be reminiscent of the mother (Aronson, this volume, Felberbaum, this volume, Moore and Fine 1990).

Transitional phenomena: Manifestations of the process of transition between objects related to *subjectively* and objects related to *objectively*, that is, of an intermediate area of experience (Aronson, this volume, Winnicott 1971). In addition to literal objects, the phenomena include behaviors such as the baby's humming, babbling, and later "rehearsing" words heard during the day, as well as fantasies and other actions that signify the mother–me relationship before boundaries are sharply delineated.

Transitional space: The potential space between inner and outer reality that is the realm of play, psychotherapy, and cultural and aesthetic experience (Aronson this volume, Chescheir this volume, Felberbaum this volume, Winnicott 1977). It is the location of the baby's maximally intense experiences between the subjective object and that which is objectively perceived. Potential space exists when the baby experiences confidence about the dependability of mother and other environmental elements. And in adult therapy, this area–somewhere between fantasy and reality–can exist only when the patient feels a context of safety. When it exists, there is room for play, illusion and creativity, and for altering the fixities that brought the person to psychotherapy.

Transitional relatedness: The ability to employ an external experience, such as an appointment card, as a symbol of relational connection and reliability between two people (Applegate, this volume).

Trauma: The disruption or breakdown that occurs when the psychic apparatus is suddenly presented with stimuli, either from within or from without, that are too powerful to be dealt with or assimilated in the usual way (Moore and Fine 1990). The experience of trauma exposes the psyche to stimuli of such high intensity as to disrupt adaptive capacities and to dissipate the power to organize. Excessive frustrations of childhood can hamper or interfere with the individual's fulfillment of nutritional, love, and security needs (Shechter, this volume).

Trauma, cumulative: Repeated minor failure to meet the infant's needs may add up to a cumulative trauma that seriously affects the child's structural development and adaptation and predisposes her or him to further trauma (Graziano, this volume, Moore and Fine 1990).

Twinship transference (*also alter-ego transference*): This form of selfobject transference represents the satisfaction in perceiving one's basic alikeness to another, hence different from the mirror transferences. It represents the need to see and understand, as well as to be seen and understood by someone like oneself (Chernus and Livingston, this volume, Moore and Fine 1990). Although Kohut originally thought that such transferences were of later origin, he came to believe that even infants enjoy a pervasive sense of security when they experience themselves as human beings among other human beings (Kohut 1984).

Unbearable agonies: Feelings of falling apart, falling forever, depersonalization, disorientation, catastrophic anxiety, or primary separation anxiety (Applegate, this volume, Winnicott 1968).

Unconscious: As an adjective it refers to the mental content that is not available to conscious awareness at a given time. As a noun the unconscious refers to one of the systems Freud described (1915) in his early topographic theory. This system comprises the early wishes and objects of these wishes and those repressed contents which are denied access to the preconscious–conscious. The domain of the unconscious is not directly accessible, but through dreams and childhood thinking we discern some of its properties, such as timelessness and spacelessness, the absence of mutual contradiction and negation, displacement, condensation, and the replacement of external by internal reality (Strean, this volume).

Some contemporary psychoanalysts are reexamining the part played by the primary unconscious in the unfolding of all of human thinking. Its symmetrical principle is active in the formation of categories, which then constitute the asymmetrical principle. The two principles are thus silently at work even in classical logic, where the asymmetrical prevails, and–depending upon their relative proportions–may make for creativity or pathology (Matte-Blanco as described in Steger, this volume).

Valency: Involuntary blending of one individual's personality with another (Freedman, this volume, Scharff and Scharff 1991).

Verbal Self: The sense of self that comes into existence with the emergence of language, usually in the second year of life. Although this makes for advances in the quantities and qualities of "being with" others, it also makes for a potential split between experiences as lived and as they can be verbally represented (Clark, this volume, Stern 1987).

Working alliance: is similar to the therapeutic alliance and refers to the realistic, cooperative, and collaborative partnership between patient and therapist (Coleman, this volume, Greenson 1967, Moore and Fine 1990, Siskind, this volume).

GLOSSARY REFERENCES

Applegate, J. (1996). The good enough social worker: Winnicott applied. (This volume).

Austin, M. (1996). Recovered memories of childhood sexual abuse. (This volume).

Balint, M. (1968). Primary love. In *The Basic Fault: Therapeutic Aspects of Regression*. New York: Brunner/Mazel.

Benedek, T. (1938). Adaptation to reality in early infancy, *Psychoanalytic Quarterly* 7:200–214.

Bion, W. (1967). *Second Thoughts*. London: Heinemann.

Blanck, G. (1984). The complete Oedipus complex. *International Journal of Psycho-Analysis* 65:331–339.

Blanck, G., and Blanck R. (1974). *Ego Psychology, Theory and Practice*. New York: Columbia University Press.

—— (1979). *Ego Psychology II: Developmental Psychology*. New York: Columbia University Press.

Diagnostic and Statistical Manual of Mental Disorders, Fourth Edition. (1994). Washington, D.C.: American Psychiatric Association.

Edward, J. (1996). Listening, hearing, and understanding in psychoanalytically oriented treatment. (This volume.)

Edward, J. Ruskin, N., and Turrini, P. (1990). *Separation-Individuation: Theory and Application*. New York: Bruner/Maezel.

Casement, P. (1990). *Learning from the Patient*. New York: Guilford.

Chescheir, M. (1996). From holding to interpretation. (This volume.)

Clark, K. (1996). The beginning phases of treatment of the schizoid disorder of the self. (This volume.)

Deri, S. (1984). *Symbolization and Creativity*. New York: International Universities Press.

Felberbaum, S. (1996). Psychoanalytically oriented psychotherapy with the HIV-infected patient. (This volume.)

Frank, M. (1996). A clinical view of the use of psychoanalytic theory in front-line practice. (This volume.)

Freedman, E. (1996). Psychoanalysis and the world of two: object relations couple therapy. (This volume.)

Freud, S. (1911–1915, 1912) Papers on technique. *Standard Edition*: 12:85–173. London: Hogarth, 1975.

—— (1914) On narcissism: an introduction. *Standard Edition* London: Hogarth.

Gill, M. (1982). *Analysis of the Transference*, volume 1. Madison, CT: International Universities Press.

Graziano, R. (1996). The adult survivor of childhood sexual abuse. (This volume.)

Hartmann, H. (1939). *Ego Psychology and the Problem of Adaptation*. New York: International Universities Press, 1958.

Jacobson, E., (1964). *The Self and the Object World*. New York: International Universities Press.

Jones, D. M. (1991). Alexithymia: inner speech and linkage impairment. *Clinical Social Work Journal* 19:237–249.

Kaplan, L. (1978). *Oneness and Separateness: From Infant to Individual*. New York: Simon and Schuster.

Khan, M. (1963). The concept of cumulative trauma. In *The Privacy of the Self*. New York: International Universites Press, 1974.

Klein, M. (1940). Mourning and its relationship to manic depressive states: contributions to psycho-analysis. *International Journal of Psycho-Analysis* 21:125.

—— (1946). Notes on some schizoid mechanisms. In *Envy and Gratitude and Other works*, pp. 1–24. New York: Delacorte, 1975.

Kohut, H. (1971). *The Analysis of the Self*. New York: International Universities Press.

—— (1977). *The Restoration of the Self*. New York: International Universities Press.

—— (1984). *How Does Analysis Cure?* Chicago: University of Chicago Press.

Kramer, P. D. (1990). Dino or Dodo. *The Psychiatric Times*, November.

Krystal, H. (1978). Trauma and affects. *Psychoanalytic Study of the Child* 33:81–116. New Haven, CT: Yale University Press.

Loftus, E. (1992). The reality of repressed memories. Paper presented at the American Psychological Association annual meeting, Washington, DC.

Loftus, E., and Ketchum, K. (1991). *Witness for the Defense*. New York: International Universities Press.

Mahler, M. (1972). On the first three subphases of the separation-individuation process. In *The Selected Papers of Margaret S. Mahler*, pp. 119–130. New York: Jason Aronson.

—— (1979). *The Selected Writings of Margaret S. Mahler*. Vol. II. New York: Jason Aronson.

Mahler, M., Pine, F., and Bergman, A. (1975). *The Psychological Birth of the Human Infant*. New York: Basic Books.

Masterson, J. F. (1981). *The Narcissistic and Borderline Disorders*. New York: Brunner/Mazel.

—— (1985). *The Real Self: A Developmental, Self and Object Relations Approach.* New York: Brunner/Mazel.

Matte-Blanco, I. (1975). *The Unconscious as Infinite Sets: An Essay In Bi-logic.* London: Duckworth.

—— (1988). *Thinking, Feeling and Being.* London: Routledge.

Miller, J. (1996). A psychoeducational-psychodynamic approach to the treatment of drug addicts. (This volume.)

Moore, B., and Fine, B. (1990). *Psychoanalytic Terms and Concepts.* New Haven: Yale University Press.

Natterson, J., and Friedman, R. (1995). *A Primer of Intersubjectivity.* Northvale NJ: Jason Aronson.

Paris, S. and Lindauer, B. (1977). Constructive Aspects of Children's Comprehension and Memory. In *Perspectives on the Development of Memory and Cognition*, ed. R. V. Kail, Jr. and J. W. Hagen. Hillsdale, NJ: Lawrence Erlbaum.

Ross, J. M. (1995). King Oedipus and the Postmodern Psychoanalyst. *Journal of the American Psychoanalytic Association* 43(3):553–571.

Rothenberg, M., and Chapman, C. (1989). *Dictionary of Medical Terms for the Nonmedical Person.* New York: Barron's Educational Series.

Sandler, J. and Rosenblatt, B. (1962). The concept of the representational world. *Psychoanalytic Study of the Child.* 17:128–145. Quadrangle Books.

Sanville, J. (1987). Theories, therapies, therapists: their transformations. *Smith College Studies in Social Work*, March, pp. 75–92.

Scharff, D., and Scharff, J.(1991). *Models of Therapy in Object Relations Couple Therapy.* Northvale, NJ: Jason Aronson.

Segal, H. (1964). *Introduction to the Work of Melanie Klein.* London: Heinemann and Institute of Psycho-Analysis.

Shane, M. (1977). A rationale for teaching analytic technique based on a developmental orientation and approach. *International Journal of Psycho-Analysis* 58:95–107.

Sifneos, P. (1967). Clinical observations on some patients suffering from a variety of psychosomatic diseases. *Acta Medica Psychosomatica*: 452–458. Proceedings of the 7th European Conference on Psychosomatic Research, Rome.

Spitz, R. (1965). *The First Year of Life.* New York: International Universities Press.

Steger, G. (1996). Leaking walls: a tale of the unconscious. (This volume.)

Stern, D. (1985). *The Interpersonal World of the Infant.* New York: Basic Books.

Stolorow, R., and Atwood, G. (1987). *Psychoanalytic Treatment: An Intersubjective Approach.* Hillsdale, NJ: Analytic Press.

Strean, H. (1996). Applying psychoanalytic principles to social work practice: an historical review. (This volume.)

Waelder, R. (1936). The principle of multiple function. *Psychoanalytic Quarterly* 5:45–62.

Winnicott, D. (1952). Anxiety associated with insecurity. In *Through Paediatrics to Psycho-analysis*. New York: Basic Books.

—— (1953). Transitional objects and transitional phenomenon: a study of the first non-me possession. *International Journal of Psycho-Analysis* 34:89–97.

—— (1956). Primary maternal preoccupation. In *Through Paediatrics to Psycho-Analysis*. New York: Basic Books.

—— (1968). Communication between infant and mother, and mother and infant, compared and contrasted. In *Babies and Their Mothers*. Reading, MA: Addison Wesley, 1988.

—— (1971). The use of an object and relating through identification. In *Playing and Reality*. London: Tavistock.

—— (1977). *The Piggle: An Account of the Psychoanalytic Treatment of a Little Girl*. Madison, CT: International Universities Press.

Zinner, J. (1989). Developmental spectrum of projective identification. Unpublished paper.

Bibliography: Related Clinical Social Work Writings

Alperin, R. M., and Hollman, B. C. (1992). The social worker as psychoanalyst. *Clinical Social Work Journal* 20:89–98.

Anechiarico, B. (1990). Understanding and treating sex offenders from a self-psychological perspective: the missing piece. *Clinical Social Work Journal* 18:281–292.

Applegate, J. S. (1989). The transitional object reconsidered: some sociocultural variations and the implications. *Smith College Studies in Social Work* 6:38–51.

Atwood, R., and Safyer, A. W. (1993). The autonomous self vs. the relational self: implications for clinical assessment and treatment in child psychotherapy. *Journal of Analytic Social Work* 1:39–54.

Bellow, G. (1986). Self psychology and ego psychology: a historical perspective. *Clinical Social Work Journal* 14:199–212.

Bingham, R. L. (1987). The interpretation of illusion: the role of illusion in psychoanalytic psychotherapy. *Smith College Studies in Social Work* 57:218–231.

Blanck, G., and Blanck, R. (1987). The contribution of ego psychology to understanding the process of termination in psychoanalysis and psychotherapy. *Journal of the American Psychoanalytic Association* 36:961–984.

—— (1994). *Ego Psychology: Theory and Practice,* second edition. New York: Columbia University Press.

Boniello, M. (1990). Grieving sexual abuse: the therapist's process. *Clinical Social Work Journal* 18:367–379.

Brandell, J. (1992). Psychotherapy of a traumatized 10-year-old boy: theoretical issues and clinical considerations. *Smith College Studies in Social Work* 62:123–138.

Burch, B. (1989). Melanie Klein's work: an adaptation in practice. *Clinical Social Work Journal* 1:15–42.

Burke, M., and Dawson, T. A. (1987). Temporary care foster parents: motives and issues of separation and loss. *Child and Adolescent Social Work Journal* 4:30–38.

Clark, K. (1993). Season of light/season of darkness: the effects of burying and remembering traumatic sexual abuse on the sense of self. *Clinical Social Work Journal* 2(1)25–43.

Cole, A. B. (1992). Frame modifications with a dying client. *Smith College Studies in Social Work* 63:314–324.

Dean, R. G. (1984). The role of empathy in supervision. *Clinical Social Work Journal* 12:129–138.

——(1993). Constructivism: an approach to clinical practice. *Smith College Studies in Social Work* 63:127–146.

De LaCour, E. (1985). Aspects of transference interpretation. *Smith College Studies in Social Work* 56:1–14.

Eisenhuth, E. (1981). The theories of Kohut and clinical social work practice. *Clinical Social Work Journal* 9:80–90.

Elson, M. (1989). Kohut and Stern: two views of infancy and early childhood. *Smith College Studies in Social Work* 59:131–145.

—— (1991). Entering the developmental spiral: the work of Michael F. Basch applied to clinical social work. *Clinical Social Work Journal* 19(2):149–162.

Federn, E. (1992). From psychoanalysis to clinical social work: an evolutionary process. *Clinical Social Work Journal* 20(1):9–16.

Fraiberg, S. (1955). *Psychoanalytic Principles in Casework with Children.* New York: Family Service Association of America pamphlet.

——(1955). Teaching American theory to social work students. *Social Casework* 36:243–252.

——(1978). Psychoanalysis and social work: a reexamination of the issues. *Smith College Studies in Social Work* 48:87–91.

Fraiberg, S., Shapiro, V., and Adelson, E. (1976). Ghosts in the nursery: a psychoanalytic approach to the problems of impaired infant–mother relationships. *Journal of the American Academy of Child Psychiatry* 14:337–342.

Frederickson, J. (1991). From delusion to play. *Clinical Social Work Journal* 19(4):349–362.

Freed, A. O. (1985). Linking developmental family and life cycle theories. *Smith College Studies in Social Work* 55:169–182.

Freeman, L., and Strean, H. (1981). *Freud and Women.* New York: Ungar.

Gabriel, M. A. (1991). Group therapists' countertransference reactions to multiple deaths from AIDS. *Clinical Social Work Journal* 19(3):279–292.

Genende, J. (1988). A therapist's pregnancy: an opportunity for conflict resolution and growth in the treatment of homosexual men. *Clinical Social Work Journal* 19:23–33.

Gilfillan, S. S. (1985). Adult intimate love relationships as new editions of symbiosis and the separation-individuation process. *Smith College Studies in Social Work* 53(3):183–196.

Green, L. (1993). Containing and the patient's observation of the therapist's countertransference. *Clinical Social Work Journal* 21:375–383.

Hanna, E. (1994). The relationship between psychic reality and trauma with special reference to an adult patient who was sexually abused as a child. *Clinical Social Work Journal* 23:355–368.

Heiman, M. (1913). *Psychoanalysis and Social Work.* New York: International Universities Press.

Kanter, J. S. (1983). Reevaluation of task centered social work practice. *Clinical Social Work Journal* 11:228–244.

Lukton, R. (1992). Gender as an element in the intersubjective field: the female therapist and the male patient. *Clinical Social Work Journal* 20(2):153–168.

Martin, M. L., and Henry-Feeney, J. (1989). Clinical services to persons with AIDS: the parallel nature of the client and worker processes. *Clinical Social Work Journal* 17:337–349.

May, R. (1985). Observations on the psychoanalytic theory of mourning. *Clinical Social Work Journal* 57:3–11.

Meers, D. R. (1993). The pragmatism of ego psychology. *Journal of Analytic Social Work* 1:55–74.

Meyer, W. (1991). A case of restricted entitlement. *Clinical Social Work Journal* 19(3):232–236.

Mishne, J. (1983). *Clinical Work with Children.* New York: Free Press.

—— (1984). Trauma of parent loss through divorce, death and illness. *Child and Adolescent Social Work Journal* 1:74.

—— (1992). The grieving child: manifest and hidden losses in childhood and adolescence. *Child and Adolescent Social Work Journal* 9:471–490.

Natterson, I. (1993). Turning points and intersubjectivity. *Clinical Social Work Journal* 21:45–56.

Nover, G. (1989). Treatment of a four-year-old and her mother. *Child and Adolescent Social Work Journal* 6:38–51.

Palombo, J. (1981). Parent loss and childhood bereavement: some theoretical considerations. *Clinical Social Work Journal* 9:3–33.

Paradis, B. A. (1993). A self psychological approach to the treatment of gay men with AIDS. *Clinical Social Work Journal* 21(4):405–416.

Perlman, H. H. (1971). *Perspectives on Social Casework.* Philadelphia: Temple University Press.

—— (1979). *Relationship: The Heart of Helping People.* Chicago: University of Chicago Press.

Raines, J. C. (1990). Empathy in clinical social work. *Clinical Social Work Journal* 18:57–72.

Ranan, W., and Blodgett, A. (1983). Using telephone therapy for "unreachable" clients. *Social Casework* 64:39–44.

Rosen, H. (1991). Child and adolescent bereavement. *Child and Adolescent Social Work Journal* 8:15–26.

Rosenberg, D. D., and Jensen, C. (1993). Listening and meaning in the psychotherapy of borderlines. *Journal of Analytic Social Work* 1:7–28.

Rosenblatt, A., and Waldfogel, D. (1983). Commitment to disenfranchised clients. In *Handbook of Clinical Social Work.* San Francisco: Jossey-Bass.

Rosenthal, E. S. (1990). The therapist's pregnancy: impact on the treatment process. *Clinical Social Work Journal* 18:213–226.

Rubin, C. (1980). Notes from a pregnant therapist. *Social Casework* 25:210–215.

Ryan, C. C. (1988). The social and clinical challenges of AIDS. *Smith College Studies in Social Work* 59:3–20.

Saari, C. (1983). On the place of reality in social work and psychoanalytic theory. *Clinical Social Work Journal* 7:21.

—— (1986). The created relationship: transference, countertransference and the therapeutic culture. *Clinical Social Work Journal* 14:39–51.

—— (1994). Empathy in clinical social work: playing in transcontextual space. *Journal of Analytic Social Work* 2:25–42.

Shapiro, V. B., and Gisynski. (1989). Ghosts in the nursery revisited. *Child and Adolescent Social Work Journal* 6:19–37.

Shepard, P. (1987). Telephone therapy: an alternative to isolation. *Clinical Social Work Journal* 15:56–65.

Shernoff, M. (1989). Integrating safer sex counseling into social work practice. *Social Casework* 69:334–339.

Siebold, C. (1991). Termination: when the therapist leaves. *Clinical Social Work Journal* 19(2):191–204.

Siegel, J. (1991). Analysis of projective identification: an object relations approach to marital treatment. *Clinical Social Work Journal* 19(1):71–82.

Socor, B. J. (1989). Listening for historical truth: a relative discussion. *Clinical Social Work Journal* 17:103–115.

Springer, C. (1991). Transference and countertransference issues. *Clinical Social Work Journal* 19:405–415.

Stewart, J. M. (1984). Deficit and negative influence: their effect on oedipal and pre-oedipal positions. *Smith College Studies in Social Work* 54:166–180.

Strean, H. (1990). Profiles in independent social work. *Journal of Independent Social Work* 4(14):81–90.

Super, S. I. (1982). Successful transition: therapeutic interventions with the transferred client. *Clinical Social Work Journal* 10:113–122.

Teitelbaum. A. (1991). Countertransference and its potential for abuse. *Clinical Social Work Journal* 19(3):267–277.

Thompson, T. E. (1991). The place of ego building work in psychotherapy with children. *Child and Adolescent Social Work Journal* 8:351–367.

Tuohy, A. I. (1987). Psychoanalytic perspectives on child abuse. *Child and Adolescent Social Work Journal* 4:25–40.

Weintraub, C. G. (1990). Telephone sessions in the treatment of a child during the therapist's absence because of threatened miscarriage. *Clinical Social Work Journal* 18:227–241.

Winter, F., and Easton, F. (1983). *The Practice of Social Work in Schools.* New York: Free Press.

Zerbe, D. H. (1990). The therapist at play and the patient who begins to play. *Clinical Social Work Journal* 18(1):9–22.

Zuckerman, E. (1983). *Child Welfare.* New York: Free Press.

Index

Abstinence, communication and, 29–31
Abuse. *See* Childhood sexual abuse; Filicide
Ackerman, N., 5, 13
Action, social work training and, 407
Adams-Silvan, A., 214
Adelson, L., 388
Adler, A., 7
Adult survivors, of childhood sexual abuse, 195–211
AIDS. *See* HIV infection
Alexander, I., 230
Alexander, J., 355
Amiel, H. F., 261
Anderson, S., 355, 356
Anorexia, 163–178
  countertransference, 172–175
  developmental factors, 167–168
  discussion of, 175–177
  overview of, 163–165
  patient growth, 175
  presenting problems, 165–166
  previous treatment, 166–167
  psychotherapy, 169–172
Applegate, J. S., 88, 89, 93, 423
Argyris, C., 81
Arlow, J. A., 28, 31, 32, 33, 41, 43, 153, 253
Aronson, J. K., 164
Atchley-Simonton, S., 247
Atkinson, R., 190

Bakhtin, M., 253
Balint, M., 107, 122, 330
Bandler, B., 11
Barol, B. I., 93
Bass, E., 186
Beatrice, J., 355
Beebe, B., 165
Behavior, social work training, 406
Benedek, T., 297, 301, 312, 320
Beres, D., 32, 33
Bettelheim, B., 373–374
Biestek, F. P., 406
Bi-logic, unconscious and, 271–272

Bion, W. R., 117, 330, 333
Blanck, G., 11, 17, 60, 257, 302, 354, 355, 358
Blanck, R., 11, 17, 60, 257, 302, 354, 355, 358
Boardroom Classics, 373
Bollas, C., 48, 90, 107, 172–173, 333
Borenzweig, H., 13
Bowlby, J., 406, 413
Brenner, C., 153, 407, 419
Breuer, J., 198
Brewer, W., 190
Brill, L., 5
Bruner, J. S., 26, 407, 408, 410
Burnham, D. L., 359, 361, 362

Campion, J. F., 389
Caruth, C., 195
Casement, P. C., 26, 30n1, 112, 113, 115, 116, 122, 248, 365
Castelnuevo-Tedesco, P., 373, 375
Centered holding, couples therapy, 334
Chassler, L., 164
Chernus, L. A., 387n2
Chescheir, M. W., 84, 93, 425, 432
Childhood sexual abuse. *See also* Filicide
  adult survivors of, 195–211
  recovered memory and, 179–194
Child therapy, parents and, 293–311
Clancier, A., 80
Clark, K. R., 133, 137, 143, 426
Clinical social work, psychoanalysis and, 14–15
Coady, N. F., 84
Colarusso, C., 312, 321
Coleman, D., 423
Communication, 23–45
  diagnosis and, 26–29
  listening therapist and, 24–25
  psychoanalysis and, 23–24
  safety and, 29–31
  theory and, 25–26
  understanding and, 31–42
Compassion, psychoanalysis and, 8
Compromise formation, defined, 264
Condensation, unconscious and, 267–268
Consciousness, therapy and, 262
Containment, interpretation and, 116–121
Context, social work training and, 409–410
Contextual holding, couples therapy, 334
Cooper, A., 47, 49
Council on Social Work Education, 411
Countertransference. *See also* Transference
  anorexia, 172–175
  child therapy and, 305, 307–308
  empathy and, 386–388
  filicide and, 386–403. *See also* Filicide
  Freud on, 304–305
  front-line practice, 61–62
  HIV infection, 246–247
  psychoanalysis and, 428–431
  sex and gender in, 431–434
  termination, 362–363
  working relationship, 435–438
Couples therapy, 327–352
  case example, 335–350
  object relations theory and, 329–330
  overview of, 327–328
  projective identification, 330–333
  treatment approach, 334–335

Dale, P., 389
Daly, L., 184
Davis, L., 186
Davis, M., 91
Dawes, R., 187, 189
Dean, R. G., 81
DeAngelis, T., 373
Defenses, social work and, 10–11
DeJonghe, F., 84
Denial, drug addiction, 232–233
Deri, S., 84, 105
Developmental factors
  anorexia, 167–168
  schizoid disorder of the self, 134–135
Dewald, P. A., 237
Diagnosis
  communication and, 26–29
  psychoanalysis, 438–440
Dicks, H. V., 334
Displacement, unconscious and, 267
Dream analysis
  unconscious and, 262
  violence and, 212–225
Drug addiction, 226–243
  denial, 232–233
  discussion of, 240–242
  guilt and shame, 228–230
  outpatient care, 226–227
  overview of, 226
  psychodynamic therapy, 235–239
  psychoeducation and, 230–232, 233–235
  treatment issues, 228
  treatment review, 239–240
Duncan, D., 112, 113, 122

Edelson, M., 408
Education. *See* Social work training
Edward, J., 27, 29, 256, 297, 312, 322, 422
Ego assessment, foster parenting, 319–321
Ego psychology, social work and, 10–11, 12
Ego relatedness, social work and, 86–87
Ellenberger, H., 261, 266
Emde, R. N., 239, 406, 413
Empathy
  communication and, 32–33
  countertransference and, 386–388
Erikson, E. H., 11, 297, 312, 321
Ethic, of psychoanalysis, 422–424

Fairbairn, W. R. D., 329, 330, 332, 341
False self
  schizoid disorder of the self, 133–134
  social work and, 90–91
  therapeutic management of, 136–149
Family therapy, transference, 47
Fantasy, HIV infection, 253–258
Farley, O., 5
Federn, P., 11
Feinstein, H. M., 390
Felberbaum, S., 245, 257
Feminism, psychoanalysis and, 13
Ferenczi, S., 196, 198, 202
Filicide, 386–403
  case example, 391–396
  discussion of, 396–402
  empathic mode and, 386–388
  psychodynamics of, 388–391
Fine, B. D., 32, 153
Fine, R., 4, 13, 14
Fischer, J., 13
Fisher, S., 4
Flavell, J. H., 190
Forced termination. *See* Termination

Foster parenting, 312–326
case example, 313–319
ego assessment, 319–321
narcissistic enhancement, 321–323
overview of, 312–313
transference, 323–325
Fragmentation
adult survivors of childhood sexual abuse, 197–199
trust versus, 199–202
Frank, M. G., 61, 424
Free association, communication, listening therapist and, 24–25
Freedberg, S., 82
Freeman, L., 13
Freud, A., 10, 11, 12, 112, 187, 188, 300, 321, 358
Freud, S., 2, 3, 7, 8, 23, 24, 26, 29, 30, 31, 32, 47, 49, 79, 81, 154, 161, 184, 185, 188, 198, 213, 262, 266–268, 287, 288, 300, 304, 406, 422, 424, 435
Friedman, D., 189
Friendly visitor, social work and psychoanalysis, 6–9
Fromm, M. G., 92
Fromm-Reichman, F., 227
Front-line practice, 59–76
case example, 62–73
discussed, 73–75
overview of, 59
psychoanalytic concepts and, 60–62

Gage, K., 324
Ganaway, G., 191
Gardner, R., 180
Garrett, A., 10
Gavazzi, S., 355, 356
Gay, P., 7, 9
Gaylin, W., 230
Gender, transference and countertransference, 431–434
Genetic reconstructions, intersubjectivity and, interpretation, 112–116
Germain, C., 5
Gill, M., 50, 51, 61, 250
Gillian, L., 324
Ginsberg, L., 5
Glenn, J., 23
Glenn, M., 355
Glick, R., 355, 366
Gloor, P., 189
Goldman, D., 79, 82
Good, P. R., 373
Greenacre, P., 161
Greenberg, R., 4
Greene, M., 366
Greenson, R., 227, 296
Grolick, S. A., 80, 82
Grosskurth, P., 81
Guilt and shame, drug addiction, 228–230
Guntrip, H., 83, 133, 135
Gutheil, T., 355

Halpert, E., 374, 375
Hamilton, G., 5, 50
Haney, P., 257
Hartmann, H., 11, 196, 254, 303, 304
Hellenbrand, S., 6
HIV infection, 244–260
case examples, 247–253
countertransference, 246–247
couples therapy, 338. *See also* Couples therapy
drug addiction and, 226–243
overview of, 244–246
relaxation exercises and imagery, 253–258

Holding, containment contrasted, 116–117
Holding environment
  interpretation and, 98–99
  long-term treatment and, 372–385. *See also* Long-term treatment
  social work and, 84–86, 377–378
  transference and, 48–49
Hollis, F., 5, 17, 50, 252
Homosexuality, couples therapy, 327–352. *See also* Couples therapy
Horner, A., 202

Imagery, HIV infection, 253–258
Inhelder, B., 187, 190
Institutional transference, foster parenting, 323–325
Interpretation, 97–124
  case example, 100–105
  containment and, 116–121
  discussed, 121–123
  holding environment and, 98–99
  intersubjectivity and genetic reconstructions, 112–116
  meaning and, 111–112
  overview of, 97–98
  schizoid dilemma, 142
  transference and, 49–52
  transitional area, 105–111
Intersubjectivity
  front-line practice, 61–62
  genetic reconstructions and, interpretation, 112–116
Intrapsychic structure, schizoid disorder of the self, 135–136

Jacobson, E., 60, 303
Jones, D. M., 199
Jones, E., 7, 9
Joseph, B., 170

Kadushin, A., 1
Kafka, E., 213
Kahn, A., 5
Kahn, M., 51, 53, 57
Kalmanovitch, J., 80
Kanter, J., 80, 93, 378
Kanzer, M., 23
Kaplan, B., 86
Kaufman, E., 226
Kaufman, P., 226
Keith, C., 355
Kernberg, O., 329, 333
Ketcham, K., 191
Khan, M., 80, 83, 196, 197
Khantzian, E. J., 227
Kiersky, S., 165
Klein, M., 81, 82, 329, 330, 331
Klein, R., 135, 137, 144
Knight, R. P., 28, 419
Kohut, H., 16, 41, 196, 198, 386
Kramer, P. D., 383, 384
Kris, A., 24
Kris, E., 60, 188
Krystal, H., 198, 199, 203, 209
Kupferman, K., 202

Lakoff, G., 410
Laub, D., 195, 199, 209
LeShan, E., 246, 258
LeShan, L., 246
Levenson, E., 50
Levitan, H., 214
Lewis, C. S., 131
Lidz, R. W., 357
Lidz, T., 357
Lifton, R. J., 397
Lindauer, B., 190
Lipton, S., 52

Listing
Listening
  theory and, 25–26
  by therapist, communication and, 24–25
Litowitz, B. E., 407
Litowitz, N. S., 407
Little, M. I., 83, 85, 201
Loewald, H. W., 33, 154, 258
Loewenstein, R. M., 214, 237
Loftus, E., 180, 184, 189, 190, 191
Loftus, G., 184, 189
Long-term treatment, 372–385
  case example, 378–382
  discussion of, 382–383
  holding environment and, 376–377
  overview of, 372–375
  short-term psychotherapy and, 375–376
  social work and, 377–378
Luepnitz, D. A., 92

MacIsaac, D. S., 386
Mackenzie, K. R., 375, 376
Mackler, G., 245
Mahler, M., 34, 43, 134, 240, 297, 312, 358, 361
Mahoney, K., 13
Mahoney, M., 13
Markson, E., 170, 174
Martin, H., 324
Masterson, J. F., 131, 135, 137, 142, 426
Matte-Blanco, I., 262, 263, 269–283, 287, 288–290, 431
McCormack, C., 334
McDougall, J., 363
Meaning
  interpretation and, 111–112
  science versus, social work training, 407–409
Meissner, W. W., 333
Menninger, K., 154
Meyer, W. S., 93
Michaels, E., 373
Mikkelson, E., 355
Miller, J., 227
Minahan, A., 13
Mishler, E. G., 408
Mitchell, C., 239
Mitchell, S. A., 329, 330
Modell, A., 106, 377
Moore, B. E., 32, 153
Moore, M., 50
Multiple personality disorder, adult survivors of childhood sexual abuse, 198

Nader, K., 191
Nagera, H., 153
Narcissistic enhancement, foster parenting, 321–323
Nelson, K., 410
Nemiroff, R., 312, 321
Neutrality
  communication and, 29–31
  psychoanalysis and, 422–423
Novick, J., 170, 171
Novick, K., 170, 171

Object relations
  couples therapy, 327–352. *See also* Couples therapy
  social work and, 89–90
  theory of, transference, 47
Oedipal conflict, resolution of, in transference, 152–162
Ogden, T., 329, 332, 335
Okun, B. F., 92
Olson, E., 397
Omin, R., 256
Oremland, J., 51
Ornstein, P., 52

Pacifico, J. F., 184
Pao, P.-N., 28
Parents, child therapy and, 293–311
Paris, S., 190
Pedhazur, E., 186, 189
Penfield, W. G., 190
Penn, L., 355, 356
Perlman, H. H., 5, 23, 406
Phillips, A., 78, 79, 90
Piaget, J., 186, 187, 190
Pincus, A., 13
Pine, F., 26, 43, 67
Play, interpretation, transitional area, 108–111
Post-partum depression, 261–292
  discussion of, 283–285
  overview of, 261–266
  symptom, 285–287
  unconscious and, 266–283
    Freud, 266–268
    Matte-Blanco, 269–283
Potential space, HIV infection, 255
Poverty
  psychoanalysis and, 7–8
  social work and, 12–13, 15
Projective identification
  couples therapy, 330–333
  developmental spectrum of, 328
Psychoanalysis, 1–22
  communication and, 23–24
  concepts of, 421–422
  countertransference and, 428–431
  described, 2–4, 419–420
  diagnosis, 438–440
  ethic of, 422–424
  front-line practice, 59–76
  purpose of, 46
  social work and
    historical perspective, 6–19
    overview of, 417–421
  social work training and, 404–415. *See also* Social work training
  transference and, 424–428
  working relationship, 435–438
Psychoeducation, drug addiction and, 230–232, 233–235
Pulver, S., 52
Pumpian-Mindlin, E., 355
Pynoos, R. S., 191

Racker, H., 224, 333
Rangell, L., 27
Rape, dream analysis and, 212–225
Rayner, E., 288n3
Reality, unconscious and, 268
Recovered memory, childhood sexual abuse and, 179–194
Reed, G. S., 26
Reik, T., 31, 423
Relaxation exercises, HIV infection, 253–258
Renik, O., 213
Repetition compulsion, front-line practice, 60–61
Resistance, social work and, 10
Resnick, P. J., 389, 390
Richmond, M., 5, 6, 7, 10
Riessman, F., 13
Riviere, J., 82
Robbe-Grillet, A., 187
Rodman, F. R., 84, 378
Rose, D. S., 216
Rosenblatt, A., 6, 16
Rosenblatt, B., 60
Rosenfield, I., 189
Rosenthal, H., 258
Rowe, C. E., 386
Rudnytsky, P. L., 79, 80
Rusczynski, S., 335
Ruskin, N., 27, 312

Saari, C., 48, 81, 405, 408, 409, 410
Safety, communication and, 29–31
Sandler, J., 60, 305, 307
Sanville, J., 26, 33, 49, 50, 61, 88, 93, 253, 254, 359, 362, 367, 432, 440
Sashin, J. I., 227
Schafer, R., 29, 30, 51, 188, 239, 240, 355, 407, 410
Scharff, D. E., 333, 334, 335
Scharff, J. S., 333, 334, 335
Schimek, J. G., 407
Schizoid disorder of the self, 125–151
  case example, 126–132
  developmental hypothesis, 134–135
  false self, therapeutic management of, 136–149
  intrapsychic structure, 135–136
  overview of, 125–126
  schizoid compromise, 133–134
  schizoid dilemma, 132–133
  treatment, 136
Schmelkin, L., 189
Schon, D. A., 81
Schumaker, J. F., 187
Science
  meaning versus, social work training, 407–409
  psychoanalysis and, 4
Segal, H., 332
Seibold, C., 355, 364
Seinfeld, J., 332
Semrad, E., 373
Sexual abuse. *See* Childhood sexual abuse
Sexuality, transference and countertransference, 431–434
Shame and guilt, drug addiction, 228–230
Shane, M., 321
Shapiro, J., 17
Shapiro, R. L., 328n1
Sharpe, E. F., 283
Shengold, L., 188
Shiffrin, R., 190
Shor, J., 88, 432, 433
Shore, B., 411
Short-term psychotherapy, described, 375–376
Siegel, J., 329
Sifneos, P., 199
Silvan, M., 214
Siponin, M., 5
Siskind, D., 296
Slipp, S., 47, 328n1, 334
Smaldino, C., 202
Smith, B. L., 92
Smith, S., 355
Social work, 1–22
  described, 4–6
  front-line practice, 59–76
  holding environment and, 377–378
  interpretation and, 97–124. *See also* Interpretation
  psychoanalysis and
    historical perspective, 6–19
    overview of, 417–421
  theory and, 1–2
  transference and, 52–53
  Winnicott and, 77–96
Social work training
  changes in, 15
  psychoanalysis and, 404–415
    action, 407
    behavior and, 406
    common ground, 410–413
    context, 409–410
    overview of, 404–406
    science versus meaning, 407–409
    therapeutic relationship and, 406–407
  Winnicott and, 91–93

Somer, S. P. S., 229
Sontag, S., 246
Spence, D. P., 407
Spitz, R. A., 28, 60, 300, 430
Stein, R., 329, 331
Steiner, J., 329
Stern, D., 49, 134, 239, 254, 406, 407, 413
Stolorow, R., 62, 406
Stone, L., 375
Strean, H., 4, 13, 18, 418, 419, 420, 421
Substance abuse. *See* Drug addiction
Sullivan, H. S., 3
Supervision, filicide and, 386–403. *See also* Filicide
Symmetrical thinking, unconscious and, 269–283, 289

Tavris, C., 186
Telephone, as transitional space, in treatment of anorexia, 163–178. *See also* Anorexia
Termination, 353–371
  case overview, 356–358
  countertransference, 362–363
  developmental diagnosis, 358–360
  literature review, 355–356
  overview of, 353–355
  process of, 364–368
  treatment process, 360–362
Therapeutic alliance, psychoanalysis, 435–438
Therapeutic relationship
  social work training and, 406–407
  transference, 46–58. *See also* Transference
Third-party payers, long-term treatment and, 374–375, 384
Timelessness, unconscious and, 268
Toffler, A., 373, 384
Toland, K., 187
Training. *See* Social work training
Transference, 46–58. *See also* Countertransference
  clinical example, 53–56
  couples therapy, 334–335
  epistemology, 47–48
  foster parenting, 323–325
  front-line practice, 61–62
  holding environment and, 48–49
  interpretation and, 49–52
  oedipal conflict, resolution of, 152–162
  overview of, 46–47
  psychoanalysis and, 3, 420, 424–428
  sex and gender in, 431–434
  social work and, 52–53
  working relationship, 435–438
Transitional process, social work and, 87–89
Transitional space
  interpretation, 105–111
  telephone as, in treatment of anorexia, 163–178. *See also* Anorexia
Trauma, dream analysis and, 212–225
Trevor-Roper, H. R., 192
Treyens, J., 190
True self. *See* False self
Trust
  adult survivors of childhood sexual abuse, 196–197
  fragmentation versus, 199–202
Tuckett, D., 288n3
Turner, F., 1, 5, 6, 13
Turrini, P., 28, 312

Unconscious
  communication and, 31, 32
  Freud and, 266–268
  therapy and, 262
Understanding, communication and, 31–42

Valenstein, A., 61
Violence
  dream analysis and, 212–225
  filicide, 386–403. *See also* Filicide
Vygotsky, L. S., 410

Wald, E., 298n1
Waldfogel, D., 6, 16
Wallbridge, D., 91
Wapner, J., 356
Watzlawick, P., 189
Weiner, I., 355
Werner, H., 86
White, R., 312
Whyte, L. L., 266
Wielawski, I., 184, 190
Williams, H. A., 333
Wilson, A., 227
Wilson, C. P., 174
Winnicott, C., 80, 83, 84, 98
Winnicott, D. W., 48, 49, 65, 77–96, 98, 105, 106, 107, 111, 112, 116, 117, 121, 122, 123, 161, 164, 176, 183, 196, 197, 201, 202, 231, 255, 256, 324, 330, 359, 360, 366, 369, 376–377, 378, 383, 413, 423, 424, 426, 431
Winters, F., & Easton, F., 5
Wolfenstein, M., 372
Woods, M., 50
Woolf, V., 125
Working relationship, psychoanalysis, 435–438
Wurmser, L., 227

Young, C., 192
Young-Bruehl, E., 184

Zinner, J., 328, 333
Zuckerman, R. L., 5, 375